S0-AGA-938

Guidance Services

PROFESSIONAL GUIDANCE SERIES

Under the Editorship of CLIFFORD P. FROEHLICH

Associate Professor of Education,
University of California, Berkeley, California.

GUIDANCE SERVICES

STUDYING STUDENTS

OCCUPATIONAL INFORMATION

COUNSELING ADOLESCENTS

16275
H85
B

Guidance Services

BY J. ANTHONY HUMPHREYS, PH.D.

Director of Personnel Services and Registrar,
Woodrow Wilson Junior College, Chicago, Ill.

AND ARTHUR E. TRAXLER, PH.D.

Executive Director, Educational Records Bureau,
New York, N.Y.

SCIENCE RESEARCH ASSOCIATES, INC.

CHICAGO

LIBRARY C. C. N. Y.

COPYRIGHT 1954 BY SCIENCE RESEARCH ASSOCIATES, INC.

All Rights Reserved under International Copyright Union.

This book may not be reproduced, in whole or in part, in any form (except by reviewers for the public press) without written permission from the publisher.

371.422
H927G

Library of Congress Catalogue Card Number: 53-12579

PRINTED IN THE UNITED STATES OF AMERICA
AMERICAN BOOK—STRATFORD PRESS, INC., NEW YORK

TO

M. H. H. and B. T.
For their loyal support
and steadfast encouragement

JE 27 '55

Foreword

IN THE preparation of textbooks, perhaps no task is more difficult than the writing of a text for a basic course. On the one hand, an author is faced with the problem of selecting those topics which are truly basic to an understanding of the field. On the other hand, he must deal with a multitude of facts and concepts if he is to give his reader an overview of the field. Humphreys and Traxler, in this volume, have struck a delicate and efficient balance between selectivity and inclusiveness.

Over the six years' period in which this book has been in preparation, the authors have diligently reworked their manuscript to make certain that it portrays the ever-expanding field of guidance services in a clear, straightforward, and interesting manner. The carefulness of their work is reflected in the accuracy and clarity of this text.

This volume was designed as the basic course text in the Professional Guidance Series. The other volumes in the series are listed on the page that faces the title page. The series is unique in the guidance textbook field in that each volume was planned to cover a specific area in a counselor preparation curriculum. There is no unnecessary duplication of content among the volumes; each complements the others to bring the reader of the series a comprehensive picture of the areas covered. Hence, when used as a set the four books in the series which are now available will help students organize and synthesize the field of guidance services. For this reason their use as a set in the core curriculum for either pre-service or in-service counselor education programs is recommended.

CLIFFORD P. FROEHLICH
Editor, Professional Guidance Series

Authors' Introduction

AS A companion function to the instructional activities in classroom and laboratory, guidance services to students are now widely accepted as an indispensable part of the process of education. In this book the authors present basic concepts and procedures for guidance services at all educational levels in elementary and secondary schools and in colleges and universities.

This presentation is intended to serve as an introduction to the field of student guidance services. It is meant to be simple and direct in treatment. It should serve both the needs of students of education who wish to become acquainted with guidance work at all levels and the needs of those faculty members who are potential counselors and who require in-service instruction in the essentials of guidance services. Leaders of youth in out-of-school activities also will find this book of practical help.

Although the treatment is simple and direct, the content is extensive and detailed. The organization of the book is intended to take account of what are believed to be the five broad, general needs of beginning students of guidance. In the first place, persons entering this field need to be introduced to the point of view held by guidance workers, to the sociological and psychological bases of guidance, to the principles and aims of guidance, and to the origin and history of guidance services. These background essentials are presented in Part I.

A second need of students of guidance is introduction to and some understanding of a wide variety of indispensable tools and techniques. They need to know how to collect and record information for guidance purposes, how to approach and carry on counseling through the interview, how to use group work in increasing the coverage and efficiency of a guidance program, how to follow up students and school-leavers, how to carry out continuous research on and evaluation of the guidance program, and how to get help from other research studies. Part II covers the basic elements of these tools and techniques and at the same time recognizes that these procedures are treated at greater length in two of the more advanced books of the professional guidance series: Froehlich and Darley's *Studying Students* and Hamrin and Paulson's *Counseling Adolescents*.

A third need of new workers in the field of guidance services is understanding of principles, procedures, and materials used in helping students solve major problems. These problems include especially those having to do with educational choice and adjustment, vocational choice, job placement, and the personal and social life of the individual. Part III treats these phases of guidance at considerable length and helps to lay a foundation for the student's use of a later book in the series: Baer and Roeber's *Occupational Information*.

Persons entering the guidance field need, in the fourth place, an understanding of the administration of a guidance program. They need to know how guidance services are organized and staffed under different plans in schools and colleges and how these services are coordinated with the rest of the educational program. These aspects of guidance are thoroughly discussed and illustrated in Part IV.

Finally, students of guidance services need information about the future of this field that they are about to enter. They need to have sketched out for them, as well as persons already experienced in the field can do it, some predictions of what the years to come will bring to this still comparatively young field of professional work. It may be a source of some encouragement to those at the threshold of service in this growing area of educational endeavor that the book ends on a carefully considered, but nevertheless strong, note of optimism.

We wish to express appreciation and thanks to Clifford P. Froehlich, editor of the Professional Guidance Series, and to James E. Mendenhall, book editor for Science Research Associates, Inc., for their helpful counsel and competent assistance in editing the manuscript. We are also grateful to the publishers of other books and journals for their generous permission to quote certain materials.

J. ANTHONY HUMPHREYS
ARTHUR E. TRAXLER

Table of Contents

PART I

Understandings Basic to Guidance Work

CHAPTER ONE

The Guidance Point of View

INDIVIDUALS ARE constantly beset by problems which must be met and solved. These problems are as varied as life itself. Some arise in everyday work; others emerge in home and family life. Many of these problems have their roots in relationships with other people.

Problems, moreover, differ in the degree of their complexity. Some are easy to solve; others are difficult. Because persons differ in their experiences and abilities, the same problem may be more intense in the life of one individual than it is in that of another.

The individual may confront certain problems because he has set a goal that he cannot attain. He also may be confused because he discovers that there is more than one road to his goal. This person may also be blocked because he finds that his familiar ways of behavior are not adequate to the problem situation. If he does not have within himself the required resources, he may seek help from friends or acquaintances in whom he has confidence. He may search for assistance in printed materials. Or he may confer with an expert in the area of his difficulty.

GUIDANCE MAY BE INFORMAL OR FORMAL IN NATURE

On many occasions, the individual seeks or receives help that is informal in character. With a friend, he may have a casual conversation about his difficulty or about a similar difficulty encountered by another person. Through such informal discussions, the individual may gain facts and opinions that are helpful to him.

3

At other times, the individual needs the benefits of relatively formal methods of securing help. He may consult a person who is professionally qualified to analyze his problem, to interpret the relevant facts, and to point out the possible solutions. In this way the individual makes use of guidance procedures that are systematically organized.

Many high schools and colleges have definite provisions for guidance including qualified personnel for aiding students to solve their problems. Today organized guidance services are regarded as among the essential functions of an educational institution.

Instruction, the principal function of the school, is facilitated or hindered by social, economic, and other key factors in the student's life outside the classroom. The student may have the *social* problem of making a satisfactory adjustment to his fellow students. He may face the *economic* problem of financing his present and future education. He may have the *vocational* problem of deciding upon his career. He may have the *emotional* problem created by continued failures in school subjects.

If the school is conscious of such student problems, it is more likely to provide help toward solving them. And this help is likely to be most effective if it is carried on by competent counselors.

WHAT IS THE GUIDANCE POINT OF VIEW?

In guidance work in an educational institution, the basic attitude should be that *the individual is of central importance.* The institution, of course, must have general regulations that protect and advance the good of all the persons involved as well as of the institution itself. Nevertheless, in guidance work, the individual, his problems, his adjustments, and his progress must be regarded as the main concern.

The guidance point of view may be defined more specifically as the attitude that aims to help the *individual*

1. To understand himself
2. To make the most of his capacities, interests, and other qualities

3. To adjust himself satisfactorily to the varied situations within his total environment

4. To develop the ability to make his own decisions wisely and to solve his problems independently

5. To make his own unique contributions to society to the fullest possible extent

The viewpoint just presented emphasizes the development of the individual to the limit of his potentialities. This objective implies that the individual needs to learn how to adjust himself to situations so that he achieves maximum satisfactions therein.

Cowley described this point of view as "a philosophy of education which puts the emphasis upon the individual student and his all-round development as a person rather than upon his intellectual training alone, and which promotes the establishment in educational institutions of curricular programs, methods of instruction, and extra-instructional media to achieve such emphasis." [1]

According to Brouwer, "the individual is not a disembodied mind, nor is he a body without a mind. He is a psychobiological organism in constant interaction with a complex array of environmental forces. As an organism he necessarily responds to his environment as a 'whole being.' . . . If both personnel work and education have to do with the whole student, then there is no instructor, administrator, or laborer on the campus who is not engaged in personnel work. . . . If all faculty members have a personnel philosophy of education, they see the interrelatedness of what they are doing to the development of the student as a whole being." [2]

The late President L. B. Hopkins of Wabash College stated a similar viewpoint when he wrote: "In education the administration is beset with many serious problems and certain of these problems become so acute at times that there is danger that they may be met and solved without sufficient consideration for their ultimate effect upon the individual student. One

---

[1] W. M. Cowley, "The Nature of Student Personnel Work," *The Educational Record*, XVII (April, 1936), 222.

[2] Paul J. Brouwer, *Student Personnel Services in Education* (Washington, D.C.: American Council on Education, 1949), pp. 280-283.

of the functions, therefore, of personnel administration in education is to bring to bear upon any educational problem the point of view which concerns itself primarily with the individual. Thus, in this particular, as in all others, personnel work should remain consistent with the theory and purpose of education by tending constantly to emphasize the problem that underlies all other problems of education—namely, how the institution may best serve the individual." [3]

Underlying these quotations is the concept that decisions involving general administrative or instructional matters should be based on their impact on the individual student. Thus, the point of reference should be the student. As Wrenn has stated, the institution exists fundamentally for the sake of the student, and not the student for the institution. Schools are established to fulfill the desire of society that potential leaders and future members of society be educated. Therefore, they must decide immediate administrative or instructional problems with an eye toward the future. A broad, farsighted attitude is demanded.[4]

Now consider the opposite of the guidance point of view. There was a time when American elementary schools, high schools, and colleges assumed that they had fulfilled all of their educational responsibilities when they had provided instruction for students. Whether the students profited or could profit from the instruction given was of secondary consideration. This survive-or-perish attitude might be characterized as "let the students swim or sink." All too many students did the latter, dropping out of school before they should.

As a school has increased its knowledge of individual differences in learning and has become more aware of the aids and hindrances to learning, it has paid greater attention to the individual. In doing so, the school raises and tries to answer such questions as these:

1. Is the student ready for the kind of instruction that is "normal" for his present age and grade level? Has the student

---

[3] L. B. Hopkins, "Personnel Procedure in Education," *The Educational Record*, Supplement No. 3 (October, 1926), 5.

[4] C. Gilbert Wrenn, *Student Personnel Work in College* (New York: The Ronald Press Company, 1951), pp. 4-7.

the skills and the knowledge necessary for making reasonably good progress in his schoolwork?

2. Is the course presented in such fashion that the student can be led successfully from the easier to the more difficult aspects of the subject under study? Has the student mastered the principles and procedures of effective study?

3. What is the level of motivation of the student? Does the student work only because he is forced to do so? Or, does he work because he sees the real values of what he is doing?

4. What is the student's physical condition? Does he have physical handicaps? Is he stable emotionally? What factors outside the classroom affect the student's progress toward physical and emotional health?

These and many other queries are investigated by a school that gives its attention to the individual student. Thus, the modern school considers more than the organization of its curricula and the content of the courses therein. It attends closely to the personal background, experience, and mental and emotional functioning of the learner as a developing and maturing individual.

WHAT ARE THE IMPLICATIONS OF THE GUIDANCE POINT OF VIEW?

According to the guidance point of view just expressed, the school helps to bring to bear on the individual those influences that stimulate and assist him, primarily by his own efforts, to develop to the maximum degree consistent with his capacities. In other words, the institution offers activities and employs procedures through which the individual is encouraged to make the most of himself.

In line with the guidance viewpoint, the school recognizes that the effectiveness of the entire group depends upon the effectiveness of each individual who is a member of that group. If the individual is not achieving as well as he might, he to that extent handicaps the development of the group as a whole.

Consider, for example, the class that has a student who is a slow learner; this student, say, is deficient in the required fundamental skills. If the teacher adjusts the speed with which group instruction is given to this slow learner, he retards the growth of other students, particularly of those who are brighter and better-equipped academically. As a result, the progress of the entire class is impeded.

Another example is a class made up of students who have varying degrees of motivation. At one extreme, some students know exactly why they are in the particular course and what they are to do; they work diligently in preparing their lessons and they participate extensively in discussions and other class activities. At the other extreme, some students are poorly motivated; they do little or nothing in classwork or homework. Until this situation is improved, the learning of the entire student group is hampered.

To promote maximum achievement by each individual and by the group as a whole, the teacher with the guidance point of view tries to know each student—his abilities, interests, attitudes, and motives. Such a teacher realizes that his effectiveness in working with the entire class is often aided or hindered by the influence of some of its members. Therefore, he focuses much of his attention on those students who are slowing up the group's progress. He may be able to help these students within the classroom. Or, he may have to devote time to them outside the regular class period. Or, he may find it necessary to refer these students to others on the staff of the institution; such faculty members may be able to assist these students individually in making the adjustments necessary to solve their learning problems.

Although the teacher strives to help the so-called "slow" or "problem" students, he devotes only a reasonable proportion of his time to them. Thus, he makes sure that he gives all the other students in his group the attention that they need and deserve.

WHAT IS GUIDANCE?

Historically, the term *guidance* has been used in the field of education to designate the assistance given to students in the solution of problems that lay outside the area of classroom teaching situations. For instance, ever since the first decade of the present century, *guidance* has meant, to a large extent, the guidance of students in the area of vocational problems.

By about 1925, a growing number of colleges and universities were providing guidance services for their students. These activities were more commonly referred to as student personnel services. Today these services constitute an all-embracing program of assistance to students; this program, of course, includes guidance services. At the high-school level as well as at the college level, these services have more and more included assistance to students in solving their educational, vocational, and personal problems.

In its early years, the vocational guidance movement was initiated and conducted primarily by semipublic, philanthropic agencies; it also was fostered by some of the public school systems in larger cities. The guidance services thus furnished were offered mainly to young people of high-school age.

For decades, teachers in the elementary grades have aided their pupils in adjusting themselves to their problems. Although these teachers have been most concerned with training pupils in the essential skills and content fields, they have rendered aid in nonacademic as well as academic fields both inside and outside the classroom. For this reason, some elementary schools were slow to recognize that pupils should have special services over and above those normally provided by classroom teachers. As recognition of this need has grown, however, elementary schools have employed school psychologists, adjustment teachers, and child guidance workers to give attention to the whole child and to his special needs and wants.

HERE ARE EXPLANATIONS OF IMPORTANT GUIDANCE TERMS

In the opinion of some people, the term *guidance* implies too much detailed direction of the students' choices, or too much coddling and spoon-feeding of young people. Such implications are not well-founded, however, if the objective of guidance is the stimulation of the individual to take increased responsibility for self-direction. Also, in the opinion of these same people, the word *adjustment* carries the connotation that the individual is adjusted mechanically to a situation. Although *adjustment* has not yet gained a definite or permanent place for itself in the terminology of the guidance field, this concept implies an adaptation that is dynamic and functional rather than mechanical.

Despite the criticisms directed at the term *guidance,* this term seems appropriate at all levels of the school and college ladder. At any level, guidance implies that the individual attains self-direction just as fast and as far as his mental, social, and emotional abilities permit. Guidance of the younger or less mature individual, of course, calls for closer direction than does guidance of the older or more mature individual. The term *guidance,* moreover, aptly applies to working with an individual all along the line from early childhood into adulthood.

Definitions of Guidance Terms

In any field, a common terminology is necessary if the discussion is to be mutually understandable. Toward this goal, definitions of the key terms within the guidance field are presented next.

Matériel and *personnel* need clarification first. According to the dictionary, *matériel* is "the aggregate of *things* used or needed in carrying on any business, undertaking, or operation." *Personnel* is "the body of *persons* employed in any work, undertaking, or service." The contrasted concepts are "things" and "persons."

Student personnel services in a school or college are the systematically organized and operated services that provide assistance to the individual in the realization (a) of his own best adjustments to problems and situations, and (b) of his own highest possible achievements.

The over-all program of student personnel services offers assistance to the individual in all phases of his personal development: intellectual growth, aesthetic appreciation, emotional maturity, physical condition, social and civic relationships, vocational potentialities and skills, financial needs, and moral and spiritual values.

Guidance services make up a major part of student personnel services. Guidance services embrace the cluster of activities or experiences that assist the individual student to grow in self-understanding, to make wiser decisions, and to do increasingly effective planning.

Counseling, interviewing, and *testing* are processes, or tools, used in the program of guidance services. They are basic features of guidance services.

Counseling is the process of individualizing the assistance given the student toward achieving the maximum of his potentialities.

The *interview* is the direct face-to-face contact that occurs when the counselor and counselee meet to deal with the counselee's problems. It is the essential means whereby all the information concerning the individual can be directed toward the diagnosis of his situation and the improvement of it.

Testing is an important part of the process of appraising the individual, because it is a relatively objective means of determining the individual's characteristics. For this purpose, testing employs psychological measuring devices.

The terms *guidance* and *counseling* are not synonymous. Guidance includes counseling. In the process known as counseling, testing and interviewing are parts or tools.

One of the important types of guidance services involves assistance to high-school students in planning their educational programs. In working toward this objective, counseling is the essential means. Through counseling, the counselor endeavors to become well-acquainted with the counselee's total situation and varied characteristics; he does this through direct observation, tests, ratings, and academic records. If the information thus obtained is systematically recorded on a cumulative record where it is readily available for both study and discussion, this information can be brought into even sharper focus by means of interviews. In an interview, the skillful counselor uses this information to assist the counselee to evaluate himself and to gain clear insights into his situation.

GUIDANCE SERVICES IN THE ELEMENTARY SCHOOL

In the elementary school, the classroom teacher is actually both teacher and counselor. He is responsible for helping the pupil master fundamental skills and knowledge within

LIBRARY C. C. N. Y.

school subjects. He is responsible also for guiding the pupil progressively toward maturity in the social and emotional aspects of personality.

The elementary-school teacher is in a good position to know the pupil's physical, mental, and emotional strengths and weaknesses. More than the teacher at any higher level, he is likely to be familiar with the whole pupil, in all aspects of his personality. In schools where classes are very large, however, the elementary-school teacher may find it difficult to gain a close acquaintanceship with every pupil in his class. Yet he should continue his efforts to do so.

Whether classes are large or small, modern elementary schools provide specialists who work with, and through, the classroom teacher. Together they guide the individual pupil. In some of these schools, the school psychologist administers, scores, and interprets group and individual tests of many kinds. Through such tests and other means, the psychologist studies pupils who are experiencing various kinds of difficulty. In others of these schools, the counselor works individually with pupils in much the same way that an elementary-school psychologist or a high-school counselor does. In still other elementary schools, both the psychologist and the counselor work with the teacher on matters related to the guidance of pupils. In modern schools, furthermore, the school physician or nurse helps the teacher understand the physical and emotional needs of children and also, when appropriate, refers them to other specialists—to the family physician or dentist, to an oculist, or to a social worker, for example.

If pupil guidance is to be most effective, it must be thoroughly integrated with the total school program. By combined efforts, the teacher and the available specialists, inside and outside the school, can make a continuous and enlightening study of the status and progress of pupils, both as individuals and as groups. Through such a study, these staff members can aid pupils in many areas—in their mastery of essential skills, in their acquisition of fundamental information, in their building of desirable attitudes toward school tasks, and in their development of the ability to adapt themselves socially. In addition, through cooperative effort, teachers and specialized personnel can assist each child to be physically strong and healthy, emotionally stable, and well-adjusted.

The elementary school with superior guidance services keeps cumulative records that summarize the progress of individual pupils. Such a school, moreover, conducts research and evaluation that improve the procedures and techniques of its guidance services.

PERSONNEL SERVICES IN THE HIGH SCHOOL

At the high-school level, student personnel services (including guidance services) involve many types of activities, as follows:

1. Preregistration advising of students—that is, advising them just prior to their entering high school

2. Admission and registration procedures

3. Orientation of new students to the school—its offerings, its requirements, and its methods of work

4. Other guidance services such as (a) collection of significant, comprehensive information about students; (b) provision of a large body of authentic and up-to-date educational and occupational information for the use of students and counselors; (c) testing and counseling students; (d) job placement of students; and (e) follow-up of students

5. Health services—advice on physical and mental hygiene, for instance

6. Extracurricular activities—student government and clubs, for example

7. Student personnel records—vital statistics, family and home background, school marks, and the like

8. Personnel research, including evaluation of the total program of personnel services

9. Coordination of all the efforts of teachers and other staff members to provide the best possible services to students

At the high-school level, the program of personnel services is broader in scope and more varied in content than it is at the elementary-school level. For this reason, the high-school program requires more specialists. Because of the departmental organization of the typical high school, the teacher therein has less opportunity to become fully acquainted with the individual student than does the elementary-school teacher.

The high-school situation, moreover, demands a systematic organization of personnel services in general and of guidance services in particular. Sufficiently trained personnel and adequate time both are required to assist students in solving problems of an educational, vocational, social, or personal nature.

In many high schools, the teachers who have the interest, training, experience, and other requisite qualities act as teacher-counselors; they are usually allotted time to perform the counseling function. In smaller high schools, teacher-counselors do all or nearly all of the guidance work. In larger high schools, however, full-time specialists are responsible for guidance and related personnel services. In these schools, the guidance specialists usually work closely with teacher-counselors.

STUDENT PERSONNEL SERVICES IN COLLEGE AND UNIVERSITY

In a collegiate program of personnel services, the essential activities do not differ markedly from those in a high-school program. At the college level, however, these services are more extensive. They are provided by a greater variety of specialists; these specialists are better trained than are those working at the high-school level.

The large colleges and universities tend to delegate student personnel functions on a highly specialized basis. As a result, the typical college teacher is less likely to be a counselor in the full sense of the term. Rather, because this teacher is trained and interested in a particular academic field, he is inclined to be solely a specialist in subject matter. In some institutions, however, certain teachers also serve as counselors. To the extent that these teachers have the necessary qualities of personality and the requisite background of training, they are able to participate in and contribute to the college's guidance services.

Student personnel services in colleges and universities involve the following types of activities:

1. Admissions
2. Registration

3. Orientation—opportunities offered, extracurricular organizations, effective study habits

4. Guidance services—responsibilities of providing help to students whose needs include improvement of skills in fundamental subjects (reading or mathematics, for example); choice of appropriate curricula and elective courses; choice of suitable vocations; and betterment of personal and social adjustments

To meet the foregoing responsibilities, guidance services in colleges and universities provide for (a) the collection of significant and comprehensive information about students; (b) the assembly of a large body of authentic educational and occupational information for the use of students and counselors; (c) the testing and counseling services; (d) the job placement services; and (e) the follow-up of students. These guidance services help students to solve their educational, vocational, and personal problems, and to achieve sound, emotionally stable, and mature personalities.

5. Health services—physical and mental hygiene

6. Extracurricular activities—student government and student clubs

7. Housing and boarding

8. Financial assistance—scholarships and loans

9. Religious activities (in some colleges)

10. Personnel records services

11. Personnel research and evaluation of the program

12. Coordination of all aspects of personnel services

WHAT IS THE ROLE OF THE GUIDANCE EMPHASIS?

The counselor will clarify his thinking about guidance services if he regards these services not only as a major part of but also as a necessary emphasis in the total program of student personnel services.

The general purpose of all student personnel services is to assist the individual in self-direction and self-development. In line with this purpose, the staff member who renders a "nonguidance" service such as instruction may also provide a guidance service. The teacher of a science course, for example, may discuss careers in scientific fields with students in his class.

In keeping with the guidance emphasis, personnel services must be varied and interrelated if they are to deal adequately with the human personality. The typical person finds that his different problems often bear upon one another. For example, a student's difficulty in solving his financial problem hampers his academic achievement or stands in the way of his development of important social skills. Because of the interrelationships among a student's problems, it is essential that all the various staff members concerned with personnel services cooperate in every way. Although specialists and nonspecialists in the field of guidance each must have a clear-cut responsibility, they must work together as a team. This requires flexible cooperation and close coordination in the highest possible degree. Otherwise these staff members will fail to reach the main goal of helping the individual student to attain maximum self-development and self-realization.

WHY IS THE SCIENTIFIC ATTITUDE ESSENTIAL IN GUIDANCE WORK?

If guidance work is to be professional in character, it must be based on the scientific method, attitude, or point of view. In other words, the scientific method not only can be applied to problems in the fields of the exact sciences such as physics and chemistry. It also can be used to solve problems arising in the field of guidance.

According to the scientific method, conclusions are drawn from facts—facts that have been objectively obtained, analyzed, and evaluated by the use of the best available devices and techniques. The scientific method entails the use of recognized processes of clear and sound thinking.

In the guidance field, the professional worker relies on logical analysis, on rational hypotheses, on mathematical preciseness, on controlled scientific experiment, on conclusions based on exact observations, and on consideration of all the facts, without regard for his personal opinions or wishes.

From these statements, the reader should *not* infer that, if the scientific method is employed, guidance services are cold and impersonal. Rather, he should understand that, according to the scientific method, the *facts* concerning an individual are systematically collected, objectively examined, and realistically faced in common by the counselor and the counselee.

Guidance services sprang from a commendable desire to assist individuals toward maximum fulfillment of their potentialities. The early leaders in this field were motivated primarily by a philanthropic or even missionary spirit—advancement of the welfare of individuals. These leaders did not have an organized body of scientific knowledge or a complete kit of scientific tools.

Slowly, and then more rapidly, during the past 25 years, workers in the guidance field have developed scientific procedures for determining and for assessing facts about individuals. As a result, they have made genuine progress in many aspects of guidance—for instance, in the understanding of human abilities, aptitudes, achievements, interests, and attitudes. Toward understanding human behavior, psychologists as well as guidance workers have made many significant contributions.

In the last 15 years, guidance workers have increasingly employed scientific methods and statistical procedures in their techniques of studying the individual. Also, these workers have more and more used so-called projective techniques. Although these techniques were not quantitative or statistical, they threw new light on ways to make guidance work more effective. And finally, guidance workers and teachers have taken pre-service and in-service training programs that have substantially raised the level of their competence in the area of personnel services.

Guarding Against Pseudo-Scientists in the Guidance Field

In spite of the contributions of psychology and psychometrics, and notwithstanding the high professional competence of many guidance workers, there are a considerable number of pseudo-guidance specialists who offer their services to individuals and institutions. These "specialists" carry on their practices under many different self-assumed titles.

Guidance workers with the scientific point of view, of course, place no credence in the so-called sciences of phrenology, astrology, or physiognomy, for example. These professional workers in the guidance field know that a person's abilities, potentialities, or interests cannot be determined scientifically by the phrenologist from a study of the conformation of the skull. These workers also recognize that neither the lines in the palm of a person's hands nor the pattern of the stars and planets at the time of his birth give scientific evidence as to his past, present, or future.

Every year gullible Americans waste many thousands of dollars going to these pseudo-scientists for advice. On occasion, moreover, people of above-average intelligence pay high fees to pseudo-guidance workers—practitioners who have the technical vocabulary but lack technical competence required in the guidance area.

Because these pseudo-guidance specialists are still offering their services, anyone who needs assistance should select his guidance consultant as carefully as he chooses his physician. When in doubt, he should seek the advice of a psychologist, guidance director, or other specialist who is, for example, on the staff of a school system, college, or university. This specialist or his institution is probably affiliated with a professional organization such as the American Psychological Association, the National Vocational Guidance Association, the American College Personnel Association, or the Educational Records Bureau. These organizations have developed standards by which to judge the competence of a guidance specialist.

Combining the Scientific and the Human Approaches

Although the scientific method is highly important in professional guidance services, it is not the only method. The best guidance work calls for a combination of the scientific approach and the human approach.

In practice, some guidance workers overemphasize the human approach. They may even refuse to use scientifically-based techniques or the findings therefrom. Other guidance workers overstress the scientific approach. They may rely solely upon scientific techniques and the results thus obtained.

According to the best theory and practice today, neither the human approach nor the scientific approach by itself is adequate. Many situations require the fusion of these two useful approaches. In some situations, the one or the other approach is mainly indicated. For certain aspects of a given situation, the appropriate techniques may be scientific; for other aspects, those techniques may be nonscientific.

When, then, should the counselor rely chiefly upon the human approach? The answer may well be: "During an interview." At that time, the student is analyzing himself and his situation and is developing insights related thereto. Not only during an interview but also during all other contacts with the student the counselor should display an understanding attitude.

GUIDANCE INSIDE AND OUTSIDE THE SCHOOL

Guidance workers who are on the staff of schools or colleges should, of course, recognize that their work can be related to similar work being carried on outside their institutions. Both educational institutions and noneducational organizations, for example, can employ the same or similar procedures, tools, and devices. Both can exchange information and experience as these bear upon the welfare of the persons being guided. More specifically, guidance or personnel workers in schools or colleges can render important assistance to personnel workers in business, industry, and government, and *vice versa*.

If personnel work is well done in a school or college, that work contributes to the success of the personnel program of a business organization. If the school has helped a student to develop certain attitudes toward himself and toward his school responsibilities, then the business employing that youth finds it easier to orient and train him for effective performance in an actual job. Moreover, if the school has aided the student to do his schoolwork well and to achieve up to his capacity, these patterns of behavior will help him later to succeed in a full-time occupation.

Whether personnel services are conducted in an educational institution or in a business organization, these two types of establishments should endeavor to meet the common needs of individuals for guidance. These include the needs for placement, orientation, adjustment, rating, and promotion. In their guidance services, these establishments often use similar principles, tests, and techniques in counseling and in other personnel work.

Much more than obtains at present, personnal workers in educational and in noneducational organizations need to understand and appreciate their mutually interrelated tasks. If the guidance worker in education and the guidance worker in business each understands what the other is doing, both can perform their own jobs better. Each can face his problems more realistically; through cooperation both can solve problems that neither working alone could master.

Personnel workers in a school or college realize that one of their main functions is to help prepare youth for adult work activities. Accordingly, these workers should be familiar with business and industry. To help youth to find jobs and to succeed in them, personnel workers in business and industry should know educational institutions—their instructors, curricula, policies, and guidance services. By knowing one another's problems, resources, tools, and procedures, guidance workers in education and in business can materially enhance their effectiveness.

SUMMARY

In professional, systematic guidance work in an educational institution, the basic attitude should be that the individual is of central importance. In line with this attitude, the chief objective of the guidance point of view is the development of the individual in all-round fashion to the limit of his potentialities. The task of the school is to make all of its resources available to the individual student so that he learns to make wise decisions and to solve his problems independently.

In an educational institution, the program of guidance services, through the central activity of counseling, is the means whereby the guidance point of view is implemented. The success of this program depends upon whole-hearted cooperation among teachers and specialized guidance workers within the educational institution; and between guidance workers in schools and colleges and in business and industry.

If the worker in an educational organization is to acquire and practice the guidance point of view, he should be familiar with the sociological background of guidance. This is the subject of the next chapter.

SUGGESTED READINGS

American Council on Education. *The Student Personnel Point of View.* American Council on Education Studies, Series VI, No. 13. Washington, D.C.: American Council on Education, Rev. ed., 1949.

Brouwer, Paul J. *Student Personnel Services in General Education.* Washington, D.C.: American Council on Education, 1949. Pp. 274-283; 310-317.

Brumbaugh, A. J. "Better Student Personnel Services in Junior Colleges," *Junior College Journal,* XXI (September, 1950), 37-41.

Crow, Lester D., and Crow, Alice. *An Introduction to Guidance: Principles and Practices.* New York: American Book Company, 1951. Chapters 1-3.

Davis, Frank G., and Norris, Pearle S. *Guidance Handbook for Teachers.* New York: McGraw-Hill Book Company, Inc., 1949.

Detjen, Ervin Winfred, and Detjen, Mary Ford. *Elementary School Guidance.* New York: McGraw-Hill Book Company, Inc., 1952.

Federal Security Agency. *Pupil Personnel Services in Elementary and Secondary Schools.* Washington, D.C.: Superintendent of Documents, 1951. Catalog No. FS 5.4:325.

Froehlich, Clifford P. *Guidance Services in Smaller Schools.* New York: McGraw-Hill Book Company, Inc., 1950. Pp. 1-21.

Hatch, Raymond N. *Guidance Services in the Elementary School.* Dubuque, Iowa: William C. Brown Company, 1951.

Hopkins, E. H. "The Essentials of a College Personnel Program," *College and University,* 23 (July 1948), 549-567.

Johnson, B. Lamar, *General Education in Action.* Washington, D.C.: American Council on Education, 1952. Pp. 54-77.

Jones, Arthur J. *Principles of Guidance.* New York: McGraw-Hill Book Company, Inc., 1951. Chapters 1-3.

Lefever, D. W., Turrell, A. M., and Weitzel, H. I. *Principles and Techniques of Guidance.* New York: The Ronald Press Company, 1950.

Mathewson, Robert Hendry. *Guidance Policy and Practice.* New York: Harper and Brothers, 1949.

Smith, Glenn E. *Principles and Practices of the Guidance Program.* New York: Macmillan Company, 1951. Pp. 1-35.

Willey, Roy DeVerl. *Guidance in Elementary Education.* New York: Harper and Brothers, 1952.

Williamson, E. G. *Counseling Adolescents.* New York: McGraw-Hill Book Company, Inc., 1950. Pp. 30-50.

Williamson, E. G. (ed.) *Trends in Student Personnel Work.* Minneapolis: University of Minnesota Press, 1949. Pp. 7-11.

Wrenn, C. Gilbert. *Student Personnel Work in College.* New York: The Ronald Press Company, 1951. Pp. 4-7; 22-28.

Zerfoss, Karl P. (ed.) *Readings in Counseling.* New York: Association Press, 1952. Pp. 39-167.

CHAPTER TWO

Sociological Bases for Guidance Work

CONCEPTS BASIC to the development of guidance work have roots in such fields as religion, philosophy, psychology, and sociology. These fields deal in varying degrees and from different points of view with the individual and with his interpersonal relationships. So, too, does the field of guidance work. It emphasizes assistance to the individual in adjusting to his own needs and wants and to the situations in which he finds himself. Through guidance services, the individual is aided in self-development and self-realization, and in the achievement of maximum effectiveness in his relationships with others.

Through the fields of knowledge just mentioned, certain basic sociological concepts of importance to guidance workers have been developed. These concepts include *the fundamental worth of the individual,* the concept that will be discussed next.

THE FUNDAMENTAL WORTH OF THE INDIVIDUAL

Among sociological bases for guidance work, first if not foremost is the belief in, and the respect for, the fundamental worth of the individual. This attitude should always be kept in mind by the guidance worker no matter with whom he is counseling. With such an attitude, the guidance worker is imbued with the desire to serve the person in need of assistance; he relegates all other considerations to their proper place in the total setting.

In the field of guidance as well as in other fields, this basic concept cannot be overemphasized. There is general agreement among historians, philosophers, and sociologists that the level of development of a civilization is measured by the degree to which it respects the value or worth of the individual.

Civilizations that have minimized and even degraded the individual may have apparently progressed, at least in certain aspects. Yet, sooner or later, these civilizations declined and then disappeared. Their collapse was due, in no small part, to the fact that they failed to give each person (including the most capable) the right to develop as an individual to his fullest potentiality.

In contrast, civilizations that gave the individual a good chance to improve and to express himself as a person have tended to flourish and to persist. Because respect for the worth of the individual was of central importance, each of these civilizations as a whole benefited.

THE CONSERVATION OF HUMAN BEINGS

A second basic concept of guidance work is the desire of society to conserve human beings and human energy; this concept, of course, implies the wise use of human resources.

In civilizations where human life was cheaply held, human resources have been wasted and even destroyed. This was true in nearly all of the ancient civilizations. In certain respects, the Athenian civilization was an exception, but even there the welfare of the individual depended upon his position in the socioeconomic system. That social system had as its base a large slave population.

In those modern civilizations which have attained high levels of development, however, human beings and human energy are guarded, respected, and conserved. Toward this goal, contributions are made by governments, including their legislative, executive, and judicial branches. Among these contributions are genuine, well-considered, well-administered social legislation. This legislation has aided materially in the conservation of human beings and in the prevention of their wastage.

The concept of the conservation of human beings implies that society has the obligation to help the individual to live the kind of life that is both individually satisfying and socially effective. To help meet this obligation, the school as a societal institution must provide sufficient guidance services to the individual when, as, and if he needs them. The school, moreover, must supply for each individual the kind of education that best fits his abilities and other potentialities. Thus the school aids the individual to attain his own maximum development, a benefit both to himself and to society.[1]

THE INCREASING COMPLEXITY OF SOCIETAL DEMANDS

The third sociological basis for guidance work is the fact that society itself and its demands on the individual are continually changing and are becoming more and more complex.

Any thoughtful observer of the modern scene is impressed by the startling changes in our modes of living. Both our store of knowledge and our techniques for getting and using it are expanding in range and depth. Technological changes pervade industry. They bring shorter hours of work that in turn bring increased leisure and attendant problems. Communication and transportation attain new and astounding speeds. Willy-nilly, international contacts become closer. Diverse political and economic problems arise.

The keystone, serving to hold a society together in this period of rapid and complex changes, is the slow but sure development of a social consciousness. In spite of social conflicts and tensions, there is a growing attitude that the individual *is* his brother's keeper.

To keep pace with societal changes, the thoughtful person recognizes that he must speed up and multiply his activities. He must have contacts with more people and with a greater variety of people. He must adjust himself to many new ideas and to the pressures they impose. In addition, this person must change his methods of work on the job; if he does not do so, he falls behind in his competition with others. This observer also realizes that the average length of life expectancy is greater than ever before; this trend poses new problems for a growing number of persons.

The thoughtful person knows that along with many other

---

[1] *Counselor Preparation* (Washington, D.C.: National Vocational Guidance Association, 1949), p. 5.

changes there are changing concepts in the home, in the school, and in the church. All these institutions are responding to the impact of new conditions, new ideas, and new attitudes.

The Increasing Need for Guidance Services

The complexities of modern life and the changes therein mean that people confront more problems than formerly and that they have more difficulty in achieving satisfactory solutions. They find that older patterns of thinking and acting and that older stocks of knowledge are inadequate guides in the new situations. For these reasons, people as individuals are in greater need of assistance today than they were in the past. To obtain this assistance, they look to various organizations that have assumed responsibility for guidance services. These organizations may be the school, the church, the place of work; they may be private or public service agencies.

These agencies of society operate on the principle that the individual has a right to receive assistance in making choices and adjustments. Through such assistance, these agencies believe, the individual is helped continually to increase his ability to guide himself by his own thought and effort.[2]

Help in Solving Emotional Problems

An enlightened and forward-looking society must provide means whereby individuals of all ages may be aided in learning how best to adjust themselves emotionally.

In all too many families, children face emotional problems that they alone or they with their parents cannot solve. These youngsters are often confused. They do not know what causes their difficulties. Often they take undesirable steps to effect their adjustments. As a result, these youngsters may become so-called "problem children." "Normal" boys and girls as well may fail to develop the most desirable behavior patterns—patterns that have emotional stability.

Toward gaining emotional stability, many pupils in the elementary grades need help from persons outside their imme-

---

[2] *Ibid.,* p. 4.

diate families. And the same is true of many high-school students. Their emotional difficulties may be more intense and serious than those of younger children for two main reasons. First, high-school students feel the cumulative effects of inadequate adjustments during elementary-school years. And second, they undergo the strains and stresses of adolescence.

Because the student in college is older chronologically than he was in high school, theoretically he has grown up emotionally. Yet all too many college students have not achieved sufficient emotional maturity.

When the young person leaves school and takes a full-time job as an adult, he often needs assistance in meeting brand new situations. Even after this youth has become oriented to his work and has learned something about its demands, he may confront new conditions and situations that upset him emotionally. Then, again, he needs assistance to guide him through his troubles.

An Example of Adjustments to a Postwar Situation

As society's demands change, so do the services required to help meet those demands. To illustrate, after the end of World War II, the government discharged millions of men from the military services. Since V-J Day, both public and private agencies have been endeavoring to organize their resources so that these veterans could adjust satisfactorily and quickly to civilian life.

On their own or with little agency help, most veterans had a relatively easy time in becoming civilians again; their problems of readjustment were not nearly as acute as predicted. However, among all veterans there were thousands who required assistance from one or more agencies before they achieved reasonably satisfactory civilian adjustments.

Whether or not a veteran needed agency assistance, he faced such tasks as these—finding an adequate job, a job in which he could succeed; earning enough money to live decently; locating a home during a period of housing shortages; and adjusting himself to the feeling that he had "lost" valuable years from his life during military service. The nature and size of these tasks tended to slow down, and at times to stop, veterans in their efforts personally to adjust to civilian living. Without society's help, in all probability, many thousands still would be maladjusted.

THE SPECIALIZATION OF FUNCTION

The fourth sociological basis for guidance work is the emphasis in modern society on specialization of function. As society has become more complex, its functions have become more highly specialized.

In the production and distribution of goods, for example, the specialization of functions among workers has become essential. In the past, the cobbler performed all the functions required to make a shoe from cutting the leather to turning out the finished product. Today these functions are performed by specialists, each of whom has particular responsibilities. In the modern shoe factory, employees are assigned narrow specialties. In these, they become highly proficient. Thus, through specialization, the factory produces more and better shoes per man-hour of labor and reduces the production cost per unit.

A similar trend is noticeable in the professions. Due to the great advances within the medical sciences, for example, no man can master all the existing knowledge and techniques in all medical fields. Therefore, some physicians have become specialists in some one field of medicine.

The trend toward specialization is also occurring in other professional fields. These include such fields as chemistry, physics, biology, home economics, law, and accounting.

Although specialization exists within skilled and semi-skilled occupations, there are fairly common misconceptions about the nature and implications of specialization at these levels of work. One misconception is that the worker who has become skilled in a certain kind of specialized job cannot succeed in another kind of specialized job. Because of this misconception, the worker may find it difficult, particularly during an economic depression, to change from one type of job to another.

Another misconception is that each worker is suited to only one given job or type of job. According to this idea, each worker has certain skills that fit him for only one particular kind of work; also, each particular kind of work requires certain activities which that individual only can effectively perform. This misconception is implied in the popular saying, "A square peg in a round hole."

As a matter of fact, most persons can become proficient in a variety of types of work. This is true partly because many individuals have the basic skills, the personal adaptability, and the other traits that are needed to succeed in a number of different jobs, and partly because many jobs which are superficially different in their requirements actually have many common elements.

Many people, furthermore, can be trained to do new jobs. During World War II, for example, war production plants recruited thousands of persons who were formerly housewives, farm laborers, and workers in service occupations. The plants trained these new employees to run machines and to perform other skilled and semiskilled operations. Their training programs were highly successful; within short periods of time, employees learned jobs that were considerably different from the jobs they had worked at previously. Also, during World War II, the military services trained millions of men for jobs that were far different from those that they had had before. Young men who had been shipping clerks, farm workers, soda-fountain workers, delivery boys became skilled airplane mechanics, pilots, navigators, bombardiers, meteorologists.

Recognizing the adaptability of people to job and jobs to people, the fact remains that the work of society is best organized and accomplished on the basis of specialization of function. To meet the requirements of specialization, individual aptitudes and job requirements must be carefully coordinated. This can best be done through an effective program of guidance services.

THE IMPORTANCE OF RIGHT PLACEMENT

The foregoing emphasis on specialization of function leads to the fifth sociological basis for guidance work. This basis implies the following premise: The stability and progress of society require that each member of society find his most appropriate place. Only if each member does so can he contribute most to the work of the group as a whole.

The very existence of a complex society such as ours depends on the optimum distribution of workers among a diversity of activities. On the one hand, suppose that all of our gainfully employed workers, or even a sizable number of them, insisted on performing the same type of work, such as cotton farming. Or suppose that they had only the abilities for cotton farming. Then, obviously, our working force would be unable to provide the goods and services that are necessary to achieve a high standard of living generally, let alone to support human life itself. On the other hand, assume that our gainful workers are placed in jobs that are right for them and for society as a whole. Then, individuals gain greater personal satisfactions; and society gains in terms of living standards and social stability.

In our society, being placed in the right job means that the individual has some freedom of job choice. Each individual has his own preferences for work activities. He also has certain economic, social, and personal resources and limitations that bear upon his ability to get the kind of work that he wants. With his preferences, resources, and limitations in mind, the individual may reach the conclusion that a certain occupation is the one for him. He believes that in this occupation he can function most efficiently and with greatest personal satisfaction. If this individual through appropriate placement enters the occupation of his choice, he gains respect in his own eyes and in those of others.

The worker who is engaged in the occupation he likes and succeeds in tends to remain in that occupation. Therein, he obtains increasing monetary and other satisfactions. Moreover, if this worker is ambitious and intelligent, and if he has the other requisite personal characteristics, he finds better ways of doing his work—he becomes more efficient. As a result, this worker may be promoted to a more responsible and better-paying position.

When the right man is placed in the right job, he himself benefits both materially and in less tangible but equally important ways. And society, of which this man is a member, also benefits; through his achievements and satisfactions, society both maintains stability and makes progress.

THE EMPLOYMENT OF WOMEN

Still another sociological basis of guidance work is the trend in the employment of women. During the past three decades, particularly, society has changed its attitude toward women in so-called gainful employment.

For generations, society held the idea that woman's place was in the home. Slowly this idea underwent change. At first, social mores accepted and then encouraged the employment of unmarried women and widows, usually women who had to support themselves in whole or in part. Yet, according to these mores, women might fill certain kinds of jobs only—jobs in such fields as domestic service, or perhaps office work or teaching. After marriage, these young women expected to leave their jobs and to confine their work to their homes.

Gradually society's attitude toward the employment of women changed even more. This change was due to many factors including the pressures exerted by women themselves. Through gaining the vote and through other means, for example, women more and more won the right to become gainfully employed persons. Some women advocated and won the right to pursue "careers" and to care for their families simultaneously.

A number of factors other than those already mentioned contributed to the growing acceptance of women in increasing numbers as members of the labor force. Among these factors, the following were important:

1. Women received longer periods of education; this education fitted them for more and better jobs in gainful occupations.

2. Women demonstrated their abilities to do certain kinds of jobs even better than men did; in some jobs women proved to be more adaptable than men.

3. Women, in increasing numbers, expressed their desire to become more self-sufficient financially; some felt that women could gain greater social independence only through greater economic independence.

4. Some women had to work outside the home to help

their husbands to support their families; others wanted outside work to raise their families' standard of living.

5. Women found that labor-saving devices decreased their home work; to fill in the time thus saved, they sought outside employment.

6. Women had increasing opportunities in gainful employment especially in wartime when there was a manpower shortage.

Since the turn of the century, the number of women in the labor force has risen sharply, from 5,000,000 in 1900 to over 17,000,000 in 1949. Among women 14 years of age and older, the proportion who were employed increased from 20 percent to a little less than 33 percent. This rise was due primarily to the entry of married women into the ranks of gainfully employed workers. To illustrate, during the past 50 years, the number of employed married women rose more than eleven times. In the same period, the number of employed single women merely doubled.[3]

It is common knowledge that women today can gain entrance to a greater variety of occupations than was true even 30 years ago. Their choices are no longer limited mostly to homemaking and teaching. Because of this fact, young women, like young men, need help in studying and choosing occupations. The situation now faced by young women places a genuine responsibility on the guidance services of every school or college. Typically the young woman's problem is somewhat more complex than that of the young man. She must steer a course that may involve two jobs—pursuit of a career and management of a home.

THE INCREASING NUMBER OF YOUTH IN SCHOOLS AND COLLEGES

The seventh sociological basis of a guidance services program is the increasing proportion and number of children and youth of school age who are attending elementary schools, high schools, colleges, and other training institutions.

---

[3] Max F. Baer and Edward C. Roeber, *Occupational Information: Its Nature and Use* (Chicago: Science Research Associates, 1951), pp. 34-36, 123-125.

According to the most reliable figures available, more than 65 percent of all high-school-age youth are enrolled in secondary schools. From 15 to 16 percent of all college-age youth are attending colleges and universities.[4]

During the past two decades, the numbers of children and youth in schools and colleges have been rising. In Table 1, note that the increases in enrollment between 1929–30 and 1952–53 were as follows: elementary schools 10 percent; secondary schools, 30 percent; and higher education, 118 percent.

TABLE 1

SCHOOL AND COLLEGE ENROLLMENTS:
1929–30 and 1952–53 *

SCHOOL	YEAR		INCREASE 1929–30 TO 1952–53 (PERCENT)
	1929–30 (NUMBER)	1952–53 (NUMBER)	
Elementary schools (including kindergarten)	23,588,000	26,064,000	10.5
Secondary schools (high schools)	4,800,000	6,263,000	30.5
Higher education (colleges and universities)	1,101,000	2,400,000	118.0
Other schools	(No data)	216,000	
Totals	29,489,000	34,943,000	

* Source: U.S. Office of Education, Washington, D.C. The figures for 1952–53 are estimates.

Concerning projected trends in college enrollments, Edwards and Richey state:

It is true that the number of young persons of college age may be expected to decrease in the future except for a short period during which the large numbers born during the war years will reach college age. It does not necessarily follow, however, that college enrollments in the long run will be smaller. With only 15 or 16 percent of the youth of college age attending college, it is possible to increase the total number materially by a moderate increase of the percentage and this does not appear

---

[4] Newton Edwards and Herman G. Richey, *The School in the American Social Order* (Boston: Houghton Mifflin Company, 1947), pp. 654-655.

unlikely. In fact, it appears very probable that the junior-college enrollments will be greatly expanded.[5]

Since the long-range predictions of high-school and college enrollments are on the side of mounting numbers, these institutions will probably experience a growing demand for guidance services.

SUMMARY

The sociological concepts discussed in this chapter present some of the most compelling reasons for guidance services. Our modern society holds in high esteem the fundamental worth of the individual. It has the strong desire to protect and develop human beings. It needs to use specialization to meet its increasingly complex demands. If society is to progress on an even keel, it must provide opportunities for each individual to make his unique contribution. To help him do so is a great and continuing challenge to all those engaged in guidance work. To meet this challenge, guidance personnel must understand not only the sociological bases but also the psychological bases of their work. The latter are treated in the chapter that follows.

SUGGESTED READINGS

Brouwer, Paul J. *Student Personnel Services in General Education.* Washington, D.C.: American Council on Education, 1949. Pp. 284-309.

Froehlich, Clifford P. *Guidance Services in Smaller Schools.* New York: McGraw-Hill Book Company, Inc., 1950. Pp. 22-39.

---

[5] *Ibid.*, p. 665.

CHAPTER THREE

Psychological Bases of Guidance Services

GUIDANCE not only has sociological bases—its growth has been due to the changing needs of society. Guidance also has psychological bases—its progress has depended upon studies of the individual and of his development. These studies have dealt with differences between individuals, differences within the individual, relationships between abilities and requirements, growth or learning curves, the nature of personality, and the role of adjustment.

THE IMPORTANCE OF DIFFERENCES
BETWEEN INDIVIDUALS

As guidance workers, we recognize that individuals differ in ordinary physical characteristics, such as height, weight, color of hair and eyes, and strength and endurance. In addition, we realize that individuals differ in their mental abilities— in general intelligence and in specific aptitudes such as verbal, quantitative, mechanical, and clerical.

We also know that individuals differ in their emotional characteristics. Some are more optimistic than others. Some are easily irritated; others are not. To some individuals, social contacts are easy to establish and are a continuing source of feelings of well-being; to others, social relations are difficult to initiate and are maintained or endured only by great effort.

Some individuals, moreover, have relatively little variation in their emotional tones. Others have sharp and frequent changes in their emotional states, ranging from feelings of exhilaration to feelings of despondency. In terms of emotional adjustment, one person lives on a uniformly low level; another, on a generally high level; and still another, at a level some-where between the two extremes.

As just pointed out, individual differences exist in par-ticular characteristics whether these characteristics are phys-ical, mental, social, or emotional. Furthermore, certain of these characteristics including height, weight, speed of running, gen-eral intelligence, and reading power can be measured.

If individuals are measured in the characteristic of general mental ability, for example, their measurements tend to dis-tribute themselves according to what psychologists call the

FIGURE 1

DISTRIBUTION OF TOTAL SCORE QUOTIENTS OF NINTH-GRADE STUDENTS
ON THE SRA TESTS OF PRIMARY MENTAL ABILITIES

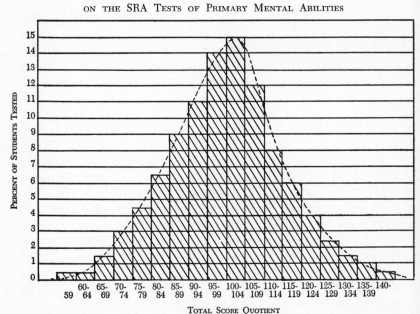

TOTAL SCORE QUOTIENT

normal curve. Such a curve is pictured in Figure 1. This figure pictures graphically the distribution of the intelligence quo-tients of ninth-grade students who took the battery of tests known as the *SRA Primary Mental Abilities.*

In Figure 1, note that the distribution is in the form of a bell. This is the shape of the normal curve that is obtained when a large number of measurements are combined and classified according to intervals—60-64, 65-69, for example.

The quotients of the largest number of students are at or near the average (100) of the distribution. At successive intervals either above or below the average, the numbers of quotients are smaller and smaller. At either extreme, there are only a few quotients, perhaps only one or two.

The distribution shown in Figure 1 is typical of the normal curve that is found when a large number of individuals are measured and classified in any one of many different characteristics—height, reading ability, scientific interest, or emotional stability, to mention a few. If the guidance worker fully understands the normal curve, he can determine approximately where an individual stands in a given measured characteristic in comparison with other individuals. He can also advise that individual with greater confidence regarding the latter's problems and potentialities.

THE IMPORTANCE OF DIFFERENCES
WITHIN THE INDIVIDUAL

There are not only differences between one individual and another in a given characteristic; there are also differences among characteristics within a given individual. The latter are called *trait differences*. An example of the trait differences of each of two individuals appears in Figure 2. In this figure, the solid line is the profile of the scores made by Student A; the broken line, the profile of the scores made by Student B.

As can be seen in Figure 2, Student A is highest in the mental ability designated as "Word Fluency." In this ability, his score of 63 is at the 97th percentile of all the 15-year-old students who took this same test. Student A is also very high in "Verbal Meaning"; he is at the 95th percentile. However, he is relatively low in the mental abilities of "Space" and "Number." In contrast, Student B is highest in "Number" and "Word Fluency." He is lowest in "Verbal Meaning" and "Space."

As the standings of Student A and of Student B in the five mental abilities tested indicate, these two students probably should consider different educational programs and different career choices. Student A appears to have the abilities needed

FIGURE 2

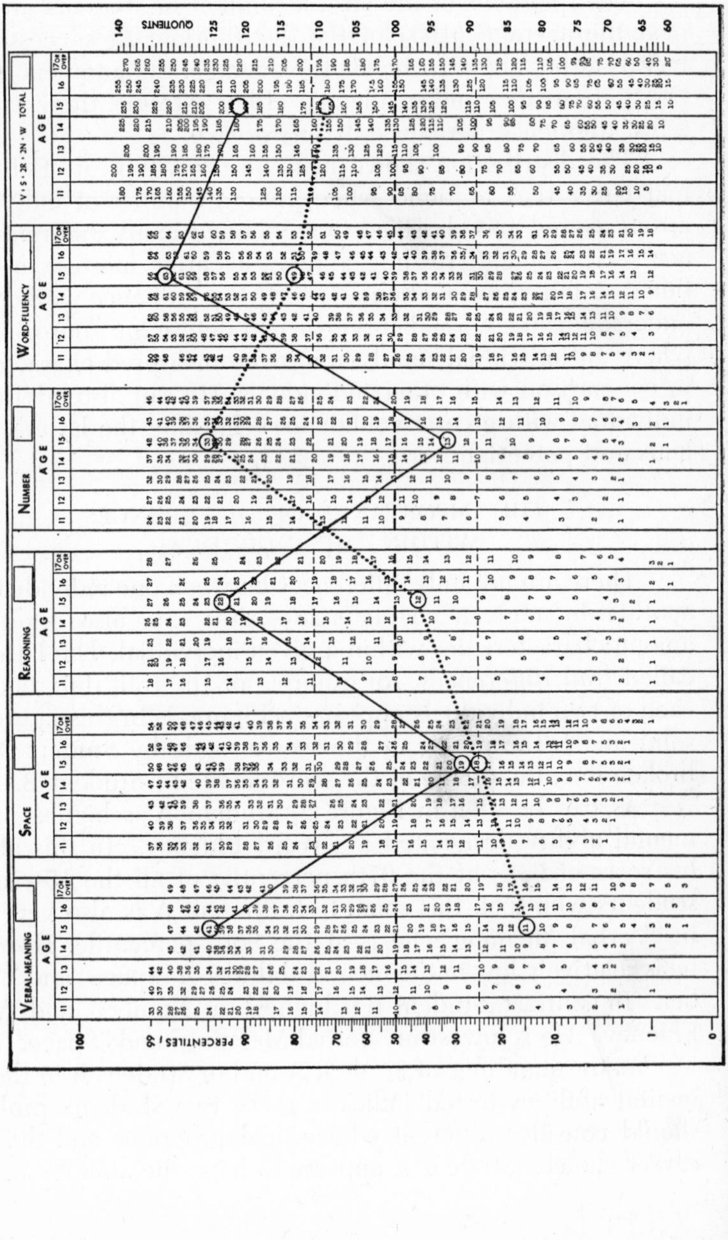

PROFILES OF THE SCORES MADE BY TWO 15-YEAR-OLD STUDENTS ON THE SRA TESTS OF PRIMARY MENTAL ABILITIES

to succeed in school subjects and careers that require facility in speaking and writing. Student B seems to have the abilities needed to succeed in subjects and careers that call for skill in handling numbers and words. More specifically, Student A might consider such an occupation as reporter, salesman, or publicity man. Student B might consider becoming a sales-clerk, cashier, bookkeeper, or accountant.

The guidance worker, of course, does *not* advise an individual solely on the basis of a single test or test battery. Rather, before counseling an individual on educational and vocational plans, the guidance worker determines the individual's standing on a mental test and other types of tests; he also obtains other information about the individual.

The informed guidance worker recognizes that an individual possesses varying amounts of different kinds of personal and social characteristics. To illustrate, Student A may be highly introverted, highly self-sufficient, low in dominance, and low in sociability. Student B, however, may be highly extroverted, highly dependent, highly dominant, and highly sociable. Because these two individuals differ in their patterns of personal characteristics, they may be expected to differ markedly in their adjustments to similar situations. Nevertheless, through conscious effort on the part of the individual and through assistance from a guidance worker, each individual can modify his personality pattern to some extent.

Knowledge of the differences between individuals in a single trait and of the differences among traits within an individual serves as a key to effective guidance services in the school or in any other organization. If the guidance worker takes the nature and extent of these differences into account, he is best able to contribute to both the immediate and the long-term adjustments of the individuals and groups with whom he works. How the guidance worker does this will be discussed, in greater detail, later in this book.

THE RELATIONSHIPS BETWEEN ABILITIES AND REQUIREMENTS

In measuring, interpreting, and otherwise considering individual differences, the beginning guidance worker should guard against a tendency to oversimplify and to mechanize the application of his findings. He should realize that there is no natural or arbitrary consistency between the characteristics that individuals have and the requirements that they must meet. In all probability, a composite of abilities, interests, and other personal traits is necessary for success in a complex educational, social, or vocational situation. To make valid assessments of composites of traits and to relate these composites realistically to educational, social, or vocational requirements entail intricate and highly specialized tasks.

Difficulties in performing these tasks are due to two main facts: First, human nature has changed with relative slowness over a period of thousands of years. And second, the human environment has changed with increasing rapidity, particularly during the past 50 years. Moreover, because the individual and his environment each is so complex, the guidance worker should realize that no single trait such as mechanical aptitude, clerical aptitude, or scientific aptitude will guarantee success in a given vocation.

In appraising the fitness of an individual for a vocation or other situation in the present-day world, the guidance worker should assess a variety of factors both within the individual and within his environment. By relating these two sets of factors, the worker is able to make reasonably sound judgments concerning the individual's pattern of traits and the pattern of traits required for success in the situation. In so far as possible, these judgments should be based upon the application of scientific methods and upon the findings of scientific studies. Up to the present time, unfortunately, all too few of these studies have dealt with the relationships between individual differences or trait differences and social adjustments or vocational success.

THE IMPORTANCE OF GROWTH OR LEARNING CURVES

Individuals display differences among themselves not only at a given time but also over a period of time; in other words, they have different rates of growth. Most obvious are the differences in the rates of physical growth. These differences are most striking soon after the onset of adolescence. For instance, consider two six-year-old boys who have about the same height and weight. They continue to grow in height and weight at about the same rates until they reach the age of 13. At that age, the first boy enters adolescence; he shoots up in height and weight. By the age of 15, he may be six inches taller and 20 pounds heavier than the other boy. At the age of 15, the second boy enters adolescence. At the age of 17, he may catch up with the first boy. Meanwhile, however, the differences between the two boys in physical development are usually accompanied by other differences, particularly in the degree of interest in members of the opposite sex. These latter differences require different modes of adjustment on the part of the two boys.

Such differences and irregularities in physical growth may at any point in the growth pattern have very important implications for the guidance of individuals. Yet these differences are so commonplace that they are likely to be disregarded. Take, for example, an early-maturing girl or a late-maturing boy in a class of average-maturing children. That girl or boy is liable to be a social misfit, at least for a time, unless that individual is wisely guided; he or she must be helped over a period which may otherwise present difficult adjustment problems.

The rates of growth in mental ability and in achievement of junior and senior high-school youth are not so clearly related to the onset of puberty as are the rates of physical growth. In fact, clear-cut evidence of an adolescent spurt in mental or educational growth is lacking. Nevertheless, there is convincing evidence that individuals differ appreciably in their rates of mental growth.

The truth of this statement can be demonstrated by a comparison of the scores that individuals make over a period of years on equivalent forms of a test of mental ability. As an illustration, consider Figure 3; it shows the mental growth curves of three high-school students as indicated by their total scores on the *American Council Psychological Examination*. These students took four equivalent forms or editions of this test—the 1946 edition in Grade 9, the 1947 edition in Grade 10, the 1948 edition in Grade 11, and the 1949 edition in Grade 12.

Figure 3 points out that the three students tested were growing in mental ability at significantly different rates. The differences among these students in their rates of mental growth were virtually certain to be reflected in their schoolwork and other activities. If the teacher or guidance worker recognized these differences, he was better able to adjust his instruction or counseling to the pattern of each student's mental development.

FIGURE 3

MENTAL GROWTH CURVES OF THREE STUDENTS IN TOTAL SCORE ON AMERICAN COUNCIL PSYCHOLOGICAL EXAMINATION

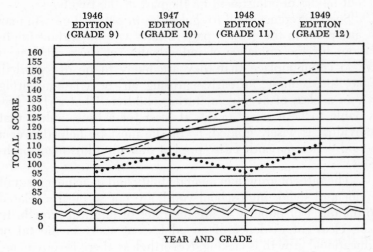

There is a question whether individual patterns of mental growth, such as those pictured in Figure 3, can be influenced appreciably by instruction or guidance. Within limits, they probably can be so influenced. The typical mental test has items that measure verbal ability and items that measure quantitative thinking. If a teacher gives considerable attention to the analysis of words in the technical vocabulary of his subject-matter field, the student will probably grow in his power to answer correctly the vocabulary items of a mental test. Likewise, if a teacher concentrates on reasoning problems in mathematics, the student will likely increase his ability to give correct answers to the arithmetic problems in a mental test. Even so, the two kinds of training just cited may not produce permanent gains in the student's verbal ability or in his ability to do quantitative thinking. In the end, therefore, the student may be no higher in one of these two mental factors than he would have been if he had not had such special training.

With reference to any mental ability test, the tester must assume that all the persons taking the test have had the same or similar opportunities to acquire the ability being measured. To the extent that this is true, the test scores obtained are sound indicators of the relative standing of these persons in that mental ability.

The foregoing discussion bears upon remedial work, with which both instruction and guidance are concerned. Although no definite or final statement on the matter can be made on the basis of present evidence, the most tenable hypothesis seems to be as follows: If an individual's growth in such skills as reading or arithmetic has fallen behind his mental growth in the verbal and numerical abilities, then properly applied remedial work is likely to be effective in raising the levels of that individual's skills; also, a considerable proportion of his growth in these skills is likely to be permanent. However, if an individual's growth in the aforementioned two skills has been slow but has kept pace with or even exceeded his growth in the corresponding mental abilities, remedial work is less likely to increase his levels of ability in these particular skills.

Whatever an individual's deficiency in a skill is and whatever remedial program is undertaken, the teacher or guidance worker should never press the individual to reach a standard that is above his mental ability. Such pressure may create an emotional upset that retards or blocks the individual's development. The better instructional or guidance procedure is to recognize and accept the fact that individuals differ in their levels of mental ability and in their rates of mental growth. If this procedure is used, each individual is treated in such a way that he makes the largest possible gains in needed skills and achieves the best possible adjustments to his situation.

With further regard to this matter, it is important to note that the average curve of mental growth as measured by intelligence tests is virtually a straight line from about age 6 up to about age 13; from year to year the increments of growth appear to be approximately equal. At about age 13, however, the curve of growth begins to slow down; year by year the increments of growth become smaller and smaller. Near age 16, the curve tends to become a horizontal line.

The curve of mental growth appears to flatten out at an earlier age for some persons than for others. There is an accumulating body of evidence that some individuals (particularly those who attend college) continue to grow mentally, as measured by tests, up to age 21 or 22 and perhaps even thereafter. The foregoing example implies that the average curve of mental growth represents the growth of the typical individual, not that of the individual who is substantially above or below average in his mental ability.

Regardless of the shape that the curve of mental growth of an individual may take, the guidance worker should keep in mind that basically growth is an *active* process. If an individual were unable to react to his environment in a positive way, he would not likely rise above an infantile level of mental ability even though he was growing older chronologically. Only if the individual experiences numerous opportunities for optimum mental and other growth will he develop his mental and other abilities to the maximum.

Because growth is an active not a passive process, the guidance worker should so far as possible place the responsibility for thinking through problems and for making decisions upon the individual. As the individual develops, he should be given increasing responsibility. For him the ultimate goal should be mature self-guidance.

THE NATURE OF PERSONALITY

The understanding of an individual's personality is basic to guidance procedures. Toward this objective, the guidance worker should recognize that an individual's personality is complex and yet behaves as a whole. This complexity and this wholeness tend to complicate the guidance process.

Personality is inextricably interwoven with the structure and functioning of the human organism. Psychologically, the parts of the human body are interrelated in a most intricate fashion. Therefore, an abnormality in one part of the body structure or of its functioning often has an effect on other parts. Note, for example, the effect of a malfunctioning endocrine gland on a person's general physical health and on his emotional reactions. More specifically, if a person's thyroid gland is not functioning properly, it may cause noticeable changes in his behavior or personality.

In considering the concept of the wholeness of personality, the guidance worker should have in view certain important psychological concepts, particularly that of the stimulus-response theory of learning. This theory appears to be most clearly applicable to learning processes that are on the physiological level (the patella reflex, for example) and on the level of lower mental processes (the rote learning of the alphabet, for instance). On the level of the higher mental and emotional processes, however, the S-R relationship is often somewhat obscure; a specific stimulus may not bring about a specific response. A stimulus, moreover, may affect not just one aspect of but rather the whole of personality.

The same stimulus, furthermore, may evoke different responses in different individuals. Consider the variations in emotional response to a frustrating situation such as this: A person is waiting to meet a friend, but the friend fails to appear. In this situation, one person is amused, another annoyed, another angry, and a fourth worried. Furthermore, in the same situation, an individual may react in different ways on different days, depending on such factors as his physical well-being, his general emotional tone, and his most recent experiences. In short, although the stimulus is apparently the same, the individual's response to it on different occasions is highly variable.

All the foregoing leads to the key question: *What is personality?* Among the many definitions of personality, that by Bingham is particularly illuminating:

> Personality . . . is one of the most comprehensive of psychological concepts embracing as it does the whole system of dy-

namic tendencies which differentiates one person from another. Inclusive of physique, temperament, intellect, and character, it is more than the sum of an individual's traits, physical and mental, emotional and intellectual, social and temperamental, passive and active; for "personality" refers also to the way in which all the traits are organized and integrated, the pattern according to which they function together. Personality is what a person is.[1]

An individual's personality is the result of all the influences of both heredity and environment, past and present. It is, in a real sense, the whole dynamic complex developed by the accumulated reactions of the individual to his environment (including people). In other words, personality is the resultant of many factors, operating over a long period of time. Some of these factors may have contributed to the stability of personality; others may have had the opposite effect.

An individual's personality, furthermore, is relatively stable. It is sufficiently so that it is correct to say of an individual that his personality is agreeable, calm, poised, or self-assured. As indicated earlier in the chapter, however, personality including the traits just mentioned may be modified within limits.

The idea of the wholeness of personality deserves special emphasis in guidance work. According to this emphasis, guidance services should be directed toward the "whole" person—that is, they should take into account that the individual is not only an intellectual being but also a physical being, a social being, and a being with emotions. Only if the "whole" individual is kept in mind will the guidance program be fully effective.

During the last 15 years, school people have directed increasing attention to educating the whole child. As a result, they have developed new theories of education and have put these theories into practice. Although such attention is highly desirable, it should not exclude attention to the following fact: In a given situation at a particular time in a student's progress through school, the guidance worker or teacher may concentrate upon the modification of a specific trait—that is, a limited

---

[1] Walter Van Dyke Bingham, *Aptitudes and Aptitude Testing* (New York: Harper and Brothers, 1937), p. 21.

segment or aspect of that student's behavior. Likewise, in working with a group of students, he may study closely the individual differences among these students in a given trait. Even so, the wise counselor or teacher keeps in mind the nature and development of each individual's personality as a whole.

THE ROLE OF ADJUSTMENT

In a guidance program, the day-to-day work of counseling should be conducted according to what is known about the psychology of individual adjustment. To illustrate, each individual has a concept of self; he tends to behave, or desires to behave, in a manner that is consistent with this concept. Frequently, when the individual's behavior is not in harmony with his self-concept, this self-concept can be used to lead him to change his behavior—for example, to substitute mature for immature behavior.

Such a desirable change in an individual, however, may be relatively difficult. The adoption of a new mode of behavior is often an uncomfortable if not a painful process because it requires both mental and emotional effort. The typical individual finds it more pleasant to drift along, maintaining his present habits and patterns of living. This is often the case even though he may be aware that some other way of behavior is better. Nevertheless, the guidance worker may rightly appeal to the individual's self-concept in order to bring about desirable adjustments in behavior.

The application of the individual's self-concept to a given problem situation may be difficult because of any one of a number of reasons. The individual may not understand the problem. He may be unwilling to face the problem realistically. He may be unable to state the problem both meaningfully and objectively.

The typical individual often finds it easier to minimize or to ignore a troublesome problem. If that problem is highly emotionalized, he may employ such psychological devices as repression, rationalization, or projection. Through one or more of these devices he "solves" the problem, but his "solution" is usually temporary and inadequate.

If an individual is to solve such a problem, he must see it clearly. He is most likely to do so if his counselor provides an optimum adjustment situation. In this situation, the counselor creates an atmosphere in which the individual brings his problem to the surface, verbalizes that problem, and works out his own promising solutions to it. At the same time, the counselor is alert to all bypaths to the problem's solution. The individual, for example, may talk about a secondary or "facade" problem perhaps because he does not yet feel secure enough in his relations with the counselor to discuss his main problem.

Once the guidance worker has discovered the individual's concept of self and has checked this concept with other information about the individual, he has a solid psychological foundation upon which to build his counseling relationships with that individual. Through these relationships, the counselor is able to help the individual to achieve the adjustments that best meet his needs and wants.

SUMMARY

As this chapter has pointed out, the psychological bases of guidance services should include such important points as the following:

1. Individuals differ widely in any given personality trait —ability, achievement, and interest, for example. In each measurable trait, the scores or ratings of individuals are distributed according to the normal curve.

2. The typical individual has different amounts of different traits. Even in a standardized test of mental abilities, he stands higher in certain abilities than in others.

3. Individuals differ greatly in their rates of growth. And this is true in many different aspects of development—physical growth, mental growth, and emotional growth, to mention only a few.

4. The personality of an individual is very complex, yet it functions as a whole. In higher-level mental activities and in highly personal emotional situations, the individual tends to react to a stimulus not only with a specific response but

also with a complex of responses—that is, with his whole personality.

5. Each individual has a concept of self, and he tends to behave according to that concept. An understanding of the individual's self-concept is essential to effective counseling.

This summary of the psychological bases of guidance work highlights the need for a discussion of guidance principles and aims, the subject to be treated next.

SUGGESTED READINGS

American Council on Education. *Exploring Individual Differences.* Washington, D.C.: American Council on Education, October, 1948.

Bingham, Walter Van Dyke. *Aptitudes and Aptitude Testing.* New York: Harper and Brothers, 1937.

Cattell, Raymond B. *Personality.* New York: McGraw-Hill Book Company, Inc., 1950.

Cronback, Lee J. *Essentials of Psychological Testing.* New York: Harper and Brothers, 1949.

Freeman, Frank S. *Theory and Practice of Psychological Testing.* New York: Henry Holt and Company, 1950.

Gulliksen, Harold. *Theory of Mental Tests.* New York: John Wiley and Sons, 1950.

Harsh, Charles M., and Schrickel, H. G. *Personality: Development and Assessment.* New York: The Ronald Press Company, 1950.

Lindquist, E. F. (ed.). *Educational Measurement.* Washington, D.C.: American Council on Education, 1951.

Segel, David. *Frustration in Adolescent Youth.* Federal Security Agency, Office of Education, Bulletin 1951, No. 1. Washington, D.C.: U.S. Government Printing Office, 1951.

Shostrom, Everett L., and Brammer, Lawrence M. *The Dynamics of the Counseling Process.* New York: McGraw-Hill Book Company, Inc., 1952.

Stagner, Ross. *Psychology of Personality.* New York: McGraw-Hill Book Company, Inc., 1948.

CHAPTER FOUR

Guidance Principles and Aims

JUST AS the motorist needs highway markers to get to his destination, so the guidance worker needs signposts along the way to reach his goal. This chapter presents a number of signposts, in the form of suggested principles and aims of guidance services.

The principles, given later, serve to direct the attitudes and activities of the person engaged in guidance work. These same principles have value for the person being guided or counseled. If the counselee is relatively mature, he should know in general what these principles are and how they apply to his own situation. If the counselee is immature, he may not need to know them. During an interview, the guidance worker should explain only those principles that can be made meaningful to the counselee. Such explanations, of course, should be worked into the counseling process in an informal and natural way.

BASIC PRINCIPLES

The section that follows presents seven fundamental principles of guidance work. Each principle is stated and then discussed.

Take Time to Solve Problems and Make Decisions

The process through which an individual makes wise decisions and adjustments with reference to important matters seldom occurs within a few seconds, or minutes, or even overnight. It usually requires time—considerable time.

There are several reasons why this process is often slow-moving. First, the individual has a complex personality that may not be easily or quickly understood either by himself or by his counselor. Second, that individual confronts problems and situations that to him may be intense. The more complex the personality and the more intense the problem, the longer it takes the individual to make a wise decision or a satisfactory adjustment.

Because the trained guidance worker is familiar with the foregoing principle, he regards with suspicion any judgment that is hastily conceived, or any solution that is quick or ready-made. The trained guidance worker also knows that a wise solution does not come from putting a few facts together and then jumping to a conclusion.

The guidance worker needs time to know the counselee, to become acquainted with him and his situation. The counselee needs time in which to know himself and his problem. If the time is too short, neither the counselor nor the counselee gains the knowledge and insight required to help the latter to understand, let alone to solve, his problem.

Further, this principle of taking time to solve problems implies that the process of assisting individuals is a continuous one. In a very real sense, guidance work with an individual is never finished. The counselor may help that individual to solve a particular problem and to adjust to the new situation thus created. Yet that individual may have other problems, then or later; these problems may involve adjustments within the person himself or between him and others. If so, he may need more help from his counselor. However, as the individual gains maturity, including growth in ability to solve problems and to adjust to situations, he requires less assistance from his counselor.

Let the Counselee Develop His Own Insights

The second basic principle of guidance work is that the process of assisting the individual should be conducted in such a way that he gains his own insights and makes his own decisions. The individual should be helped to take increasing responsibility for self-discovery, self-development, and self-management. As he accepts greater responsibility, he gains in the feeling of self-confidence and the power of self-direction. As the individual thus matures, he needs less and less assistance from the counselor or from anybody else.

The foregoing does not mean that in guidance work the individual in need of assistance should be coddled. He should not become so dependent on the counselor that he makes no plans and decisions on his own. If the counselor allows this to happen, he has failed to aid the counselee in growing toward independence.

To the individual being counseled, the counselor should serve as a general guide, a stimulating force, an interpreter of facts, ideas, and attitudes. He should never be the dictator who says, "You must do this." He should never take the position expressed by "I know better than you do."

At times, the counselor may believe that he should tell the individual exactly what to do. The counselor may feel that thereby he can give the individual a quick answer and a good one, saving the time of all concerned. But the counselor who acts in this way may propose to the individual a solution that sooner or later proves to be incorrect. And even worse, the counselor may retard the individual in his efforts to gain self-confidence, or to strengthen and sharpen his skills in self-direction. As a result, the individual's immaturity is prolonged.

Consider Most Individuals As Average, Normal Persons

The third basic principle of guidance work is the assumption that most individuals are average, normal persons. Recognizing the soundness of this assumption, the counselor is concerned mainly with the development of persons who are so-called "normal"; they are relatively normal in intelligence, normal in emotional stability, and normal in physical constitution and ability.

At times, of course, the counselor advises with persons who are abnormal—these include individuals who are extremely slow learners or who are emotionally unstable to a serious degree. So far as possible, the wise counselor soon refers such persons to appropriate specialists. Thus, he helps them most; thus also he is able to devote most of his time to normal individuals.

All too often, students gain the impression that the guidance staff is primarily interested in serving individuals who are not normal—"the troublemaker" or "the dumb-bell," for example. If students hold this impression, deservedly or not, the chances for the guidance staff to do its real job well are greatly reduced, perhaps even to the zero point. For this reason, staff members concerned with guidance should continually make clear, by both word and deed, that their services are available to all students, not just to those who are atypical.

It is a commonplace occurrence for an average or normal person to be confronted by a problem in which he needs assistance. His problem may arise from a new situation at school, at home, or on the job. The fact that he has this problem and feels the need for help, however, does *not* indicate that he is a strikingly abnormal person. Almost any normal person may become temporarily abnormal in the face of a frustrating or an insurmountable problem, particularly if that problem is of crucial importance to him.

In almost every sizable group there are a few persons who deviate so much from the average or normal that they may rightly be designated as *abnormal.* Some of these abnormal persons may be dull mentally; some may be extremely unstable emotionally or maladjusted socially; and some may be seriously handicapped physically. These abnormal persons may include the child who cannot learn to read, the child who cries all the time, the child who has no friends, and the child who has to use crutches.

On the basis of the qualifications of its staff members, each guidance department must decide to what extent it can offer help to children who are very abnormal. The department may have available in the school the personnel and the facilities to assist these children—for example, an ungraded class for very slow learners, a clinic for very poor readers, a psychological clinic for emotionally disturbed children, or a special gym class for the physically handicapped. If the school cannot provide such special services for these exceptional children, the guidance department may be able to find other agencies in the community to help them.

A given school may handle the problem of slower learners

in one or more ways. It may decide that it should make special provisions for pupils whose mental abilities lie within a certain range, say, pupils whose mental abilities lie between 70 and 80 I.Q., on the Stanford-Binet Scale. The school may place these pupils in special classes where the content and methods of teaching are fitted to the needs and abilities of these children.

If the school is a private institution, it may refuse to admit children who are much below average in mental ability, emotional stability, or social adjustment. If the school is public, it may according to a state law or an administrative policy admit nearly all children who apply, no matter what their abnormalities may be.

In a school or college, all staff members should be familiar with the more common symptoms of abnormalities. If they know these symptoms, they are better able to identify those students who are in need of special assistance. Obviously these staff members are usually not qualified to diagnose such abnormalities and to prescribe courses of treatment therefor. Yet, having identified students with abnormalities, the staff members can refer these persons to experts either inside or outside the school. After the experts have made their diagnoses and prescriptions, staff members can make recommendations as to what is to be done. For example, a given student may be transferred to an outside agency or institution that provides help in the field of his abnormality—this agency may be a special school. Or, the student may continue in school where he receives special help from an expert in the field of his need.

In serving students who are very abnormal mentally, emotionally, socially, or physically, the counselor (particularly one who is inexperienced) should avoid two main dangers, as follows:

First, the counselor should guard against developing the attitude that most of his counselees are maladjusted. This attitude may be an outgrowth of his uncritical acceptance of the professional literature on the subject of deviates, that is, of those whose personalities are distinctively abnormal. The counselor, moreover, should avoid "reading into situations" revealed by counseling more than actually exists. If this counselor encounters in rapid succession a few cases of personalities with serious emotional disturbances, he may unconsciously but wrongly conclude that many other people are similarly disturbed. Thereafter, because he consciously looks for such abnormalities, he usually finds them in situations that come to his attention.

In counseling as in other fields, "a little knowledge is a dangerous thing." [1] Whether the counselor is a beginner or is one with considerable experience, he should check his early impressions of counselees to make certain that first impressions were correct impressions. Before the counselor designates a counselee as abnormal, he should have definite evidence bearing on the latter's deviations from normal. Otherwise, in handling the case, the counselor may use procedures that prove to be inadequate or even harmful to the counselee.

Second, the counselor should avoid devoting an undue amount of time to counselees who are considerably abnormal in their abilities to achieve. When the counselor is almost completely absorbed in serving such counselees, he does not have enough time to provide normal counselees with the services that they need and want. As already indicated, many normal persons have problems that call for guidance. Because there are more normal than abnormal persons, the counselor should give more time to the normal group.

Each educational institution must, of course, set its own policies with reference to the extent it should, within its resources, give attention to those who are not relatively normal. These resources include the number of guidance workers, their qualifications, and the time at their disposal. If these resources are comparatively limited, the institution may rightly decide to allocate its guidance services as equitably as possible among all its students; this means that the institution will not be able to provide all the assistance needed by every abnormal student.

If the institution is a college or an independent school, it

---

[1] Regarding this matter, Thomas Henry Huxley once wrote: "If a little knowledge is dangerous, where is the man who has so much as to be out of danger?"

may, as a last resort, have to drop a student who is a deviate. This action, however, need not be summary or negative in character. Before such a student leaves the institution, his counselor should offer positive suggestions as to a possible course of procedure. For example, he might name and describe other schools that are better fitted to the counselee's personal characteristics and needs. Or, the counselor might refer the student to a psychiatrist or psychologist, or to another qualified specialist.

According to the basic principle just discussed, guidance services should be concerned mainly with the development of persons who are relatively normal—mentally, physically, emotionally, and socially. These persons make up the great majority of all persons needing such assistance. Thus guidance services help many individuals to develop their characteristics to higher levels and to achieve better adjustments all around.

Problems Arise Out of Situations

The fourth basic principle is that specific problems arise out of situations. They do not appear without cause, or without advance notice. The present behavior of an individual depends upon his heredity and his experiences—in other words, upon the interactions between two main factors, the individual and his environment.

Although the counselor cannot exactly ascertain which of the two factors just mentioned contributed more to the individual's behavior, he can be reasonably sure that such behavior has a cause or causes that originated in the past. For example, a child does not suddenly become an inefficient reader, an obstructionist, a fearful person, a rowdy, or a "shrinking violet." Or, an employee does not overnight become obnoxiously aggressive, highly uncooperative, exceedingly stubborn, chronically tardy, emotionally wrecked. The present behavior of such an individual has roots that grew, year by year, in his past.

A guidance worker who is trying to help an individual solve a problem must delve far enough into that individual's history to discover what the problem is, why the problem arose, and when the problem began. This entails finding out the point at which the individual's difficulty first showed itself, the place where the individual went definitely off the track, and the steps the individual took in the development of his problem. With such facts and insights, the guidance worker is able to act intelligently in diagnosing and treating the individual's problem.

In examining such an individual's problem, the guidance worker should not mistake symptoms for causes. In fact, he should always be on guard against doing so. If the guidance worker treats symptoms as causes, his approach is bound to be superficial and may even be harmful; it will almost surely lead to no lasting solution of the individual's problem.

If the counselor is working with a counselee who is sufficiently mature, he may inform the latter that he is searching for the underlying causes of the problem; he may also seek the conscious assistance of the counselee. The counselor may try to help the counselee to be aware of the differences between symptoms and causes. With this distinction in mind, the counselee is more likely to gain insight into his situation.

Both the counselor and the counselee need to get as close as possible to the causes of the latter's present difficulty. For instance, here is a youth who is continually quarreling and fighting with others in his group; he is known as a constant troublemaker. These symptoms may be summed up as over-aggressiveness. The underlying cause of this pupil's aggressiveness may be a feeling of rejection and insecurity; it may be his strong desire for acceptance and recognition—a desire that manifests itself in socially maladjusted behavior.

A considerable portion of the adjustment aspect of guidance work should be preventive rather than therapeutic. A counselor who is alert to symptoms of maladjustment may often identify the causes of an individual's problem while that problem is still relatively minor; then, by dealing promptly with the causes of the problem, he may prevent it from becoming serious.

Problems Are Interrelated

The fifth guiding principle is that interrelationships exist among the various kinds of problems experienced by the individual. From one point of view, this principle can be said to be a corollary of the principle just cited—that problems arise out of situations and that these situations have earlier causal factors.

In dealing with an individual, the counselor is more effective if he holds steadily in mind the fundamental fact that personality is a complex but integrated whole. In actual functioning, the human personality cannot be divided into neatly labeled compartments or aspects. The counselor may find it necessary and proper to identify the various aspects of personality for purposes of organization, analysis, rating, and discussion. Yet he realizes that in actuality these aspects manifest themselves in interrelated ways.

Consider, for example, the student in high school or college who has reached the stage where a choice of a vocation is a live problem to him. After a preliminary analysis, the counselor and the counselee agree that educational as well as vocational plans must be considered. Suppose that this counselee has chosen a definite occupation. Then he must take the necessary steps toward developing an educational plan that will prepare him for the occupation of his choice. This plan must take into account all the costs involved.

As a specific example, take the case of a counselee who is considering three different, but allied, occupations. He must weigh the factors related to training for these occupations. Training for one occupation may entail a much greater financial outlay, and a much longer period of education, than training for either of the other two occupations. To help this counselee in selecting the training most appropriate for him, the counselor has the responsibility of making certain that the counselee has definite and complete information about the cost of the required training in both money and time. Whether the counselee is able to finance a certain educational program may prove to be the decisive factor in his final selection of an occupation. Other decisive factors related to a counselee's final occupational choice may be his present age, abilities, and interests.

Another important type of interrelationship exists among the counselee's various problems—for example, between his vocational problem and his personal problem. To the counselor, the counselee may bring a situation which to the counselee appears to be a problem mainly of the choice of an occupation, but which, in reality, is a problem of personality adjustment. The counselor in his own mind may decide rather quickly that the counselee's basic problem is his general attitude toward himself and his environment; this attitude may involve feelings of great inferiority that are revealed by symptoms of extreme submissiveness or shyness. This counselee's outlook and consequent behavior might well prove a major obstacle to success in almost any vocation he might select.

In this case, the counselor's first tasks are to find the underlying causes for the counselee's attitude and behavior, to assist the counselee to gain insight into his situation, and to help him to accept appropriate therapeutic measures. If the counselor were to concentrate his attention on the counselee's vocational problem or were even to give it any direct attention before understanding the counselee's basic difficulty in personality, he would lead the counselee toward no satisfactory or permanent solution to his over-all problem. If the counselee were to choose an occupation without clearing up his personal maladjustment, he would likely face continuing discouragement and frustration.

It is a serious mistake to think of vocational, educational, and personal problems as entities and to set up a program of guidance services accordingly. Rather, these problems should be considered as distinguishable but related. For this reason, all staff members who have responsibility for guidance services should be designated as "counselors." They should not be labeled "educational counselors," "vocational counselors," or "personal counselors."

Certainly, any counselor who works in the area of vocational problems should be well-versed in educational requirements and opportunities. He should also be sufficiently informed in the field of mental health to recognize maladjustments in a counselee's personality, and to refer that counselee, if necessary, to the specialist who is best qualified to help him. The specialist and the counselor can then work together to help the counselee to achieve a better adjustment.

The Integration of Effort Is Essential

The sixth guiding principle is that guidance services should be organized according to integration of effort. This means that although each staff member should contribute according to his abilities, all staff members should coordinate their efforts.

The integration of effort has three implications:

1. Guidance services should have a logical form of organization.

2. The separate functions of guidance services should be assigned to staff members on the basis of their unique qualifications.

3. All staff members who have direct or indirect responsibilities for guidance services should cooperate wholeheartedly.

These implications have important meanings in terms of an institution's guidance program, as follows:

First, staff members must determine and agree upon the specific objectives of the guidance services to be provided. They must also decide, together, upon the persons who will have major responsibilities for the program and upon the persons who will have minor but no less essential duties in making this program fully effective.

In a high school or college, the objectives and the general plans for operation of the program of guidance services should be determined by the following staff members: the administrative head, the principal administrative assistants, the person in charge of the guidance program, and representatives of the teaching faculty. The guidance program should promote the understanding and participation of students and parents and of community organizations and agencies.

In the institution itself, the director of guidance services, of course, is best qualified to suggest objectives and procedures for their realization. Nevertheless, he should both seek and welcome ideas from other staff members. Otherwise, the guidance services program may become a "one-man program." Such a program is limited because all or most of the staff is not participating in it. And such a program may fail eventually because the support of other "key" people in the institution is not enlisted. The foregoing, however, does not imply that the direction or supervision of the guidance program should be in the hands of a number of people. Rather, it implies that one person should *head* the program.

Second, the person who is especially well-fitted to perform a specific function in the guidance program should be assigned to that function. In any institution, no one person is sufficiently expert or qualified by personality or skills to handle competently all of the varied functions of the guidance program. Because genuine guidance services are diverse in nature, broad in scope, and extensive in character, many persons should have the opportunity to make contributions according to their abilities and interests.

Even in a small organization, a few guidance workers, working alone, do not have the time or energy required to provide the optimum guidance program; they must have the active assistance of other staff members.

To some staff members in a small institution, the amount of money spent on the guidance program may seem unnecessarily large. Yet if these staff members are brought into guidance activities, they will soon discover that guidance work when well-conceived and well-executed pays tangible and intangible dividends to the institution as a whole.

Third, effective guidance services are the result of the smooth, wholehearted cooperation of many persons. One may liken this cooperation to the operation of a machine. Such a machine has many parts, each of which has a special function and each of which meshes with the other parts. To produce the desired goods, these parts must work together efficiently as a total unit. If one part fails to perform both its special and cooperative functions, the entire machine slows down and may even stop. As a result, it does not produce what it should. If any faculty member or administrative head falls down on his guidance job, the institution will fail to help all its students to make the progress they should.

Full information about an individual is an extremely important aspect of guidance services, particularly in counseling. According to the principle of integration of effort, the guidance worker who is counseling that individual should, within limits, exchange information about that individual with all others who have contacts with him.

The clearing house for data about an individual is the guidance department. To assist that individual most intelligently, the department must have a wide variety of information about him. It obtains such information not from just one staff member, say, the individual's counselor, but rather from a number of persons—his counselor, his teachers, and his parents, for example. These persons have had contacts with the individual in diverse circumstances.

The individual being counseled has many facets, so to speak. He reveals these facets in a variety of situations that have different conditions and different observers. Therefore, the guidance department should have a definite plan for gathering varied and significant data about the individual and for disseminating these data. All information except that which is highly confidential should be accessible to any staff member who has responsibility for helping an individual. Only if this arrangement exists can a staff member see the different aspects of the individual's problem in relationship and in perspective; only thus can he help the individual to work out the best possible solution. It is particularly important that all the facts about the individual be available to the guidance worker. He can readily get these facts if his institution has records that are comprehensive, cumulative, and well-organized.

Although the full and free interchange of information is essential to wise guidance, some of this information may be so personal and confidential in nature that it should not be written in any record. Under some circumstances, the teacher who has such information about a student may note on the latter's record, "See me about So-and-so." Then, the counselor may obtain this information in a personal talk with the teacher. Thereafter, the counselor must use his own best judgment as to whether to divulge the private information to anyone else. As a general rule, the teacher or the counselor should keep confidential all highly personal information. If this information has an important bearing upon the general welfare of his institution, however, he may ethically reveal it to the school's administrative head.

The counselor who talks unnecessarily about his counselees and about the things they have told him in confidence is not only unethical; he is also short-sighted. If counselees learn about this, they quickly lose confidence in that counselor; they may also lose faith in other counselors as well. As a result, these students will not go to a counselor for help in dealing with their personal affairs. For this reason among others, every guidance worker should consider the personal information given by a student as between him and the student only. In this regard, the guidance worker might well emulate the professional ethics of the physician.

Between the danger of reporting too much and the risk of reporting nothing about a counselee, the counselor should steer a middle course in handling information about the individual. If the information is not of a highly personal nature, the counselor should make it available to any authorized person—a staff member or a parent, for example. This practice is definitely in line with the principle of integration, a principle that calls for the collection of varied information about the individual and for the free exchange of that information. Only thus can an institution's guidance services be truly effective.

Guidance Services Must Be an Integral Part of the Organization

The seventh guiding principle can be stated positively, as follows. In order to fulfill their purposes, guidance services can function only if they are an integral part of the entire organization. Negatively stated, guidance services cannot function if they are an appendage to the general body of the organization.

From time to time, a few administrators and teachers have expressed the attitude that guidance services are "fads and frills"—nice to have but not necessary to their institution's basic educational program. In actuality, however, such a program cannot be adequate or effective unless it includes guidance services, organized and offered on an integrated basis.

Modern education is conceived of as the development of the individual in *all* aspects of his personality, not solely in the intellectual aspect. Certain institutions have been slow in recognizing this concept of education; some of them have resisted the newer ideas of psychology that apply to the individual person. In such an institution, special efforts had to be made to introduce these ideas. Often this was done through a guidance program. For a time, the institution, unfortunately, tended to operate the guidance program separately from the teaching and administrative programs. As a consequence, guidance services became an independent and somewhat isolated function of the institution.

In an educational institution, guidance services should supplement and complement instructional services, in the all-round development of individual personalities. This integration of all educational services is not always easy to accomplish. In the typical institution, most teachers are deeply concerned with the organization and presentation of their subject-matter fields. In general, they do not have the time, the interest, the knowledge, or the skills required to provide the guidance activities needed to help students to develop balanced personalities. If these teachers offer certain guidance services, these services tend to supplement their usual classroom activities.

At this point, the inference should not be drawn that many teachers are unable to participate actively in guidance work. On the contrary, every member or nearly every member of the teaching staff can and should be an active assistant in the guidance program. Ideally, each teacher ought to be imbued with the guidance point of view. And each should be a guidance worker in the sense that he renders his own best contribution to the total program of guidance services.

To be realistic, the administrator should recognize that some teachers do not desire personal contacts with students outside of their classrooms. He should also realize that, for the general good of guidance work, no teacher should be forced to participate in guidance activities if he does not wish to do so. Said another way, the administrator should never try to impose a guidance program on his teaching staff.

Instead, in introducing guidance services into his educational institution, the administration may well employ a three-fold approach, as follows:

1. The administration selects those teachers who are already most interested in the program and who are potentially most capable of developing as guidance personnel.

2. The administration works cooperatively with the selected staff members; together they work out a proposed guidance program and submit it to the entire staff for study, discussion, and decision.

3. The administration selects new teachers, in part upon the basis of their interest and skill in guidance services.

THE AIMS OF GUIDANCE SERVICES

This chapter has emphasized and explained the principles that should direct and guide the pursuit of guidance services. It will next consider the fundamental aims of these services—first, in relationship to the individual counselee; and second, in relationship to the institution's total educational program.

Aims from the Point of View of the Individual

In relationship to the individual being aided, the aims of guidance services are:

1. To help the individual, by his own efforts so far as possible, to achieve up to the level of his own capacity, to gain personal satisfactions in as many aspects of his life as possible, and to make his maximum contribution to society.

2. To assist the individual to meet and solve his own problems as they arise, to make correct interpretations of facts, and to make wise choices and adjustments.

3. To help the individual to lay a permanent foundation for sound, mature adjustments.

4. To assist the individual to live a well-balanced life in all respects—physical, mental, emotional, and social.

In line with one of the basic points of view in guidance, the individual holds the center of the stage. Because guidance services are for him, the foregoing aims are introduced by the words "to help" or "to assist." Each aim thus suggests that, during successive periods and in various aspects of his development, the individual needs help—that is, assistance from sources outside himself. At the same time, each aim states or implies that the individual is expected, *first*, to exert his own efforts toward achieving his goals and toward solving his problems, and, *second*, to increase his own power of self-direction and self-management. In other words, the individual is expected to increase his ability to stand on his own two feet, with less and less support by or direction from others; he is expected to take greater responsibility for his own insights. Each aim also means that the individual's goal is to achieve up to the limit of his capacity. By doing so, he gains the greatest personal satisfactions possible; and he makes his maximum contribution to society.

The aims just given assume that, as the individual works to solve his problems as they arise, he develops the general attitude that any and all situations should be faced realistically. In addition, he invents and uses his own improved methods of attacking his problems. Thereby, the individual lays the foundation of a highway that leads to sound, all-round adjustment. As the individual moves along this highway, he becomes increasingly mature, mentally and emotionally. He also becomes more self-confident, self-reliant, and independent. And he is better able to cope with his problems and to make optimum personal adjustments.

The Role of Adjustment

Adjustment is the process whereby the individual adapts or accommodates himself to his situation or environment. In the animal world, the thirsty deer roams from place to place until he finds water. The hungry infant continues to cry until his mother feeds him. These are two examples of the ways in which an animal makes adaptations or adjustments in his behavior to satisfy his basic internal need through his environment. These adjustments occur not alone in physical behavior but in mental and emotional behavior as well.

In his book *The Human Mind*, Dr. Karl A. Menninger clearly points out that we must think of the mind as an adjustment process—"a process of constantly changing itself in an effort to make itself more comfortable, constantly changing its environment for the same purpose, and constantly being changed by its environment, sometimes for better, sometimes for worse." [2]

Any adjustment in human behavior involves the interaction of a situation and a personality. The nature of these two forces and their roles in human adjustment have been cogently described by Dr. Menninger, as follows:

> The situation is the thing to which the personality has to adjust himself. It is the particular phase of life presented at the particular moment. It is a composite of requirements, a game with a set of rules. It is a game we must play in order to live. The rules of life are made up of physical laws, chemical laws, economic laws, social customs, legal enactments, and many regulations. . . . The laws grow more and more complicated. It is no wonder that there are so many failures.[3]
>
> All the things that go to make up the personality of the individual are potential resources for making or not making an adjustment to the situation. These include his physical, mental, social, and emotional resources. In his effort to make the best adjustment, the individual may call upon his memories of past experiences; he may also call into play the devices that worked successfully in the past. His attempted adjustment to the situation may be a success, a failure, or in-between; it also may be a compromise between what he wants and what he can get. If the individual makes an adaptation without injuring himself or the environment, his adjustment is considered successful. Because he believes that everything is working smoothly, he feels satisfied with his adjustment. But if the individual fails to adjust to the situation so that it meets his felt needs, he may flee from the situation, or he may attack it. In doing so, he may become a "broken personality" (break-down, suicide) or he may create a "broken situation" (crime of some sort, murder).[4]

The foregoing clearly implies that the guidance worker should assist the individual to achieve not only physical health but also mental health. Dr. Menninger has aptly defined mental health as "the adjustment of human beings to the world and to each other with a maximum of effectiveness and happiness. Not just efficiency or just contentment—or the grace of

---

[2] Karl A. Menninger, *The Human Mind* (New York: The Literary Guild of America, 1930), p. 20.

[3] *Ibid.*, p. 23.

[4] *Ibid.*, p. 25.

obeying the rules of the game cheerfully. It is all of these together. It is the ability to maintain an even temper, an alert intelligence, socially considerate behavior, and a happy disposition." [5]

With the adjustments that develop mental health as a major goal, guidance services can be evaluated in terms of their effectiveness by the extent to which they help an individual (1) to develop the proper attitudes toward his problems, (2) to learn and use the appropriate techniques for solving his problems, and (3) to achieve successful solutions to these problems.

Aims from the Point of View of the Institution

Within a school or college, the guidance program not only provides services to the students directly. It also renders services to the institution in the educational work it is carrying on. These services can be classified as services to the instructional staff, services to the administration, and research services. [6]

According to Froehlich, the guidance program should facilitate the work of the instructional staff along three main avenues:

1. The program should assist teachers in their efforts to understand students.

2. It should offer teachers systematic in-service training activities.

3. It should provide for referrals of students by teachers.

Within a school, the guidance department has all the accumulated information concerning individual students and concerning groups of students. The guidance head can and should place this information at the disposal of teachers. Because many teachers do not have the skills possessed by trained counselors, the guidance head should assist them to acquire such guidance skills. He can do this through a systematic program of in-service training. Until a sufficient number of teachers are qualified to deal with students who have problems, many teachers will have to refer these students to the

---

[5] *Ibid.,* p. 2.

[6] By permission from *Guidance Services in Smaller Schools,* by Clifford P. Froehlich. Copyright, 1950. McGraw-Hill Book Company, Inc., pp. 16-20.

guidance department. Its staff members are usually able to give such students the help they need.

In serving the administration of the school, the guidance program should perform at least two important functions:

First, because the guidance department has a wide variety of data about individual students, it can identify the needs of many of them. Some of these needs can be met through individual counseling. Others of these needs can be met through classroom or group instruction.

Second, the guidance department can play a liaison role between the administration and the community. Guidance workers are continually gathering valuable information about the community, and about its resources and its opportunities. They have frequent contacts with employers and with other community leaders, and with the families of students. During these contacts, guidance workers can not only obtain information; they also can convey information. They, for example, can help interpret the school's program to the school's community—a genuine service to the school's administration.

Because research contributes to guidance and to the school's total educational effort, the guidance program can and should carry on research activities. These activities should include community surveys that yield general information and specific data concerning occupational opportunities. They should also include follow-up studies of school-leavers—of both graduates and drop-outs. By such activities, the school obtains facts and figures whereby it can judge the soundness of its curricula, courses, and guidance program.

The school's standing in the community depends upon its contributions to the education of young people. Through research, undertaken as part of guidance services, the school evaluates its own work and makes it possible for the public to do likewise.

SUMMARY

To the end that the guidance program may function most effectively, all the resources and activities of the school related to guidance must be coordinated. The main responsibility for this coordination belongs to guidance workers. The basic goal of the coordinated effort—guidance services—is to assist the individual student to achieve up to the level of his capacity, to meet and solve his problems, and to become a well-balanced and increasingly mature person in all the varied and interrelated aspects of his life.

The principles and aims of guidance that are accepted today were developed over a period of many years. Their history and the history of guidance practices and organizations are discussed in the succeeding chapter.

SUGGESTED READINGS

Crow, Lester, and Crow, Alice. *An Introduction to Guidance: Principles and Practices.* New York: American Book Company, 1951. Chapter 4.

Erickson, Clifford E. *A Basic Text for Guidance Workers.* New York: Prentice-Hall, Inc., 1947.

Lefever, D. W., Turrell, A. M., and Weitzel, H. I. *Principles and Techniques of Guidance.* New York: The Ronald Press Company, 1950.

Mathewson, Robert Hendry. *Guidance Policy and Practice.* New York: Harper and Brothers, 1949.

Wrenn, C. Gilbert, and Dugan, Willis E. *Guidance Procedures in High School.* Minneapolis: University of Minnesota Press, 1950. Pp. 1-11.

CHAPTER FIVE

The History of Guidance Services

WHEN WE hear the term *guidance services*, we usually think that such services are provided only by and for man. Yet it is commonly observed that many of the lower animals give their young the guidance necessary to enable them to survive and to grow toward adulthood. Witness birds teaching their young to fly and wolves training their pups to stalk prey.

Some of us may believe that guidance services are relatively new in the history of Western civilization. But if these services are broadly defined, their origin antedates recorded history. In all probability, certain kinds of guidance were devised and used not only by primitive man but also by his even more primitive ancestors.

IMPACT OF CHANGING CONDITIONS
ON GUIDANCE NEEDS

For hundreds of thousands of years, guidance was undoubtedly a natural, everyday process in the life of the family. Even as late as 1900, the typical American family provided nearly all the guidance that its children received.

When adult work was relatively unspecialized or undifferentiated, the vocational aspects of guidance were usually performed by parents, with occasional advice from friends. This type of guidance was reasonably adequate in meeting the vocational needs of youth and in satisfying the vocational demands of society. When society itself was simple, the problems of young people were comparatively easy to solve. Because of

71

this, these youth needed little if any help from guidance workers who were expert in the various fields of life adjustment.

By the end of the nineteenth century, the industrial revolution had created profound changes in living conditions in civilized countries throughout the world. Growing concentrations of population in industrial areas created new social and economic problems. The factory system of production called for new types and gradations of work for which special training was required.

Faced with many occupational opportunities instead of few and with the need for specialization in order to get a job and succeed in it, young people found it more and more difficult to choose and to prepare for a vocation. Inevitably, large numbers of young men and some young women began to experience frustration if not failure.

In a world where many new occupations emerged, the very names of which were strange, most parents were unprepared to give adequate vocational guidance to their children as parents had done in a simpler society. A problem that had been primarily a family problem gradually became one of growing concern to schools and other institutions outside the home.

Naturally, because urban industrial life was becoming more and more complex, the large cities felt the need for vocational guidance of young people before the more sparsely settled areas did. As we shall see next, several cities widely separated geographically, recognized the need and began working to meet it.

THE BEGINNINGS OF ORGANIZED GUIDANCE

The forerunners of today's programs of organized guidance developed more or less independently out of local conditions in several different places. Although no one place can be given sole credit for originating the guidance movement, professional literature mentions the city of Boston most frequently as "the cradle of vocational guidance," and New York City next most frequently. In these two cities, various organizations worked together to help guide young people in planning their careers and in finding jobs. During the early years, however, the vocational guidance movement may have had more sustained vigor in certain Midwestern cities, particularly Cincinnati and Chicago, than in any of the cities on the Eastern seaboard.

To get a correct perspective of the multifarious activities of modern guidance programs in secondary schools, it will be helpful to examine the characteristics and motivations of those who fostered the beginnings of organized guidance in urban communities. In such communities, the leaders of civic, charitable, philanthropic, and, in some cases, business organizations had more to do with initiating guidance work than did educational leaders and much more than did psychologists.

The Role of Civic-Minded Leaders

Civic-minded leaders were concerned with the need to aid young men in finding the right jobs and in achieving vocational security, both within an economic society of growing complexity. Some of these early leaders had vision enough to recognize that guidance should *not* be limited to the relatively narrow field of job training and job placement; such guidance, they believed, should be extended to cover the development of the whole individual. Most leaders, however, thought of guidance as being primarily vocational in its goal and in its content. Because of this, the guidance movement appealed widely and strongly to the heads of many community organizations; as a result, they eagerly supported the introduction of guidance into the schools.

As the public began to realize the long-term values of guidance in terms of its vocational contributions to the individual and to society, it was increasingly willing to assume the financial burden entailed in the addition of this field of education to the school program. The vocational aspect of guidance has continued to have greater public appeal than any other aspect—for example, guidance designed to help the individual to achieve better personal and social adjustment.

After about 1895, vocational guidance was stimulated by a number of writers. Among Americans who wrote popular editorials, articles, and books on the subject of how to succeed in business or life were Elbert Hubbard, Russell Conwell, Horatio Alger, and William M. Thayer. Among the earliest books on vocational guidance were Nathaniel C. Fowler's *Starting in Life,* published in 1906, and Frank W. Rollins' *What Can a Young Man Do?* published in 1907. All these writers helped bring the need for guidance to the attention of the public; all gave impetus to the guidance movement at about the turn of the century.

Initiation of Guidance in Welfare Agencies and in High Schools

In the first decade of the 1900's, the conditions in various cities were favorable for the beginning of programs aimed toward the planned guidance of youth. In these communities scattered over the United States, a number of philanthropic and civic-minded leaders started work, at about the same time, on the introduction and expansion of guidance services. Outstanding among such leaders was Frank Parsons of Boston; he is generally regarded as the man who, more than any other, might be called "the father of the vocational guidance movement."

Early guidance work in Boston. As a volunteer worker in the Civic Service House in Boston, Parsons came into contact with many young people who were out of school. He was increasingly impressed by the fact that a large proportion of these youth were poorly adjusted to their work and lacked the foundation for it. To help these young men and women, Parsons organized the Bread Winner's Institute in 1905–06. Through this organization, he began to develop vocational guidance on the basis of a planned program; he stated the basic principles of this program in a book, *Choosing a Vocation.*

In 1908, Parsons organized the Vocation Bureau of Boston, which was supported by contributions from interested citizens. In his first and only report to the bureau's directors in May, 1908, Parsons used the term "vocational guidance" and gave his official title as "director and vocational counselor." It is said that this was the first time on record that the terms "vocational guidance" and "vocational counselor" were used.

Parsons had a broad conception of vocational guidance; his writings indicated that his thinking in this field was both clear-cut and advanced. He believed that, in order to choose a vocation wisely, the individual had to have (1) an understanding of himself, (2) a knowledge of the conditions of and requirements for success in different lines of work, and (3) the ability to reason logically with regard to the relationships between facts about himself and facts about his potential work environment. Although Parsons was not connected with the schools, he saw that guidance was a long-term educational undertaking; for this reason, he urged that vocational counseling be provided in the schools.

After Parsons' untimely death in 1909, the work of the Vocation Bureau of Boston was carried forward by several men, including Meyer Bloomfield, David S. Wheeler, and Frederick H. Allen. As an important part of this work, they introduced the training of teachers in the Boston schools. Subsequently, the Vocation Bureau became the Bureau of Vocational Guidance of Harvard University.

As early as 1906, the High School of Commerce in Boston was giving instruction in business opportunities; this work was later expanded to include vocational counseling. It was not until 1915, however, that the Boston School Committee established the Department of Vocational Guidance in the public school system. During the years immediately thereafter, the school committee was rather slow in granting powers to the new department. As a result, the chief function of the Vocational Guidance Director was advisory; the introduction of guidance activities was left largely to the initiative of each individual school. However, the caliber of the "vocational assistants" in the schools was raised when a plan was instituted whereby they were granted credentials on the basis of examinations.

Early guidance work in New York City. While vocational guidance was getting under way in Boston, a movement to provide guidance for young people was initiated in the New York City public schools. This movement was headed by the High School Teachers Association, under the leadership of Eli W. Weaver, a teacher in the Boys' High School of Brooklyn.

At first the New York movement was entirely voluntary; it did not have official endorsement. Weaver and some of his fellow teachers in 1906 organized the "Students' Aid Committee of the Boys' High School." Because this type of organization was so successful, it was adopted by many other high schools in the city. The movement was further advanced by the High School Teachers Association in 1908, when it organized a "Students' Aid Committee" of which Weaver was made chairman.

In 1909, the High School Teachers Association made certain recommendations with regard to guidance to the superintendent of schools. The work of its "Students' Aid Committee" was recognized by Superintendent Maxwell in his *Eleventh Annual Report of the Superintendent of Schools*. In that report, Maxwell recommended that the Board of Education organize a vocation or employment bureau. Although the board did not endorse this recommendation, it did provide a small grant for the guidance program in each high school. As a further outcome of the continuing efforts of the High School Teachers Association, a guidance survey was conducted in New York City in 1911, and a number of local agencies were set up to deal with guidance and placement.

By 1910, interest in guidance had become so widespread throughout the United States that a national conference on vocational guidance was warranted. That year a two-day conference was called by the Boston Chamber of Commerce and the Vocation Bureau of Boston. It is important to note that 45 cities sent delegates. Two years later, in 1912, a national conference on vocational guidance was held in New York City.

Early guidance work in Philadelphia. In Philadelphia, the vocational guidance movement developed only a little later than it did in Boston and New York. As in Boston, the first motivation for guidance in Philadelphia came from outside the schools. In 1909, Pennsylvania passed the "Labor Law for Women and Minors." Shortly thereafter, the Consumer's League of Philadelphia became interested in the enforcement of this law. Toward this objective, the League established the Industrial Betterment Bureau. This Bureau had two main purposes: first, to report law violations; and second, to provide guidance and placement services for young people.

Soon after 1909, the Public Education Association of Philadelphia, another private organization, took an interest in vocational guidance; in 1911, the Association undertook a survey of the vocational guidance needs of youth.

In Philadelphia, the public school's need for a vocational bureau to advise pupils was recognized by Superintendent M. G. Brumbaugh in his annual report for 1912. The Philadelphia Board of Education set up a department of vocational guidance in 1914 and a school placement bureau in 1915.

Early guidance work in Cincinnati. In Cincinnati, philanthropic organizations spearheaded vocational guidance. There the Schmidlapp Fund to help self-supporting young women had been established in 1907. This fund, together with the local child labor committee, set up a Vocational Department; the department was privately financed but was administered as a public school vocation bureau. The bureau was placed under the direction of Mrs. Helen T. Woolley, a leading psychologist.

Within the bureau, Mrs. Woolley organized a psychological laboratory in which mental and physical tests were given to young people. She also instituted a program of vocational advisement and placement service for youth. In 1911, Mrs. Woolley began a detailed research study that was published fifteen years later. The study compared the rate of mental and physical development of young people in industry with those in school.[1]

While private organizations were working for guidance, the public schools of Cincinnati were also showing an interest in this field. As early as 1907, Superintendent Dyer's reports gave attention to the problems of employed youth. By 1911, educational administrators had begun to introduce vocational guidance into the public schools. During the next two years, a program of educational and vocational guidance was formulated by F. P. Goodwin, Director of the Department of Civil and Vocational Guidance. This program introduced modern procedures, including the use of personnel records, into the city's schools.

Early guidance work in Chicago. A variety of influences contributed to the development of vocational guidance in Chicago. The University of Chicago and the Chicago School of

---

[1] Helen T. Woolley, *An Experimental Study of Children* (New York: Macmillan Company, 1926).

Civics and Philanthropy undertook guidance research and stimulated the application of research findings to the vocational guidance needs of the community. The Committee on Public Education of the Civic Club of Chicago, an influential organization, became active in the guidance movement in 1911 and 1912. At approximately the same time, the Chicago Association of Commerce took an active interest in vocational education; its activities in this field were described in the Association's reports, published annually from 1912 through 1916.

While the Civic Club and also the Chicago Association of Commerce were working for vocational guidance of boys, several women's organizations were pressing for a similar program for girls. These organizations were the Chicago Women's Club, the Chicago Association of College Alumnae, and the Women's City Club. The efforts of the women's groups were unified through the Department of Social Investigation of the Chicago School of Civics and Philanthropy.

By 1913, the Chicago Board of Education had officially recognized the guidance field. At that time, all guidance work in the city schools was placed under the supervision of District Superintendent William M. Roberts. Superintendent Ella Flagg Young threw her support fully behind the guidance movement in the schools and urged expansion of the program. In 1916, the Board established the Public School Bureau of Vocational Guidance; four appointments were made to the staff of that Bureau.

Early guidance work in other cities. Other Midwestern cities which contributed to the development of guidance in the early 1900's were Grand Rapids, Saint Louis, Minneapolis, and Omaha. In Grand Rapids, as in New York City, the leadership of one man in the public schools was largely instrumental in the initiation of guidance work. In Grand Rapids, that man was Jesse B. Davis, principal of the Central High School. He inspired his teachers and others in the school system (1) to foster the development of the personality and character of students and (2) to provide vocational information in connection with the regular school subjects. In this program, Davis secured the active cooperation of the Chamber of Commerce, the public library, the Y.M.C.A., and other local organizations.

Among the cities in the Far West, vocational guidance was undertaken relatively early in Denver, Salt Lake City, Los Angeles, San Francisco, Oakland, and Seattle. In Seattle the guidance movement was led by Principal J. A. Reed and his wife, Anna Y. Reed; their interest in this field had begun as early as 1906 and 1907 when they were living in New York City. After contributing much to the establishment of guidance services in Seattle, Mrs. Reed returned to the East. For many years, she was a leader in the training of guidance personnel as a professor of education at New York University and then at Cornell University.

Effects of scientific management and cooperative education. The development of vocational guidance throughout the nation was considerably influenced by two movements—scientific management and cooperative education. Late in the nineteenth century and early in the twentieth, Frederick W. Taylor was a vigorous advocate of scientific management, which was founded on such techniques for increasing efficiency as time-and-motion studies and job analyses. The aspect of scientific management that had to do with selection, training, advancement, and other adjustments of employees became known as personnel management. By its very nature, personnel management in industry was closely related to vocational guidance in the schools.

Cooperative education had as its aim the supplementing of theoretical training in school with practical experience on the job. The pioneer in this field was Herman Schneider, dean of the College of Engineering, University of Cincinnati; his work was carried on at about the same time as that of Parsons and Taylor. Cooperative education did not call for vocational counselors who worked mainly if not solely in the school; rather, it required so-called "coordinators" who understood both the school training field and the industrial field and who could integrate these two fields in helping prepare young people for jobs.

In the early stages of the guidance movement, most attention was centered upon vocational guidance. Even so, a growing number of the early leaders in this movement recognized that vocational guidance and educational guidance should be closely interrelated. For example, wise guidance of the individual in the choice and study of courses should precede or should be carried on along with wise guidance in the selection of and preparation for a vocation. A definite contribution to understanding the nature of and the relationships between the two kinds of guidance just mentioned was made by Truman L. Kelley. His doctor's dissertation at Teachers College, Columbia University, in 1914, carried the title, *Educational Guidance*.[2] In his study, Kelley presented the values of tests in helping a student to select a high-school curriculum. He also pointed out the role of educational guidance in vocational guidance.

Beginnings of Guidance and Personnel Work in Colleges

Because college students constituted a selected group, they did not require the same kind of guidance as did noncollege youth. The needs of college youth did not appear to be sufficiently outstanding to arouse widespread public demand for guidance services to meet them.

College students, moreover, seemed to need practical guidance in vocational choice and adjustment much less than did noncollege youth—for instance, adolescents who had dropped out before completion of high school. As a result, the development of guidance received little or no attention within the colleges themselves or from "outside" organizations. For some years, the only group that was greatly interested in this matter was the Association of Collegiate Alumnae. Its work is described later.

Guidance role of the dean of women. Whereas early programs of vocational guidance for noncollege youth gave more attention to the vocational needs of boys than of girls, guidance at the college level began mainly with the needs of young women. After the Civil War, women began applying for admission to college in increasing numbers. Many of the Eastern colleges for men steadfastly refused to consider the admission of women. Colleges in newer regions, particularly the state-supported universities and other institutions of higher learning

---

[2] Truman L. Kelley, *Educational Guidance* (New York: Teachers College, Columbia University, 1914), Teachers College Contributions to Education No. 71.

in the Middle West and in the Far West, however, rapidly became coeducational.

Many college administrative officers tended to view with misgiving the invasion by women of what had been primarily men's institutions. Although their alarm was sometimes greater than it need have been, they recognized correctly that the development of coeducational colleges created new social and moral problems.

In order to "protect" women students and to provide them with guidance, colleges began the practice of appointing a new staff officer, known as a lady principal, a lady assistant, or a matron, and occasionally as "the warden." During the latter part of the nineteenth century, many women's colleges and many coeducational colleges had such a lady staff officer.

From this early group of lady administrators, there gradually emerged the well-known functionary who carried the title *dean of women*. A dean of women was appointed at the University of Chicago in 1892, and at the University of Michigan in 1896. The first national convention of deans of women was held in 1903. As more and more colleges appointed deans of women, they assigned more and more responsibilities to these officers. The forward-looking college placed greater stress upon the advisory and personnel functions of the dean of women and less emphasis upon her administrative functions; such a college, however, usually continued to assign to this dean some administrative responsibilities.

Between 1882, when the Association of Collegiate Alumnae was formed, and 1915, that organization contributed in various ways to personnel services for college women. Early in its history, the association carried on a series of studies designed to indicate (1) whether college women were physically and mentally capable of meeting college requirements and (2) whether college education tended to make women unfit for homemaking. Also, the association encouraged and helped to support collegiate bureaus of occupational guidance.

Increasing need for guidance of college men. During their early history, most American colleges concentrated upon the preparation of young men for the professions. Because the number of these professions was limited, the problem of vocational choice was not difficult. Furthermore, in these early colleges, the major educational goal was the development of the character and the intellect of young men. The student body was small and so were the classes. This made it possible for faculty members to pay close attention to the all-round development of their students. Because the head of the institution and his faculty felt that they were already handling the advisory needs of students reasonably well, they did not see the need for special guidance services—the services as we know them today.

After 1900, the number of college students began to increase rapidly because more and more young men as well as young women wished to obtain the benefits offered by institutions of higher learning. This rise in college enrollments was due partly to the improvements in economic conditions and partly to the increased demand for college-trained personnel. Because the standards of training for admission to many occupations were rising, it became more and more difficult for young untrained men to get and hold responsible jobs in such occupations.

More and more college students came from the middle and lower income families—families that previously had had few or no children in college. The vocational aims of these students were not confined to the professions; their aims frequently were either indefinite or were directed toward a variety of business and industrial pursuits.

Within a typical college, the increased size of the classes created difficulties of adjustment for many students. Because of large classes, all too many faculty members could not become well-acquainted with their students. In instruction and in personal contacts, these teachers were unable to carry on the informal advisement and guidance of students that teachers had conducted almost naturally in the earlier colleges. To meet such conditions as the foregoing, there arose a need and a demand for organized personnel services for all college students.

The college dean—disciplinarian or counselor? Today the typical coeducational college has an organization of personnel and guidance services that is differentiated somewhat according to sex. We have already noted that such a college designated the lady principal, later known as the dean of women, to work with women students. A little later in point of time, it became customary for a college to appoint a man to handle personnel work with men students. This officer was most often entitled the "dean of men"; sometimes he was called "dean of student affairs" or "dean of students."

The word "dean" itself carried a connotation of administrative if not disciplinary authority. Whether a dean had such authority or not, this connotation tended to interfere with the development of good rapport between the dean and a student; without such rapport it was difficult for the dean to provide the best possible counseling service.

The aforesaid difficulty was experienced particularly by the officer who was the dean of women. Prior to a counseling interview with a student, she probably had had to exercise her authority as a dean "over" women students. Time and again she had had to take disciplinary action to insure that women students observed the relatively strict rules applying to their social activities.

In more recent years, colleges have somewhat reduced the disciplinary aspects of the work of the dean of women. This has been done mainly through a carefully planned program of personnel work. Such a program starts when young women enter the institution and continues until they graduate. This program allocates guidance services among a number of faculty advisors. To the extent that the guidance program thus becomes widely effective, the necessity for disciplinary action on the part of the dean of women is lessened.

Since the offices of deans of men were established, these deans have usually had fewer and less-detailed disciplinary responsibilities than the deans of women have had. Also, the deans of men have had greater opportunity to develop personnel work with students. In certain colleges and universities, the deans of men have set up and conducted programs of student counseling with such skill and understanding over a period of many years that their names have become renowned. Among these outstanding deans are or were Briggs of Harvard, Coulter of Purdue, Clark of Illinois, Goodnight of Wisconsin, Straub of Oregon, and Hawkes of Columbia.

The Beginnings of Guidance in Elementary Schools

Guidance work at the elementary-school level has no such clearly identifiable history as has guidance in high schools and colleges or as has out-of-school guidance of adolescent and post-adolescent youth. Vocational guidance, as commonly understood, is scarcely of significance below the junior high-school level where the first exploratory courses in occupations may be offered. The guidance needs of elementary-school pupils are mainly in the fields of learning basic skills, facts, and habits including those related to health and social adjustment. Much of this kind of guidance is undifferentiated from the classroom activities having to do with instruction.

Although guidance services in the elementary school are not distinct from instruction, these services are just as important as are those in the high school or college. As a matter of fact, some of the most skillful guidance to be found anywhere is carried on in the elementary school, particularly in the nursery school, the kindergarten, and the primary grades. At these very early levels of schooling, there is an intimate relation between teacher and pupils. This provides the teacher with an excellent opportunity to integrate personnel work and daily classroom activities. In some elementary schools, the guidance programs for children have an effectiveness that is not equalled by programs at any higher level of the school.

The Expanding Concept of Guidance

In the early history of the guidance movement, as we have seen, great stress was placed upon vocational guidance; educational guidance was regarded as a concomitant and necessary phase of this work. From time to time, emphasis was given to other forms of guidance designated as follows: civic guidance, health guidance, moral guidance, social guidance, religious guidance, leadership guidance, and recreational guidance.

As the years went by, educational leaders increasingly recognized that all these forms of guidance were closely interrelated and that, in reality, they belonged under the general heading of student personnel work, or, more simply, student guidance. Also these leaders recognized more and more that educational institutions had to accept responsibility for a program of student personnel work covering all the important forms of guidance. This recognition was based on the fact that schools and colleges were, and still are, the only institutions normally in a position to perform all the essential guidance services for all children and youth.

The Influence of National Organizations

Since about 1910, a number of organizations in the United States have made positive contributions to the guidance movement. Among these organizations was the National Education Association; it was potentially in a strategic position to foster guidance. Although the N.E.A. cannot be said to have maintained sustained interest in the movement, it has from time to time made definite and real contributions to the development of guidance. In this connection, it is interesting to note that in 1910 President Eliot of Harvard University addressed the annual meeting of the N.E.A. in Boston on the subject, "The Value During Education of the Life Career Motive."

By 1912, there was considerable national interest in the guidance movement. In its meeting that year in Chicago, the N.E.A. took account of this interest. Addresses on different aspects of guidance were given by Jesse B. Davis, Meyer Bloomfield, and Charles A. Prosser. A committee on vocational education and vocational guidance was appointed. Interest in guidance remained high in the 1913 meeting of the N.E.A. in Salt Lake City.

In the N.E.A. meetings after 1913, however, attention to guidance declined. This may have been due, in part, to the fact that certain other national organizations specifically devoted to the guidance field had been set up and had begun to function. Within the last decade, however, the N.E.A. has shown a tendency toward renewal of active interest in the guidance field. For instance, this organization has recently published one of the most useful systems of personnel records now available to secondary schools.

The National Society for the Promotion of Industrial Education, formed in 1907, became another organization that was active early in the guidance movement. This organization grew out of the interest of employers in developing more practical public education. It carried on and published vocational surveys; it consistently urged the enactment of federal legislation to foster vocational education. Partly as a result of the efforts of this society, the Smith-Hughes law was enacted in 1917. This act provided for federal aid to certain types of vocational education carried on in public schools.

Reference was made earlier to the first national conference on vocational guidance, the meeting called by the Boston Chamber of Commerce in 1910. That meeting was the forerunner of the National Vocational Guidance Association. The organization of the N.V.G.A. was completed in a meeting at Grand Rapids, Michigan, in 1913. Especially after 1920, the N.V.G.A. grew in membership and influence. Its annual meetings drew representatives from secondary schools and colleges throughout the United States. Its official publication, called *Occupations, The Vocational Guidance Journal*, was widely read. The N.V.G.A. met educational needs in the guidance area at the secondary-school level similar to those met at the college level by the American College Personnel Association. The latter association, formed during 1923–24, was very influential in the development of personnel work at the college level.

So many independent guidance associations were formed in the first 25 years of the guidance movement that the Council of Guidance and Personnel Associations, an organization to coordinate their work, was set up in March, 1934, at a meeting in Cleveland. The constituent groups of the C.G.P.A. were the Alliance for Guidance of Rural Youth, the American College Personnel Association, the National Association of Deans of Women, the National Association of Guidance Supervisors, and the National Vocational Guidance Association. In 1951, the American College Personnel Association, the National Association of Guidance Supervisors and Counselor Trainers, and the National Vocational Guidance Association merged to form a new organization, the American Personnel and Guidance Association. The A.P.G.A.'s official magazine, successor to *Occupations*, is the *Personnel and Guidance Journal*.

From the beginning, the nonschool organizations that provided placement services inevitably contributed to and applied practical principles of guidance. And so did organizations of representatives from these services. One of these organizations was the American Association of Public Employment Offices, organized in 1913. It approached employment problems in a professional manner; it also showed much concern over the social needs of pupils leaving school before graduation.

In the ten-year period between the first attempts at organized guidance and the entry of the United States into World War I, some 50 high schools had launched programs of vocational guidance. Most of these programs were somewhat tentative and experimental; many were under attack by unsympathetic elements in the community. There were only 14 full-time vocational guidance officers employed in the high schools of the United States in 1916. Nevertheless, by that year, the bases of guidance programs, which later were to exert wide influence, had been laid in various communities. These communities included Cincinnati, Minneapolis, Oakland, Denver, Pomona (California), and especially Providence. In the last-named city, a thoroughgoing program was adopted in 1918 and placed under the direction of Dr. Richard D. Allen.

RECENT DEVELOPMENTS IN THE GUIDANCE MOVEMENT

The development of guidance was greatly facilitated by World War I. In that war, a great deal was learned about the scientific selection and training of men. The psychological section, set up in the War Department, constructed intelligence tests and administered them to millions of men. This was the widest and most representative sampling of the intelligence of the male population of the country up to then. The findings obtained made possible many important studies in subsequent years. Among these were studies of the intellectual levels required for different occupations. These studies had significant implications even though the data and interpretations thereof evoked disagreements among psychologists and others. After World War I, the rehabilitation of disabled veterans led to the beginning of attempts at aptitude appraisal; these attempts yielded information that was valuable to guidance programs.

Other noteworthy and salutary influences on the develop-

ment of guidance were the establishment of national professional organizations (already mentioned), the measurement
movement, the introduction of cumulative records, the growing
interest of professional societies in the improvement of the personnel in their respective fields, and the provision of guidance
services by the federal government. In some cases there was
an interplay of influences. For instance, measurement and cumulative records not only influenced the guidance movement;
they were in turn influenced significantly by this movement.
So close has the relationship between testing and guidance become that neither can flourish, or even exist, without the
other.

THE CONTRIBUTIONS OF THE MEASUREMENT
MOVEMENT TO GUIDANCE

The measurement of mental functions has had two main
lines of development. One is represented by intelligence tests;
the other, by achievement tests. Both of these lines antedate
the beginning of organized guidance.

The Development of Mental Tests

During the latter part of the nineteenth century, studies of
individual differences led to the development of the first objective mental tests. About 1905 Binet and Simon in France devised an intelligence test that they administered to individual
school children. Binet developed the use of the mental age
(M.A.) as a means of interpreting the performance of children
on his test. In the United States, Terman began experimenting
with the Binet test about 1911; he developed the concept and
first applied the technique of the intelligence quotient (I.Q.)
about 1916.

Full-scale work on group tests of mental ability was begun in the United States between 1910 and 1920. During
World War I, the Army gave considerable impetus to group
intelligence testing when it developed the *Army Alpha* test
and the *Army Beta* test (nonverbal); these tests were used
throughout the American Army. Since that time, many such
tests have been constructed; as a result, there are now nu-

merous group tests of mental ability at all levels from the kindergarten level into adulthood.

Nearly all individual and group intelligence tests yield a single undifferentiated mental age and an intelligence quotient based thereon. These indicators of absolute and relative mental ability of a student have been very useful in broad educational and vocational guidance. They also have served as mental yardsticks that can be applied to other abilities as measured by achievement tests, for example. Valuable as mental tests that yield only an M.A. and an I.Q. have been, they have one major limitation—namely, the scores on these tests do not provide measures of more or less discrete mental abilities.

The development of intelligence tests that measure specific mental abilities has come through two main sources: (1) the application of factor analysis techniques by Spearman, Thurstone, Kelley, Holzinger, Hotelling, Flanagan, and a number of other specialists in psychology and statistics; and (2) the application of logical analysis procedures by Crawford and Burnham, Bennett, Seashore, Wesman, and others. As an outcome of research by these experts, the concept that intelligence consists of a single mental factor is being replaced by the concept that intelligence is composed not only of a general mental factor but of a number of different and discrete mental factors as well. In line with this new concept of intelligence, for example, Thurstone employing the technique of factor analysis developed measures of primary (basic) mental abilities. The Thurstone tests measure six fairly independent factors: number, verbal, spatial, reasoning, word fluency, and memory.

In a practical school situation, it is usually not feasible to attempt to measure all the mental factors that are now measurable, because of the amount of time and money involved if for no other reason. Yet there is a definite tendency for a school to use tests of at least two or three of the more important mental factors, such as verbal, numerical, and spatial.

These differential intelligence tests, providing somewhat diagnostic measures of mental functions, have great potential guidance values. More research needs to be done to serve as a basis for guidance workers to interpret the scores on these tests in terms of their power to predict success in different educational and vocational areas. Even so, their increased use in the schools should be encouraged.

The Development of Achievement Tests

Modern achievement testing may be traced back to the work of Dr. J. M. Rice, beginning in 1894. Rice had been a student in Germany; he returned to America with the idea that the careful methods used by German scientists for the study of the psycho-physical field of human behavior might well be adapted to the study of other fields of behavior. To try out his idea, Rice devised a spelling test, gave it in a large number of schools, and published his results. In, the beginning, school people in general were greatly opposed to Rice's work, but certain young students in education and psychology were considerably stimulated by it. One such student was Dr. E. L. Thorndike; shortly after 1900, Thorndike began to make exceedingly important contributions to the science of measurement in education.

Early in the twentieth century, Thorndike, Courtis, Freeman, Stone, Kelley, Buckingham, Ayres, Monroe, Judd, and other psychologists became very active in the promotion of the scientific movement in education. They, and large numbers of their students, worked on the construction of a wide variety of objective and standardized achievement tests. Today such tests are indispensable to educational guidance at all levels; they have real values for vocational guidance as well.

The Development of Interest Inventories and Personality Tests

Although intelligence tests and achievement tests have constituted the two main lines of test development, several other important types of tests have been constructed and used. One of these types was the interest inventory.

Starting about 1925, Dr. E. K. Strong, Jr., developed vocational interest blanks for men and for women. Through his test, Strong made it possible to appraise objectively the vocational interests of individuals of each sex with regard to a variety of occupations. More recently, Dr. G. Frederic Kuder and other psychologists have constructed instruments designed to measure vocational interests and other types of interest. These instruments are employed to ascertain the interests of high-school pupils, college students, and adults, according to broad areas or categories.

Through techniques somewhat similar to those employed in constructing interest inventories, psychologists have devised a considerable number of paper-and-pencil inventories of personality. These inventories have potential values for guidance only when they are used by persons who are thoroughly trained in their interpretation and who are fully aware of their limitations.

Psychiatrists have also constructed projective devices for personality assessment such as the Rorschach test. Since these devices were first made available generally, they have been widely used in research on personality. But these projective devices, it should be emphasized, call for more expert knowledge and more mature judgment on the part of the tester than do the paper-and-pencil personality questionnaires.

It was perhaps inevitable that many of the new tests of intelligence, achievement, interests, and personality were of inferior quality. For many years, the idea of using measurement in the schools ran ahead of technological developments in this field. The result was that many tests were hastily constructed and poorly validated. These inferior tests were offered to schools along with the good ones. The schools found it difficult if not impossible to choose from the mass of available tests those that were reasonably satisfactory in quality.

Even though schools selected good tests, they were not in a position to use the results to greatest advantage. The typical school, for example, did a great deal of testing before it had trained counselors to interpret tests results. Sometimes the school filed test findings, and then forgot them. Even worse, the staff, untrained in the testing field, misinterpreted the results or otherwise used them to the detriment of the individual.

The Development of Testing Programs

The poor quality of tests and their misuse by school people pointed up the great need for centers of leadership to organize and direct test construction and use. To meet this need, a number of agencies have arisen within the last 20 years.

State testing programs. One of the first and most influential of the efforts directed toward the organization and unification of testing efforts is to be found in various state testing programs. Testing on a state-wide basis has been undertaken in at least 16 of the 48 states. Among the best organized and best known of these is the Iowa State Testing Program, carried on under the direction of Dr. E. F. Lindquist.

The state-wide testing program has been of definite help to the guidance programs of the schools that have cooperated. For the most part, the state program has used tests that have been carefully constructed and that have been selected with the needs of the schools clearly in mind. Through the preparation of norms for the state, the state-wide program has given the cooperating schools meaningful yardsticks for comparing the scholastic aptitude and achievements of their pupils with other pupils in the state. This program has also contributed to the development of more representative national norms for the given tests.

Commercial testing activities. As the testing movement progressed, it attracted the attention of commercial publishers. A number have established themselves as "test publishers." [3] These companies have, for years, published many different types of tests and have sold them to schools and colleges throughout the country. The tests distributed by these publishers have varied considerably in quality. The better tests issued by these companies have helped materially to objectify guidance data and to facilitate their use at all school levels.

The Cooperative Testing Service. While commercial companies were publishing and distributing more and more tests, a need was recognized in the 1920's for nonprofit organizations that would provide testing services on a nationwide scale. Toward meeting this need, the most ambitious venture designed to produce tests and to provide services related thereto for secondary schools and colleges throughout the country was the Cooperative Test Service.

---

[3] Among the leading commercial test publishers are California Test Bureau, Los Angeles, California; Educational Test Bureau, Minneapolis, Minnesota; Psychological Corporation, New York, New York; Public School Publishing Company, Bloomington, Illinois; Science Research Associates, Chicago, Illinois; and World Book Company, Yonkers, New York.

The Cooperative Test Service was founded under the auspices of the American Council on Education through a subvention from the General Education Board. Under the direction of Dr. Ben D. Wood, this service undertook, starting in 1932, to produce annually an extensive series of comparable forms of tests covering all academic fields for the secondary school and the junior college. In 1947, when the Cooperative Test Service was merged with the testing services of certain other organizations to form the Educational Testing Service, there were more than 60 different tests in the Cooperative series; many of these tests were available in from four to ten different comparable forms. Today the Cooperative tests are widely used in educational guidance programs, particularly at the high-school level.[4]

The Educational Records Bureau. In addition to the need for a noncommercial test-making agency whose activities would be nationwide, there was need for an organization that would assist schools in test usage—in selecting, administering, scoring, and interpreting tests in individual guidance. For sound interpretation of tests results, schools required annual comparable measurements of students.

To meet the need, a small group of educational institutions formed the Educational Records Bureau in 1927. The Bureau was chartered by the State of New York as a nonprofit service and research organization for schools and colleges. Since its organization, the Bureau has grown steadily; in 1953, it had 570 member institutions, of which 25 were colleges.

The Educational Records Bureau is in no sense a closed corporation; rather, its services are available to schools throughout the country. Year by year, new schools are being added to the Bureau's list of members. Today, 90 percent of these members are independent or private institutions; the rest are public institutions. These schools carry on fall and spring testing programs each year. Through its testing and test-related services, the Bureau continually stresses the use of test results in the guidance of individual pupils.

Two other organizations of national scope have played im-

---

[4] The Cooperative Achievement Tests are now published by Educational Testing Service, Princeton, New Jersey.

portant roles in the history of educational measurement in the United States. These are the College Entrance Examination Board, and the Carnegie Foundation for the Advancement of Teaching. For the most part, these organizations have served colleges and universities rather than the lower levels of the educational ladder.

The latest development in cooperative nonprofit testing in the United States was the merger in December, 1947, of the testing services of the College Entrance Examination Board, the American Council on Education, and the Carnegie Foundation for the Advancement of Teaching. The Educational Testing Service, the organization resulting from the merger, is having much influence on the measurement and guidance programs of schools and colleges throughout the country.

Test-Scoring Devices. The use of objective tests has been greatly facilitated by the International Test Scoring Machine, which was made available about 1935. This device, developed by the International Business Machines Corporation, has encouraged increased participation in programs of cooperative testing. By 1953 a number of centers were working on new electronic devices designed to increase markedly the speed and accuracy of machine-scoring.

Some persons have feared that a test-scoring machine would force teachers and other educators to construct their tests in objective forms, the only forms that can be machine-scored. Fortunately, the producers of the machine and most of its users have approached the testing problem in a professional and forward-looking manner. For example, they have recognized that, to measure certain abilities, some kinds of examinations should probably not be changed into completely objective form. Thus, the producers and users of the test-scoring machine support the flexibility in measurement that is so essential if tests and other means of evaluation are to serve guidance objectives.

The Development of Personnel Records

The use of records, except of some very simple forms, is a comparatively recent development in American education.

The main purpose of the earlier school records was systematic pupil accounting rather than personnel or guidance services.

Early types of school records. The first type of record was the school register. The movement for the adoption of the school register was led by Horace Mann of Massachusetts, Henry Barnard of Connecticut, and Samuel Lewis of Ohio, in the 1830's and 1840's. In time, nearly all states followed the lead of Massachusetts in passing laws requiring the school register to be kept in all districts.

Throughout the nineteenth century and well into the twentieth century, the personnel records in the majority of schools of this country showed little advance over the school register. In a large number of schools, the records were gradually changed from bound volumes to loose cards or sheets, but they still were almost devoid of personnel data. They were maintained primarily to comply with school laws and to account for the time of the pupils rather than to serve as a means of contributing to pupil development. Such development depended upon the recognition of individual differences, a trend that began about the turn of the century.

The awareness of the need for guidance which started to grow in the early 1900's directed attention toward the individual pupils; this awareness led educators to view records in a different light. As a result, the pupil register including the record of pupil attendance began to be supplemented by various kinds of individual pupil record systems. One of the first such record systems was prepared about 1909 by Charles M. Lamprey, Director of the Boston Model School. Lamprey's system was adopted by the Boston Public Schools in 1910.

A few of the independent or private schools took a leading part in the development of personnel records. In the Park School, Baltimore, for example, Eugene R. Smith and Margaretta R. Voorhees worked out and then published materials dealing with methods of studying and recording the personality characteristics and the other aspects of the developmental behavior of pupils. Smith and Voorhees began their work in this field about 1912.

From the end of World War I up to about 1930, several comprehensive systems of child accounting records with personnel features were made commercially available and were widely used. Four of the best known were the *Strayer-Engle-hardt Record System;* the *Child Accounting Practice,* by Mc-Alister and Otis; the *Heck-Reeder Uniform School Accounting System;* and the *Flynn-Utne Simplified Record System.*

The construction of cumulative record forms by educational organizations. The various systems of published record forms, helpful though they were, did not fully meet the needs of educational institutions for records whose central and controlling purpose was personnel work. Toward serving this purpose, the modern type of cumulative record did not become generally available until 1928. That year the American Council on Education published a supplement to *The Educational Record,* entitled "Personnel Methods."[5] The supplement, later published separately as a brochure, presented a new cumulative record card and the philosophy underlying it. This card, devised primarily as a guidance instrument for the Council's Committee on Personnel Methods, was prepared by Ben D. Wood of Columbia University and E. L. Clark of Northwestern University. The card was the first of the American Council Cumulative Record Forms. The publication of the card and the brochure constituted a landmark in the history of individual guidance in the United States.

In 1928 and in the years immediately following, the American Council on Education published for general use a cumulative record folder for college students and a cumulative record folder for secondary-school pupils. It also printed a briefer form of the latter on two sides of a card suitable for a letter-size file. In 1933, Eleanor Perry Wood and Winston B. Stevens of the Educational Records Bureau prepared for independent schools an adaptation of the American Council folder for high-school students. A little later, the Council published an elementary-school cumulative record card devised by Anna L. Rose Hawkes and Margaret Moore.

All four forms issued by the American Council on Education were widely distributed. Because they were not copyrighted, schools and colleges were free to reprint them or to

---

[5] *Personnel Methods.* The Educational Record, Supplement No. 8, IX. (July, 1928).

adapt them to their own needs. Subsequently, various aspects of the American Council forms appeared in literally hundreds of the cumulative record cards that were printed and used by educational institutions.

About 1938, ten years after the publication of the first American Council cumulative record form, it became apparent that, because of new developments, certain improvements in the American Council forms could well be made. Accordingly, a committee for the revision of these forms was set up, with Eugene R. Smith as chairman. Working in a series of meetings from 1939 to 1945, the committee issued four cumulative record folders in revised editions—a form for the primary grades; a form for Grades 4, 5, and 6; a form for junior and senior high schools; and a form for colleges. For these forms, the Council in 1947 published an unusually thorough manual.[6]

Other organizations that have taken a leading part in the development of personnel records are the American Association of Collegiate Registrars and Admissions Officers, National Association of Secondary-School Principals (National Education Association), and Progressive Education Association. The last-named association made its most important contribution to the development of records during the so-called "Eight-Year Study" which began in 1934. The high schools cooperating in this study undertook to record about their students the most significant information that could be sent on to colleges. To conduct the study, several committees were set up under the chairmanship of Eugene R. Smith. These committees made an especially sustained, coordinated, and fruitful attack upon the problem of designing meaningful pupil personnel records for use in educational guidance.[7]

Since 1940, numerous committees of administrators, teachers, and counselors throughout the country have devised and printed cumulative record forms for their own schools or school systems. Although published forms such as those issued

---

[6] *Manual for the American Council on Education Cumulative Record for Schools and Colleges* (Washington, D.C.: American Council on Education, 1947), p. 28.

[7] Eugene R. Smith and Ralph Tyler, *Appraising and Recording Student Progress* (New York: Harper and Brothers, 1942).

by the American Council on Education presented many valuable ideas, each school system usually found that it was highly desirable to prepare its own form, keeping in mind its objectives and program.

To the setting up of cumulative record systems in schools throughout the country, the Office of Education of the Department of Health, Education, and Welfare of the United States Government has made many substantial and continuing contributions. That office has studied available record forms and has served as a clearing house of information in this field. It has issued two helpful publications: *Nature and Use of the Cumulative Record,* by David Segel; [8] and *Handbook of Cumulative Records,* a report of a national committee on cumulative records.[9] As a service to interested educational institutions, the Office of Education and the Educational Records Bureau each makes available loan kits consisting of collections of sample personnel records. These kits may be borrowed by schools and colleges that are working on the revision of their guidance record forms.

The Pennsylvania Study and the Educational Records Bureau Demonstration Project

A study of the relations of secondary education and higher education in Pennsylvania was carried on for about a decade by the Carnegie Foundation for the Advancement of Teaching. This study, popularly known as "The Pennsylvania Study," demonstrated the importance of cumulative objective measurements of an individual student's attainment and progress to an institution's program of educational and vocational guidance.[10]

The Pennsylvania Study involved the establishment and maintenance of cumulative records for some 30,000 students. These records included the results of a succession of objective

[8] David Segel, *Nature and Use of Cumulative Records.* Bulletin 1938, No. 3 (Washington, D.C.: Office of Education, 1938).

[9] *Handbook of Cumulative Records.* Bulletin 1944, No. 5 (Washington, D.C.: Office of Education, 1944).

[10] William S. Learned and Ben D. Wood, *The Student and His Knowledge* (New York: Carnegie Foundation for the Advancement of Teaching, 1938), Bulletin No. 29.

tests that were given starting in the seventh grade and extending through college. Analyses of the results of these tests pointed clearly and sharply to the fact that pupils classified at the same grade level are too heterogeneous to attain like goals or to profit equally from the same or similar types of instruction or guidance. According to the findings from every achievement test used, there was great variability among the scores made by students within a given grade. Moreover, there was considerable overlapping between the distribution of scores in a given grade and the distribution of scores in the grade below or in the grade above it. Analyses of the test results also indicated the urgent need for the careful, continuous recording and study of the aptitudes, attainments, and interests of each student.

The preliminary findings of the Pennsylvania Study were so significant that they began almost immediately to influence the guidance procedures in forward-looking schools. The final results impelled these and other schools to make considerable revisions in their guidance techniques. All too many schools, however, had not yet reached the place where they were prepared to take full advantage of the study's findings and recommendations.

Nevertheless, the Pennsylvania Study definitely helped to bring the need for cumulative guidance records to the attention of the schools of the country. It was, in a sense, the first step—a step in which the work of measuring and recording was done *for* the schools rather than *by* them. The next step called for was a study related to how public schools, on their own, could best obtain and use objective data in their cumulative records—all as an integral part of their programs of educational guidance. Such a study was set up under the direction of the Public Schools Advisory Committee of the Educational Records Bureau, with financial support from the Carnegie Foundation for the Advancement of Teaching.

The purpose of this study project was to encourage and assist a small representative group of public schools to plan and conduct demonstration programs in educational guidance and curriculum adaptation. Such programs, then, might serve as models for other public schools to follow. This large gen-

eral purpose of the project was subdivided into the following
major aims:

1. Maintenance of cumulative records
2. Systematic use of comparable tests
3. Development and observance of a system of continuous
teacher education
4. Study of the relationship between curriculum requirements and individual needs
5. Improvements in procedures for marking pupils and
reporting their progress to parents

The project was carried on for a period of five years at
the junior-senior high-school level in seven selected school
systems. These systems had been chosen on the basis of their
geographical distribution and their willingness and ability to
cooperate in such an extensive program. The seven participating centers were the Billings Public Schools (Billings, Mon-
tana); the Groton Public Schools and the Robert E. Fitch High
School (Groton, Connecticut); the Plainfield Public Schools
(Plainfield, New Jersey); the Rochester Public Schools (Rochester, Minnesota); the San Antonio Public Schools (San Antonio, Texas); the Scarsdale Public Schools (Scarsdale, New
York); and the secondary school of the Colorado State College of Education (Greeley, Colorado). The keynote of the
entire study was freedom on the part of each school to work
out its own guidance program to fit its local situation, utilizing
cumulative records based on comparable objective and other
data so far as they were applicable. The results of the project
were reported in *Guidance in Public Secondary Schools*.[11]

Work of Professional Societies in Improving Personnel

An important contemporary trend within the professions
is to turn a critical eye upon themselves, to observe the
strengths and weaknesses of their members, and to look for
ways of improving the competence of these members through
such means as in-service training and pre-service selection
and training. For some years, several professional groups have

---

[11] Arthur E. Traxler (ed.), *Guidance in Public Secondary Schools* (New
York: Educational Records Bureau, October, 1939), Educational Records
Bulletin No. 28.

conducted such programs of self-evaluation and self-improvement; in these programs, they have employed measurement and guidance techniques.

Since about 1930, for example, the Association of American Medical Colleges has carried on studies that used the *Moss Medical Aptitude Test* and other devices to select candidates for admission to medical schools. (Since 1948, this association has utilized the testing facilities of the Educational Testing Service.) Various law schools, including those of Columbia, Yale, Harvard, the University of Illinois, and the University of Minnesota, have sponsored experiments in the preparation of law aptitude examinations. Recently these examinations have been administered at regular intervals through the Educational Testing Service.

For a number of years, the League for Nursing Education has been active in the preparation and use of objective tests designed to measure the aptitude and the achievement of nurses in training. Since 1940, the National Committee on Teacher Examinations cooperated with teacher-training institutions in a well-organized annual program of testing candidates for teaching positions. In 1943, engineering societies with the assistance of the Carnegie Foundation for the Advancement of Teaching launched a project of measurement and guidance in the field of engineering education. Since then, this program has expanded rapidly; it is now one of the testing projects of the Educational Testing Service.

The profession that has most recently introduced a program aimed toward the improvement of its personnel is public accounting. In 1943, the American Institute of Accountants appointed a Committee on Selection of Personnel. This committee set up a project designed to carry on measurement and evaluation at the college and professional levels. The project was supported financially by the Institute and certain public accounting firms; it was directed by Dr. Ben D. Wood of the Educational Records Bureau. During a four-year period of research, the Bureau constructed tests of orientation and achievement and prepared special accounting norms for the *Strong Vocational Interest Blank*. This testing program, operated by the Bureau, was placed on a full service basis in 1947.

These testing programs in professional fields have much significance for testing and counseling practices in colleges and universities. They facilitate guidance toward or away from a given profession with the objective validity that was formerly lacking, particularly under conditions where students must be counseled on a large scale.

Up to now, however, these testing programs have had little significance for guidance in high schools. Such measurement programs could make valuable contributions not only to the professional societies themselves but also to the guidance procedures of secondary schools. For example, a high-school student who is interested in becoming a public accountant could take the screening tests for that profession; on the basis of his performance on these tests, he could decide more realistically whether he should take an accounting course in a college or university. Along this line, the American Institute of Accountants, in 1953, prepared an accounting orientation test for high-school seniors.

Federal Aid to Guidance

The federal government has assisted the guidance movement in various ways. One of the most important has been through the U.S. Office of Education. It has published numerous bulletins and other materials relating to guidance. In 1938 this office established the Occupational Information and Guidance Service, with Harry A. Jager as director. The Service's publications and advisory work have been and still are of material help to the schools in keeping abreast of new developments in the guidance field.

A second way in which the federal government has aided guidance is by making federal funds available to the states. Through the Office of Education, the federal government has made and is still making grants in aid to the states to pay half the salaries of state guidance directors and to help pay the salaries of state supervisors and counselor trainers and of local supervisors and counselors. Under the provisions of the George-Barden Act, the federal government appropriates funds for the program. The program itself is administered by the Guidance and Pupil Personnel Service of the Office of Education.

A third guidance-related contribution of the federal government has to do with employment service. The Wagner-Peyser Act of 1935 set up the United States Employment Service; since then its larger offices have offered counseling services related to employment. As a result of this act, the states were encouraged to establish employment offices; to support these offices, the federal government matched state funds. During World War II, the federal government took over and operated these offices and extended their services within the several states. In 1943, it provided in each office a special counselor to advise returning war veterans. Soon after the close of the war, the federal government returned the administration of these employment offices to the states.

THE INFLUENCE OF WORLD WAR II ON GUIDANCE

Soon after the United States entered World War II, the development of guidance in high schools was temporarily checked and even set back, according to data gathered by the Office of Education. Some of these data are presented here.[12]

Year	Number of Schools	Number of Guidance Officers	Number of Students Served
1939	1,297	2,286	2,062,344
1942	1,233	1,662	1,659,744

As was to be expected, the war interrupted the guidance movement in several ways. For example, the draft of young men for military service and the job opportunities in war industries considerably reduced the number of boys enrolled in the last year of high school. Because of military and other war-related demands for personnel, most schools experienced shortages of teachers and counselors. They lost staff members and could not replace them. When this situation arose, these

[12] Oscar J. Kaplan (ed.), *Encyclopedia of Vocational Guidance* (New York: Philosophical Library, 1948), p. 477.

schools tended to reduce or even to eliminate their guidance services. Sometimes they assigned a guidance worker to teaching where the demand was insistent and inescapable.

By the end of the war, however, guidance programs were again forging ahead. Their progress was noted by Froehlich [13] in a study based on Office of Education figures for 1939, 1942, and 1945. The data for these years indicated a notable increase both in the number of schools having counselors and guidance officers and in the number of guidance personnel employed. In 1945–46, 3,990 out of 24,314 public high schools, or 16 percent of all the schools reporting, stated that they employed counselors or guidance officers. The total number of such guidance workers reported was 8,299—3,618 men and 4,681 women.

Although World War II appeared to retard or even to set back the guidance movement, war-related developments had a salutary effect upon guidance and personnel services. During the war, great strides were made in the development of measurement procedures connected with the appraisal of men for different kinds of military service. These procedures, for example, led to the construction of many new and better aptitude tests. Also during the war, many men in military and other wartime services were trained in counseling and guidance techniques; they found that this training was valuable in civilian guidance work.

In the last years of the war and since then, the Veterans Administration has carried on an active program of readjustment and rehabilitation. This program has made considerable use of evaluation and counseling. An important part of the V.A.'s work has been the advisement of veterans who wanted to enter or to return to college. In the comparatively small number of cases of veterans who wished to complete their high-school education, the V.A. has provided individual counseling that was even more thorough than that provided for those wanting to go to college.

The new testing techniques that were devised, the experiences that numerous young men had in the fields of measure-

---

[13] Clifford P. Froehlich, "Counselors and Guidance Officers in Public Secondary Schools," *Occupations*, XXVI (May, 1948), 522-27.

ment and guidance, and the awareness of the need for guidance that spread and grew especially among those whose schooling had been interrupted—all these war-related developments helped to advance the guidance movement and to raise it to a level of service never before approached.

THE INFLUENCE OF OUTSTANDING GUIDANCE PROGRAMS

Since the organized guidance movement was started about a half century ago, much progress has been made in all areas of personnel work, and the outlook for further progress is favorable. Lest we become complacent, however, we should note two points: *First,* vast numbers of schools in the United States have no planned systematic guidance of any kind. And *second,* all too many schools that profess to give educational and vocational guidance to their pupils have programs that fall short of the mark. In fact, objective observation indicates that it is the rare public school or college that has fully adequate services for evaluating and for otherwise assisting individual students.

If the guidance services of an educational institution are fully adequate, they include (1) the scientific collection and interpretation of test data and other important information about the individual, (2) the provision for his use of extensive and reliable information concerning educational and vocational opportunities, (3) the relating of the information about the individual to the opportunities available to him, and (4) the counseling with the individual so that he is able to participate actively and intelligently in working out his own plans.

The communities whose public school systems have guidance practices that have reached the stage where they are sufficiently outstanding to deserve national attention include Cincinnati (Ohio); Denver (Colorado); Los Angeles (California); Minneapolis (Minnesota); Pasadena (California); Plainfield (New Jersey); and Providence (Rhode Island).

THE DEVELOPMENT OF GUIDANCE IN OTHER NATIONS

Economic and social conditions similar to those which led to the development of organized guidance programs in the

United States have existed in all of the more highly civilized countries of the world. It is, therefore, not surprising that a number of such countries have developed guidance movements that are similar in many respects to that within the United States. In these countries, it should be noted, attention to guidance needs was directed mainly to elementary-school and secondary-school pupils and to out-of-school youth. Practically no attention was given to guidance in colleges mainly because these countries had no counterpart of our liberal arts college. In the United States, such colleges enroll large numbers of students.

To get a better understanding of guidance services here, it is worth-while to observe briefly the origin and growth of organized guidance in certain other nations.

Australia

Vocational guidance was first advocated in Australia in the 1920's, but it was not accorded official recognition until the 1930's. The state of New South Wales, containing the large industrial city of Sydney, made more progress than any other state.

World War II influenced guidance in Australia in several ways. To illustrate, the war directed attention to problems of scientific selection and placement of men and thus stimulated the further growth of psychological methods. The war also led to the development of new procedures by the Vocational Department of Labor and National Service and to the use of these procedures elsewhere. After the close of the war, the extensive testing and counseling of men being separated from the military services resulted in improved guidance techniques.

The success of psychological personnel work in the military services, the vocational guidance provided in the rehabilitation of service men and women, and the availability of counselors trained during the war and immediately thereafter—all, it is anticipated, will tend to make a permanent place for vocational guidance in postwar Australian life. Although the techniques used there are mainly those developed in the United States and England, a considerable amount of test construction is carried on by such agencies as the Australian Counsel for Educational Research.

Canada

The growth of vocational guidance in Canada has been considerably influenced by the guidance movement in the United States. Because the control of education in Canada is vested in the governments of the nine provinces, the development of vocational guidance in the schools has varied from one province to another. In the main, the provincial departments of education have formally recognized, developed, and directed vocational guidance only within the last ten or twelve years. However, the federal government has, to some extent, provided for the guidance of school children and youth through the Dominion-Provincial Youth Training Program.

In Canada, communities and schools have introduced guidance on a local basis. The development of these local guidance programs has been due to the leadership of interested individuals and to the concern of the general public for the vocational orientation of youth. In Canadian colleges and universities, there is little systematic guidance. Some deans of women, however, have made attempts at nontechnical guidance of their students.

In Canada, one school of thought concerning guidance stresses occupational guidance and job analysis. Another school emphasizes mental hygiene—that is, the point of view that regards guidance as adjustment and development. There is an apparent trend toward the latter approach.

Although the Canadian Psychological Association had developed many useful techniques in the field of personnel selection and other forms of guidance, Canada was slow to adopt these techniques during the early years of World War II. In 1941, however, the Army and the Air Force introduced personnel selection procedures and, in 1943, the Navy did likewise. Toward the end of the war, the government began to offer vocational guidance to men being separated from the services. These war-related developments gave considerable impetus to vocational guidance. Even so, one of Canada's outstanding needs in the guidance field continues to be trained personnel.

France

Those responsible for the guidance of youth in France have had to keep in mind that occupational adjustment begins at different levels for different types of work. For the lower and middle positions in the fields of trade and commerce, the beginning of occupational training is usually at the end of the elementary-school period when the youth is about 14 years old. For the higher positions in these same fields, such training usually starts at the end of the higher elementary-school period when the youth is about 16 years of age. For the professions, occupational training gets under way at the end of the secondary school when the youth is approximately 18 years of age.

Although vocational guidance in France is not a function of the public schools, it is provided by agencies that cooperate with these schools. National recognition of vocational guidance was first given by government decree in 1922. Under the decree, vocational guidance offices were established. They cooperated with the national public placement offices (under the Board of Trade) in a program to place adolescents, particularly, in appropriate occupations. The vocational guidance offices were so organized that their officers collaborated with the following persons: (1) elementary-school teachers who supplied information on the mental and moral characteristics of their pupils; (2) physicians who provided data on the health and physical development of counselees; and (3) staff members of placement offices who furnished information regarding occupational opportunities.

The National Institute of Vocational Guidance was founded in Paris in 1928 and was recognized by decree in 1930. It functions under the Division of Vocational Education and the Ministry of Education. A leading responsibility of this institute is the training of vocational counselors.

In France, just as it has in the United States, private philanthropy has influenced the development of guidance. The Chamber of Commerce of Paris, for example, has created a central office of vocational guidance for the benefit of all children leaving school.

Vocational guidance in France is carried on under the supervision of the Ministry of Education and in cooperation with the Ministry of Labor. This plan is different from that in most of the other European countries, where guidance is customarily placed under the supervision of the Ministry of Labor.

Germany

Different influences contributed to the origin and development of vocational guidance in Germany. An important influence so far as the guidance of women was concerned was exerted by forward-looking women's organizations; these groups, about 1900, created special information services for women who wished to get started in a vocation.

An even more important influence toward the provision of guidance was World War I. To meet wartime needs, the government set up a public agency that provided employment services and vocational guidance services, particularly for apprentices. The legal base for this agency was a government edict, issued in 1918.

For a number of years, both governmental and private agencies provided guidance in the field of employment. But in 1927 the government enacted the Unemployment Insurance Law. This law made vocational guidance an obligatory part of public employment services; it also stipulated that no charge was to be made for such services. The 1927 law tended to reduce the importance of the services offered by private agencies.

Prior to 1933, Germany developed a fairly extensive system of vocational guidance. The government established vocational guidance offices in more than 500 cities; many of these offices provided psychological services including aptitude testing. However, Germany failed to develop comprehensive vocational guidance programs in either its elementary or its secondary schools. To assist the counselor in a guidance office, these schools were expected to give him reports on pupil conduct and pupil progress (mainly in academic subjects). Although some aptitude questionnaires and tests had been prepared, the schools usually gave these tests in doubtful cases only. They rarely employed objective group achievement tests.

When the Nazis came into power, they continued to carry on vocational guidance work but only for purposes related to service to the State. They paid most attention to the mental and physical capacities of an individual so that he could be placed where he could work most effectively for the Nazi regime.

Germany has never had a systematic training program for guidance counselors. Persons were usually appointed as counselors on the basis of satisfactory experience in this field and of several years of practical experience in an occupation.

Vocational guidance, even the type that was conducted by the Nazis, broke down before the end of World War II. After the war, one of the cardinal objectives of the educational program in the American Zone of Occupation in Germany was the rebuilding and extension of guidance services for youth, according to democratic principles.

In the newly formed West German state, the development of guidance programs in which objective information about individuals will be utilized has been stimulated by the establishment of centers for test construction and research. Among the more important centers is the Institute for Educational Research in Frankfort on the Main; this institute is directed by Professor Erich Hylla.

The public employment services now employ psychologists in most offices in major cities. Their work is largely testing and evaluation. The counseling is done by employment interviewers.

Great Britain

Great Britain began to feel the need for systematic guidance of young people at about the same time as did the United States. In Britain, however, the development of guidance was left largely to local initiative and responsibility. An important exception has been the program carried on by the juvenile departments of the national employment exchanges; these exchanges were set up by the Ministry of Labor in the early 1900's.

In Great Britain there has been some tendency to regard vocational guidance as a general part of the broad educational program rather than as a specific educational program related to occupational advisement, training, and placement. The British concept of guidance, however, has probably been changing due mainly to the Education Act of 1944. This act raised the age of compulsory school attendance immediately to 15 and later to 16. Because the law requires youth to stay in school longer, the schools and the public will probably seek ways to improve and to extend vocational guidance services.

In Great Britain, interest in vocational guidance is greatest in the secondary schools. Many such schools have "career masters"; they are responsible for conveying vocational information to students. In general, the introduction of the position of career master has come about naturally and gradually. The headmaster of a school, for example, has often appointed a career master mainly because certain subject-matter masters have become conscious that their students require the help of a specialist to solve their vocational problems.

Secondary schools have also focused their attention on the need to provide adequate guidance services for those students who will leave school just as soon as they pass the compulsory attendance age. As a result of such attention, many schools have made considerable progress in this field of guidance.

Although the job advisement and placement of British youth is carried on mainly under the Ministry of Labor, similar guidance services are provided by some private groups and institutions. Among the latter is the National Institute of Industrial Psychology in London. Active since 1922, this organization is perhaps the most notable private agency in the guidance field. Therein, the institute provides counseling, carries on research, and conducts training courses for vocational advisors and career masters.

In Great Britain, both public and private vocational guidance services were much disturbed by World War II. Staff members who normally provided these services were overloaded with other duties. Because the wartime demand for labor was so great, young workers readily obtained positions without vocational assistance. As a result, the demand for guidance services declined.

Since the war, guidance services throughout the country have been going through a period of reconstruction and expansion. During this period, one of the key questions yet to be decided is whether vocational guidance, in the main, should be conducted by the educational system or by other agencies.

Japan

Because Japan had consistently built up its school system during the first third of the twentieth century, by the time of World War II this system was relatively modern and efficient, particularly at the elementary-school level. As an important outcome, the country's percentage of literacy was extremely high.

Interest in vocational guidance in Japan began to develop comparatively early. The impetus for this development came from two main sources—the Department of Education, and the Department of Domestic Affairs. In 1922, for instance, the education department established a lecture class in vocational guidance; and in 1927 it formed a National Association of Vocational Guidance. In the 1920's, the education and the domestic affairs departments reached an agreement on a program of vocational guidance; since then, they have worked cooperatively to carry out this program on a nation-wide basis.

In Japan, vocational guidance has, from the beginning, been regarded as a national policy designed to advance the nation's welfare. In line with this policy, vocational guidance has been a part of general guidance under the direction of the government.

Since 1927, Japanese elementary schools have offered extensive vocational guidance. Secondary schools, however, have devoted relatively little attention to such guidance because they felt that at their level of education this type of guidance was not needed. This feeling was probably due to the following situation. In Japan, the maximum compulsory school age was so low that comparatively few young people attended high school. Because most of these high-school youth had already decided to go into government work or into professional work, they did not require vocational guidance.

For young people of high-school age who were not in school, Japan has carried on a systematic program of vocational guidance. General responsibility for the guidance of these boys and girls has been taken by the Department of Education.

In guidance work with pupils, Japanese teachers have tended to stress personal relationships and inspirational qualities. Few of these teachers have had training in the scientific procedures for studying children. Although several standardized intelligence and achievement tests have been made available, comparatively few teachers have used these tests.

Another important aspect of Japan's guidance program, in its broader sense, has been conducted by the Bureau of Thought Supervision, and since 1937 by its successor, the Office of Educational Reforms. The purpose of this bureau was to provide moral training and to combat personal and social unrest including that due to Communist activities.

During World War II, because of Japan's manpower needs, the government dominated the programs of occupational training and employment. As a result, the type of vocational guidance carried on before the war virtually disappeared. During the postwar period, Japan's educational program has given increasing attention to the development of a new and democratic philosophy and technique of guidance. In connection with this program, Japanese educators have been studying guidance procedures in the United States; they have tried to adapt some of these procedures to the guidance of Japanese youth.

During the 1951–52 school year, a team of American guidance experts under the leadership of Wesley Lloyd conducted a series of seminars for Japanese educators. A national association of guidance workers was organized and is now active in the field.

SUMMARY

The foregoing descriptions of the history of guidance in the United States, Australia, Canada, France, Germany, Great Britain, and Japan have indicated that guidance developed in different parts of the world out of somewhat similar influences. These accounts, however, have made clear that, on the whole, guidance programs in the United States are considerably more advanced than such programs in other countries. Moreover, nowhere else in the world, with the possible exception of Canada, is personnel work and guidance so closely identified with the schools as in the United States.

The progress made in the guidance field in our nation has been due to the continuous development and use of improved tools and techniques. Among these are systematic methods of collecting and recording information about individuals, the subject of the next chapter.

SUGGESTED READINGS

Allen, Wendell C. *Cumulative Pupil Records.* New York: Bureau of Publications, Teachers College, Columbia University, 1943.

Brewer, J. M. *History of Vocational Guidance.* New York: Harper and Brothers, 1942.

Hamalainen, Arthur E. *An Appraisal of Anecdotal Records.* New York: Bureau of Publications, Teachers College, Columbia University, 1943.

Handbook of Cumulative Records. Bulletin 1944, No. 5. Washington, D.C.: Office of Education, 1944.

Kaplan, Oscar J. (ed.). *Encyclopedia of Vocational Guidance,* "Apprenticeship Training in the United States" (J. W. Kelly and Ansel R. Cleary), pp. 20-21; "Australia" (D. Cunningham), pp. 75-78; "Canada" (Stephen R. Laycock), pp. 137-43; "France" (Franklin J. Keller), pp. 402-08; "Germany" (Herbert S. Lewin), pp. 409-12; "Great Britain" (F. M. Earle), pp. 412-22; "History of Vocational Guidance in the United States" (James H. Bedford), pp. 469-78; "High School Guidance, History of" (Charles M. Smith), pp. 461-69; "Japan" (H. L. Smith), pp. 641-45. New York: Philosophical Library, 1948.

Keller, F. J. *Vocational Guidance Throughout the World.* New York: W. W. Norton and Company, 1937.

Manual for the American Council on Education Cumulative Record Folders for Schools and Colleges. Washington, D.C.: American Council on Education, 1947.

Reed, Anna Y. *Guidance and Personnel Services in Education.* Ithaca, N.Y.: Cornell University Press, 1944.

Segel, David. *Nature and Use of the Cumulative Record.* Bulletin 1938, No. 3. Washington, D.C.: Office of Education, 1938.
Smith, Eugene R., and Tyler, Ralph W. *Appraising and Recording Student Progress.* New York: Harper and Brothers, 1942.

PART II

Guidance Tools and Techniques

CHAPTER SIX

Collecting and Recording for Guidance Purposes

MANY SCHOOLS provide a considerable number of guidance services regardless of whether these services are organized as guidance programs. As a rule, however, the schools that have organized guidance programs are doing a better job of helping individuals than are schools that have unplanned and uncoordinated guidance services. The schools with organized programs obviously have effective methods of collecting and recording information for various guidance purposes.

When a school undertakes a guidance program, the members of its staff may, in the beginning, be motivated mainly by a desire to help students solve problems and attain goals that the staff members feel are important—at least as important as the learning of subject matter. At first, these staff members may have only a vague idea of how to begin a guidance program or of what steps to take in making this program successful.

As staff members study this matter, they will increasingly realize that *all guidance services properly begin with an understanding of the individual.* To acquire and apply this understanding, they must conduct a cooperative project—a project that enlists the school, the students, and the home. Such a project calls for the thorough study of the individual including his history and present status; the collection of a variety of facts concerning his aptitudes, achievements, and interests;

119

and the recording of all the information about him in an organized and cumulative form.

THE USE OF INFORMATION-GETTING TECHNIQUES [1]

In obtaining information for guidance purposes, observation, rating scales, autobiographies, and sociometric devices form a valuable group of related techniques. To illustrate, observation of the individual while he is engaged in uncontrolled or unsupervised play activities may reveal many meaningful facts about him. This technique is particularly useful in collecting information about a young child.

The Roles of Observation and of the Autobiography

To observe the individual casually is one thing; to observe him scientifically is another. The former is relatively easy; the latter, much more difficult. To observe behavior, to record it objectively, and to interpret it soundly, the observer must have considerable skill and insight. He also must have had adequate training and sufficient experience. All are essential if the observer is to assess behavior—to determine its nature and motivation, for example.

In securing information about individuals, staff members of a school can employ not only observational techniques but also autobiographies. In fact, the latter can be used much more effectively than they are being used at present.

The autobiography is a natural and readily available means of obtaining data on the personal qualities of an individual. To illustrate, the writing of an autobiography is a common requirement in high-school English classes. In such a class, the teacher often uses the autobiography as a vehicle for training a pupil in written expression. If the pupil respects and has confidence in the teacher, he is likely to write freely about himself. If he does so, his autobiography may reveal important aspects of his personality, aspects that are valuable leads in counseling.

---

[1] For a fuller discussion of these techniques, see Clifford P. Froehlich and John G. Darley, *Studying Students* (Chicago: Science Research Associates, 1952); also see Arthur E. Traxler, *Techniques of Guidance* (New York: Harper and Brothers, 1945).

Although autobiographies are relatively easy to obtain, their interpretation calls for considerable expertness. To draw reliable inferences from an autobiography, the interpreter must use keen insight and sound judgment.

The Nature and Uses of Rating Scales

Another technique for getting facts about the individual is the rating scale. Rating scales may be divided into two general types: self-rating scales, and scales for rating others. Occasionally the same scale may be used both for self-rating and for rating by another person.

Some self-rating scales are informal, locally-constructed devices. Their main purposes are to stimulate the individual's analytical thinking concerning his strengths and weaknesses and to provide his counselor with the counselee's judgments about himself.

Other self-rating scales are standardized in such a way that they yield grades or scores for a number of personal qualities. Often these grades or scores are portrayed on a single profile sheet.

Studies have indicated that self-ratings are of questionable validity. Therefore, the counselor should use such ratings only as suggestive, for example, of the aspects of an individual's personality that should be further investigated. By studying the individual's answers to specific questions in the rating scales, the counselor obtains leads that he can follow up in an interview. This is one of the main values of self-rating scales, whether standardized or not.

The scales used in rating others usually have a scale for each quality to be rated. The rater may indicate his rating on a scale that consists of a number of steps. These steps may be designated by numerals, say, from "0" (low) to "10" (high). Or they may be identified by phrases such as "takes no responsibility whatever" to "displays high and consistent responsibility." In using either of these types of scales, the counselor or teacher indicates on a given scale his opinion of the amount of the quality possessed or exhibited by the individual.

Measurement and guidance specialists prefer the graphic type of rating scale pictured in Figure 4. In this figure, for

FIGURE 4

A Graphic Scale for Rating a Student

Rate the student in each of the qualities given here. For example, on the scale for the quality, "Ability to learn," mark a check (✓) to show your rating of the student. If the student is average in the quality, mark your check at or near the center of the scale—that is, just below the number "3." Please do not attempt to rate a student on a quality unless you feel that you have sufficient knowledge to make a reliable rating. In rating each student, try to rate each quality as independently as possible of any other quality. It is suggested that you rate each student in your group on the first quality, then, on the second quality, and so forth.

STUDENT _____
CLASS _____
DATE OF RATING _____

QUALITY	RATING SCALE				
	1	2	3	4	5
A. ABILITY TO LEARN	Unable to learn	Learns slowly	Shows average ability in learning	Above-average ability in learning	Learns with exceptional ease and speed
B. QUALITY OF WORK	Generally unsatisfactory	Sometimes inferior	Average quality	Above-average	Work is of exceptionally good quality
C. RATE OF WORK	Extremely slow	Rather slow	Completes regular assignments in reasonable time	More than average speed of work	Completes very large amount of work quickly
D. DEPENDABILITY	Needs watching	Sometimes unreliable, particularly if he thinks he can "get by"	Generally dependable	Very dependable—needs only occasional supervision	Exceptionally dependable—no supervision required
E. INITIATIVE	Lazy—needs prodding	Indifferent	Does ordinary assignments of own accord	Industrious and energetic	Does much more than is expected
F. COOPERATION—ABILITY TO GET ALONG WITH OTHERS	Inclined to make trouble	Gives limited cooperation	Usually cooperates willingly	Above-average cooperation—well-liked	Cooperates cheerfully—inspires others
G. OVER-ALL	Very low	Below average	Average	Above average	Very high

example, the scale for the quality "ability to learn," indicates five different degrees ranging from "unable to learn" to "learns with exceptional ease and speed." With the degrees of the quality thus designated, the rater is best able to indicate his opinion of how much of the given quality the rated individual possesses.

A rating scale has considerable value in counseling, particularly if it is employed systematically. This means, to illustrate, that a student should be rated on the same rating scale at regular intervals, say, once each school year. It also means that the counselor and the other staff members who know the student well should rate him. These staff members should use separate copies of the same scale so that their ratings are independent. These independent ratings of each given quality should then be summarized. This summary should show both the spread and the central tendency of staff ratings.

The Place of Sociometric Devices

Still another technique for getting information about an individual is that of sociometric devices. Although these devices have been used increasingly in recent years, little objective information appears in professional literature regarding their value.

One of the few studies giving information with reference to the validity of sociometric devices was made by Wrightstone.[2] Wrightstone obtained data about a group of pupils from two sociometric techniques and from the *California Test of Personality*. One of these techniques involved pupils' nominations of classmates as friends; the other, their nominations of classmates as naturally suited to roles in class plays. For these same pupils, Wrightstone secured ratings on personal qualities by teachers and supervisors—these ratings were based on careful observations.

The findings of this study by Wrightstone were as follows: The pupils who were "rejected" by their classmates (that is,

[2] J. Wayne Wrightstone, "Assessing Pupil Adjustment by Self-Description and Sociometric Technics," *Growing Points in Educational Research,* Official Report of American Educational Research Association (Washington, D.C.: American Educational Research Association, 1949), 330-35.

who received no or few nominations by classmates as friends) tended to be rated low in peer acceptance by teachers; the correlation was .72, relatively high. The correlation between pupils' scores on the qualities measured by the *California Test of Personality* and pupils' ratings by teachers on these same qualities were also fairly high, .66 and .74.

Apart from the scientific evidence now at hand, some teachers and counselors feel that sociometric techniques are definitely useful in guidance. Others, however, believe that more research is needed to establish whether these techniques really add to the information available through other devices.

A TESTING PROGRAM FOR GUIDANCE PURPOSES

Staff members of a school can get many valuable impressions of individual students from observations, ratings, and other subjective devices. But they can obtain a thorough understanding of these students only if subjective information is complemented by objective data, from a well-thought-out program of measurement. The results of such a testing program can be recorded, studied, and used to help guide children year after year as they progress through school.

It should be understood at the outset that a school will find it uneconomical or undesirable to set up a testing program for guidance purposes alone. Nearly all tests have many different potential values. For this reason, a school should design its measurement program so that the results therefrom will help to improve instruction and guidance for students as a group and as individuals.

In the typical school or college, the testing program may be composed of two main parts: (1) an all-school program made up of the tests that all students take, and (2) a supplementary program consisting of special tests that only certain students take.

The first part of this program should include tests that will provide information the school needs concerning all students, regardless of their goals, general intelligence, educational levels, special abilities, or specific interests.

The second part of this program should have tests that yield facts the individual student needs or wants. Such tests should be given as the occasion demands. They should aid the student to determine his long-term goals, his special abilities, and his unique interests; they should also aid him in solving his specific and immediate problems.

The All-School Testing Program

The tests that a school finally decides to administer to all students nearly always represent a compromise between what the school would like and what it can afford. In developing an ideal testing program, the school assumes that its resources of money and time are unlimited. In working out a practical program, the institution takes fully into account its limited resources for testing purposes.

As far as is consistent with the objectives and content of the school's curricula and with the improvements in tests and testing techniques, the all-school testing program should include the same or similar tests from year to year. If a school administers several forms of the same test during a given academic year or over a period of several years, it can readily determine a student's progress. If the different tests used have comparable age, grade, or percentile norms, a student's standing in one test can be compared directly with his standing in another test.

A school should administer certain tests to all students at least once a year. If for financial or other reasons a school cannot do this, it should give these tests every other year or every third year.

A good testing program should, as a minimum, include the following types of tests: (1) a test of scholastic aptitude; (2) a test of reading ability; (3) tests of achievement in English, social studies, mathematics, science, foreign languages, and other important subject-matter fields; and (4) a test of interests. If the last type of test, particularly that dealing with vocational interests, can be administered only once to each student, it should be given in the upper grades, in Grade 11 or Grade 12 of the high school, for example. The other types of tests, however, should be administered when appropriate in any grade of the school.

If a school can afford to give only one type of test to all

students, it should probably select a test of scholastic aptitude. Such a test yields results that have more extensive guidance uses than the results from any other type of test. A scholastic aptitude test, for example, is of great help to the counselor in advising a student concerning both the present and expected level of his educational attainment and the vocational level toward which he should aspire.

Measurement of Scholastic Aptitude

A word of explanation is needed with regard to the term "scholastic aptitude." As used here, tests of scholastic aptitude include tests of general ability to do schoolwork. These tests have various titles; they are commonly called *scholastic aptitude tests, mental tests, tests of mental ability, intelligence tests,* or *psychological examinations.* Whatever their titles are, these tests are primarily designed to measure general scholastic ability.

Among all possible titles for such tests, the term "scholastic aptitude" is regarded as preferable, for these reasons. *First,* unlike such terms as "mental ability" or "intelligence," the term "scholastic aptitude" carries no connotation that the capacity measured is solely native and is therefore inflexible. *Second,* the term "scholastic aptitude" is most nearly descriptive of the purpose and content of these tests—that is, the measurement of the aptitudes required to succeed in schoolwork. The term "intelligence" is too broad; it implies that these tests measure all the important types of mental ability, which is definitely not the case.

The content of scholastic aptitude tests. Nearly all scholastic aptitude tests are highly verbal and numerical; most contain more verbal than numerical items. Both verbal and numerical aptitudes are the types of ability that have the closest relationships to the majority of school subjects. Because aptitude tests measure the kinds of intelligence needed to succeed in the usual school subjects, such instruments tend to predict fairly well what an individual will achieve academically.

Valuable as scholastic aptitude tests are, the majority of them do not measure certain kinds of intelligence, such as ability to deal with spatial relations or ability to succeed in social relationships; these abilities may be very important to success in certain situations not only within the classroom but also outside.

The types of scholastic aptitude tests. Tests of scholastic aptitude may be grouped roughly into two main types. The first type yields a single score indicating general mental ability. The second type yields a number of scores indicating different kinds of mental abilities. For either type there are norms that can be employed to convert a score into a mental age or a percentile.

Both the general and the differential types of aptitude tests provide data that are useful in the school's instructional program. Nevertheless, the differential aptitude test seems to be preferable for guidance purposes. In guidance, the counselor is more interested in an individual's relative strengths and weaknesses than in his general mental ability. Because the differential type of test helps to reveal both strengths and weaknesses, it has important diagnostic values in guiding the individual.

Techniques have been devised for making an extensive and reliable diagnostic measurement of scholastic aptitude. Through the application of these techniques, three extensive batteries of such tests have been developed—SRA *Primary Mental Abilities,*[3] the *Yale Educational Aptitude Tests,*[4] and the *Differential Aptitude Tests.*[5] These tests are available generally to schools. To illustrate the content of these batteries, the *SRA Primary Mental Abilities* (for ages 11 to 17) is designed to measure the following mental factors: verbal-meaning, space, reasoning, number, and word-fluency. It is believed, as mentioned earlier, that a test of this kind has noteworthy potential values for guidance.

In a minimum testing program, the typical school prefers a scholastic aptitude test that can be administered within a single class period, usually ranging from 45 to 55 minutes. During

---

[3] Published by Science Research Associates, Chicago, Illinois.
[4] Published by Department of Personnel Study, Yale University; distributed by Educational Records Bureau, New York, New York.
[5] Published by Psychological Corporation, New York, New York.

this limited time, such a test can adequately measure only a few different mental abilities.

Because of the foregoing and because of the need to appraise more than one mental factor, psychologists have in recent years developed the "two-axis" mental test. According to research, verbal aptitude and quantitative aptitude are the two types of mental ability that are especially important in most school subjects and in many vocations. The most widely used test which measures separately these two aptitudes is perhaps the *American Council on Education Psychological Examination*.[6] Another test is the *California Test of Mental Maturity;*[7] it yields separate scores for language and for nonlanguage mental abilities.

In general, the verbal and the quantitative scores on a two-axis aptitude test have comparatively high validities. Therefore, the verbal scores can be used to predict a student's chances of success in school subjects and in vocations that require the extensive use of language. And the quantitative scores can be employed to forecast a student's chances of success in mathematics and physical science courses, in certain professions including engineering, and in clerical vocations that call for the manipulation of numbers. Although quantitative ability is important in many school subjects and occupations, verbal ability is probably even more important. Verbal ability is helpful if not essential in nearly all subjects and occupations.

What scholastic aptitude tests measure. Some of the psychologists who developed the first tests of general intelligence claimed that their tests measured native capacity. The testmaker usually based this claim upon two related assumptions: *First,* that every person who took the test had had the same or similar opportunities to learn what the test measured. And *second,* that the person's test score therefore represented his native ability to learn—that is, his intelligence.

At the present time, however, psychologists recognize that the items (or tasks) in a scholastic aptitude test measure a

---

[6] Published by Educational Testing Service, Princeton, New Jersey.
[7] Published by California Test Bureau, Los Angeles, California.

composite of native learning ability and acquired learning ability. This composite has been determined or influenced by both heredity and environment. Because a test score reflects learning to a certain extent, it is not a pure measure of native intelligence. Even though such a test is perfectly valid and reliable, the intelligence quotient (the index of ability to learn) derived therefrom may not be absolutely stable. A child's I.Q., for example, may fluctuate somewhat from year to year because it is affected by environmental factors, especially schooling.

Today psychologists and test specialists believe that the I.Q. is only a rough index of native intelligence. From careful studies, they know that the I.Q. is not entirely constant over an extended period of years. They also know that the I.Q.'s derived from different tests are not always the same numerically.

Measurement of Reading Ability

If a school's resources permit the use of only one test in addition to a test of scholastic aptitude, that second test should probably be a reading test. As most teachers realize, ability to read is of paramount importance in nearly all schoolwork; also, it is probably related to success in numerous vocations.

Measurement in the field of reading is difficult not only because the reading process itself is very complex, but also because reading tests vary in the reading abilities they purport to measure. Some of these tests provide three or four scores; others, as many as ten or more scores. Each score represents a specific kind of reading ability. Such tests are usually in the form of a test battery that yields a composite or total reading score based on all the specific reading scores. These test batteries can usually be used for both survey and diagnostic purposes.

A school will find it desirable to administer a reading test battery of the survey type to all students annually, or at least every other year. As just suggested, this survey test should provide a total reading score that gives a general picture of a student's reading ability. The test also should furnish subscores (scores on the tests in the battery) because they have diagnostic values. If a student's total score on the survey test is low, the subscores will indicate the abilities that he needs to strengthen.

An illustration of a test that shows a student's general reading ability and that also is broadly diagnostic is the *Cooperative Reading Comprehension Test*.[8] This test battery supplies separate scores for vocabulary, for speed of comprehension, and for level of comprehension, and a total score. The norms are in the form of Scaled Scores; these facilitate comparisons among scores made on the battery's subtests and with the scores made on other Cooperative Achievement Tests.

There are other diagnostic reading tests that are especially useful to counselors. One of the most promising is the test battery that was constructed by an independent committee, the Committee on Diagnostic Reading Tests; its work was originally subsidized by the Blue Hill Foundation. The Committee's upper-level test battery consists of a *Survey Section* and of several *Diagnostic Sections*.[9] All are designed for the range, Grade 7 through the college freshman year. The *Survey Section* measures rate, vocabulary, and comprehension; it is intended to be given to all students as a screening test to identify good, average, and poor readers. There are at present eight forms of the *Survey Section*, and two forms of each of the *Diagnostic Sections*.

Recently, the Committee on Diagnostic Reading Tests issued a third type of reading aid, a remedial manual; it is to be used by teachers and counselors in following up the findings from the *Diagnostic Reading Tests* with appropriate training materials and methods. In 1952, the Committee published a lower level of the *Survey Test*, for Grades 4, 5, and 6.

Measurement of Achievement

A school that is able to administer more than a test of scholastic aptitude and a reading test will probably find that

---

[8] Published by Cooperative Test Division, Educational Testing Service, Princeton, New Jersey.

[9] Published and distributed by the Committee on Diagnostic Reading Tests, Inc., 419 West 119th Street, New York, N.Y. They are distributed by Educational Records Bureau (New York) to its member schools. The *Survey Section* is also published and distributed by Science Research Associates (Chicago).

tests of achievement are the next most valuable contributors to its guidance program. Although the relative importance of tests in the different subject fields continues to be a debatable matter, the experience of schools taking part in the testing program of the Educational Records Bureau suggests the following rank order: English, mathematics, science, social studies, and foreign languages.

In cooperation with subject-matter teachers, the person who has the main responsibility for a school's testing program should carefully examine the available achievement tests. Together they should choose those tests which seem best suited to the objectives and the curricula of that school. In selecting tests, they should recognize that the majority of the existing achievement tests in such a field as mathematics, science, or social studies cover specifically the subject matter that schools commonly teach in that field of study. Some of these achievement tests, however, measure broad rather than narrow outcomes in a given field.

Among the test batteries designed for the measurement of achievement in basic skills and in other elementary-school subjects, five are worthy of special mention. These are the *Metropolitan Achievement Tests*,[10] the *Stanford Achievement Test*,[11] the *California Achievement Tests*,[12] the *Iowa Every Pupil Tests of Basic Skills*,[13] and the *Coordinated Scales of Attainment*.[14] Among these, the Metropolitan and Stanford tests include the most subjects, the California tests cover the widest range of grades, and the Iowa tests are the most diagnostic. The *Coordinated Scales of Attainment* have a separate booklet for each grade level, an advantage to the user.

Above the elementary school level, the Cooperative tests [15] are, without doubt, the outstanding series of achievement tests presently available on a nationwide basis. For this reason, secondary schools may seriously consider using these tests. In cer-

---

[10] Published by World Book Company, Yonkers, N.Y.
[11] Published by World Book Company.
[12] Published by California Test Bureau, Los Angeles, California.
[13] Published by Houghton Mifflin Company, Boston, Mass., and Science Research Associates, Chicago, Ill.
[14] Published by Educational Test Bureau, Minneapolis, Minn.
[15] Published by Educational Testing Service, Princeton, N.J.

tain states, however, high schools may find it preferable to use the achievement tests that are administered on a state-wide basis; if a school uses such tests, it can compare the scores of its students with those of students in other schools in the state.

The Cooperative Test Service, as mentioned earlier, was set up in the early 1930's through a grant from the General Education Board to the American Council on Education. Under the direction of Dr. Ben D. Wood, the Cooperative Test Service prepared forms of tests in nearly all the academic subjects annually during a ten-year period. Construction of new test forms was discontinued temporarily during World War II; soon after the war, however, their preparation and publication were resumed. The Educational Testing Service, which now publishes the Cooperative tests, maintains several forms of each of the more important Cooperative tests on its active list.

The Cooperative tests have a uniform system of derived scores, known as Scaled Scores.[16] Such scores materially enhance the usefulness of these tests in both instruction and guidance. If counselors who use the Cooperative tests will inform themselves thoroughly concerning the interpretation of Scaled Scores, they will be well repaid for the time and effort expended. An understanding of these scores is well within the reach of anyone with an elementary knowledge of statistics. The Scaled Scores system for the Cooperative tests was introduced more than 15 years ago. As yet, unfortunately, all too few users of these tests adequately comprehend these scores.

Although most of the Cooperative tests are designed to measure specific achievements in academic subjects, some of these tests measure general achievement in broad fields such as mathematics, science, and social studies. Other tests that measure general achievement in broad fields at the secondary-school level are the batteries known as the *Iowa Tests of Educational Development*[17] and the *General Educational Development*

---

[16] John C. Flanagan, *The Cooperative Achievement Tests: A Bulletin Reporting the Basic Principles and Procedures Used in the Development of Their System of Scaled Scores* (New York: Cooperative Test Service, December, 1939).

[17] Published by Science Research Associates.

Tests,[18] issued by the United States Armed Forces Institute (USAFI). Both batteries are widely used. Some states have made it possible for mature individuals who scored well on the USAFI tests of general educational development to obtain certificates that are equivalent to high-school diplomas. Colleges and universities have used the scores on the USAFI tests extensively in evaluating the fitness of veterans without the required high-school credits to enroll in college.

Measurement of Interests

It is well known that if an individual is interested in an educational or vocational pursuit, he is more likely to be successful in it. It has been scientifically established that within a group of individuals there is, in general, a positive correlation between interest and aptitude. Usually, however, this correlation is not especially high; moreover, it varies greatly according to the individuals involved and according to the fields concerned. In short, the correlation between interest and aptitude is not large enough to infer aptitude from a measurement of interest or interest from a measurement of aptitude. For this reason, the results of an objective scholastic or other aptitude test should be supplemented with the findings of an objective measure of interests. An interest inventory, in other words, is a valuable feature of a school-wide testing program.

A number of good interest inventories are now available. These inventories yield kinds of scores that indicate interests according to three types of classification: (1) interests in specific occupations, (2) interests in families of occupations, and (3) interests in broad fields, which may cut across vocational groups.

The outstanding example of an inventory of the first type is represented by the occupational scales of the *Strong Vocational Interest Blank for Men*.[19] Examples of the second type of inventory are the group scales on the *Cleeton Vocational In-*

---

[18] The civilian form of the USAFI tests is distributed by Educational Testing Service.

[19] There is a comparable blank for women. The blank for men and the blank for women are published by Stanford University Press, Stanford, California.

terest Inventory,[20] the *Brainard Occupational Preference Record* and the *Lee-Thorpe Interest Test.*[21] The third type is illustrated by the *Kuder Preference Record-Vocational.*[22] This inventory provides a profile of scores in 10 interest areas: mechanical, computational, scientific, persuasive, literary, artistic, social service, musical, clerical, and outdoor interests.

The use of the results of an interest inventory may be illustrated by reference to the scores of an eleventh-grade girl on the *Kuder Preference Record-Vocational,* as shown in Figure 5. There it will be observed that the girl, whom we shall call Mary, had percentiles of 100 in the computational and clerical areas. In these areas, her percentiles were much higher than they were in the other areas. Because Mary showed extremely high interests in the computational and clerical areas, she might well give first consideration to occupations within these areas. Specifically, some of these occupations are: billing clerk, bookkeeper, calculating machine operator, cashier in a store, invoice clerk, payroll clerk, posting clerk, statistical clerk, statistician, stock clerk, tabulating machine operator, and bank teller.

In advising a student, the counselor should, of course, supplement the results of an occupational interest inventory with the findings of tests of ability in the areas in which the interest ratings are highest. For example, he might compare Mary's percentiles in computational and clerical interests on the Kuder test with her percentiles on one of the following aptitude tests or subtests: (1) the Q-score (ability to deal with quantitative concepts) on the *American Council Psychological Examination;* (2) the N-score (numerical ability) on the *SRA Primary Mental Abilities;* and/or (3) the scores on the *Minnesota Clerical Test.* By means of this comparison, Mary can readily determine whether her aptitudes are consistent with her interests. If Mary is high in aptitude as well as in-

---

[20] Published by McKnight and McKnight, Bloomington, Illinois.

[21] The Brainard record is published by Psychological Corporation; the Lee-Thorpe test, by California Test Bureau.

[22] Published by Science Research Associates. This company also publishes the *Kuder Preference Record-Personal.* This inventory yields scores in five interest areas.

SELF-INTERPRETING PROFILE SHEET FOR THE KUDER PREFERENCE RECORD-VOCATIONAL—FORM C

0 24	1 32	2 48	3 21	4 39	5 31	6 28	7 24	8 52	9 96
OUTDOOR	MECHANICAL	COMPUTATIONAL	SCIENTIFIC	PERSUASIVE	ARTISTIC	LITERARY	MUSICAL	SOCIAL SERVICE	CLERICAL

terest within a given field, her chances of success within that field are relatively good.

Studies have shown that the scores on interest inventories with multiple-scoring features, such as the Strong and the Kuder blanks, are about as reliable as those obtained with aptitude and achievement tests of equal length. In the interest inventories, the scores in many of the areas or fields have not yet been checked against adequate criteria, mainly because such criteria are difficult to establish. Even so, the studies made in certain interest areas indicate that the scores therein are sufficiently valid for guidance purposes.

Supplementary Tests for Individuals

In addition to the tests to be given regularly to all students, a school occasionally needs in its guidance program at least three general types of supplementary tests: achievement and general aptitude tests administered individually; tests of specific aptitudes; and measures of personal qualities.

A school, for example, may wish to check upon a student's performance on a group test of mental ability or scholastic aptitude by giving him an individual intelligence test. If this student is a poor reader, his group test score may not be a true indicator of his level of mental ability. To follow up this possibility, the school psychologist may administer an individual test such as the *Stanford-Binet Scale* [23] or *Wechsler-Bellevue Intelligence Scale*,[24] or a nonlanguage test such as the *Revised Beta Examination*.[25] Each of these tests requires little or no reading.

As another example, a school may find that a student's score in social studies on a group achievement battery is at the 25th percentile according to national norms, but his social studies marks average B+. Therefore, the school may verify the group test score by giving the pupil individually another form of the test or another test designed to measure his achievement in the social studies field.

As a third example, a school may wish to supplement the

[23] Published by Houghton Mifflin Company.
[24] Published by Psychological Corporation.
[25] Published by Psychological Corporation.

results of the vocational interest inventory used in its regular program with the results of another inventory of interests. The latter inventory, given individually, may be particularly helpful to a student who is in a state of great doubt and worry about his vocational choice.

For the kind of supplementary individual testing indicated by the foregoing examples, the guidance department should have a small supply of a wide variety of scholastic aptitude, achievement, and interest tests. At least one of its staff members, furthermore, should be fully capable of administering any of these tests to an individual or to a small group and of interpreting the findings therefrom.

Tests of Specific Aptitude

The second type of supplementary tests for use by counselors includes tests of aptitude in such specific fields as art, music, foreign languages, mechanical work, clerical work, and science. In this aspect of guidance testing, the counselor should keep in mind the following important point: The measurement of aptitudes for specific vocational pursuits is complicated by the fact that there are thousands of occupations and several hundred occupational families. Even if a good test for each of the latter families or areas were available, a school obviously could not test students in all of the hundreds of areas. The time and cost alone would be prohibitive.

The typical school, however, has alternate procedures that are practical. *First,* the school measures the vocational interests and the general aptitudes of all students in its regular school-wide testing program. And *second,* the school gives specific aptitude tests to a student only in those fields which seem to be in line with his interests and general aptitudes.

As an illustration, consider a student who on the *Kuder Preference Record-Vocational* stands at the 95th percentile in the area of mechanical interest. Assume that this student is definitely higher in nonlanguage I.Q. than in language I.Q. as measured by the *California Test of Mental Maturity.* Therefore, the school gives the student a test of mechanical aptitude; thus it obtains a sounder basis for predicting his success or failure in the field of his particular interest.

To provide this type of special service, the guidance department of the school should have tests of specific aptitudes, such as these: the *Meier-Seashore Art Judgment Test*,[26] the *Seashore Measures of Musical Talent*,[27] the *Stanford Scientific Aptitude Test*,[28] the *Revised Minnesota Paper Form Board Test* and the *Bennett Mechanical Comprehension Test*,[29] the *Wrightstone-O'Toole Prognostic Test of Mechanical Abilities*,[30] the *Minnesota Clerical Test*,[31] and the *Symonds Foreign Language Prognosis Test*.[32]

Among the more recently developed tests are the *Flanagan Aptitude Classification Tests*. In this battery, the tests (published separately) are designed to measure the 14 following aptitudes: inspection, coding, memory, precision, assembly, scales, coordination, judgment and comprehension, arithmetic, patterns, components, tables, mechanics, and expression. An individual's scores on these tests can be employed (1) to indicate his general level of performance and his specific strengths and weaknesses in terms of the 14 job-element aptitudes, and (2) to provide information concerning his composite aptitude for some 240 specific occupations grouped into 30 broad occupational areas. (Science Research Associates publishes these tests.)

Measures of Personal Qualities

The third class of supplementary measures consists of inventories of personality and adjustment. For testing purposes, an individual's personality may be defined as the totality of his behavior.

Subjective methods of appraisal. As suggested near the beginning of this chapter, one procedure for appraising personality is that of observation. In a school, the teacher or counselor makes careful observations of the behavior of a child. A

---

[26] Published by Bureau of Educational Research and Service, State University of Iowa, Iowa City, Iowa.

[27] Published by Psychological Corporation.

[28] Published by Stanford University Press.

[29] Both the Minnesota test and the Bennett test are published by Psychological Corporation.

[30] Published by California Test Bureau.

[31] Published by Psychological Corporation.

[32] Published by Bureau of Publications, Teachers College, Columbia University, New York, N.Y.

young child is often observed in a play situation; an older child in that and many other situations.

A valuable technique in connection with the process of observation is that of the anecdotal method. It has been used with noteworthy success in a number of schools. In the anecdotal method, a teacher, counselor, or other observer jots down instances of a child's behavior that he regards as significant in the course of the child's day-to-day activities. From time to time, the observer assembles, analyzes, and summarizes the information that appears in these anecdotal notes. He thus obtains a clear developmental picture of the child's personality.

Still another procedure is to make use of sociometric devices. One of these is the "guess who" device [33] for obtaining information concerning which children are accepted by their group and which are "isolates."

A widely-used procedure for estimating personal qualities is the rating scale. As pointed out previously, the teacher rates a student on a scale ranging from low to high for each personal quality rated. Such ratings become more reliable if the quality to be rated is carefully defined in advance and if several persons who know the student well make independent ratings. If these ratings of a student on a given quality are combined, they show not only the central tendency (the average) but also the range of all ratings. Because this average and this range have a fair degree of objectivity, they form a useful basis for guidance.

The merits of observation, sociometry, and rating scales have been demonstrated. Because of the time, expense, and training involved, however, these methods of personality appraisal are not being employed sufficiently in many schools.

The global versus the atomistic approach. Ideally, in the measurement of personality, the test-maker sets up test conditions that provide adequate samples of an individual's behavior in various situations. He can obtain these samples, however, only in a detailed, elaborate, and usually costly research study. The best that the test-maker can do to meet school needs and resources is to try to devise a test whose scores represent rea-

---

[33] See Clifford P. Froehlich and John G. Darley, *Studying Students* (Chicago: Science Research Associates, 1952), 339-40.

sonably typical samples of behavior, samples that correlate relatively highly with the ratings of that behavior by qualified persons.

In attempts to reach this objective, test-makers have developed two general approaches to personality assessment or measurement. These are known as *the global approach* and *the atomistic approach*. As the designations indicate, the former deals with the whole personality; the latter, with a small part of it. In general, the global approach makes use of so-called projective techniques; the atomistic approach, of nonprojective techniques.[34]

According to the global approach and its projective procedures, the tester endeavors to assess personality as a whole through one or more test situations; he makes an analysis or interpretation of that total personality.

Projective-type tests. Until recently, projective tests were nebulous in their structure and content; they required involved and technical interpretations. For these reasons, such tests could be used successfully only by highly trained and skilled experts, psychiatrists and clinical psychologists, for example. Within the last few years, however, some of these projective tests have become much more usable in school situations. One of these tests is the *Rorschach*.[35] This test is based on a series of ink blots that Hermann Rorschach, a Swiss psychiatrist and psychoanalyst, first developed and experimented with about 1920. Since then, as a result of the huge amount of research on the *Rorschach*, it promises to become more widely useful than was previously believed.

School people generally have been slow to accept the *Rorschach* test, partly because the interpretations made seemed obscure to the layman, and partly because the terminology used meant little to the uninitiated. This skepticism was

---

[34] The term "nonprojective technique" is used here because it has been in wide use in recent years and will no doubt be familiar to many readers of this book. The term, however, is not a very appropriate one, for almost any test may, under certain conditions, be employed as a projective technique. Most of the measurement devices loosely grouped under the heading, "nonprojective techniques," are *structured inventories;* therefore, it is believed, this class name should preferably be applied to them.

[35] Published by C. H. Stoelting Company, Chicago; also distributed by Psychological Corporation, New York.

healthy. It would have been very unfortunate if persons untrained in the proper use of the *Rorschach* had administered a test of this kind, clearly a clinical instrument for the use of specialists only.

Another projective device for the assessment of personality is the *Murray Thematic Apperception Test*.[36] This test, commonly known as *T.A.T.*, may be somewhat better suited to school use than is the *Rorschach*. The *T.A.T.* probably does not require as much training on the part of the administrator as does the *Rorschach*. Moreover, research has indicated that the *T.A.T.* has considerable value in the study of adolescent personality.

Designed for use with pre-adolescents (children 8-14) is the *Michigan Picture Test*.[37] Administered individually, this projective test reveals the child's major personality conflicts.

Disguised personality tests. Most of the experimentation with personality tests suitable for school use has been directed toward the atomistic or nonprojective approach. The term, nonprojective, covers a variety of tests, with their own techniques for accomplishing their several purposes. According to their techniques, these tests may be classified into three main groups:

1. Tests whose purposes are fairly obvious to the test-taker, assuming that he is a moderately intelligent person;

2. Tests whose purposes are partly disguised, or hidden from the test-taker; and

3. Tests whose purposes are completely disguised, or hidden from the test-taker.

The possibility of preparing disguised personality tests that were both reliable and valid was explored in the Character Education Inquiry some 25 years ago. The Inquiry's staff developed such tests as the *Character Education Inquiry Tests of Honesty* and the *Maller Self-Marking Test*.[38] Both of these tests, designed to measure honesty, proved to be useful in appraising a limited segment of personality or character. Even

---

[36] Published by Harvard University Press.
[37] Published by Science Research Associates.
[38] Published by Bureau of Publications, Teachers College, Columbia University.

so, at the present time, there are almost no paper-and-pencil tests of character that can be recommended for general use.

Personality inventories. During the last 20 years, the majority of those constructing personality tests have employed the technique of the self-inventory, a structured type of questionnaire. In such an inventory, the individual usually responds with "yes," "no," or "doubtful" to each of a series of questions concerning how he acts or feels in a variety of situations.

Some of the earlier personality inventories yielded only a single score. Many of the present inventories, particularly those developed since 1930, provide a number of scores, representing measurements of a variety of personality factors. The individual's scores are usually entered on a profile sheet that pictures comparisons among his scores in the factors measured and between his scores and the percentile norms for these factors.

Among the paper-and-pencil inventories of personality that have been constructed with considerable care and that are based on scientific methods and data are the following: the *Bernreuter Personality Inventory;* [39] the *Bell Adjustment Inventory;* [40] the *Guilford-Zimmerman Temperament Survey;* [41] *Aspects of Personality,* by Pintner, Loftus, Forlano, and Alster (for elementary schools) and *Washburne Social Adjustment Inventory* (Thaspic edition); [42] the *Adams-Lepley Personal Audit;* [43] the *Thurstone Temperament Schedule;* [44] the *Heston Personality Inventory;* [45] the *SRA Youth Inventory* and the *SRA Junior Inventory,* both by H. H. Remmers; [46] the *Behavior Preference Record,* by Hugh B. Wood; [47] the *Minnesota Multiphasic Personality Inventory;* [48] and the *California Test of Personality,* [49] by Thorpe, Clark, and Tiegs.

---

[39] Published by Stanford University Press.

[40] Published by Stanford University Press.

[41] Published by Sheridan Supply Company, Beverly Hills, California.

[42] Both the Pintner and the Washburne inventories are published by World Book Company.

[43] Published by Science Research Associates.

[44] Published by Science Research Associates.

[45] Published by World Book Company.

[46] Both inventories are published by Science Research Associates.

[47] Published by California Test Bureau.

[48] Published by Psychological Corporation.

[49] Published by California Test Bureau.

Two of the foregoing personality tests are very suitable for general school use. One is the *Bell Adjustment Inventory* that yields scores in these five areas: home adjustment, health adjustment, social adjustment, emotional adjustment, and vocational adjustment. The other is the *SRA Youth Inventory* that provides scores in these eight areas: My School; Looking Ahead; About Myself; Getting Along with Others; My Home and Family; Boy Meets Girl; Health; and Things in General.

One of the newer tests that enjoys wide favor among psychologists is the *Minnesota Multiphasic Personality Inventory*. In recent years, there has been much more research on this inventory than on any other structured device of its type. Originally, this test was set up and standardized for clinical use. Because this test has been adapted and published as a questionnaire-type inventory, it is suitable for use by well-trained counselors outside the clinical situation.

The majority of the published personality inventories are intended for use with a wide range of individuals, from youth who are beginning high school to adults who are no longer in school or college. Few such inventories, however, have been designed to serve young children. One battery of personality tests that is designed for all levels from Grade 1 into adulthood is the *California Test of Personality*. This test provides a profile of scores grouped under two main headings: self-adjustment and social adjustment. Another battery, for children in the upper elementary grades, is the *SRA Junior Inventory*.

Needed improvement in personality tests. For years, test-makers have attempted to measure many different aspects of personality. Today these test-makers are not completely agreed upon the major aspects of personality, although many of them include scales purporting to measure aspects to which they have given the same names. An analysis of 10 of the more widely used personality tests showed that these tests yield scores on 56 different aspects of personality. This indicates that, despite the large amount of research in the field of personality, there is still a definite need for comprehensive studies designed to discover the most important aspects of personality.

Although some personality tests are low in reliability, others are sufficiently high in this respect to justify their use.

The average split-half reliability reported for nine of the better-known paper-and-pencil tests is approximately .85. This coefficient of reliability is of about the same magnitude as that of many tests of scholastic aptitude and achievement; it is not as high as that of the best tests in the latter two fields. The research literature in this field indicates that some personality tests do yield scores that are fairly consistent or reliable over a considerable period of time.

Most studies of the validity of personality tests have yielded disappointing or inconclusive results.[50] In schools, colleges, and other civilian-type situations, studies that compared the scores made by individuals on these tests with certain criteria such as ratings of these individuals by others have revealed coefficients of validity that are relatively low. The lowness of these coefficients may have been due to one or more factors, as follows: (1) the subjective nature of the criteria employed to establish the validity of the test; (2) the lack of sufficient rapport between the test-giver and the test-taker to induce the latter to answer all test items as truthfully as he could; and (3) the fact that the test was administered to a group that was considerably different from the groups on which the test was standardized. In the military services during World War II, however, studies of the personality inventories used showed that these tests had relatively high coefficients of validity. For this and for other reasons, such tests were of considerable value in the neuropsychiatric screening of personnel.[51]

Considered as a whole, the research studies related to personality inventories indicate rather definitely that these tests are somewhat more useful in military situations than in civilian situations. This may be due to the fact that in military situations the researcher can obtain better criteria for the validation of personality inventories; he also can exercise better control over testing conditions.

---

[50] Albert Ellis, "The Validity of Personality Questionnaires," *Psychological Bulletin*, XLIII (September, 1946), 385-440.

[51] Albert Ellis and Herbert S. Conrad, "The Validity of Personality Inventories in Military Practice," *Psychological Bulletin*, XLV (September, 1948), 385-426.

At the present time, the greatest single need in personality measurement is probably that of more extensive and better-controlled studies of the validity of the existing instruments in this field. Until the results of these studies are in hand, very few personality inventories can be confidently recommended for general school use. Before a school thus employs such tests on a mass basis, it needs more evidence than is now available that these tests actually measure what they purport to measure —also, that they measure the most important personality traits of children and adolescents.

ADMINISTERING AND SCORING TESTS

To manage a comprehensive testing program involving scholastic aptitude, reading, achievement, and interest tests, a school should carefully plan all the necessary steps. These steps include selecting tests; scheduling tests; administering tests; scoring tests; converting test scores into age, grade, or percentile equivalents; tabulating test scores or their equivalents; interpreting test results; and reporting test findings. Too often, a school does not realize the potential values of tests because it is not careful or competent in taking one or more of the steps just mentioned. Any test, regardless of its excellence, may yield results that are worthless if it is poorly administered, scored, or interpreted.

In a given school, one member of the faculty should have full responsibility for the general testing program. This staff member should confer with the principal and the department heads in choosing the tests to be given, and in making up the testing schedule. He should order these tests several weeks ahead of the testing dates; he will then have the tests on hand in ample time to sort them into groups and otherwise to make sure that all materials are ready. He should make out a detailed written test schedule and duplicate it for distribution to the faculty and students. He should carefully select the examiners and proctors; he should make sure that they have the necessary general directions and specific instructions for administering the tests to be used.

Beforehand, each examiner should study the test he is to administer and the manual of instructions for it. Preferably, he himself should take the test; for practice, he should give the test to one or two individuals, before administering it to a group of students.

The examiner will find that the typical group test is not difficult to administer. During the examination, however, he should use great care to see that students follow all directions to the letter. He should time the test accurately to the second; and he should not help any student to answer a test item. In these and other ways, the examiner makes all the conditions under which the test is given as uniform as possible. If these conditions are the same as those specified in the test manual, the scores made by students are more likely to be accurate. This is a prerequisite for converting these scores into equivalents as given in the test's norms.

In a typical school, it is not feasible to give all the tests recommended for a systematic and comprehensive school-wide testing program during the same week or even month of the academic year. If a school attempts to do this, there is danger that the staff will be overburdened, that too many consecutive class periods will be appropriated for testing purposes, and that staff members will not have time to study all the results in detail as these results become available. For these reasons among others, a school should administer tests at different times during the year. Many schools follow the plan proposed by the Educational Records Bureau. According to this plan, a school administers the scholastic aptitude, reading, and interest tests in the early fall, two or three weeks after the first semester starts. The school administers the achievement tests in the spring, say a month before the end of the second semester.

The scoring of the tests may be done either inside the school by a staff of clerical workers who are competent and carefully-trained or outside by an agency that is specially prepared and equipped to render this type of service. Desirably, the school should not load teachers and counselors with the heavy burden of scoring tests.

It is sometimes assumed that while a teacher or a counselor is scoring a student's tests, he can and should study that student's responses to obtain insight into strengths and weaknesses. But such a diagnosis while scoring a test tends to slow down the scoring process and, even worse, to produce errors therein. Although diagnosis is a necessary step in the interpretation of test results, diagnosis and scoring are essentially different procedures; each can be carried on more efficiently if it is completely divorced from the other.

With further reference to test scoring, the typical school pays its teachers considerably more than it pays its clerks. Whether that school realizes it or not, it is financially advantageous to have clerks, not teachers, do the clerical work of scoring tests. Under such an arrangement, teachers and counselors are able to use all their work time for productive activities of a professional nature.

To save teacher time and to economize on clerical expenditures, a large school system may well consider the possibility of using an electrical test-scoring machine. It can rent this device usually for a reasonable annual fee. A small school system may be able to arrange to have its tests machine-scored, at nominal cost, at a near-by college or university. Or a small school may pool its funds for test-scoring with those of several neighboring small schools. Together they can pay the annual rental of a test-scoring machine. They can place this machine in one of the schools which serves as a scoring center for the group of schools.

As soon as a school has obtained the scores made by students on a given test, it should take the following steps: (1) For each class, the names, scores, and equivalent percentiles of the individual students should be recorded. (2) Distributions of the scores and percentiles of students within each class should be made. (3) The ranges, medians, and quartiles of scores and percentiles for each class should be found. (4) For each class, a typed list showing the names, scores, percentiles, and other data should be prepared.[52] (5) For all classes in each grade within the school or within the school system, the ranges,

---

[52] Some agencies, such as the Educational Records Bureau (New York), provide complete scoring and related test services. The Bureau is prepared to do all the clerical and statistical work needed in connection with a testing program. It furnishes the school with typed class lists and distributions showing test scores, percentiles, medians, quartiles, and any other statistical data desired. Similar services for the *Iowa Tests of Educational Development* are available from Science Research Associates, Chicago.

medians, and quartiles of scores and percentiles should be computed.

The staff member in charge of testing should distribute copies of the class lists giving students' scores and percentiles to all the teachers concerned—subject-matter teachers as well as homeroom teachers. This staff member should then explain the results to teachers both in group and individual conferences. If a classroom teacher has such test data about his students and if he is trained in the interpretation of these data, he is able to function more effectively both as an instructor and as a counselor. And what is true of a teacher is equally true of any other guidance worker.

In order to do a thorough job of guidance, full-time or part-time, counselors must have the understanding and cooperation of the rest of the faculty. That understanding and cooperation can be best achieved if the entire staff has dependable objective information about the aptitudes and achievements of individual students.

THE ROLE OF CUMULATIVE RECORDS

A single test score for an individual may be of little value. For example, that score may be relatively low in reliability or in validity; if so, it may give an incorrect and misleading impression of the individual. Even though that score is high in both respects, it represents only one measurement (sample) of one aspect of the individual's life. For this reason, that score should be related to and compared with the individual's scores on other tests of the same aspect and of different aspects. That score should also be supplemented by nontest information about the individual. Then and then only does the score become really meaningful to the counselor and helpful to the individual.

The collection and comparison of a variety of scores and other information concerning a student may be very confusing to his teacher or counselor unless all this information is carefully accumulated and organized. The best device for arranging this information about an individual is the cumulative record form. This means that the school which wishes to make the most effective use of tests as part of its guidance program must install and keep up-to-date a system of cumulative records—at least one record for every student.

The typical school usually keeps a permanent record for each student of the subjects or courses taken, the marks earned, and the credits received. Although this record is in a sense cumulative, it is inadequate. The modern type of cumulative record is much more comprehensive. How comprehensive a school's cumulative record should be depends mainly upon its clerical resources.

In planning a cumulative record, the school should make sure that each student's record covers minimum essentials, is filled out completely, and is kept up-to-date. Such a record is preferable to a record that is so extensive and elaborate that those responsible for it cannot complete it or keep it current.

As a minimum, the cumulative record for a student should include the following information: courses taken and the marks therein; test data, including scores and age, grade, or percentile equivalents; information concerning personal qualities, home background, extracurricular activities, work experience, health and physical development; vocational and other interests; summaries of interviews; and over-all appraisals by counselors and teachers. (See Figure 6 and Figure 7.)

The student's cumulative record should be kept up-to-date both by occasional entries and by regular entries, annually or semiannually. Thus the record presents the student's status at each successive stage of his development; thus also, it portrays the student's growth during his school years. Such a record gives the teacher or the counselor a valuable basis for predicting the student's future development including his probable success in academic work.

The schools of this country have a wide variety of cumulative records for their students. After considering the available forms of such records, a school may select a published form, such as one of the series issued by the American Council on Education or an adaptation of that form. Or, a school may design its own record form perhaps including certain features or items that appear in the forms being used by other schools.

In the selection or construction of a cumulative record

FIGURE 6

ERB Cumulative Record for Independent Schools

(Front of card)

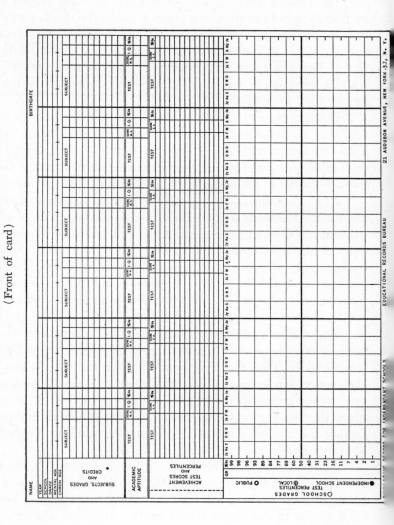

ERB Cumulative Record for Independent Schools

(Back of card)

NAME	M. F.	BIRTHDATE—PLACE	GEN'L HEALTH	RELIGION	RACE or NAT'L'TY	OCCUPATION	ADDRESS	
FATHER							RES. BUS.	
MOTHER							RES. BUS.	
STEP-PARENT OR GUARDIAN							RES. BUS.	
LANGUAGE SPOKEN IN HOME BEFORE 10—		AFTER 10—	TYPE OF COMMUNITY BEFORE 10— ,			AFTER 10—		IF PARENTS SEPARATED GIVE DATE
YEAR AND AGE								
ADVISER	A	T	A	T	A	T	A	T
ATTENDANCE								
DISCIPLINE								
HOME INFLUENCES AND COOPERATION								
MENTAL AND EMOTIONAL								
PHYSICAL AND ATHLETIC								
EXTRA-CURRICULAR ACTIVITIES AND INTERESTS								
NOTABLE ACCOMPLISH-MENTS AND EXPERIENCES								
EDUCATIONAL PLANS								
PERSONALITY RATINGS	+2 +1 0 -1 -2							
REMARKS								

FIGURE 7

SRA Cumulative Form

(Front of card)

Simplified SRA CUMULATIVE RECORD FORM created by Arthur E. Traxler. Published by SCIENCE RESEARCH ASSOCIATES, INC., 57 West Grand Ave., Chicago 10, Ill. Reproduction Permitted. Printed in the U.S.A. 1947

SRA CUMULATIVE FORM

(Back of card)

NAME		BIRTH DATE		BIRTHPLACE		RELIGION			ADDRESS		TELEPHONE
FAMILY	OCCUPATION	EDUCATION	RELIGION		HEALTH		DECEASED DATE				
FATHER											
MOTHER											
STEP PARENT OR GUARDIAN											
SIBLINGS			BIRTH DATE						Note here anything of significance concerning the family or conditions in the home.		
YEAR AND AGE											
INTELLIGENCE QUOTIENT											
COUNSELOR											
ATTENDANCE											
DISCIPLINE ACADEMIC / PERSONAL											
INTERESTS IN SCHOOL / OUT OF SCHOOL											
VOCATIONAL EXPERIENCES											
NOTABLE ACCOMPLISHMENTS											
HEALTH AND PHYSICAL VIGOR											
EDUCATIONAL AND VOCATIONAL PLANS											
RESPONSIBILITY DEPENDABILITY											
CREATIVENESS AND IMAGINATION											
INFLUENCE											
SOCIAL ADJUSTMENT											
COUNSELOR'S NOTES											
REMARKS											

BEHAVIOR DESCRIPTION

form, a school's staff should have in mind such important points as the following:

1. The cumulative record form for a pupil or a student should agree with the objectives of the local school.

2. The form should be the result of the group thinking of a faculty committee.

3. The form should provide for a continuous record of the development of the student from the first grade to the end of his formal education; for this purpose, a series of forms may be used.

4. The form should be organized according to the customary sequence of academic years; for each year, the same or a similar kind of information should be recorded for a student.

5. The form should contain carefully planned spaces in which to record the results of standardized tests including date of test, title of test, student's score, his standing in terms of norms, and the like.

6. The form should provide for the annual recording of the personality ratings or behavior descriptions that represent the consensus of the student's counselor and teachers.

7. The form should be as comprehensive as possible, but it should not overburden the clerical or teaching staff of the school.

8. The form should be accessible to the teachers as well as to the principal and counselors. If a counselor has recorded highly confidential information about a student, this record should be filed outside the regular form.

9. The form should be re-evaluated periodically; it should be revised as needed to take account of educational developments.

The aforementioned points were taken into account in the preparation of the two sample record forms that appear in Figures 6 and 7. Each of these forms, shown somewhat reduced, is an 8¼ x 11¾-inch card.

The record card shown in Figure 6 is the *Educational Records Bureau Cumulative Record for Independent Schools.* This form, usable over a six-year period, is suitable for an elementary school or a secondary school; it is, however, intended mainly for the latter level. Note especially that the front of this form provides for a written and graphic record of the results of tests taken by the pupil, and that the back of the form calls for other important information of various types about him.

The record card appearing in Figure 7 is an adaptation and simplification of the 1941 Revision of the *American Council on Education Cumulative Record Card for Junior and Senior High Schools*. The form in Figure 7 is somewhat similar to that in Figure 6; both, for example, provide a six-year record for the pupil. The former card, however, does not have a graph of test results; instead, it has more space for notes, for example, about the home background and behavior of the pupil.

Training of Counselors for Use of Tests and Records

The guidance values of a school's testing program depend largely upon the competence of its counselors in the use of measurement devices and in the interpretation of resulting scores. Toward developing a high level of competence in the area of measurement techniques, a counselor should have the following kinds of experience and of understanding:

1. The counselor should have had several courses in the fields of psychological measurements and statistical procedures.

2. The counselor should be broadly acquainted with different types of tests. He also should know where to find detailed information on specific tests. Such information appears, for example, in test manuals and in the Buros' *Mental Measurements Yearbooks*.[53]

3. The counselor should be thoroughly familiar with the test portion of the cumulative record form. He should be able to interpret accurately the data therein.

4. The counselor should know how to supplement the test and other data that appear on a student's cumulative record form. This may require the administration of special tests to the student. At all times, this supplementary testing should be

---

[53] Oscar K. Buros (ed.), *The Fourth Mental Measurements Yearbook* (Highland Park, N.J.: Gryphon Press, 1953). For earlier editions of this yearbook, edited by Buros, see the following: *The Nineteen Thirty Eight Mental Measurements Yearbook; The Nineteen Forty Mental Measurements Yearbook;* and *The Third Mental Measurements Yearbook* (New Brunswick, N.J.: Rutgers University Press, 1949).

planned and carried on in accordance with clearly-defined student needs and counselor purposes.

5. The counselor should understand the administration, scoring, and interpretation of the more frequently used standardized tests. He should prepare carefully before he undertakes to give a new test; preferably, he himself should take the test.

6. The counselor should understand elementary statistical measurements, such as these: range, median, quartile, and percentile; and mean, standard deviation, and standard score. He should also be able to compute these measures when needed.

7. The counselor should improve his use of tests and records through the reading and study of professional books and magazine articles that describe and illustrate the application of measurements to guidance work.

8. The counselor should keep in mind the fact that his first duty is to understand and help the individual to gain insight as to his own abilities, interests, and goals so that he is better able to orient and guide his life in a mature fashion. The counselor should be aware that tests are but one of several kinds of techniques designed to facilitate his understanding of the individual.

SUMMARY

This chapter has indicated such key points as the following:

1. In guidance, the emphasis is on understanding of the individual.

2. All aspects of a school's testing program should be carefully planned and supervised.

3. The tests employed in guidance and instruction are of two main types—those used in a systematic all-school testing program; and those used in a supplementary individual testing program. The purpose of both types of tests is to serve the needs of individual pupils.

4. In a regular all-school program, the main kinds of tests are, in order of importance, a test of mental ability, a test of reading ability, tests of achievement, and an inventory of interests.

5. The supplementary testing program should consist of

tests of specific aptitudes and personality. Many of these tests can be administered individually to check on the results of tests previously given in the regular program.

6. A well-organized cumulative record should be employed if test results are to be used effectively.

7. A training program for counselors should stress the understanding and use of measurement, recording, and interpreting techniques.

All the key points just mentioned contribute to the enlargement of the school's knowledge of the individual and of his understanding of himself. They also increase the effectiveness of counseling and interviewing, the subject of the next chapter.

SUGGESTED READINGS

Bingham, Walter V. *Aptitudes and Aptitude Testing.* New York: Harper and Brothers, 1937.

Buros, Oscar K. (ed.). *The Fourth Mental Measurements Yearbook.* Highland Park, N.J.: Gryphon Press, 1953.

Cronbach, Lee J. *Essentials of Psychological Testing.* New York: Harper and Brothers, 1950.

Donahue, Wilma T., and others. *The Measurement of Student Adjustment and Achievement.* Ann Arbor, Mich.: University of Michigan Press, 1949. P. 256.

Froehlich, Clifford P., and Darley, John G. *Studying Students: Guidance Methods of Individual Analysis.* Chicago: Science Research Associates, 1952. Chapters 5-8.

Greene, Edward B. *Measurements of Human Behavior.* New York: Odyssey Press, Inc., 1949.

Greene, Harry A., and others. *Measurement and Evaluation in the Elementary School.* New York: Longmans, Green, and Company, 1941.

Greene, Harry A., and others. *Measurement and Evaluation in the Secondary School.* New York: Longmans, Green, and Company, 1943.

Handbook of Cumulative Records. A Report of the National Committee on Cumulative Records, Bulletin 1944, No. 5. Washington, D.C.: Superintendent of Documents, U.S. Government Printing Office, 1945. P. 40.

Lindquist, E. F. (ed.). *Educational Measurement.* Washington, D.C.: American Council on Education, 1951.

Mursell, James L. *Psychological Testing*. New York: Longmans, Green, and Company, 2nd ed., 1949.

Paterson, Donald G., and others. *Student Guidance Techniques*. New York: McGraw-Hill Book Company, Inc., 1938.

Traxler, Arthur E.; Jacobs, Robert; Selover, Margaret; and Townsend, Agatha. *Introduction to Testing and the Use of Test Results in Public Schools*. New York: Harper and Brothers, 1953.

CHAPTER SEVEN

Counseling and Interviewing in Guidance Work

COUNSELING IS the application of the personnel resources of the school or other institution to the solution of the problems of individuals. Counseling usually takes place between two individuals, a counselor and a counselee.

Some authorities on personnel work hold that counseling is always a relationship between just two individuals, but their view does not appear to cover all possible cases. For example, a counselor may, on occasion, counsel a boy and his parents simultaneously; or, two personnel officers—a counselor and a psychologist—may sometimes work together in counseling a student. Although counseling is normally more effective when only two persons are present and participating, the term *counseling* cannot be restricted to a situation in which only two persons are on hand.

At times, counseling and guidance are referred to as though they were synonymous. However, counseling is one part of guidance, not all of it. Another part is so-called *group guidance*. Although group guidance is not counseling, there is a close relationship between the two. Where group guidance is carried on effectively, individual guidance through counseling and other means can be conducted in ways that bring the greatest benefits to the largest number of counselees.

At other times, counseling is regarded as synonymous with *interviewing*. But the two terms are not interchangeable. Interviewing is a face-to-face discussion between the counselor and the counselee. It is nearly always the central process of counseling, but it is not the only counseling process. Others include telephone conversations and correspondence between the two persons concerned. Intelligent counseling, moreover, cannot be carried on by the interviewing process alone. It requires that the counselor make a thorough study of the counselee before the interview and that he carry out a systematic follow-up thereafter.

Because counseling lends meaning and purpose to guidance, it is absolutely essential to a guidance program. Yet, as just suggested, counseling in itself is not a complete guidance program. To illustrate, during an interview, the skilled counselor will sometimes be able to help an individual through the application of so-called intuitive procedures alone. But more often, he will be able to work most effectively with that individual if his insights are illuminated by measurements, personnel records, and various other data about the individual's personal qualities.

THE INTERVIEW IN COUNSELING

An interview, as Bingham and Moore have stated succinctly, is *"a conversation with a purpose."* [1] Accordingly, general conversation carried on for the enjoyment which comes from talking with another person is not an interview. Nevertheless, such a conversation, on the initiative of one of the two persons concerned, may be changed into an interview—a conversation with a purpose. Similarly, after the objective of an interview has been achieved, an interview may change into general conversation.

Furthermore, an interview may develop casually or it may be planned. Because the guidance worker has limited time available, however, he must definitely plan and schedule most of his interviews.

The Role of the Counselor in the Interview

In recent years, professional literature in the guidance field has included considerable discussion of the role of the counselor in interviewing. This literature has presented three

---

[1] Walter V. Bingham and Bruce V. Moore, *How to Interview* (New York: Harper and Brothers, 1941), p. 1.

main positions that are indicated in the questions that follow. (1) On the one extreme, should the counselor decide definitely in advance the kind of advice that should be given to the counselee? Should he then take firm control of the interview for the purpose of seeing that the counselee receives the advice he needs? (2) On the other extreme, should the counselor serve merely as "a sounding board" for the counselee as he thinks aloud in an attempt to solve his own problems? (3) Or, should the counselor take a middle course that lies somewhere between these two extremes?

Directive counseling. There can be little doubt that the typical untrained or inadequately trained counselor is all too ready to give advice to his counselee. Drawing on his fragmentary knowledge of scientific findings and applying his superficial mastery of counseling techniques, such a counselor predicts with certainty the vocational future of a high-school boy, for example. On the basis of what this boy tells him, the counselor also diagnoses the emotional maladjustment of the boy's sister—all in the same 40-minute period. The cocksureness of such a counselor may arise partly out of his ignorance of the complexity of problems of the youth with whom he is dealing and partly out of the sense of insecurity that he feels in the counseling situation.

Leaders in guidance and personnel work are almost universally agreed that the solution of the immediate problems of the individual often is a comparatively minor function of counseling. The major controlling and long-term function of counseling including the interview is to help the individual reach a stage of maturity where he will be able to make his own decisions intelligently.

The counselor should always employ the interview in such a way that it becomes a growth experience for the counselee. He may permit or even encourage the counselee to "blow off steam"—to express freely his emotionalized attitudes. This expression is often a prelude to learning. By word, by gesture, by action, the counselor should try to get the counselee to take the lead in thinking through his own problems, for growth is an active process that comes from within. From time to time, however, the counselor may rightly assume leadership in the interview; at strategic points, he may provide information and other direct aid to the counselee.

For years, guidance specialists have taken the position that the counselee should be encouraged to assume as much initiative and responsibility as is consistent with his stage of maturity. Nevertheless, there are still all too many instances of unskilled, highly directive, and dogmatic counseling. This tendency of the counselor to "play god" to his counselee can be corrected only through a strong, even dramatic, movement within the guidance field.

Nondirective counseling. Since about 1940, such a corrective movement has been spearheaded by Dr. Carl R. Rogers, a leading exponent of the nondirective theory and technique of counseling. This movement grew out of the need for better counseling in schools and colleges; it had its origins in psychotherapy.

In nondirective counseling, the counselee has the primary role; the counselor, a secondary one. The latter's part in the interview is to create a "permissive" atmosphere; in such an atmosphere, the counselee may think aloud concerning his problems until independently he arrives at a solution or a course of action.

At all times during the interview, the counselor avoids directing or taking the lead in the discussion. In fact, his expressions may consist almost solely of noncommittal remarks, such as, "Tell me more about that," "So you feel that you are being picked on?" or "Hm!" The purpose of these remarks is to encourage the counselee to continue talking. According to Rogers' techniques, however, the counselor may provide information, give and interpret tests, and perform other services *at the request of the counselee.*

In present-day personnel work, the nondirective counseling movement may be likened to the progressive movement in education in the 1930's. Both movements represented protests against stodgy, hidebound, dogmatic practices. Both stressed the freedom of the individual and his right to develop an integrated personality. Both movements have had an extreme left wing; this sect is made up of enthusiasts who contended with religious fervor that their creed would solve all educational or guidance problems.

In one sense, nondirective counseling uses a time-tested technique similar to that of the confessional. The latter's therapeutic values have been recognized and put to good use by churchmen for hundreds of years; these values have also been recognized by laymen. For instance, ministers have been aware that if an individual is encouraged to talk freely about his troubles, he brings his repressed thoughts to the surface and thereby relieves his tensions.

From the point of view of therapy, as the foregoing has indicated, nondirective counseling is on solid ground. But from the viewpoint of practicability in school or college, this type of counseling raises the following important question: Can all the counseling needs of all individuals be met if counseling is limited to a series of interviews in which the counselee "talks himself out" and the counselor makes encouraging remarks from time to time?

At this juncture, it should be recalled, the strongest reason for public support of guidance programs is that these programs help all or nearly all individuals to find the opportunities that are *right* for them. Because nondirective counseling techniques are relatively time-consuming, their exclusive use may deprive many individuals of the counseling services they need. If this occurs, public support of guidance may not continue to grow as it has in the past.

Valuable as nondirective counseling may be, it poses these questions: How can an individual better solve a problem of educational and vocational choice? By drawing solely on the resources within himself? Or, by using not only his inner resources but also the resources available through his counselor? The counselor can give this counselee tests that measure the latter's aptitudes, achievements, interests, and other personal qualities. From the counselor's knowledge and experience in the field, he can supply the counselee with worth-while information as to the available educational and vocational opportunities. In this situation, the counselor clearly has the obligation to provide the counselee with the help needed to relate his aptitudes to the opportunities open to him. The counselee himself, of course, should have the right to make the final decision as to what his course of action will be.

Further to clarify thinking with reference to this discussion, the authors cite Wrenn's distinction between advising and counseling. Wrenn has defined these terms as follows:

> *Advising*—The adviser accepts responsibility for the quality of the decision with the emphasis placed upon the immediate decision.
>
> *Counseling*—The student is assumed to be responsible for the decision with the emphasis placed upon what the student learns in the process.[2]

Eclectic counseling. The point should be stressed here that guidance experts generally are in favor of giving the counselee a great deal of freedom in the interview. They believe that the counselor should allow the counselee to take the initiative and to do most of the talking, so long as the latter does not become completely sidetracked from the main line leading to the objectives of the interview.

The foregoing belief, of course, raises the main question: How much freedom should the counselee be allowed? Most experts in the guidance field are not willing to give full endorsement to the nondirective techniques that give the counselee complete or nearly complete freedom in all kinds of interviewing situations. Yet these same guidance experts do not recommend the sole use of the directive techniques in which the direction comes from the counselor. Rather, these experts tend to take a middle position between the exclusively nondirective and exclusively directive positions; their position has been designated appropriately as that of "eclectic counseling." [3] According to this "eclectic" position, the counselor considers the personality and needs of the individual he is counseling; he then selects the nondirective or directive technique that seems to be most applicable and most helpful to the counselee at a particular time and in a particular situation.

---

[2] C. Gilbert Wrenn, "Training of Vocational Workers," *Occupations,* XXIX (March, 1951), 414-19.

[3] See Shirley A. Hamrin and Blanche B. Paulson, *Counseling Adolescents* (Chicago: Science Research Associates, 1950), chapter 4.

PROBLEMS FOR WHICH COUNSELING IS NEEDED

Counseling may occur at fairly regular intervals, intermittently as needs arise, or both. An individual's needs for counseling will usually fall within one of five general fields: (1) educational orientation and guidance, (2) vocational orientation and guidance, (3) educational achievement, (4) personal and social adjustment, and (5) health adjustment.

With regard to the first three of these fields of counseling, the individual's needs therein are often interrelated. The individual may face problems of educational orientation and guidance because he has chosen an inappropriate field of study. If so, he may also confront problems concerning his vocational objectives.

In the light of the example just given, *educational counseling* and *vocational counseling* usually must be considered as a unit. As soon as an individual reaches a level where some choice is allowed among various courses, the counselor should help him to choose the courses that are in line with his abilities and interests and that lead toward his vocational and other life goals.

In considering a possible field of study, the individual will find that both his aptitudes and his interests are important. If the individual is to succeed in this field, he must have the required aptitudes. These aptitudes may be revealed by a test or tests that measure such abilities as **verbal, numerical,** and **spatial.** To do well in the field, the individual should also have relatively strong interests, for these serve as a drive toward success.

Counseling in Educational and Vocational Fields

Many studies have shown that more persons desire vocational counseling than counseling in any other field within the whole guidance area. This demand is not surprising, for the selection of a vocation is undoubtedly one of the two or three most important decisions that an individual makes during his entire lifetime.

Vocational counseling is so complex that probably no one can be said to have attained full mastery of the knowledge and the techniques that are available in this field. Yet therein, the alert counselor constantly tries to add to his knowledge and to improve his techniques. He does all possible to keep on tap an adequate and reliable fund of information about various occupations; this information deals not only with present conditions but also with past trends and future outlook. This counselor also does his best to appraise accurately the aptitudes, achievements, and vocational interests of the individual.

No matter how well-qualified a counselor is in educational and vocational guidance, he will discover that one of the most difficult cases is that of the individual whose vocational ambition is much above his general mental aptitude. To help that individual, the counselor must use great skill and tact. In interviews with the individual and his parents, he must judiciously interpret the results of the individual's mental aptitude test as these results bear upon the latter's occupational aspirations.

Many counseling problems, varying in duration from those of immediate moment to the student to those extending over the larger part of his school history, are related to educational achievement. In this field, the three most common general problems are underachievement, ineffective study skills and habits, and retarded reading ability. Each of these problems will be considered next.

Counseling the Underachieving Student

In underachievement, the individual's accomplishment may be below the accepted standard for a class or other group, or it may be below his general scholastic aptitude. The former may be primarily an instructional rather than a counseling problem. The solution to this problem may call for one or more of the following actions: removal of the student's handicaps in tool subjects, such as reading or number; adjustment in the curriculum to put the work within the range of the limited ability of the student; or assignment of the student to a special class.

Even though the actions just cited are mainly instructional, the counselor has important functions to perform for the underachieving student who is in need of assistance. For example, the counselor should provide objective information concerning the scholastic abilities of the student who requires special instructional procedures. This information will help the student and the teacher involved, as well as each administrative officer, to understand the nature of the student's difficulties and to decide upon the best methods of easing these difficulties.

Thus, in aiding the student whose achievement is below his general scholastic aptitude, the counselor has the special responsibility of trying to find the cause or causes of that underachievement. The student's underachievement may be due to lack of effort or persistence. Or, it may be due to lack of interest or ambition. If so, the counselor may help the student to correct the situation through a conference. During this talk, the counselor may inform the student of his standing in a scholastic aptitude test and may then compare that standing with his standing in achievement as indicated by school marks and standardized tests. Occasionally, such a conference in itself is sufficient to bring about the desired changes in the student's attitudes and efforts. More often, however, the counselor may also have to seek the development of better relations between the student and his teachers or to arrange for a revision in the student's program of studies.

The counselor should *not* assume, in all cases or even in most cases where a student's achievement is notably below his scholastic aptitude, that the student's difficulty has only one cause, say, lack of application or effort. Rather, the counselor should recognize that a student's underachievement is usually the result of a number of causes, causes that are probably interrelated. For this reason, a "good talking to" or a "slap on the back" is not enough to remedy the student's situation.

At all times, the counselor should be on the alert for the basic causes of a student's underachievement. As possible causes, he should look first for physical factors, such as eyestrain, hearing difficulty, or nutritional deficiency. He should then look for mental factors, low mental ability or poor study skills.

After the counselor has eliminated the foregoing as possibilities, he should search for less obvious factors. He may discover that the student's underachievement is due to a long history of poor general health, to a serious maladjustment at home, or to a complex emotional disturbance; these may call for the assistance of medical or psychiatric specialists.

Counseling for Better Study Methods

The experienced counselor recognizes that study skills and habits have an important bearing upon achievement. Students who know how to study and who practice what they know are more likely to succeed in their academic work and in their other school adjustments. But students who are deficient in study skills and habits make up the large proportion of school failures, particularly in college where students are expected to have relative maturity and independence in study situations.

In the field of how-to-study, group guidance procedures can be highly effective, of real benefit to many students. Through group work, students not only can learn good study methods but also can apply these methods in their courses. Group guidance in study methods, however, should be supplemented by individual counseling. Thereby, the counselor can help each student to analyze the shortcomings in his study skills and habits, and to plan and carry out a program to improve these abilities.

Before initiating group or individual programs related to study, the counselor or teacher should determine which students need which study skills or habits. To make this determination, all students should fill out a self-inventory of study procedures, such as the *Wrenn Study Habits Inventory*,[4] or the *Survey of Study Habits Blank*.[5] The teacher can use the responses of all students to the inventory's items as a basis for setting up a group instructional program on how to study. The counselor can use a student's responses to the inventory items as a basis for an individualized program to improve study methods.

---

[4] Published by Stanford University Press, Stanford, California.
[5] Published by Educational Records Bureau, New York, N.Y.

Counseling for Reading Improvement

Because a student's level of study efficiency and his reading ability are so closely related, the counselor cannot deal with one without considering the other. In working with a student who has a reading difficulty, however, the counselor should realize that the field of remedial reading is more highly developed and specialized than is that of corrective study procedures.

Remedial reading calls for expert knowledge and techniques that are usually outside the field of training of the typical counselor. The counselor may be able to help students who have mild reading difficulties, but he should refer students with serious reading problems to a reading specialist; this specialist may also be an English teacher in the school or college.

The counselor, however, has the important responsibility of helping to identify cases of reading disability and of lending assistance in their treatment. The counselor often administers and interprets the results of reading tests. Thereby he locates students who are deficient in reading abilities. While such a student is taking a remedial reading course, the counselor may from time to time confer with him relative to his reading progress. If the counselor has had some training in the reading field, he is better able to identify the student who is a poor reader and to assist him in strengthening his reading abilities.

Counseling for Better Adjustment

It is generally recognized that one of the most crucial areas of counseling is that of *personal adjustment*. At times, the student's emotional problem is relatively minor; it is an everyday, short-term problem. If so, the counselor is usually able to handle that problem with ease and competence. At other times, the student's problem is moderately severe and involved. If so, the counselor should work with the student in cooperation with the school physician, psychologist, or other specialist on the school's staff.

At still other times, the student's emotional problem is both persistent and serious. It is so deeply rooted and so relatively complex that the typical counselor should not attempt to treat the student's case; rather, he should refer the case immediately to the school psychologist. The psychologist, in turn, may refer the case to a psychiatrist or psychiatric social worker. It is imperative that the counselor recognize the symptoms of the three types of cases just mentioned and that he refer each case to the professional person who is best equipped to handle it.

In a school or college, *health adjustment* problems calling for counseling are less frequent but no less important than those of emotional adjustment. In helping a student who has a health problem, the counselor, of course, works closely with that student's physician. On the basis of the physician's recommendations, the counselor assists the student to make adjustments that solve or ease the latter's problem.

Health adjustment problems and personal adjustment problems are often interrelated. The former may be caused by the latter. A student, for example, may have frequent migraine headaches. During a thorough physical examination, the physician may be unable to find any physiological causes for these headaches. In that event, he with the help of the counselor should search for other causes. They may find that the underlying cause is a fear of failing school tests, an unhappy relationship with parents, or another emotionally-involved problem.

Counseling the Whole Person

It should be clearly understood that, although counseling techniques should be adapted to the various needs of the counselee, counseling should never be compartmentalized. The counselor should work with the whole person in all the different aspects of his life. For this reason, the school should not set up separate counseling programs—for instance, programs of vocational counseling, educational counseling, and adjustment counseling. Instead, the school should have one counseling program, a program that includes counseling in all of the areas just cited.

The competent counselor works with a counselee in all the important areas of the latter's life. The counselor rarely if ever deals with a specific vocational problem or a specific educational problem, in isolation; rather, he considers that problem in its relationships to the other problems or adjustments that the counselee is facing or will face.

THE EXTENT AND NATURE OF COUNSELING

As indicated in Chapter 5, nearly all counseling of young people was, until comparatively recent years, incidental and unorganized. In secondary schools, counseling developed slowly from its beginning about 1910 up to World War II. The Office of Education reported that in the years 1937–38 less than 10 percent of all secondary schools had staff members who gave half or more of their time to counseling. The American Youth Commission estimated that in 1940 not more than six percent of the secondary schools surveyed had full-time counselors.

Even today, only a relatively small proportion of the high schools of the country have planned, organized counseling. In a survey carried on in 1945–46, Froehlich [6] found that only 16.4 percent of the 24,314 secondary schools polled had counselors. The percentages of schools having counselors varied greatly according to states. The states with the highest percentages were as follows: The District of Columbia had counselors in 85.7 percent of its schools; New Jersey, 59.7 percent; and Rhode Island, 58.1 percent. The following states had the lowest percentages: Alabama had counselors in 3.2 percent of its schools; Arizona, 4.7 percent; Maine, 4.8 percent; and Mississippi, 4.9 percent.

With regard to the proportion of high-school pupils having access to counseling services, however, Froehlich found that the situation was somewhat better than that indicated by the preceding figures. This was due to the fact that many of the schools with large enrollments had counselors on their staffs. Thus, although only 16.4 percent of the nation's secondary schools had counselors, 44.7 percent of all secondary-school pupils were enrolled in these schools. Nevertheless, as

---

[6] Clifford P. Froehlich, "Counselors and Guidance Officers in Public Secondary Schools," *Occupations,* XXVI (May, 1948), 523-27.

recently as 1945–46, less than half of all the high-school pupils in the United States were in schools employing counselors.

What, then, are the prospects of an improvement in this situation? On the favorable side, various colleges and universities are now training fairly sizable numbers of counselors. Yet will many of these counselors be employed in high schools that at present do not have counseling programs? It appears unlikely that, in many states, large numbers of secondary schools will employ counselors until school administrators and taxpayers are more aware of the great need of young people for counseling services.

Degree of Specialization of Counselors

In their training and functions, counselors in schools and colleges vary according to a scale. At one extreme of the scale are counselors who have had relatively little training in counseling and who have to give a large share of their time to teaching and other noncounseling duties. At the other extreme of the scale are counselors who are well-trained in the field of counseling and who devote all or nearly all their time to counseling work.

At or near the less specialized end of the scale are registration advisors; their main function is to advise students concerning choice of courses. Next to the advisors are teacher-counselors. In a high school, the typical teacher-counselor has 25 to 30 pupils assigned to him for counseling services.

This teacher-counselor may have taken one or two courses in guidance; he may have had most of his training in counseling on the job—that is, in "the school of experience." Although such training is valuable, it is no substitute for systematic training at the college or university level.

At the specialized end of the scale just given are the school counselors who give half or more of their working time to counseling. As a rule, such a counselor has had graduate training in counseling and related techniques. He also has had a variety of work experience, both in school and outside. Because of this training and experience, his services in the field of counseling are likely to be effective.

Most highly specialized of all counselors are those who

have had thorough training in the philosophy and principles of guidance, in the methods of individual analysis, in the techniques of gathering and interpreting occupational data for guidance purposes, and in the administration of guidance programs. In addition to this specialized training, many of these counselors have had extensive training in the fields of psychology of adolescence, mental hygiene, statistics, and clinical psychology. Some hold the doctorate in guidance or have had training equivalent thereto.

FUNCTIONS PERFORMED IN THE INTERVIEW

In the personal interview, the counselor performs five main functions. His first function during an interview is to get acquainted with the counselee and to establish friendly relations with him; then the counselee will feel free to talk about his problems and to return to the counselor when again in need of help. In short, the counselor must develop *rapport*.

The counselor's second function is to secure information about the counselee. The counselor may obtain this information from the counselee himself through the interview or from other sources—the counselee's cumulative record and the anecdotal reports of teachers, for example. If the interview is a fact-finding interview, the counselor aims to get a better understanding of the counselee so that he can assist this individual with his problems.

The counselor's third function is to impart information to the counselee and otherwise to instruct him. During an interview, for example, the counselor may present and interpret the counselee's test scores and cumulative record; the counselor may also call the counselee's attention to reading materials on the occupations in which the counselee has both interest and aptitude.

The counselor's fourth function is to motivate the counselee. He does this mainly through giving the counselee information about himself and about opportunities available to him. In motivating the counselee, the counselor seldom if ever uses direct pressure or persuasion. Rather, he tries to aid the counselee in developing his own inner motive power.

The counselor's fifth function is to help the counselee in

the fields of adjustment and long-term planning. Of all the mentioned functions, this is by far the most complicated and the most subtle. To perform this function successfully in working with a typical counselee, the counselor must have a series of interviews rather than just one interview.

In considering interviewing techniques, the counselor should understand himself as a person; he is a person who has definite attitudes and prejudices, and who has habitual modes of approaching people and of working with them. The counselor can seldom if ever see completely or take fully into account the idiosyncrasies of his own personality—nor should he be expected to do so. However, the counselor can strive to look at himself realistically; he can, moreover, seek to improve the objectivity of his work. The counselor can do this, for example, by constantly using care to avoid asking questions or making comments that reveal or transfer his own bias to the counselee during an interview.

SCHEDULED AND UNSCHEDULED INTERVIEWS

Interviews with students may be divided into three general classes: (1) interviews that are regularly scheduled, (2) interviews that are initiated by the counselor because of special problems that he has observed or concerning which he has been informed, and (3) interviews that are voluntary on the part of the student.

The school or college counselor usually tries to see each student assigned to him at least once during the academic year. If the counselor has a relatively small number of counselees, he may be able to interview each of them once a semester.

No matter how often the counselor can confer with each counselee, he should plan his interviews according to a regular schedule. By scheduling interviews, the counselor maintains systematic contacts with each counselee, informs him concerning his progress, helps him make further educational and vocational plans, and gives him an opportunity to discuss any matter of great concern to him. Regarding the last, the counselee may confront an important matter that has not been sufficiently pressing to cause him on his own initiative to seek a special interview with his counselor. He will, however, often raise this matter during a regular interview.

Whatever matters are covered in a regular interview, the counselor may well devote some time to a discussion of the counselee's cumulative record; the counselor, of course, will have examined that record in advance of the interview.

Because the total interviewing time is limited, the counselor should ask himself such questions as these: In making out my schedule, how much time should I allow for each interview? During an hour of interviewing time, can I handle effectively one, two, three, or more interviews?

Although there are no hard-and-fast answers to these questions, the counselor should schedule interviews, on the average, at 20-minute intervals—that is, at the rate of three interviews an hour. He should then keep to this time schedule. If the first counselee is making good progress and has no special problems, the counselor may successfully complete the interview in from five to ten minutes. But if the first counselee uncovers problems that will require much more than the 20-minute period allotted, the counselor should arrange for a follow-up interview and then should end the interview as per schedule. The counselor, however, may prolong the interview if there are very special circumstances that make it imperative to do so. By adhering to his interviewing schedule, the counselor makes sure that he interviews all of his counselees at regular intervals. No counselee has to wait for his interview to begin or to postpone its date.

IMPORTANT CONSIDERATIONS IN INTERVIEWING STUDENTS

Often as a follow-up of reports or suggestions from teachers, the counselor may ask students to come in for special interviews for a variety of reasons. One student may be doing schoolwork much below the level of his scholastic aptitude. Another student may be "a disciplinary problem" in some of his classes. Still another student may have emotional adjustment problems.

In starting the interview with such a student, the counselor should carefully avoid giving this student the impression that he is being "called on the carpet." If the counselee feels on the defensive, he is not likely to cooperate. Instead, the counselor should begin the interview by talking with the student about the general purpose of the guidance program in the school. He should then make clear that his help is available if the student needs and wants it. In these ways, the counselor tries to get the student to understand (1) that the counselor's job is in no sense disciplinary, and (2) that the student is not required to avail himself of the counselor's services.

In his work, the counselor should definitely not confine his special interviews to students who are called in because of one kind of difficulty or another. Although the counselor, of course, should invite such students to visit him, he should invite other students as well. Among the latter are individuals who are doing outstanding schoolwork, who have achieved noteworthy success in special projects, or who have displayed unusual leadership in the school's community. Through such interviews, the counselor has opportunities to show his sincere recognition of the worth of these "successful" students. He may even enlist their aid and cooperation in helping other students. And he makes his services more readily available to all students in the school.

If an interview is to be successful, there must be good rapport between the counselor and the counselee. If the interview is initiated voluntarily by the counselee, it usually begins auspiciously. In some instances, a student comes to a counselor simply to discuss his program in a general way and to be reassured that he is on the right track. In such a situation, rapport usually starts at a high level and remains so throughout the interview. More often, however, a student visits a counselor to discuss a definite, and sometimes a very pressing, special problem. In this situation, rapport may be good at the beginning of the interview but may deteriorate rapidly unless the counselor keeps his functions clearly in mind and makes sure that the counselee understands them.

Toward the foregoing objective, the counselor may during the interview say or imply the following: The counselor is *not* a person who has on hand a ready-made panacea for all of the counselee's troubles; moreover, he is *not* a troubleshooter either for the counselee or for the school. In this discussion, moreover, the counselor must avoid letting the counselee unload his problems on the counselor's shoulders or challenge the counselor to solve these problems for him.

From the outset of the interview, both the counselor and the counselee should definitely understand that the primary responsibility for working out the solution to the counselee's problems belongs to the counselee—that, in discharging this responsibility, the counselee can obtain the counselor's aid and advice as needed.

In connection with each special problem brought to him during an interview, the counselor should decide, at least tentatively, the time interval between the counselee's first presentation of his problem and his arrival at a workable solution, a solution that is reasonably acceptable to the counselee. If the counselee's problem is one of emotional adjustment, it may call for intensive effort to discover some way to alleviate the difficulty. If the counselee's problem is one of vocational choice, as so many student-initiated special problems are, the pressure for its solution is likely to be less intense. In the latter type of problem, it may be desirable for the counselor and counselee to work the matter out in a series of interviews. These interviews, interspersed by reading and by discussions with others, may extend over a period of a school year or longer.

Helping the Counselee with Personal Problems

The counselor should keep in mind that the real problem troubling a counselee may not be the one he says it is when he appears for the interview. At the beginning of the interview, the counselee who has a highly personal problem naturally hesitates before telling that problem to another person. During such hesitation, the counselee is likely to talk about matters that are comparatively impersonal. He continues to do so until he feels that his listener is an understanding person.

More specifically, such a counselee often raises a vocational problem or some other problem that he believes is "acceptable" to the counselor. He asks questions and makes comments about this problem ostensibly to get advice but in reality to "sound out" the counselor. If the counselor appears to be an understanding and trustworthy person, the counselee begins to talk about his highly personal problem.

In view of the foregoing, the counselor should avoid closing an interview too quickly after the counselee has stated his problem and the two participants in the interview have arrived at a promising course of action. Rather, the counselor should wait a while, filling in the gap with small talk for a moment or two; thus he gives the counselee an opportunity to talk about anything else he may have on his mind. That "anything else" may be a problem that is very personal and important to the counselee.

The experienced counselor often becomes proficient at using subtle cues for locating deep-seated problems, problems that the counselee would "like to get off his chest." Such a cue may be the unusual tension displayed by the counselee—a level of tension that is higher than that ordinarily shown by a person who is discussing a problem of educational or vocational choice, for example. Or, this cue may be a preoccupied attitude on the part of the counselee; the counselee, to illustrate, seems to be giving only a small part of his attention to the matter under discussion; or he seems to be waiting for the right moment to introduce a subject that is more important to him.

One of the most essential functions of the counselor is to help the counselee to bring his hidden and disturbing problems to the surface. There the counselee can see these problems clearly and can discuss them freely. After this occurs, the counselor can help to find or to create environmental situations in which the counselee is able to work out successful solutions to his personal problems.

ADDITIONAL SUGGESTIONS FOR INTERVIEWING

Various principles that apply to interviewing have been stated or implied in earlier sections of this chapter. It will be helpful next to present some of these principles more definitely, in the form of suggestions to the interviewer.

1. *Prepare carefully for each regularly scheduled interview.* Study the counselee's cumulative record if one is avail-

able. Make notes of significant items. Consult with other staff members if they can provide information that will round out the picture. Try to obtain up-to-date information, particularly about any recent achievement of the counselee; this information may provide a promising starting point for the interview.

2. *Remember that emergencies will arise where the individual needs an interview almost immediately and where there is little or no time to prepare.* Do not let the habit of careful preparation for interviews prevent you from seeing persons when they greatly need counsel, even though you must "meet them cold." Follow the practice of being available when needed even though requests for interviews cause interruptions in work that you regard as important. Remember that counseling is likely to be most effective when the counselee comes to you with a feeling that he needs your help.

3. *Be natural.* Meet each counselee pleasantly, but do not assume a forced heartiness. Be yourself. Do not try to adopt the manner of another interviewer, even though he is known to be very successful. His personality is different from yours.

4. *Take a few moments at the beginning of the interview to put the counselee at ease.* This is time well spent. At the very start of the interview, you may justifiably do most of the talking until the counselee gets accustomed to his surroundings. Your opening comments need not be on the subject of the interview. These comments are often the initial steps in establishing rapport. Refer to mutual acquaintances, to the news of the day, to tomorrow's football game, or to anything else that will help to build friendly relationships.

5. *Come to the point of the interview as quickly as circumstances permit.* Remember the definition of an interview— "a conversation with a purpose." Never lose sight of that purpose, even though the conversation may temporarily be sidetracked.

6. *Hold your interviews in as favorable a physical setting as possible.* Although offices vary greatly, make your office as attractive as possible. Try to assure privacy and freedom from interruption. Arrange chairs and desk informally, to avoid a stiff, cold atmosphere.

7. *Create a permissive atmosphere so that the counselee*

feels free to express his feelings without fear of criticism or censorship. Take the attitude that the interview is a cooperative relationship.

8. *Be a good listener.* Talk only as much as is necessary to keep the counselee's conversation within the general area of his problem and to assist him in thinking his situation through. Help him to understand the implications of factual evidence. Seldom offer advice directly to the counselee. Never use pressure to get him to agree with you.

9. *Let the counselee take the lead in making decisions.* Do not try to give him all the answers in the first ten minutes; they will very probably be wrong. Even when you feel sure of the right decision for the counselee, it is much better psychologically if he himself can be led to formulate that decision.

10. *Always maintain an objective point of view.* An elementary but cardinal rule of interviewing is that the counselor must never become emotionally involved with the counselee. A poorly adjusted person often craves emotional experiences with others. If the counselee is such a person, he may try to arouse your sympathy, your admiration, your anger, or your disgust. For example, he may derive satisfaction from seeing that he is upsetting you emotionally. If he does, this type of satisfaction may become a primary objective for the counselee. Then, during the interview, nothing constructive will be accomplished toward the ultimate solution of the counselee's problem.

11. *Avoid being placed on the defensive.* The counselee may insist upon unloading his problem upon you. He in effect says: "All right, there it is. You are a counselor, aren't you? What do I do now?" You may present him with a solution, your solution. Then you may find yourself in the position of having to defend your proposed solution. Instead of answering the counselee's questions, reflect his questions back to him. This suggestion does *not* say that you as the counselor should disclaim all responsibility for the solution. Rather it implies that both you and the counselee should recognize that the problem is and remains the counselee's at all times. Said another way, the counselee should take the leading role in working on his problem, with you as the counselor lending assist-

ance to him in arriving at a decision and in planning a course of action.

12. *Respect the personality of the counselee.* Let him take the lead in revealing his inner life. Avoid prying, sarcasm, or superiority. Help the counselee to maintain dignity and self-respect.

13. *Be aware of your limitations.* Do not try to counsel an individual whose problems are beyond your depth. Frankly recognize that some cases must be referred to persons who have greater specialized knowledge and techniques than you have.

14. *End the interview upon a constructive note—one that is as optimistic as circumstances allow.* Send the counselee away with a feeling that he has accomplished something worth-while and that he can accomplish even more by his independent, conscientious efforts.

SUMMARY

Counseling and interviewing provide an unusual opportunity to blend scientific techniques with artistic skills. The outstandingly successful counselor is a scientist who constantly studies human psychology and the tools of his craft. At the same time, this counselor is an artist who is sensitive to those subtle cues in personal relationships that make possible the expert application of promising techniques. The able counselor, moreover, is a professional person who is skilled not only in individual but also in group techniques of guidance, the subject of the next chapter.

SUGGESTED READINGS

Bell, Hugh M. *The Theory and Practice of Personal Counseling with Special Reference to the Adjustment Inventory.* Stanford, California: Stanford University Press, 1935.

Berg, Charles. *The Case Book of a Medical Psychologist.* New York: W. W. Norton and Company, 1948. P. 260.

Bingham, Walter Van Dyke, and Moore, Bruce Victor. *How to Interview.* New York: Harper and Brothers, 1941.

Blum, Milton L., and Balinsky, Benjamin. *Counseling and Psychology.* New York: Prentice-Hall Inc., 1951.

Cassidy, Rosalind, and Kozman, Hilda Clute. *Counseling Girls in a*

Changing Society. New York: McGraw-Hill Book Company, Inc., 1947.

"Counselor Competencies in Occupational Information." Washington, D.C.: Federal Security Agency, Office of Education, February, 1949.

"Counselor Competencies in Analysis of the Individual." Washington, D.C.: Federal Security Agency, Office of Education, July, 1949.

"Counselor Competencies in Counseling Techniques." Washington, D.C.: Federal Security Agency, Office of Education, July, 1949.

Culbert, Jane F., and Smith, Helen R. *Counseling Young Workers.* New York: Vocational Service for Juniors, 1939.

Curran, Charles A. *Personality Factors in Counseling.* New York: Greene and Stratton, 1945.

Froehlich, Clifford P., and Darley, John G. *Studying Students: Guidance Methods of Individual Analysis.* Chicago: Science Research Associates, 1952.

Froehlich, Clifford P. "Counseling and Guidance Officers in Public Secondary Schools," *Occupations,* XXVI (May, 1948), 523-27.

Garrett, Annette. *Counseling Methods for Personnel Workers.* New York: Family Service Association of America, 1945.

Germane, Charles E., and Germane, Edith G. *Personnel Work in High School.* New York: Silver-Burdett Company, 1941. Chapters 15-20.

Gordon, H. P., Densford, K. J., and Williamson, E. G. *Counseling in Schools of Nursing.* New York: McGraw-Hill Book Company, Inc., 1947.

Hamrin, Shirley A., and Paulson, Blanche B. *Counseling Adolescents.* Chicago: Science Research Associates, 1950.

Jones, Arthur J. *Principles of Guidance and Pupil Personnel Work.* New York: McGraw-Hill Book Company, Inc., 4th ed., 1951.

May, Rollo. "The Present Function of Counseling," *Teachers College Record,* XLVI (October, 1944), 9-16.

Myers, George E. *Principles and Techniques of Vocational Guidance.* New York: McGraw-Hill Book Company, Inc., 1942. Chapter 8.

Rogers, Carl R. *Client-Centered Therapy.* Boston: Houghton Mifflin Company, 1951.

Rogers, Carl R. *Counseling and Psychotherapy.* Boston: Houghton Mifflin Company, 1942.

Shostrom, Everett L., and Brammer, Lawrence M. *The Dynamics of the Counseling Process.* New York: McGraw-Hill Book Company, Inc., 1952.

Snyder, William U. *Casebook of Nondirective Counseling.* Boston: Houghton Mifflin Company, 1947.

Strang, Ruth. *Counseling Technics in College and Secondary School.* New York: Harper and Brothers, rev. and enl. ed., 1949.

Williamson, E. G. *Counseling Adolescents.* New York: McGraw-Hill Book Company, Inc., 1950.

Williamson, E. G. *How to Counsel Students.* New York: McGraw-Hill Book Company, Inc., 1939.

Williamson, E. G. (ed.). *Trends in Student Personnel Work.* Minneapolis, Minn.: University of Minnesota Press, 1949.

Williamson, E. G., and Hahn, M. E. *Introduction to High School Counseling.* New York: McGraw-Hill Book Company, Inc., 1940. Chapter 8.

Wilson, Gertrude. "Counseling in Schools and Colleges," *Journal of the National Association of Deans of Women,* X (March, 1947), 33-111.

CHAPTER EIGHT

Group Techniques in the Guidance Program

IN THE two preceding chapters, certain techniques for analyzing the important characteristics of counselees have been described and discussed. These techniques may be used with a counselee individually or with a group of counselees. In either case, the purpose of such a technique is to obtain and to apply information about each individual—his abilities, achievements, interests, and other personal characteristics.

This chapter describes and discusses a technique that is commonly used in the guidance program. This method is known by various names: group guidance, group counseling, group instruction, or group work. Whatever the name, the counselor's role is to help students help themselves by working together as a group.

Avoid Use of the Term "Group Counseling"

Strictly speaking, the term "group counseling" should never be employed. In the earlier discussions of counseling, it will be recalled, the process of counseling particularly during the interview goes on with only the individual counselee and his counselor participating. The complete attention of both is directed to the problem of that one counselee.

Contrast what happens when the guidance worker as a leader meets with a group of students. Because of the group situation, these students tend to discuss problems that are general in nature. Sometimes a student raises problems that are personal to him; if he does, there is usually insufficient opportunity to discuss and analyze these matters thoroughly. Moreover, if this student's problems are especially intense, the leader will certainly not talk about them with the group unless he in advance has secured the permission of that student to do so. Furthermore, even though the leader has obtained such advance permission, he will discuss that student's problems with the group only if he believes such a discussion will benefit many if not all of the members of the group. Otherwise the discussion will waste the group's limited time.

Because the expression "group counseling" is a misnomer for guidance activities in a group situation, it should not be used. Rather, this type of formal or informal work with a group of individuals as part of the guidance program should be called "group guidance" or "group work."

"Group Instruction" Not an Adequate Term

Sometimes the term "group instruction" is applied to group guidance. But this term is not entirely satisfactory because it means or implies only those activities that are usually carried on in academic classroom teaching. To most people, "group instruction" has no connotation of guidance activities.

The foregoing statement should not be taken to mean that instruction is not an important activity in group guidance. Certainly, some aspects of the process of group guidance are instructional. These instructional aspects are particularly appropriate in the orientation of students, a subject that will be discussed later in this chapter.

"Group Guidance" Is the Preferred Term

Of all possible terms, that of "group guidance" is by far the best. "Group guidance" has the greatest specificity of meaning, and it is most widely accepted by workers and writers in the field. Moreover, it is preferable to the term "group work" because the latter refers to work other than that dealing with guidance matters.

With reference to use of terms, Froehlich[1] has made an interesting observation: "To avoid some of the semantic difficulties, the phrase *group procedures of the guidance program* is proposed. This phrase encompasses the activities of the guid-

[1] By permission from *Guidance Services in Smaller Schools*, by Clifford P. Froehlich. Copyright, 1950. McGraw-Hill Book Company, Inc., p. 14.

ance program in providing organized group services to help students acquire needed experiences for intelligent personal planning. . . . Whether these activities are sponsored by the instructional staff or the guidance staff is a question that each school must decide. The important point is that they are essential services which, if the guidance program is to be successful, must be available to all students."

EXAMPLES OF GROUP GUIDANCE IN ACTION

What are the common school situations in which group work is used as a technique in the guidance program? This important question will be answered in the paragraphs that follow.

1. *Group guidance is employed in orienting a student to the guidance services of a new school or to new aspects of these services in his present school.* The typical high school provides an orientation program to familiarize groups of freshman students with the school's guidance services, course requirements, student activities, physical layout, and traditions. This orientation program may range from one meeting conducted on the first day of school to a course extending over the first semester of the ninth grade. The high school may also provide orientation for its students at the beginning of their junior year. At that time, students may make a special study of such key matters as college and occupational training requirements. They may also be helped to arrive at educational and other decisions that bear upon the years just ahead. In much of this orientation, group methods can be highly effective.

2. *Group guidance is used to broaden the horizons of students with reference to occupations that are available to them.* This guidance may be carried on as part of a regular course in any of several subject-matter fields—for example, in a civics course or in an English course. Such guidance may also be conducted in a special course where students, for instance, are introduced to the study of occupations. No matter where this study is offered, the student group usually makes a survey of many occupations or fields within the world of work and the general requirements of these fields. The group may

set up student committees, each of which assembles information about a particular field of work.

3. *Group guidance can lead to the discussion of the common problems of students.* To determine these common problems, the leader may have a group discussion during which students cite the matters that are of greatest concern to them; these problems may then be listed on the blackboard. Or, the leader may have each student fill out a problem check list. The problems that students agree are most important may be the subjects of further study and discussion. In a group of high-school juniors, for example, such problems as these are likely to be mentioned frequently: values of a college education; financing a college education; choice of a college or university; choice of a life work; desirability of specialized training after high school if a college degree is not the goal; boy-and-girl problems; family problems; and getting a job.

4. *Group guidance can be conducted in student extracurricular activities.* Students may benefit greatly through their participation in well-managed student activities. These activities often provide experiences that are available nowhere else. Such experiences frequently help students to grow as individuals and to develop as personalities. For this reason, group guidance includes extracurricular activities that are conducted under good sponsorship and with good direction.

WHY HAVE GROUP GUIDANCE?

Group guidance should have an important place in a school's total guidance program because such guidance yields many significant values. Some of these values are presented next.

1. *Group guidance is efficient.* Through meetings with a group of students, the teacher-counselor can convey information in much less time than if he gave the same information to each student, for instance, in an interview. Because the teacher-counselor saves time by the group approach, he can pay more attention to the more difficult and complex aspects of the situation faced by an individual student. Moreover, through group activities, the teacher-counselor can obtain general background information about his students and their prob-

lems. Through interviews, he can secure specific background information about the individual student.

2. *Group guidance multiplies contacts with students.* The teacher-counselor actually can have many more contacts with a larger number of students through group guidance than through individual interviews. During these contacts, he observes each student's behavior in the group situation and thus increases his knowledge of that student.

3. *Group guidance offers students the opportunity to discuss common problems.* Under proper leadership, students within a group can determine what their common problems are. They can then work toward general agreement as to the basic nature and causes of these problems and as to the best ways to solve them.

4. *Group guidance helps improve students' attitudes and behavior.* Students not only have common problems; they also have common attitudes toward themselves and their problems. A student's attitudes toward his problem can make that problem either easier or harder for him to solve. For example, a teen-ager often has the problem of establishing and maintaining satisfactory relationships with his parents and with other members of his family. The typical youth, moreover, has the drive for independence from his parents; this drive is sometimes the cause of unpleasant family situations. With regard to such problems, group discussion including free exchange of opinions and realistic analysis of attitudes can aid teen-agers to achieve better-balanced judgments and more desirable behavior.

For some teen-agers, group discussion many times offers at least a fresh and more promising approach to their home problems. Students frequently accept suggestions that have grown out of group discussions held with their peers. If parents, teachers, or other adults had made the same suggestions directly, their suggestions would have been ignored or rejected by these youth.

5. *Group guidance aids the normal student.* A school that attempts to carry on all its guidance activities on an individual basis usually gives too little attention to the so-called normal student. Although this student, by his own efforts, is able to

achieve fairly adequate solutions to his problems, he may not secure the attention that he deserves. Through group guidance, however, the normal student can be given the information and the direction that he needs and wants. With such assistance, he can go on from there to manage his own affairs even better than before.

GROUP GUIDANCE TECHNIQUES FOR ORIENTATION

Group guidance techniques can be classified in various ways. One system of classification that is a practical aid to better understanding of the functions and procedures of group guidance has been developed by Super.[2]

Super points out that "group guidance methods can be classified under two headings according to their purpose: as *orientation* activities and as *therapeutic* activities. They can be classified also according to the principal method used: as *activity* methods and as *discussion* methods."

According to Super, "the purpose of orientation is dual; it may be *factual,* conducted in order to disseminate information presumably needed by the participants, or it may be *attitudinal,* designed to inculcate or develop attitudes which facilitate self-orientation. Or it may, of course, be designed to do both of these things." [3]

Factual orientation. This type of orientation may be offered in one of several ways. The teacher may carefully present the information to be studied and discussed. Or, the students themselves may present this information in the form of reports of their reading and first-hand observation; these reports may then be discussed by the group. Whichever way is used, the students will become oriented to the extent that they themselves participate in the orienting activities.

Super [4] believes that activities as a method of disseminating information—educational, occupational, or other—are more promising than discussions. As one such activity, students may

---

[2] Donald E. Super, "Group Techniques in the Guidance Program," *Educational and Psychological Measurement,* IX (Autumn, 1949), Part II, 496-510.

[3] *Ibid.,* p. 496.

[4] *Ibid.,* p. 498.

make direct observations and studies of people on their jobs. As another such activity, they may take part in extracurricular programs. In certain student organizations, young people may get experiences in and information about occupations. These organizations include the student government, the school paper, the dramatics club, and the engineering club, for example. Through such participation, students may gain information that is meaningful and realistic to them and that is highly valuable in their orientation.

Attitudinal orientation. Orientation means not only the acquisition of knowledge but also the transformation of attitudes. The purpose of *attitudinal orientation,* as the term implies, is to help students develop attitudes that make for self-management and self-direction. This type of orientation involves a complex of interrelated emotions, values, and beliefs because these constitute the basis of the attitudes that individuals have and display. If a student calmly considers a possible course of action, if he has a set of values to assess the desirability of that action, and if his beliefs have a factual background for that action, he is in the best possible position to orient his attitudes and behavior toward a constructive and promising objective.

To solve a youth problem, students may employ group discussion or other group activities. Consider, for example, the problem of a high-school boy who is convinced that "white-collar jobs" are the only respectable kinds of occupations. To the suggestion that he train for jobs in which blue shirts are worn, this boy reacts negatively and with a great show of emotion. Under the leadership of a good teacher-counselor, the problem raised by this youth is discussed by the group.

During the discussion, the students present the *pros* and *cons* of the question: "Do blue-collar jobs deserve respect?" Near the close of the discussion they generally agree that the answer is "Yes." Thus, the group expresses its general attitude toward the matter; in all probability, such expression will modify the feelings of the aforementioned boy and of certain other members within the group. It may change their attitudes from outright rejection to tacit if not outspoken acceptance of the idea that "blue-collar jobs" are respectable.

Participation in other types of group *activities* such as trips to industrial and commercial establishments and exhibits can contribute to the orientation of the group. This orientation will include evaluations that influence individuals to reorient their present emotionally-toned attitudes.

GROUP GUIDANCE TECHNIQUES FOR THERAPY

During the past few years, guidance workers have been giving increased attention to meeting individuals' personal needs by group therapeutic procedures. These are the needs that cannot be satisfied by the usual methods of group orientation.

Group therapy was put into practice in mental hospitals and in mental health clinics because it had proved to be a good way of treating a large number of patients with a relatively small staff. More and more, these hospitals and clinics have found themselves swamped with patients and with applicants for treatment. Because of their large and increasing patient load, these institutions were unable to provide the services needed solely on an individual basis.

Agencies for mental care, of course, have not replaced individual with group therapy. As Moreno has pointed out, group therapeutic procedures ought not to be regarded as expedients in the absence of, or as substitutes for, individual procedures of treatment, but rather as therapy which results in values not always available through individual treatment.[5]

Through studying the group therapy techniques of psychiatrists, mental hygienists, and other clinicians, guidance workers have developed their own techniques of group therapy. In the main, they have employed two methods of such therapy: *group discussion* and *group activity*.

Four Forms of Group Therapy through Discussion

According to Super,[6] group discussion provides group therapy in the following four forms: cathartic-supportive

---

[5] Samuel R. Slavson (ed.), *The Practice of Group Therapy* (New York: International Universities Press, 1947), p. 10.

[6] Super, *op. cit.*, p. 502, 503.

group therapy; nondirective group therapy; group development therapy; and interpretive group therapy.

Cathartic-supportive group therapy is a method used by certain religious cults. According to this method, an individual finally achieves mental catharsis through the public confessional and conversion. During treatment, he is permitted to express his anxieties freely. No matter what the personal consequences may be, the person who confesses openly and with fervor is completely absolved of guilt and is accepted wholeheartedly by the group.

Nondirective group therapy offers "acceptance, reflection, and clarification of feeling" as a means of resolving personal and social problems. In this group technique as in nondirective counseling with an individual, the atmosphere is permissive. By free and frank discussion of emotionally-toned ideas, the members of the group become better acquainted with their fundamental concepts of themselves as individuals and of themselves in relationship to other people. A type of problem that can be successfully approached by this method of nondirective group therapy is that of racial intolerance.

Group development therapy (sometimes called *group interaction therapy*) helps the individual to gain insight into and deeper understanding of himself, by revelation of his behavior in the group. As a result, modification of the individual's attitudes may take place.

In this form of group therapy, a designated person employs the basic techniques of observing the behavior of the group and of making specific notations concerning the kind and degree of participation of each member. Using this written record, the observer prepares a summary of his observations and presents this summary to the group. The group then discusses the summary analytically. Thereby, the group gains a clearer view of itself as a whole and of each of its members. In this discussion, the individual has the opportunity to see himself as he is seen by others; he also has the opportunity to express his new self-insights with others who have equal opportunity to do the same. If the discussion has an atmosphere of give-and-take and of acceptance and sympathy, the individual acquires a fresh understanding of himself as a person and of his behavior. As a result, he is likely to modify his thoughts, feelings, and actions in a positive direction.

Interpretive group therapy, as Super points out, is a form of group therapy that is perhaps among the oldest approaches employed by psychiatric and psychological therapists. In this technique, the individual's behavior is observed and interpreted both by a trained group leader and by other members of the group. The individual whose behavior or personality is being discussed by the group is always supported personally by the leader in the sense that the leader has an attitude of acceptance. Thus the individual gains new insights into himself. In addition, he develops a feeling of solidarity with the group because all members are working toward the same general goal—self-insight and self-modification of behavior.

With further reference to these four forms of group therapy, a note of caution is appropriate. Each of these forms can be separately described, but each seldom if ever occurs alone or in a pure state in an actual group situation. More likely, in any given situation, these forms occur in varying combinations.

The experienced leader of a group may start off by employing one form of group therapy. He may then shift to another form of therapy—or may use a combination of two or more forms. At all times, he uses the form or forms that appear to be best in the situation that prevails within the group. To illustrate, the leader may employ interpretive group therapy and then later may supplement this form by that of group development. The leader, moreover, may use different forms of group therapy with different groups. He, of course, employs the form that is best suited to a particular group's needs.

Therapy through Group Activity

Among the best-known types of therapy through group activity other than group discussion is the psychodrama. This technique has been developed and popularized especially by Moreno.[7] It involves the "staging" of a situation in which se-

---

[7] J. L. Moreno, "The Group Approach in Psychodrama," *Sociometry* (May, 1942).

lected members of the group are "the actors," and the other members are "the spectators."

The technique of the psychodrama has been employed in certain mental institutions and mental clinics. According to Slavson,[8] "psychodrama on the stage is begun when the patient has been motivated adequately to desire to act out some aspect of his own personality, assisted by *auxiliary egos*, specially trained personnel of the institution to function in this capacity. . . . Moreno refers to it as the *spontaneity theatre*. During the course of the psychodrama the patient-spectators as well as the patient-actors are apt to be activated and take part in spontaneous play, and thus the whole group participates in the therapy, either on the stage or as spectators."

By assumption, participation in the psychodrama ("the make-believe world of the stage") permits the individual to express his inner needs and reactions to pressures. Through cathartic release of tension, better insight into his repressed self is achieved. It is assumed further that constructive forces come into play, and that, by permitting them to direct the individual's make-believe acting, he realizes more complete and realistic understanding of himself.[9]

WHAT ELSE CAN BE DONE THROUGH GROUP GUIDANCE?

Many high schools and colleges have set up specific group programs as part of their guidance services. The nature and extent of these programs differ from one school or college to another, depending on personnel, financial support, room facilities, and the other resources that are available. Oftentimes, even though a school's resources are limited, its administrative head and teaching staff, using imagination and ingenuity, are able to develop a good program of group guidance.

Whatever their resources for group guidance, high schools and colleges have worked out certain practices that have proved relatively effective. Some of these practices are described next.

1. *Presentation of information about the school to newly-arrived students.* Through an orientation program of group

---

[8] Slavson, *op. cit.*, p. 257, 258.
[9] Super, *op. cit.*, p. 505.

guidance, the school helps new students to overcome their feelings of strangeness in the new situation. It also helps them quickly to become acclimated to the school environment; within a few days, they feel at home with their new teachers and in their new classes. During this orientation program, the school gives new students factual information with reference to such matters as the following:

a. The history of the school including its most important and most interesting traditions

b. The physical layout of the campus and of the principal building or buildings thereon (A college, for example, supplies each student with a map of the campus and with floor plans of the main buildings. These show the locations of such important features as classrooms, laboratories, library, cafeteria, gymnasium, swimming pool, student lounges, and the like.)

c. The regulations applying to the academic, social, and personal life of students

d. Available educational opportunities: the various curricula and the courses therein; the prerequisites of courses

e. Student extracurricular activities: student government; student newspaper; social organizations; dramatics; clubs based on interest in subject-matter fields or professions

2. *Provision of aids to effective study.* These aids include activities, such as these:

a. Budgeting of time so that all responsibilities and activities can be adequately covered

b. Learning to read more skillfully

c. Learning to take notes on reading for courses

d. Learning to take lecture notes

e. Learning to review and prepare for examinations

f. Learning to use the library efficiently

g. Understanding external conditions that make for more effective study

3. *Determination of problems common to the student group.* The school can ascertain the common educational, voca-

tional, personal, and social problems of students by any of several methods. For example, staff members can lead student discussions of student problems. Or, they can give students a standardized questionnaire on which they specifically indicate their problems.

Among such questionnaires are the *Mooney Problem Check Lists.*[10] These check lists are available at four levels—junior high school, high school, college, and adult.

Another such questionnaire is the *SRA Youth Inventory.*[11] In taking this inventory, the student checks each statement that "expresses something that has been a problem" to him. The inventory provides scores in eight different areas. This device is applicable in Grade 7 through Grade 12. An elementary-level questionnaire, the *SRA Junior Inventory,*[12] measures the pupil's adjustments in five major areas; it is usable in Grade 4 through Grade 8.

An inventory such as those just described serves at least three purposes. *First,* it enables individual students to determine exactly what their specific problems and problem areas are. *Second,* it gives students a recognition that they have certain common problems. And *third,* it provides the school or college with information about the problems of students both as individuals and as a group.

4. *Presentation of basic information as an aid to individuals in solving their educational, vocational, and personal problems.* Through group guidance techniques, the school can convey the facts that students need and want to help them in solving their problems. If the information thus supplied is sufficiently authentic and comprehensive, students within the group are better able to make wise decisions and realistic plans.

5. *Group discussion of the experiences of students, either within the group or within other groups.* Through a study of case histories including the experiences, successes, and failures of other students, individuals in the group can get ideas

---

[10] Ross L. Mooney and Leonard V. Gordon, *Mooney Problem Check Lists* (New York: Psychological Corporation, 1950).

[11] H. H. Remmers, A. J. Drucker, and Benjamin Shimberg, *SRA Youth Inventory* (Chicago: Science Research Associates, 1950).

[12] H. H. Remmers and Robert H. Bauernfeind, *SRA Junior Inventory* (Chicago: Science Research Associates, 1951).

on good ways to meet their own difficulties and to solve their own problems. In this connection, the faculty leader and the members of his group should have access to materials written by Allen [13] and by Endicott.[14]

6. *Presentation of the principles of mental hygiene.* If students are to achieve success in their academic work and if they are to lay the foundations for happy and effective adult life, they must increasingly understand the emotional aspects of their personalities. Toward this goal, individual reading and study, viewing of films, and group discussions all can make real and widespread contributions.[15]

7. *Provision of attitudinal orientation.* In group guidance, as was mentioned earlier, there is need not only for factual orientation but also for attitudinal orientation. It is one thing for a leader to present facts to a group and quite another for him to get the group willingly to accept the personal implications of the presented facts. Because of the "mind set" (or earlier developed attitudes) of the group, some of its members may find that such acceptance is difficult if not impossible due to emotional involvements.

A group of students, for instance, may decide that it needs and wants to discuss certain problems that arouse deep-seated attitudes. These problems may deal with such emotionally-tinged matters as these: tolerance of peoples of various races and religions; social classes within the student body; economic organization of society; and present-day mores of youth and adults. Through study, discussion, and other activities, members of the group can make important changes in their attitudinal orientation.

8. *Administration and interpretation of psychological tests and inventories.* High schools and colleges often appraise stu-

---

[13] Richard D. Allen, *Case-Conference Problems in Group Guidance,* 1933, and *Common Problems in Group Guidance,* 1934 (New York: Inor Publishing Company).

[14] Frank S. Endicott, *One Hundred Guidance Lessons* (Scranton, Pa.: International Textbook Company, 1942).

[15] Among materials designed to help students in the field of mental health are the *Life Adjustment Booklets,* and *About You,* by Marjorie C. Cosgrove and Mary I. Josey. These are published by Science Research Associates.

dents by giving them group tests. Group discussion techniques can be employed to inform the group as to what a given test measures and as to how its results can be used. Sometimes the teacher may privately give each student his score. He may then, on the blackboard, present to the group a distribution of the scores that its members made on the test; he also may indicate the Q3, Q2 (median), and Q1 scores in this distribution. Thus each student can determine where he stands on the test in relationship to the standing of his classmates. The teacher, however, should *not* reveal the score made by a student to other students in the group. If the teacher wishes to discuss a student's standing in comparison with those of others in the group, he should do this later in a private interview with the student.

The foregoing point should be re-emphasized. If the teacher presents a distribution of scores to his group, he should be extremely careful that a student knows only his own score, not the scores made by other students. In using this procedure, the teacher should be well-acquainted with the group; he also should be fully aware of the possible effects of this procedure on some of his students, particularly on those whose scores were very low.

9. *A creatively-designed and systematically-operated program of extracurricular student activities.* This program is commonly a fruitful means of group guidance in high schools and colleges. It appeals to the interests of students and provides them with opportunities to follow up these interests.

In considering the group guidance values of students' activities, the following classification based on the work of Strang [16] and of Wrenn [17] is illuminating:

  a. Policy-making and governing organizations—student government, student council

  b. Service, social, and recreational groups

  c. Esthetic and religious groups

  d. Academic interest groups

---

[16] Ruth Strang, *Group Activities in College and Secondary Schools* (New York: Harper and Brothers, 1946), pp. 86-195.

[17] C. Gilbert Wrenn, *Student Personnel Work in College* (New York: The Ronald Press Company, 1951), chapters 8 and 9.

e. Athletics

f. Student publications

10. *Development of student leaders through participation in group activities.* Because group activities are the means whereby leaders emerge and leaders are trained, these activities are receiving increased attention on the part of guidance workers in high schools and colleges. As one result, professional literature in the student personnel field contains more and more reports of studies related to the development of leadership.

The need for giving all students training in some aspect of leadership is indicated by the findings of a special project sponsored by the American Council on Education.[18] On the basis of these findings, Warters [19] made three main suggestions for improving the training of students in techniques of leadership, as follows:

a. Development of concepts of leadership which include concern for good human relations

b. Training of students in the analysis of offices and of group procedures

c. Enlarging the range of leadership activities in which pupils have a chance to develop joint purposes with respect to what they want and consider important

WHERE SHOULD GROUP GUIDANCE BE INTRODUCED?

In the typical high school or college, group guidance includes a number of relatively formalized activities. One of these is the orientation program for entering students. Just prior to the opening of regular classes, for example, the institution requires all freshmen to participate in what is called *Orientation Day* or *Freshman Week*. At this time, it orients these students in an organized way to the new educational situation.

The orientation course. In addition to the foregoing, the institution may require all freshmen to attend a class in orien-

---

[18] Hilda Taba (ed.), "School Culture and Group Life," *Journal of Educational Sociology,* 21 (May, 1948), 497-556.

[19] Jane Warters, "Guidance through Groups," *Review of Educational Research,* XXI (April, 1951), 143 (Washington, D.C.: American Educational Research Association).

tation. This class meets at stated sessions each week for a varying period of time—six, eight, or ten weeks, or the entire first semester. During these sessions, the teacher presents such topics as these: techniques of effective study; educational opportunities offered by the school or college; the common problems of students; mental hygiene and personality development; procedures for choosing careers; and implications of the results of tests and inventories.

The topics just listed point to the desirability of having a required orientation course, a course that meets, say, twice a week during a semester. This length of time is probably necessary if students are adequately to cover the entire range of essential topics. For this course, some institutions give no academic credit to students. Others, however, provide such credit. The latter practice is preferable because, if credit is granted, students are more likely to take the course seriously and teachers are better able to demand high standards of work.

Certain high schools have found it practical to include certain phases of orientation as parts of academic courses. In these schools, students receive orientation with reference to their vocational and educational problems in such courses as civics and English. They obtain orientation in mental hygiene and personality development in courses in biology or general science.

The homeroom. In many high schools, the homeroom is considered a most important channel for group guidance. In theory, this arrangement is desirable; in practice, it works only fairly well. All too often, the time available in the homeroom period is absorbed by recording attendance, making announcements, taking up collections for special funds, and handling administrative matters. There is usually little or no time left for group guidance activities.

Moreover, although the entire homeroom period is devoted to group guidance, that period is usually much too short for an effective program in this important area. In some schools, this period is only 10 to 20 minutes, too few minutes to carry on a guidance project that is of real value to students.

Despite the limitations just cited, the potentiality of the homeroom for group-guidance purposes should not be overlooked. If a high school provides that its homerooms devote, say, at least one period a week to well-planned guidance activities, these homerooms can play a significant role in the institution's group guidance efforts.

Other courses. Group guidance may be offered not only in special courses or units but also in regular courses such as English, social studies, science, and mathematics. If a subject-matter teacher carefully studies the possibilities, he will find that he can systematically devote some of his class time to students' guidance problems.

The high school that has a "core curriculum" program that includes required courses in general education (sometimes known as "survey" courses) can offer many opportunities for group guidance. Without doubt, these courses can orient students to wider fields of thinking and can stimulate them to explore new areas of interests. Such courses can also help students to analyze their strengths and weaknesses in the various areas of knowledge. This analysis often aids students in solving their educational, vocational, and other problems.

Other activities. As just suggested, group guidance may be conducted formally in the regular courses of the school's curricula. It also may be offered informally in a variety of extra-curricular activities, such as the following: meetings of student clubs to pursue special interest fields; in-school gatherings of students to discuss common interests and common problems; and regularly scheduled but informal meetings of students in the same residence hall or at the same eating establishment to talk about matters of common concern.

If a teacher or a counselor can arrange to do so, he may wish to invite a small group of students to his home. There all present can talk about guidance problems. In an informal, permissive, and understanding atmosphere, the teacher can carry on highly effective group guidance. If this session is to be successful, the teacher must have the type of personality that appeals to students and that wins their confidence. He must know how to lead a group discussion in a genuinely informal fashion. He must be able skillfully to keep the discussion on the track, free from confusion and pointlessness.

WHO SHOULD HANDLE GROUP GUIDANCE?

The logical persons to carry on the formal aspects of the group guidance program in a high school are as follows: teachers in charge of homerooms; teacher-counselors; class sponsors; director of guidance services; and school psychologist. In a college or university, these persons are as follows: faculty counselors; teachers of orientation courses; director of guidance services; dean of men and dean of women; director of placement; and head of the health service.

In a high school or a college, those responsible for conducting the informal aspects of the group guidance program include the aforementioned personnel plus such persons as these: teachers who are well-liked by students and who have the personality and outlook on life that make them well-fitted for this work; and student leaders who are emotionally mature and well-balanced personalities. In a college, the heads of or counselors in student residences can also contribute to the group guidance program.

If the staff member is to conduct group therapeutic activities, he should be well-trained in the techniques required. He should be reasonably expert in this approach to group guidance. The staff member should *not* be a person who has merely read about the techniques and who is anxious "to do good by trying them out." Such a person may actually harm certain members of the group without intending to do so.

THE GUIDING PRINCIPLES OF GROUP WORK

To point up the discussion so far, the key principles of group guidance are presented next.

1. Group guidance should have motives, purposes, and points of view that are the same as or similar to those of individual guidance—for example, those that obtain in the most fruitful kind of individual counseling. In group guidance, of course, many of the techniques of counseling must be adapted to the group situation.

2. Group guidance should be regarded as a supplement to counseling, not as a substitute for it. Counseling, by its very

nature, is a more personal and more productive technique for working with an individual.

3. In group guidance, the leader should be on the alert for means of encouraging certain members of the group to seek individual counseling assistance. If group guidance is effective, it leads to the counseling of individuals from the group. (Likewise, if individual counseling is competently done, it often results in the counselee's joining a group to gain benefits from such participation.)

Through the development of a close relationship between group guidance and individual counseling, the teacher-counselor helps the student:

    a. To apply to his own situation the general information obtained during group study and discussions;

    b. To secure additional information pertinent to his own problems;

    c. To take special tests of aptitudes, interests, and the like;

    d. To discuss with his counselor the scores made on tests given to the group; and

    e. To correlate test information and other information as these bear upon his educational, vocational, or other plans.

4. In group guidance, the students constituting the group should be relatively homogeneous in certain respects. As a minimum requirement, the group should have a common purpose or interest. For example, that common interest may be vocational—the choosing of careers. Or, that interest may be social—the learning of the skills and habits needed to get along successfully with others.

At times, a school may be unable to achieve the homogeneous grouping for group guidance that its staff wants. Within his group, the teacher-counselor may have difficulty, at least at first, in finding a purpose or interest that is common to all students. As his group's work goes along, he may discover a common purpose. In line with this general purpose, he may set up committees within his group. Each committee may be composed of students who have a common special interest.

5. In group guidance, the teacher-counselor should in-

troduce a unit or project at the time that seems most appropriate for his students. In this matter, students' needs and interests are the best guides. If students do not feel the need for the unit or if they are not interested in the unit, they will get little or nothing of value from it.

6. Group guidance should be given the importance that it deserves in the school's total educational program. If such guidance is offered, in part, as a separate course, that course should have real standing in the school. In too many high schools and colleges, a course in group guidance is still looked upon by subject-matter teachers as "a course for dumbbells" and by students as "a snap course." This group guidance course can, however, earn the respect and support of nearly all teachers and students, (a) if the course is well-planned, outlined in detail, and packed full of sound content, and (b) if the course has high standards of achievement thus requiring serious work on the part of students. Such a course, however, may differ considerably in its methods from the subject-matter courses that are traditionally taught in a school.

7. In planning group guidance, the administrative head of the school should allocate an adequate amount of time and a desirable time of day for this type of education. Moreover, if the administration, by word and deed, considers group guidance important, this program is likely to be rated highly by both faculty members and students.

8. In group guidance, the administrative head should provide adequate educational materials and devices, and sufficient physical facilities for group work. Without these aids, group guidance cannot succeed.

9. The teachers or other staff members responsible for group guidance should be thoroughly qualified for this type of work. All too often, a teacher is assigned to this work solely because he is interested in it or because he does not have a full teaching load. But such a teacher cannot do the job that needs to be done. If he is to conduct group guidance effectively, he should have the technical knowledge of and skills in the processes and devices involved. Such competence does not come by chance; it is a result of technical training in group work.

10. Group guidance should be considered as one means but not the only means of guidance. Group guidance, for example, cannot produce miracles; it cannot correct all the situations that other means of guidance have failed to improve. Group guidance, furthermore, should not be regarded as a palliative measure—a treatment that eases without curing. Such guidance cannot prevent or overcome the mistakes that are made in the counseling of individuals. And it cannot substitute for counseling and other types of guidance.

Group guidance, moreover, is *not* a panacea. It is *not* equally effective with all students. It may help many students to achieve better personal adjustments and better social adaptations. But there are indications that it is only the "better-adjusted, more insightful, and more self-directing individuals who are able to profit much from group guidance." [20] Individuals who stand low in such traits require more than group guidance. They need individual guidance, particularly through counseling.

SUMMARY

Group guidance can play a significant role in the total guidance program of a school or college. This type of guidance is being employed increasingly by educational institutions; many of these institutions have reported favorable results. Even so, group guidance deserves further exploration and implementation by qualified personnel. As yet, all too little is known about its potentialities. School and college people need to conduct more research that aims to systematize, expand, and evaluate group guidance. Nevertheless, a growing number of schools and colleges have found that group guidance is a highly valuable part of the entire program of guidance services. Its effectiveness has been indicated by follow-up programs, to be discussed next.

SUGGESTED READINGS

Bradford, Leland P. Introduction to "The Dynamics of the Discussion Group," *Journal of Social Issues,* 4:3,4 (Spring, 1948).
Hinckley, Robert G., and Hermann, Lydia. *Group Treatment in*

---

[20] Super, *op. cit.,* pp. 501, 507.

Psychotherapy. Minneapolis: University of Minnesota Press, 1951.

Hoppock, Robert. *Group Guidance: Principles, Techniques, and Evaluation.* New York: McGraw-Hill Book Company, Inc., 1949

Jennings, Helen Hall. *Leadership and Isolation: A Study of Personality in Interpersonal Relations.* New York: Longmans, Green and Company, rev. ed., 1950.

Jennings, Helen Hall. *Sociometry in Group Relations.* Washington D.C.: American Council on Education, 1948.

Powdermaker, Florence B., and Frank, Jerome D. *Group Psychotherapy: Studies in Methodology of Research and Therapy.* Cambridge, Mass.: Harvard University Press, 1953.

Robinson, Francis P. *Principles and Procedures in Student Counseling.* New York: Harper and Brothers, 1950. Pp. 263-273.

Slavson, S. R. *Creative Group Education.* New York: Association Press, 1937.

Strang, Ruth. *Group Activities in College and Secondary School* New York: Harper and Brothers, rev. ed., 1946.

Wrenn, C. Gilbert. *Student Personnel Work in College.* New York The Ronald Press Company, 1951. Pp. 203-240.

Wright, Barbara H. *Practical Handbook for Group Guidance.* Chicago: Science Research Associates, 1948.

Zerfoss, Karl P. *Readings in Counseling.* New York: Association Press, 1952. Pp. 519-570.

CHAPTER NINE

The Follow-Up in Guidance Services

AN INTEGRAL part of guidance services is *the follow-up.* Through the follow-up conducted by a counselor, the counselee learns the nature and the extent of his progress. The counselee determines the areas of his life in which he has made successful adjustments and the areas in which he needs to make further adaptations.

Without the follow-up, counseling is incomplete, and so are other types of guidance services. A counselor who does not find out what has happened to his counselee is like the physician who does not check upon whether his patient recovered from an illness. Neither is providing the professional services that he should.

Desirable and necessary as the follow-up is, it is all too often omitted because a school lacks the time, money, personnel, or procedures that are needed for this purpose. In a typical school, the counselors are so busy working with their current counselees that they cannot follow up their former counselees. The main reason for this failure to follow up, as just mentioned, is that the school does not have sufficient resources to render continuing services to its counselees over a period of time.

Despite the difficulties of establishing and maintaining a systematic follow-up program, counselors in a school or college should consider, *first,* the need for follow-up, and, *second,* the practical means for meeting this need. Certainly, as long as a counselee is attending the educational institution, its staff can follow up his progress.

Examples of a Follow-Up Method and Need

Because the typical counselor has limited time, he may be able to follow up only those counselees who have relatively serious problems. For example, early in the first semester, this counselor may interview some 25 freshman students. At mid-semester, he may quickly review the academic and other records of these students. Among them, he may find six students who are experiencing difficulties in learning how to study effectively. He may immediately hold a second interview with each of these students. On the basis of this interview, he may arrange to have these students attend a how-to-study class. These students may continue this special work for a number of weeks. At the end of the semester, the counselor may hold a third interview with each of these students to check on progress. He may conclude that five of these students are able to carry on effective study independently, but that one student needs further training on an individual basis.

Even though the counselor may try to follow up each counselee who is most in need of his services, he may, at times, overlook such a counselee. Consider, for example, a senior who made a tentative choice of occupation while in his junior year. If the counselor unintentionally fails to interview this senior, the latter may choose a career that is inappropriate for him. This kind of illustration points to the importance of a well-planned and well-executed program of follow-up counseling.

THE FOLLOW-UP OF THE COUNSELEE
WHILE STILL IN SCHOOL

Ideally, as suggested earlier, the counselor should have follow-up interviews with a counselee on a voluntary basis, that is, the counselee should take the initiative in arranging for an interview. This means that in the initial interview and in each interview thereafter, the counselor should try to get the counselee to feel that the door of the counselor's office is always open to him. By so doing, the counselor may lead the counselee to decide to report his progress or his lack of progress, say, two or three weeks later. If the counselee who needs help does not voluntarily seek it, however, the counselor obviously has an obligation to take the initiative. He must do so particularly in the case of a counselee who has trouble in drafting plans or in reaching decisions, or who has serious personality weaknesses.

Follow-up activities are as complex and broad as the other activities making up guidance services. Even so, to the greatest extent possible, these services including counseling should be made available to every counselee so long as he is in school. The only way to make sure that a counselee receives the benefits of these services is through a definite follow-up program. The crux of this program is the careful review of a counselee's situation at regular intervals and also whenever such a review seems necessary.

Because each counselee is an individual whose problems are unique, the follow-up program for him should also be unique. The timing of the interview and the devices used therein should be tailored to the individual being counseled. If the counselee's problems are primarily educational or vocational, or a combination of the two, the counselor ordinarily can best review the counselee's case at certain key points in the latter's progress through school.

Ideally, for example, the counselor should confer with a counselee in the spring of the school year. Then the counselee checks upon his progress and makes up his program of courses for the year ahead. If the counselor foresees that the counselee will probably encounter difficulties with certain courses in the curriculum, he should immediately arrange a follow-up interview to try to forestall such troubles. If the counselor finds that a counselee is having serious personal problems, he should use his best judgment as to the appropriate time and way to follow up the case.

In the early interviews with a counselee, the counselor will be most helpful if he envisions the kinds of difficulties that the counselee is likely to confront in his efforts to carry out his decisions and to pursue his plans. During any of these early interviews, the counselor may or may not discuss all of the counselee's future difficulties as he sees them. He may wisely decide *not* to present all these anticipated difficulties simultaneously to the counselee particularly if many of these difficulties appear to be insurmountable. Rather, during one interview, the counselor may discuss two difficulties—one that is hard to overcome; and one that is relatively easy to manage.

In talking about anticipated difficulties with a counselee, the counselor should be convinced that the counselee's goal is a feasible one—that the counselee *can* reach his objective. If this is the case, the counselor can proceed to discuss the factors that bear upon whether the counselee will succeed or fail in working toward his objective. Some of these factors such as aptitudes, interests, and personality traits are within the counselee himself; others are to be found in the counselee's environment.

In all follow-up activities, the counselor's main objective is to obtain answers to such questions as these: (1) How well is the counselee following the plan that he developed earlier? (2) How well is he adjusting himself to his current situation? (3) In the light of new developments, does he need assistance in modifying his plan or in making further adjustments? Through the answers to these questions, the counselor tries to evaluate the counselee's progress toward the latter's chosen goal.

THE FOLLOW-UP OF THE STUDENT LEAVING SCHOOL BEFORE GRADUATION

In the school's guidance services, the counselor should give special attention to the student who has decided that he must withdraw from school or college. If this student has passed the age of compulsory attendance, he, of course, is free to leave when he wishes.

The counselor obviously has the responsibility of giving this imminent school-leaver all the assistance that he can. Toward doing so, the counselor should first explore all possible ways to keep this student in school. Then, if it appears that the student cannot or should not continue his schooling, the counselor should arrange an exit-interview with him. Preferably, this exit-interview should be conducted by the student's regular counselor. This counselor already has rapport with the student; he also knows the student and his background better than does any other staff member.

During the exit-interview, the counselor should secure from the student information pertinent to such matters as these: (1) the immediate reasons for the student's withdrawal from school; (2) the changes, if any, in the student's educational and vocational plans; (3) the various possible future effects of the student's withdrawal on his earlier and present plans and decisions; (4) the possibility of the student's transfer to another school; (5) the possibility of the student's resumption of his school program at a later time; (6) the definite steps already taken by the student to find work and their outcome; and (7) the consideration of ways to meet the student's situation other than withdrawal from school.

The counselor should employ the exit-interview not only for the purpose of obtaining the aforesaid information but also for many other worth-while purposes. For example, he can use the interview to strengthen the counselee's belief in himself and in his plans. Or, he can help the counselee to gain further insight into his earlier decisions—these may or may not have been adequate or desirable. With reference to these decisions, the counselor can lead the counselee to consider new solutions to his problems and to make new plans accordingly; these plans may be more appropriate to the counselee's present situation and to his current abilities and interests.

During the exit-interview with a counselee, the counselor should try to make suggestions that are as positive and heartening as possible. He should *not* close the interview on a note of discouragement. Rather, the counselor should help the counselee to feel that he is leaving school with promising ideas and plans, that he can succeed in what he is undertaking.

If the counselor believes that the counselee needs specialized assistance he should refer the counselee to a professional person who can best render that type of help. Such a person may be another counselor, a physician, or a psychiatrist who is on the staff of an institution or who is in private practice. As a follow-up, the counselor should invite the counselee to return for a conference at a later time.

THE FOLLOW-UP OF THE GRADUATE-TO-BE
WHO IS SEEKING FULL-TIME WORK

The counselor should definitely arrange a follow-up interview with a counselee who is about to graduate and who is looking for a position. To illustrate, consider the senior student who for more than three years has had thorough counseling with reference to his vocational problems; as a result, he has made plans to meet his career situation. When the counselor initiates the procedure of placement, he calls this student in for a follow-up interview; preferably this counselor should be the one who has been working with the student over a period of time. During this interview, the counselor may directly help the student in finding a position. Or, he may refer the student to the placement counselor for an interview. Together this counselor and the student assess the latter's potentialities and discuss the positions open to him. In placement work, the regular counselor and the placement counselor each recognizes his responsibilities; both cooperate fully in their efforts to place the student in the position that is best for him.

FILE DEVICES TO FACILITATE THE FOLLOW-UP

The "tickler" file. Whatever the purpose of the follow-up, this follow-up is facilitated if the counselor keeps a "tickler" file on his desk. On each card in this file, the counselor has written such items as these—the counselee's name; the date when he is to be seen; the general nature of the case; the student's progress up to and including the latest interview; and the possible course of follow-up for that counselee.

The counselor arranges these "tickler" cards according to coming interview dates. In planning an interview, the counselor notices the card of a given counselee who will be coming in for a conference, say, a week hence. After reading that card, he undertakes to assemble the information that he will need for the interview. He obtains a complete (up to then) record of the counselee's academic marks. He talks to the teachers and other staff members who have been closely and recently associated with the counselee. He examines again the counselee's record of performance on standardized tests. The counselor then holds the interview on the date appearing on the counselee's "tickler" card.

The card file of interview records. The follow-up of counselees is also made more effective by a card file of interview records. This file is usually kept in a central place, in the office of the guidance department. There the file is available to all authorized persons including those responsible for guidance services.

In this interview record file, there is one card for each counselee. This card gives the following information: the counselee's name, the dates of interviews, and the names of the persons who conducted these interviews. Using this interview record card, a counselor can readily determine which other persons have interviewed the counselee; he can then confer with them before a follow-up interview. Also using this card, the guidance head can better decide which counselor should work with the counselee in the immediate future.

The cumulative record. As was pointed out in Chapter 6, the most nearly complete information concerning a student should appear in his cumulative record, on a card or in a folder. This record should contain brief summaries of all the interviews by counselors. These summaries may furnish leads for following up the student's situation; it also may reveal different points of view relative to the counselee's status.

The counselor and other staff members will have to devote time and effort to maintaining the "tickler" card file, the card file of interview records, and the summaries of interviews in the cumulative record file. However, they will find that the information appearing in these files is highly valuable in follow-up guidance work. If these records are relatively simple, staff members can make entries in them quickly and with little effort. If these records are kept up-to-date, they greatly facilitate follow-up activities; they also minimize the number of cases that might otherwise be overlooked. By referring to the data in these records, moreover, counselors are relieved of the burden of remembering the details that may be needed later in guiding students. With such records at hand, counselors are able to spend more time and thought in creative follow-up work with their counselees.

THE FOLLOW-UP OF THE FORMER STUDENT

A high school or college should make every practical effort to follow up its former students. Although such a follow-up is obviously difficult to conduct, it can yield much valuable information, as will be pointed out later.

In following up its former students, a high school usually employs a questionnaire that calls for information about such matters as these: educational institutions which the former student entered; curriculum pursued; marks received; degree or degrees earned; position or positions held; and membership in organizations (community agencies, service clubs, professional associations).

Reasons for the Follow-Up of Former Students

There are a number of important reasons why a high school or college should gather information about its former students, both drop-outs and graduates. *First,* this information will indicate the achievements of these former students, achievements that are due in part to their school or college training.

Second, employing this information, the educational institution can conduct studies of the relationships between the training given these former students and the use that they later made of this training. These studies help the institution to determine the effectiveness, desirability, and fitness of its course offerings—in short, to evaluate its educational programs. On the basis of such evaluation, the institution may decide to introduce important changes in its offerings and practices.[1]

Third, by drawing upon information from former students, counselors can improve their current work with students. Counselors often find that the experiences of former students furnish useful leads toward helping their present students to solve difficult problems.

Examples of follow-up outcomes. Assume that, through a follow-up study, a counselor has definite knowledge of the successes of former students who entered certain other training

---

[1] By permission from *Guidance Services in Smaller Schools,* by Clifford P. Froehlich. Copyright, 1950. McGraw-Hill Book Company, Inc., pp. 309-313.

institutions or who entered certain kinds of jobs. This counselor can effectively use such knowledge in advising his present students. Likewise, assume that this counselor has information about the failures or shortcomings of former students in certain training institutions and in certain jobs. He can take this information into account in counseling with his present students.

Next, the counselor can "go behind" the information provided by former students. He can attempt to find out the factors that appeared to cause these previous students to succeed or to fail. These factors may have been present in the counselor's own institution, in the institutions attended later by these former students, or in the jobs entered by these young people. By ascertaining these factors, the counselor is in a better position to help his counselees in planning their educational and vocational futures.

In addition to the information collected through follow-up studies of former students, a school can compile useful local occupational information by means of surveys.[2] Thus, over a period of time, the school becomes better acquainted with the occupational opportunities for the school-leavers in the local community. The school secures more nearly accurate and complete knowledge of local job requirements in specific occupations, of rates of pay, and of trends in the demand for workers, especially for those who are seeking their first full-time jobs. Surveys to collect information on the foregoing matters must be carefully planned and directed; they must employ a prearranged form so that the data can be readily tabulated; and they must yield summaries that are useful in counseling with students.

The follow-up of former students can serve as an important technique for evaluating the school's guidance services. The proof of the worth or lack of worth of these services is, in no small part, the behavior of youth after they have left the school. In a follow-up study of these former students, they may well submit reports indicating their successes or failures

[2] Max F. Baer and Edward C. Roeber, *Occupational Information: Its Nature and Use* (Chicago: Science Research Associates, 1951), pp. 278-324.

and giving their opinions of the school's guidance and other programs.

According to these reports and other data, the failures of some of these former students may be due to circumstances outside the control of the school's guidance staff. The failures of other former students, however, may point to the inadequacy of certain aspects of the school's guidance program.

To illustrate the foregoing, consider several examples. Because the counselor did not have up-to-date information about higher educational institutions in the field of Counselee A's interests, he did not help this counselee to seek admission to the school or college that was best for him. Or, because the counselor lacked knowledge of occupations in the community and knowledge of Counselee B's occupational aptitudes and interests, this counselee while a high-school senior made an unwise vocational decision; he became an office worker when he might better have entered an apprenticeship program for machinists. Or again, the counselor failed to note that Counselee C was seriously disturbed emotionally; he, therefore, did not refer this counselee to a psychiatrist. Subsequently, this former counselee had a nervous breakdown.

Through follow-up studies of former students, the school can not only correct mistakes in its guidance program. It can also increase the effectiveness of all of its guidance services.

The Values of Follow-Up Studies to Former Students

The counselor can employ the returns from follow-up studies to help the school's former students as well as his present counselees. In studying these returns, the counselor will discover former students who are in need of guidance services. He may arrange to have these services provided by the school or by other institutions, agencies, or organizations within the community.

Stated another way, the follow-up study of former students should have as one of its major purposes the provision of further guidance services to these young people. This purpose should be made crystal clear to these youth. Otherwise, a former student who is in a serious quandary may not ask the school for its help. If the follow-up aids such a former student, however, it achieves one of its most important objectives.

DEVICES FOR FOLLOW-UP OF FORMER STUDENTS

To gather the various kinds of significant information concerning its former students, a high school or college can employ one or more techniques, such as the following: questionnaires filled out by former students; letters to and from them; telephone conversations with them; interviews with them; visits to their places of work; interviews with their employers or present counselors; and other contacts with persons and organizations who know these former students. Of all follow-up techniques, that of the questionnaire is probably most popular and most useful.

The Use of the Questionnaire Follow-Up

Each high school or college will, of course, want to design its own follow-up questionnaire to send to its former students, both graduates and nongraduates. This questionnaire, however, should have these two general purposes: *First,* to find out what further education these former students had; and, *second,* to find out where these former students were or are employed and what positions they held or hold. If the questionnaire is short enough, it can be printed on a double postal card; this device tends to increase the percentage of former students who send in replies.

In order to secure the maximum cooperation of former students, the preamble of a questionnaire should contain a statement of its general purposes and of the proposed uses to be made of the returns. The main body of the questionnaire should include such items as those appearing on page 218.

Other suggested questionnaires for use in follow-up studies appear in *Occupational Information,* by Baer and Roeber.[3]

The guidance worker who is constructing a follow-up questionnaire should consult professional publications that deal with this type of project. To make even a short questionnaire is not an easy or simple task. For example, if the questions are poorly worded, the person queried will not know

---

[3] *Ibid.,* pp. 286-296.

Date of leaving
Name _____ our high school _____

College(s) attended	Dates of attendance	Number of credit hours	Degree earned
_____	_____	_____	_____
_____	_____	_____	_____

What educational institution, if any, are you now attending?

_____

In what field or fields of study have you specialized since leaving our high school? _____

When you entered high school, did you have this specialization in mind? Yes _____ No _____ If "no," what specialization did did you have in mind?

_____

If now employed, is it full-time? _____ Part-time _____
What is the nature of your work? _____
How long have you been employed at it? Years _____ Months _____
What is the name and address of your employer? _____

_____

What full-time job, or jobs, have you held since leaving high school? _____ Nature of work? _____
How long employed at it? _____
Name of employer(s) and address(es) _____

_____

(Signed) _____ (Date) _____
Your address _____

exactly what is wanted. If the fields to be covered are not carefully thought through, important items may be omitted. For these and other reasons, the guidance worker should read and study at least one basic reference on the preparation and use of the questionnaire. One such reference is the book, *The Questionnaire in Education,* by Koos.[4]

After the guidance worker has received the filled-out copies of a follow-up questionnaire and has tabulated or summarized the data therein, he should observe certain cautions in drawing conclusions from the findings. *First,* this worker should compute the percentage of returned copies to the

---

[4] Leonard V. Koos, *The Questionnaire in Education* (New York: Macmillan Company, 1928).

number distributed. This proportion should be at least 50 percent. *Second,* the worker should study the characteristics of those who filled out and returned their copies of the questionnaire. These persons should be a representative sample of the total group to whom the copies were sent.

If the returned copies of the questionnaire are a relatively small percentage of all the copies sent out, and if the returned copies are not from a representative sample of the entire group queried, the guidance worker should clearly indicate that his findings from the study are highly tentative and may be unreliable. Although these findings may have certain values in terms of leads, they should not be accepted uncritically as the basis for changing guidance policies and practices.

The Use of the Telephone Follow-Up

The guidance worker may employ the telephone in a follow-up study of former students. He should, however, recognize that this technique has its limitations. At best, the telephone technique can serve as a means for securing only the more routine kinds of information from former students, their employers, and others. Unless the guidance worker knows these people personally, they are not likely to give him routine information, let alone confidential information, over the telephone. These persons, moreover, may refuse to give information about a former student until they have obtained his permission to reveal this information.

Nevertheless, the guidance worker can often use the telephone effectively in his follow-up study of former students. In seeking information, he should explain the school's earlier relationship with the person for whom information is sought. The guidance worker should also give the reasons for his query. At no time should he use pressure or the hint of pressure to obtain a reply. As just mentioned, if the person queried is the former student's employer, he will probably want to check with his employee before giving an answer.

Because of the time required, the guidance worker should not attempt to have a former student give his answers to a follow-up questionnaire over the telephone. The worker, however, should use the telephone to contact a former student who has not yet filled out and mailed in his copy of the questionnaire. In this way, the guidance worker may be able materially to increase the percentage that returned questionnaires represent of all questionnaires sent out. The higher this percentage, as pointed out earlier, the more reliable the findings of the questionnaire study.

The Use of the Follow-Up Letter

In a study of former students, a follow-up letter serves the same fundamental purpose as does a follow-up questionnaire. However, the letter usually covers only a few items of information; the questionnaire, many. In comparison with a questionnaire, a letter ordinarily gives the person to whom it is addressed more freedom in his reply. Preferably, the letter should ask the person certain definite questions; it should also encourage him to write as freely and as fully as he wishes in answering these questions.

Ordinarily, the guidance worker employs the follow-up letter when he wants qualitative information from former students. Usually he sends out only a small number of such letters. The guidance worker uses the questionnaire when he wishes to obtain quantitative information; he sends out copies of this questionnaire simultaneously to many former students.

Whether the guidance worker uses a follow-up letter, questionnaire, or both, he should seek the wholehearted cooperation of all of the persons who are queried. Whatever the device employed, he should explain the school's relationship to the former student, the reasons for the inquiry, and the probable uses to be made of the replies.

In situations where confidential information is being sought from someone other than the former student, the latter's permission should be obtained in advance. The school can then note that such permission has been granted in its letter of inquiry or questionnaire to that former student's employer. This procedure serves two purposes: (1) It protects the former student and all others concerned. (2) It is more likely to draw a larger percentage of replies from those who are queried.

The Follow-Up Interview

In his follow-up study, the guidance worker can use the interview technique to very good effect. He can interview the former student; or, he can interview that person's employer or other associate. In conducting any of these interviews, the worker should observe the principles that were discussed in Chapter 7. Before an interview, the guidance worker should decide exactly what questions he wants to ask, how he shall phrase these questions, and when he will present each question. During the interview, the guidance worker will, of course, adapt his questions to the interviewee's personality and to the prevailing situation. Through such practices, the guidance worker is more likely to secure the information that he desires.

If during the interview the guidance worker asks certain specific questions drafted in advance, he obtains data in a relatively standardized form. Later he can readily assemble, tabulate, and summarize these data, and draw valuable conclusions therefrom.

In all interviewing, the guidance worker faces the problem of whether or not to take notes during the conference. If his questions ask for information that is relatively objective and impersonal, he may make notes on what the person being interviewed is saying without inhibiting the latter's replies or comments. However, if he and the interviewee are discussing subjective or personal matters, he should wait until after the interview to record what was said.

SUMMARY

As this chapter has emphasized again and again, the follow-up is a very important part of guidance services. That follow-up, however, may be difficult if not impossible because a given high school or college lacks the requisite time, interest, personnel, or procedures.

Through follow-up programs, counselors, for example, can undoubtedly improve their services to former, present, and future counselees and over longer periods of time. Through a questionnaire study, counselors can find out what has happened to many of their former counselees. They can compare the information thus obtained with the school's records of what was done for these counselees. These comparisons may reveal such defects as mistakes in the use of certain testing devices, misinterpretations of test results, and faulty use of occupational information. By locating these defects and by correcting them, counselors in the school can become much more helpful to students than ever before.

Up to the present, all too little research has been done in the field of follow-up work as an integral part of guidance services. Relatively speaking, little is known concerning the usefulness of the follow-up techniques that have been discussed in this chapter.

If guidance services are to be improved, research workers in this field must conduct many more and much better studies of follow-up techniques. As a result of these studies, some of the common follow-up techniques may prove to be valuable; other such techniques may not. As a further outcome of these studies, researchers may develop new and more effective follow-up techniques. What research and evaluation can contribute to the advancement of the follow-up and to other guidance services is the subject of the next chapter.

SUGGESTED READINGS

Baer, Max F., and Roeber, Edward C. *Occupational Information: Its Nature and Use*. Chicago: Science Research Associates, 1951. Pp. 278-324.

Erickson, Clifford E. *A Basic Text for Guidance Workers*. New York: Prentice-Hall, Inc., 1947. Chapter 16.

Erickson, Clifford E., and Smith, Glenn E. *Organization and Administration of Guidance Services*. New York: McGraw-Hill Book Company, Inc., 1947. Pp. 120-128.

Froehlich, Clifford P. *Guidance Services in Smaller Schools*. New York: McGraw-Hill Book Company, Inc., 1950. Pp. 309-326.

Harden, Edgar L. *How to Organize Your Guidance Program*. Chicago: Science Research Associates, 1950. Chapter 9.

Smith, Glenn E. *Principles and Practices of the Guidance Program*. New York: Macmillan Company, 1951. Chapter 10.

Super, Donald E. *Appraising Vocational Fitness*. New York: Harper and Brothers, 1949. Chapter 24.

Traxler, Arthur E. *Techniques of Guidance*. New York: Harper and Brothers, 1945. Chapter 16.

CHAPTER TEN

Research and Evaluation in Guidance Services

ALTHOUGH GUIDANCE services make up a comparatively new function of high schools and colleges, they have expanded with increasing rapidity, especially since World War I. During the 1920's and 1930's, as cited earlier, guidance services were strengthened and improved by scientific research in the fields of psychology and education. This research led to the development of better tools and practices of guidance.

Scientific research in the guidance field was stimulated by such important factors as these:

1. The insistent demands by psychologists and others for wider application of the testing and guidance techniques that were developed by the military services during the two world wars

2. The increasing realization by business and government that better guidance contributed to the training and placement of employees

3. The growing recognition by school people that broader and more effective guidance services were needed by the increasing number and percentage of youth who were continuing in school

Despite the depression of the 1930's and partly because of it, some real progress in research and evaluation was made in the field of guidance services. This progress was due mainly to the work of psychologists, statisticians, educators, and other experts who were staff members of certain governmental agencies and of many universities and colleges.

During World War II, teams of experts carried on considerable research both in the military and civilian branches of the federal government. This research led to the development of better techniques for the selection and training of personnel. Since then, many of these techniques have been successfully adapted and applied to nongovernmental situations.

THE DIFFICULTIES OF RESEARCH AND THE NEED FOR IT

In a field as varied and complex as guidance, it is to be expected that many aspects of guidance services have not as yet been adequately studied and advanced. Up to now, more attention has been given to some aspects than to others. Quite naturally the aspects receiving the greatest attention have been the ones which lent themselves most easily to scientific study. For these aspects, workers in the field had developed the necessary research tools, techniques, and professional competence.

In an editorial in *Occupations*,[1] Kitson points out four important reasons why more research has not been conducted in the field of guidance services, as follows:

1. Because a research problem must be restricted in scope, the research worker is forced to limit himself to a small segment of the larger area at any one time. The meager result—established fact—usually helps a later investigator more than it helps a present-day worker.

2. For most significant results, a number of years of laborious research are required. Witness in other fields the extended investigations of such scientists as the Curies, Edison, and Urey.

3. Among all guidance workers, there are only a limited number of persons who are trained in the techniques of scientific research. None of them has sufficient time or facilities to maintain a large flow of productive research studies.

4. Research cannot solve all the problems of counselors or administrators. Some difficulties can be resolved only

---

[1] Harry D. Kitson, "More and Better Research in Vocational Guidance," *Occupations*, XXVI (February, 1948), 308, 309.

through administrative action or the resolution of conflicting personalities in a local situation.

Although Kitson's statements are directed particularly to research with reference to problems of choosing a vocation, they apply equally well to research in other aspects of guidance services.

As Kitson and others have said, researchers should carry on studies of certain problems rather than studies of other problems because the former yield more fruitful and practical results. For example, there is general agreement that researchers might spend less time on constructing new tests of vocational aptitudes or proficiencies and more time on establishing the degree of relationship between performance on existing tests and success in various occupations. Then, too, instead of developing new inventories of interests, researchers might better concentrate on validating the inventories that are already available and that are widely used.

More Controlled Experiments Called For

Researchers in the field of guidance, moreover, might make greater use of so-called *controlled experiments*. In this important type of scientific experimentation there is rigorous control of the factors involved in the problem under study; such control is usually difficult to establish and to maintain.

Take, for illustration, the problem of determining, under true experimental conditions, the effects of two kinds of group training in the field of vocational choice on two groups of students. Before the training period begins, the director of the study equates the two groups. As nearly as possible, a student assigned to Group A has the same characteristics as a student assigned to Group B. These characteristics include such factors as mental ability, school achievement, home background, and socio-economic status. During the training period, the two groups are taught in two different ways; both ways, however, have the same objective—leading pupils to make a wise choice of an occupation.

Although the study's director is able to keep certain factors under relative control by equating them, he is unable to take into account such factors as family pressures that bear upon choices, personal financial conditions that limit choices, and deep-seated personal attitudes that condition choices. These and other factors are outside the control of the experiment's director; they may be very influential on the end results of his study. Therefore, the study's director cannot conclude with certainty that the one method of group training is better than the other.

This example points out that human and other factors, some controllable and others not so, make scientifically controlled experimentation difficult and sometimes impossible in the field of guidance services. Nevertheless, guidance workers should increasingly try to employ controlled experiments in evaluating the effectiveness of their services, for this technique is definitely among the best.

NEED FOR STANDARDIZATION OF CONCEPTS AND OTHER TERMINOLOGY

Although some guidance services have been offered for more than 25 years, guidance workers have given too little serious attention to the standardization of terminology in their field. Due perhaps to haste to do something, thinking has been superficial and concepts have been loosely defined. As a result, a given term has meant different things to different workers; the term "counseling," for instance, has had many varied connotations.

Even the experts in the field have held heated arguments over the meanings of certain terms—to illustrate, over the distinctions between "student personnel work" and "student personnel service"; some have insisted that the term "student personnel work" should be limited to activities outside the classroom. All too many other guidance workers have used the terms "guidance" and "counseling" interchangeably.

In terminology, the situation in the field of guidance services contrasts sharply with that in the field of physics, for example. The latter field is a scientific discipline; the knowledge therein is logically organized. For these reasons, the field of physics has well-defined concepts and other standardized terminology.

If the field of student personnel services (including guidance services) is to become a science, guidance workers must develop a standardized terminology—that is, clear-cut and agreed-upon concepts and symbols. These workers must also evolve a logical organization of the content of their field. With such terminology and organization, guidance services can become a science. Then, workers in the field will be able clearly to understand each other; then also, they will be better able to cooperate in their efforts to improve and evaluate guidance services.

SOURCES OF RESEARCH INFORMATION

In the field of guidance, there are many types of problems that are approachable through research. This is demonstrated by the fact that the studies in this field have been increasing rapidly in number and variety, particularly during the last 15 years. Because some problems have been especially important, they have been the subject of repeated studies. These studies have employed old approaches, new approaches, or combinations of both.

For a comprehensive survey of research studies in the guidance field, the guidance worker should examine the special issue of the *Review of Educational Research* [2] that is entitled "Guidance and Counseling." This special issue appears once every three years. In the April, 1951, issue, the guidance topics covered are indicated by the chapter headings, as follows: Characteristics and Needs of Individuals; Conditions Affecting the Guidance Program; Programs of Guidance; Appraisal of the Individual; Counseling; Guidance through Groups; Educational and Vocational Information; and Preparation of Teachers and Specialists for Guidance Service.

For reliable information in the field of achievement tests, psychological tests, and inventories, the guidance worker should consult *The Fourth Mental Measurements Yearbook*,[3] edited by Buros. This extensive volume of more than 1,000 pages describes and reviews a large number and variety of

---

[2] Published by the American Educational Research Association, 1201 16th St., N.W., Washington 6, D.C.

[3] Oscar K. Buros (ed.), *The Fourth Mental Measurements Yearbook* (Highland Park, N.J.: Gryphon Press, 1953).

tests and inventories. It lists 429 books, articles, and other studies related to measurement, and includes reviews of many of them.

To keep up to date on research findings in his field, the guidance worker should regularly read such professional journals as these: *The Personnel and Guidance Journal* (successor to *Occupations*),[4] *Educational and Psychological Measurement*,[5] and the *Psychological Abstracts*.[6]

MORE RESEARCH NEEDED

In practically every aspect of guidance services, research is needed. For this reason, any qualified guidance worker has many opportunities to undertake scientific research studies. These studies will help him to increase the effectiveness of his own work. They also will contribute to the sum total of useful knowledge in the guidance field. Such studies may deal with old problems as well as new ones. For example, although numerous studies have been conducted in the appraisal of individual students and in the application of statistical techniques, even more such studies are needed; the findings therefrom can help to refine old methods and to develop new methods, all of value to guidance services.

The guidance worker who is "on his toes" in the field is constantly on the alert for studies or projects that he can undertake. For this worker, here is a list of worth-while research projects, stated in the form of questions.

1. To what extent do guidance services contribute to, or result in, such outcomes as the following:
   a. Decreased number and proportion of students who drop out of school before graduation?
   b. Formulation by students of sensible long-term programs?
   c. Determination by students of the relationships between current occupational choices, opportunities

---

[4] American Personnel and Guidance Association, Inc., 1534 O Street, N.W., Washington 5, D.C.

[5] Educational and Psychological Measurement, Box 6907, College Station, Durham, North Carolina.

[6] American Psychological Association, 1333 Sixteenth Street, N.W., Washington 6, D.C.

for training for those occupations, and chances for later success in those occupations?

d. Appropriateness of students' decisions about their future educational or training plans?

e. Effectiveness of the job placement of outgoing students and of former students?

f. Development of ability of students to be self-directive?

2. Are the present forms and procedures of guidance services both adequate and effective?

3. Do admission requirements permit all of the individuals who are able to profit from the educational program to enter the institution?

4. Within the school, what environmental influences other than guidance services affect individuals and the student body as a whole? In what ways?

5. What are the significant characteristics of the student body? Which of these characteristics are most important for guidance workers?

6. What are the fundamental needs of the individuals who make up the student body?

7. In terms of individual and group characteristics and needs, what changes should be made in the institution's guidance services?

8. How can the guidance worker help to adapt curricular offerings and instructional methods to the characteristics and needs of individuals?

9. What particular orientation activities do the students need to adapt themselves satisfactorily to a new educational institution?

10. What specific criteria and techniques will contribute to the selection of better faculty counselors?

11. How can guidance workers and other staff members integrate curricular and extracurricular activities so that these activities facilitate the all-round development of the individual?

12. How can techniques to follow up the institution's former students (drop-outs and graduates) be introduced, expanded, or improved?

EVALUATION OF GUIDANCE SERVICES

Because evaluation and research often go hand-in-hand, the guidance worker should not attempt to draw a hard-and-fast line between the two. Evaluation, of course, may involve research; it may be thought of logically as an aspect of research. Technically and more precisely, however, evaluation connotes an assessment of values. Such an assessment occurs, for example, when a guidance worker evaluates the extent to which the originally stated objectives of his program have been achieved.[7, 8]

As an illustration of evaluation, assume that the objective of one of the school's programs is to decrease the incidence of poor scholastic achievement. Near the end of this program, the guidance worker evaluates in detail the means used to attain the objective and the results achieved. As another illustration, suppose that the guidance worker is interested in determining the effectiveness of the school's counseling program on the scholarship of students and upon their retention until graduation.

Such an investigation in the form of a controlled experiment was made by Toven.[9] At the beginning of the experiment, Toven selected two similar groups of college students. One group received systematic counseling; the other did not. At the end of the experiment, Toven compared the two groups. He found that, in comparison with the noncounseled students, the counseled students had, on the average, achieved a greater increase in their academic marks. He also found that a substantially larger percentage of the counseled students were graduated from college.

In the evaluation of the results of counseling, scholastic achievement should not be the sole or even the most impor-

[7] Ralph W. Tyler, "An Appraisal of Technics of Evaluation—A Critique," *Official Report of 1940 Meeting* (Washington, D.C.: American Educational Research Association), 72-77.

[8] Ralph W. Tyler (edited by E. G. Williamson), "Achievement Testing and Curriculum Construction," *Trends in Student Personnel Work* (Minneapolis: University of Minnesota Press, 1949), 391-407.

[9] J. Richard Toven, "Appraising a Counseling Program at the College Level," *Occupations*, XXXIX (May, 1945), 459-466.

tant criterion, as it still is in all too many high schools and colleges. Rather, social adjustment and emotional adjustment, as well as educational adjustment, should be criteria for judging the values of a counseling program. This trend is evident in a growing number of educational institutions.

Application of the criteria of social and emotional adjustments to the evaluation of counseling was reported in a study by Hill.[10] In his experiment, Hill equated two groups of college students according to 15 variables. One group received regular counseling; the other did not. Comparing the two groups, Hill found that a larger percentage of the counseled students participated in extracurricular activities and improved their social adjustments. Although the differences between the counseled and noncounseled groups were not statistically significant, these differences suggested that systematic counseling of students contributed to their extracurricular participation and social adjustment.

Another illustration of the application of the criterion of social adjustment in the evaluation of guidance services appears in a study by Worbois.[11] Specifically, the purpose of his investigation was to ascertain the effects of guidance programs upon the emotional development of students.

In the public high schools in Flint (Michigan), Worbois matched two groups each of 233 ninth-grade pupils on the basis of sex, intelligence, achievements, and certain other factors. Over a period of three years, the experimental group was given intensive individual guidance. Careful attention and treatment were provided for whatever problems seemed significant in the adjustment of each pupil. The control group was given only the regular guidance provided by the school. This program was typical of that offered in most well-organized city high schools.

At the end of a three-year period, representative samples of 24 pupils each from the experimental and control groups were tested for "emotional adjustment" by the Luria tech-

[10] Mark H. Hill, "An Experimental Study of Social Adjustment," *American Sociological Review,* 9 (October, 1944), 481-494.

[11] G. M. Worbois, "Effect of a Guidance Program on Emotional Development," *Journal of Applied Psychology,* 31 (April, 1947), 169-181.

nique.[12] From the findings, Worbois concluded that the experimental group of pupils showed significantly less "emotional conflict" than did the control group of pupils. On some of the criteria of emotional adjustment, the averages of the experimental group were higher than those of the control group. Some of these differences between averages were statistically significant; others did not completely satisfy the test of statistical significance.

The techniques of the Worbois study are far more important than its findings. These techniques point the way to the improved methods of research that are needed in evaluating the effects of guidance programs on the adjustments of students.

In the field of guidance services, there is also a need for better techniques of appraising the procedures employed in training counselors. In this connection, Robinson[13] has reported a study of the effects of supervised work experience on a group of counselors-in-training. These counselors, all advanced college students, were assigned to help systematically two to four undergraduates. The latter were enrolled in a course in the psychology of effective study and individual adjustment.

In this experiment, each counselor-in-training aimed to help his undergraduates (1) to improve their skills and habits in the field of academic work through diagnostic and remedial measures, and (2) to solve their problems in other fields such as planning careers and making better personal and social adjustments.

At the end of the experiment, there was considerable evidence that the undergraduates progressed in many ways. For example, they improved their study skills, raised their scholastic averages, obtained higher behavior ratings, and made better social adjustments. The counselors-in-training also benefited. They reported that they had increased their knowledge and

---

[12] A. E. Luria, *The Nature of Human Conflicts*. Trans. by W. H. Gantt (New York: Liveright, 1932).

[13] Francis P. Robinson, "Two Quarries with a Single Stone," *Journal of Higher Education*, 16 (April, 1945), 201-206.

skills and had improved in their personal qualities and adjustments.

Need for Additional Evaluation Studies

The studies just cited as well as others point to suggestions for additional research designed to evaluate guidance programs. This research might include studies of matters such as these:

1. Extent to which the principal aspects of a program of guidance services are covered

2. Nature of the guidance program's contacts with the different kinds of student or youth problems

3. Relative degree of success or failure of the guidance program in meeting the needs of youth to solve their various types of problems

4. Effectiveness of interviews with counselees

5. Usefulness of tests in appraising students

6. Short-term and long-term predictive values of aptitude, achievement, and interest tests, and of test profiles

7. Efficacy of different theories and practices of counseling (including interviewing) in various kinds of situations

8. Effectiveness of counseling superior students and inferior students

9. Effectiveness of guidance through group activities

10. Effectiveness of the guidance means used to achieve articulation between secondary school and college

11. Effectiveness of placement services and follow-up procedures

12. Extent to which guidance services are understood, respected, and accepted by students and by the general community

13. Extent to which guidance services are supported or performed by staff and line officers in an educational institution

Bearing of Guidance Research and Evaluation on the Curriculum

In a school or college, the results of research and evaluation in the area of guidance services can be applied to the improvement not only of the guidance program but also of the curricula and of the courses therein. An educational institution can employ these research findings to redesign its instructional services so that they better meet the needs of its youth. The school can also use these findings to assess the adequacy of its curricula and its methods of instruction, in terms of students' progress.

Through the testing and counseling procedures of the guidance program, for example, the school may discover that its curricula and courses of study have specific gaps with reference to students' basic needs and are insufficiently adapted to the abilities, aptitudes, and interests of students. Or, the school may find that the contents and methods of teaching certain courses are not adjusted to the learning skills of students.

At present, the teaching staff in the typical school or college is relatively unwilling to give full consideration to the findings of research and evaluative studies—studies made by the guidance director or the guidance department, for example. That is why the guidance head should discuss research findings with teachers and other staff members. Thereby, guidance workers and teachers can better coordinate guidance services and instructional services. Only through this coordination can the school substantially improve its curricula, its methods of teaching, and its extracurricular activities.

With reference to what guidance and other personnel workers can contribute to an institution's curricula, MacLean [14] has stated that (1) we must know thoroughly the characteristics of the students; (2) we must know the students' sociological and cultural backgrounds; and (3) we need to know the present and probable future needs of students—individually and as a group—and the needs of our "dynamic and emerging society."

In a well-planned guidance program, the staff gathers and records extensive, objective information about students, and then places this information in the files of the guidance office. For each student, these files contain records of the following:

---

[14] Malcolm S. MacLean (edited by E. G. Williamson), "Adolescent Needs and Building the Curriculum," *Trends in Student Personnel Work* (Minneapolis: University of Minnesota Press, 1949), 29.

his school marks; his standings on scholastic aptitude, achievement, and other psychological tests; his family's characteristics including its socio-economic status; his general health and specific physical disabilities, if any; and his educational and vocational plans.

In these records, the school has important information about each individual student. By combining selected data from these records, the school obtains significant information about the student body as a whole. Such information serves as a valuable resource to staff members who are working to adapt the institution's curricula to the educational needs of its students.

Information about the student body can also be of great value to the institution in planning and conducting its program of extracurricular activities. Staff members, for example, can employ this information to adapt such activities to the interests and abilities of students. In doing so, the staff recognizes that an organized program of extracurricular activities should be based upon adequate knowledge of the abilities, achievements, interests, and needs of students. Much of this knowledge can be obtained through research studies of the data that are usually kept in the files of the guidance department.

By drawing upon the recorded information about students, the classroom teacher can improve the content and methods of his course. By consulting the cumulative records of his students, the teacher can determine such important facts as these about his students as individuals and as a class group: the levels of abilities of various kinds possessed by his students; the extent to which his students have mastered the fundamental skills needed in the course; his students' knowledge and application of the principles and practices of effective study; his students' backgrounds of success or failure in school or elsewhere; and the deficiencies in vision, hearing, or other physical capacities of certain of his students.

The teacher may have difficulty in summarizing and in interpreting the data about his students that appear in the guidance files. He also may have difficulty in applying what he has learned from these data. To overcome these difficulties, the teacher may have to devote both time and thought. Nevertheless, through such efforts, he will be better able to tailor his course to the needs and wants of his students—an important contribution to both instructional and guidance activities.

OTHER PROBLEMS AND TECHNIQUES OF EVALUATION

The evaluation of existing guidance procedures and devices is as important as the conduct of research for the development of new techniques and tools. Furthermore, unless the existing procedures and devices are evaluated in terms of their effectiveness in serving guidance purposes, there is no assurance that they have genuine worth. No matter how good these procedures and devices appear to be in and of themselves, their values can be judged only in the light of their proved contributions to guidance.

The Need for Specifically-Stated Objectives

To evaluate guidance methods and tools calls for the clear formulation of guidance objectives. These objectives must be stated in such a way that evaluation is practicable. If an objective is to serve as a criterion for evaluation, it must be relatively specific in meaning and narrow in scope.

As an example of a poorly-stated objective, consider this statement: "The purpose of our college is to provide a liberal education for all students." This objective is stated so broadly that nobody, no matter how expert, can develop and apply tests or other techniques that evaluate the extent to which students have become "liberally educated."

In contrast, a school that has specifically-worded objectives is able to develop and to apply sound processes and devices of evaluation. To illustrate, Oberlin College has stated that its aims of a liberal education are as follows:

1. To train students in the methods of thinking and in the main tools of thought;
2. To acquaint students with the main fields of human interest and to direct them in the acquisition of knowledge therein;
3. To guide students in the integration of knowledge;
4. To develop their physical and mental health; and
5. To develop their social resourcefulness.[15]

---

[15] "Aims of Oberlin College," *Oberlin College Bulletin,* 49 (July, 1951).

Although the foregoing statement of the objectives of one liberal arts college is more specific than that given previously, this type of statement can present these objectives even more definitely. An institution's statement, for instance, can include particular objectives in the areas of certain skills, knowledges, and attitudes. The institution can then select, construct, and employ the devices needed to measure and evaluate student progress toward each of the aforesaid objectives. Thus, in each skill or field of knowledge as expressed in terms of a specific objective, the school determines the degree to which students have developed mastery. In short, the narrower the stated objective and the greater its specificity, the easier it is to check upon the relative effectiveness of a particular educative process.

Methods of Systematic and Comprehensive Evaluation

A plan for the systematic evaluation of guidance programs in secondary schools was developed by a committee that reported to the Eighth National Conference of State Supervisors of Occupational Information and Guidance Services and Counselor-Trainers. To implement this plan, the supervisors prepared two publications on evaluation.[16]

One of these publications presents the criteria that are significant in evaluating guidance services. The criteria given are grouped under the following five areas: administrative bases for guidance services; guidance staff; guidance services; services complementary to the guidance program; and guidance services as an influence on total school development.

Each subarea within each of the areas just given has a list that is made up of items for use in evaluation. As an example, here is part of the check list for the subarea entitled "Procedures in Counseling."

( ) 1. The counselor prepares for each interview by carefully studying all the data pertinent to the case.
( ) 2. The interview is organized purposefully, but flexibil-

---

[16] *Criteria for Evaluating Guidance Programs in Secondary Schools, Form B,* Misc. 3317 (Washington, D.C.: Office of Education, Division of Vocational Education, Occupational Information and Guidance Service, January 15, 1949). *How to Use the Criteria for Evaluating Guidance Programs in Secondary Schools, Form B,* Misc. 3317-A (Office of Education, March, 1949).

ity is maintained to adjust to any emerging problem of the pupil.

( ) 3. The pupil is encouraged to express himself freely.

( ) 4. The counselor avoids domination of the interview or of the pupil.

( ) 5. The counselor accepts the pupil as he reveals himself, without expressing values on anything the pupil says.[17]

The other publication, in the form of a manual, suggests the procedures for applying the criteria for evaluation.[18] The manual outlines in detail each step in evaluation, such as preparation for evaluation, self-evaluation, re-evaluation by a visiting committee, and follow-up of an evaluation project.

NECESSITY OF COOPERATIVE RESEARCH AND EVALUATION

To conduct scientific research and evaluation in the area of guidance services, there must be planned cooperation among a number of qualified guidance workers. Such cooperation by competent workers is essential for several reasons.

First, in content and methods, guidance is far from simple. The personality of the individual who is being guided, the environment in which he is being guided, and the relationships between the two, all are highly complex and some are relatively intangible.

Second, guidance calls for much local research in such fields as students' needs and interests, occupational opportunities, and the like. Findings of this local research can then be coordinated with findings of similar research in other localities.

Third, guidance requires the development of an authentic, sizable body of scientific information and devices. To develop this body of knowledge, researchers must chart the guidance area of education. Then, each researcher must assume responsibility for investigating one problem or field within the area. For this investigation, he should preferably select localities that are typical or representative. If he does so, his findings are likely to be widely applicable.

---

[17] *Ibid.,* p. 24.

[18] *How to Use the Criteria for Evaluating Guidance Programs in Secondary Schools, Form B,* Misc. 3317-A (Washington, D.C.: Office of Education, Division of Vocational Education, Occupational Information and Guidance Service, March, 1949).

Up to now, the development of guidance services has come mainly through the efforts of individual researchers, each working more or less on his own. Had those researchers done more to coordinate their efforts, they would probably have advanced guidance services considerably beyond the present stage. In the immediate future, guidance workers, other personnel workers, teachers, and other staff members— all can profit from researches and evaluations that are conducted according to cooperative planning. This cooperation may be among schools and colleges; it may also be between schools or colleges and commercial, industrial, or other organizations. Such cooperation is most likely to produce continuous and widespread improvement of the guidance services offered in educational institutions and elsewhere.

SUMMARY

Scientific research and evaluation in the area of guidance services are inseparable. If guidance services are to contribute effectively to the development both of individuals and society, they must be based upon scientific research and evaluation. Only through such research and evaluation can guidance workers determine the adequacy of the principles, procedures, and tools within their area of responsibilities. Only thus can they help students to solve their major problems, the subject of the chapters in the next part of this book.

SUGGESTED READINGS

Brayfield, Arthur H. (ed.). *Readings in Modern Methods of Counseling.* New York: D. Appleton-Century-Crofts Company, Inc., 1950. Pp. 445-520.

Froehlich, Clifford P. *Guidance Services in Smaller Schools.* New York: McGraw-Hill Book Company, Inc., 1950. Pp. 308-339.

Hartley, David, and Hedlund, Paul A. "Reactions of High-School Seniors to Their Guidance Programs," University of the State of New York *Bulletin,* No. 1411 (September, 1952). State Education Building, Albany 1, N.Y.

Hoppock, Robert. *Group Guidance: Principles, Techniques, and Evaluation.* New York: McGraw-Hill Book Company, Inc., 1949. Pp. 157-224.

Monroe, W. S. (ed.). *Encyclopedia of Educational Research.* New York: Macmillan Company, 1950.

Rothney, John W. M., and Roens, Bert A. *Guidance of American Youth.* Cambridge: Harvard University Press, 1950. Pp. 202-240.

Smith, Glenn E. *Principles and Practices of the Guidance Program.* New York: Macmillan Company, 1951. Pp. 336-352.

Wrenn, C. Gilbert. *Student Personnel Work in College.* New York: The Ronald Press Company, 1951. Pp. 475-508.

PART III

Solving Students' Major Problems

CHAPTER ELEVEN

Helping Students Solve Educational Problems

THIS IS the first of four chapters that consider the major problems encountered by students. For discussion purposes, these problems are grouped according to three types: educational, vocational, and personal. In reality, however, a given problem cannot be classified as belonging to one type exclusively. Such a problem usually has a variety of aspects, aspects that are characteristic of problems of several types.[1]

Take, for example, the high-school junior whose major educational problem is to decide which elective courses to take. He wants his electives to contribute in maximum degree to his preparation for entrance into the occupation of his choice. His problem of course selection, therefore, is vocational as well as educational. That problem also involves such personal considerations as the financial status of his family, the pressure exerted by his family toward his entering a certain kind of work, or the status of his physical and mental health.

In the light of the foregoing, the present chapter discusses not only the main educational problems of students but also the noneducational aspects of these problems. At times, these aspects may become so important that they in themselves are problems. Although guidance workers deal with students whose educational problems often have vocational and personal implications, they must often give their first attention to educational problems as such. These include the problems confronted by students who are entering a new school or college situation.

---

[1] Shirley A. Hamrin and Blanche B. Paulson, *Counseling Adolescents* (Chicago: Science Research Associates, 1950), pp. 187, 188.

ORIENTATION OF STUDENTS TO A NEW
SCHOOL SITUATION

Guidance workers should provide means whereby students quickly and surely become oriented to a new educational environment. Such orientation is particularly essential at those steps on the educational ladder where students are changing from one grade to the next higher grade or from one school to another. If this orientation is skillful and realistic, it can help decrease the intensity and limit the extent of the educational problems faced by these students.

Every time a student enters the next higher grade of school, he meets a new set of circumstances. These circumstances usually include a new teacher or teachers, new fellow students, and new learning materials. Even if the student has the same teacher as the year before, many of the same fellow students, and the same or similar subjects to study, he is involved in a situation that has many new elements.

Among all transition points in a student's schooling, some are more pronounced: for example, at the end of the third grade; at the end of the sixth or the eighth grade (depending on how the school system is organized); and at the end of high school. At these points, the typical student usually has difficulties in making adjustments that are satisfying and successful. As is to be expected, students vary in the ease with which they accommodate themselves to a new educational situation. On the whole, these students adjust easily or with difficulty according to the characteristics of personality that they possess and according to the assistance that they receive from the school's staff.

Orientation of Pupils to High School

At the transition point in the elementary school when pupils enter the next higher grade, the teacher has the responsibility of orienting members of his class to the new situation early in the academic year. Usually, this orientation is a relatively easy process. Much more difficult is the orientation of eighth-grade pupils to high-school entrance.

In comparison with the elementary school, the high school

is much more complex in organization and much more diverse in curricular offerings. For this reason, the orientation of new pupils to high school should be conducted on a carefully-planned and systematic basis. Many high schools initiate their orientation program by getting acquainted with prospective pupils while they are in the eighth grade. This is usually done by the high-school's freshman counselors.

If the high school follows the practice of getting in touch with pupils at the beginning of the second semester of the eighth grade, a pupil and his parents have adequate time to become well acquainted with a high-school counselor and to consider carefully all the matters involved in that pupil's orientation before high-school entrance. Thus, all concerned can make deliberate decisions that take into account all the factors pertinent to the pupil's future school situation.

What the Freshman Counselor Should Do

As the first step in orienting eighth-graders to high-school entrance, the freshman counselor should acquaint himself in detail with all the important information about each pupil. Much of this information usually appears in the pupil's cumulative record; this record, for example, shows the pupil's marks in various subjects of study, his scores and ranks on standardized tests and inventories, and his teacher's ratings and statements on personality characteristics and behavior.

In some elementary schools, the foregoing information appears in the pupil's personnel folder. This folder is maintained by the elementary-school counselor or by the school psychologist. Such a folder contains a variety of information not only about the pupil's school marks and test scores, but also about his interests and hobbies, his home and family background, and the like. No matter where or how the information about a pupil is kept in an elementary school, the freshman counselor should obtain and study that information before he first confers with that pupil.

If an elementary school does not have adequate information about its eighth-grade pupils, the freshman counselor may arrange with the principal to secure the desired data. This arrangement may include the administration of a standardized scholastic aptitude test to all eighth-graders and the filling out of a personal data questionnaire for each pupil.

For each eighth-grader, the freshman counselor needs a summary of information that can be used currently in advising the pupil about his ninth-grade program and that can be transmitted later to the high school. To obtain this summary, the counselor may use a summary information form like that shown in Figure 8. In filling out this form, the freshman counselor or the elementary-school staff member can draw upon the information that appears in a pupil's cumulative record or personnel folder.

As the second step in orienting eighth-grade pupils, the freshman counselor should meet with each eighth-grade class. At this session, he should briefly describe the educational programs that are available in the high school. These programs consist of different types of curricula: commercial, technical, vocational, and college preparatory, for example. The counselor should then indicate the courses within each curriculum and the occupational fields toward which that curriculum leads. After this presentation, the counselor should encourage the pupils to ask questions and to make comments.

If possible, the counselor should also meet with the parents of eighth-graders. Such a meeting should be in the evening so that fathers as well as mothers can attend. At this parents' gathering, the counselor outlines the various high-school curricula and leads the discussion that should follow. He also invites interested parents to have personal conferences with him or with other high-school counselors.

If the freshman counselor arranges a personal conference with a pupil's parents, he should request that the pupil also be present. During this conference, each participant and especially the pupil should have the opportunity to express himself. In some cases, the counselor may wisely hold later conferences with the parents alone or with the pupil alone.

As the third step, the freshman counselor should arrange to have groups of eighth-graders visit the high school during the semester prior to entrance. During such a visit, the pupils can attend an interesting and informative assembly. They also

FIGURE 8

SUMMARY INFORMATION FORM FOR EIGHTH-GRADE PUPIL WHO IS
ABOUT TO ENTER HIGH SCHOOL

(Front of form)

Pupil's name_____
         Last   First   Middle

Home address_____

Date of birth_____ Place of birth_____

Father's
name_____ Father's
occupation_____

Mother's
maiden
name_____ Mother's
occupation
if employed_____

PUPIL'S SCHOOL HISTORY

Name of elementary school_____

Grades repeated,
if any_____ Grades skipped,
if any_____

Pupil strongest in these subjects _____

_____

Pupil weakest in these subjects _____

_____

Comments on pupil's school history _____

_____

_____

_____

FIGURE 8—*Continued*

SUMMARY INFORMATION FORM FOR EIGHTH-GRADE PUPIL WHO IS
ABOUT TO ENTER HIGH SCHOOL

(Back of form)

Pupil's name_____

PUPIL'S PERFORMANCE ON STANDARDIZED TESTS

Pupil's grade when test was taken	Date of test administration	Name of Test (and Form)	Pupil's standing on test		
			in local school: Percentile	on national norms: Percentile	Grade

Other information about pupil (interests and hobbies; occupational interests; physical disabilities, if any; special problems — personal, family, etc.)

_____

_____

_____

Date_____ Name of person filling in this form_____

can be taken on a conducted tour to points of interest in the high-school building.

The eighth-graders may make out their freshman programs of courses before their visit or at the time of their visit. Or, they may postpone this registration until they enter the high school at the beginning of the next semester.

As the fourth step, the freshman counselor on his own or with other staff members should conduct an orientation program for new high-school students. This program should start early in the first semester of the freshman year. During the first week of classes, to illustrate, the program should give new students the information that they need at once to understand and to adjust to high school. This part of the program can be carried on through presentations and discussions in assemblies, homerooms, or division rooms. Thereby, students can become familiar with such important matters as these: the traditions of the school; the guidance services available; the opportunities for participation in extracurricular activities; the student government; the regulations concerning absences; the use of the library; the procedures for changing programs of study; and the rules of conduct.

Information such as the foregoing may appear in a student's handbook, a guide for the youth who is entering a high school or college. The institution may distribute copies of this handbook to new students in the summer prior to registration or during the opening days of the academic year. Such a booklet should be written in an interesting style; it should have an attractive format. If the institution cannot afford a printed book, it may be able to mimeograph one. No matter what the handbook's form, this booklet can be of real service in orienting freshman students to their new high school or college.

Orientation of Students to College

Through their guidance services, many colleges and universities have orientation programs for their new students. These programs nearly always include means whereby a staff member and an incoming freshman early become acquainted with each other. Through such assistance, many of the educational problems of the new student are eased if not solved;

and certain other problems are prevented. As the staff member is learning the characteristics of the new freshman, he informs that student about the new institution and its demands.

In the typical college or university, field representatives interview prospective students usually during the so-called *College Days* that are held in some high schools. In interviewing a high-school senior, for example, a college representative tells that pupil of the educational opportunities that are available at his institution; he also learns from that pupil what the latter's interests, ambitions, and plans are. Often the main subject of discussion is the youth's problem of financing his college education.

Ideally, during such an interview, the college representative should try to help the youth to choose the higher institution that will best serve *all* his needs. If the college representative clearly feels that the young person would be better served by attending another college, he should indicate that such is the case.[2]

If a high-school pupil or graduate applies for admission to college, he is, of course, required to fill out an application form. On this form, the youth records a variety of detailed information about himself and about his family; sometimes he is required to submit a brief autobiographical statement. The youth must also provide the college with other information, for instance, a high-school transcript of all the courses he took and all the marks he received. In addition, the youth may have to take a college entrance examination. If the youth is admitted to the college, all or most of the foregoing information about him is usually made available to his counselor or advisor.

The typical college orients its new students not only through individual counseling but also through group activities. At registration time, the college conducts on its campus what is known as *Orientation Days, Orientation Week,* or *Freshman Week.* The group program carried on includes such activities as these: administration of psychological and placement tests; presentation of descriptions of the available courses (both re-

---

[2] C. Gilbert Wrenn, *Student Personnel Work in College* (New York: The Ronald Press Company, 1951), pp. 276-278.

quired and elective) and of the class schedules for various courses; explanation of the terms not usually known to college freshmen (units of credit, honor points, grade-point averages); outlines of the basic scholastic standards that students must meet to remain in the college; attendance regulations; history of the institution; discussion of the college's social regulations; discussion of effective study habits; presentation of opportunities in extracurricular activities; description of available guidance services; social affairs for freshmen and their faculty counselors; advisement of freshmen concerning their first term's or year's course programs.[3]

The activities just described provide two-way educational benefits: *First,* they brief the student on his new school. And *second,* they brief the school on the new student. Regarding the latter, if the school obtains information about the youth *before* he starts his first year in college, it is able to render the greatest possible assistance to him. As the first term progresses, the counselor or the guidance services staff will add more facts and data to its store of information about this student. The more complete this information the better prepared the counselor will be to aid the student in meeting and solving his educational problems.

STUDENTS' MAJOR EDUCATIONAL PROBLEMS

Before attempting to list the principal educational problems of students, the reader should note that none of these problems will necessarily trouble all students. Nor will the same problem trouble any two students to the same degree. Even so, studies of the problems of large numbers of students indicate that such problems can be classified according to a few major types. Each of these problem types will be presented and discussed next.

Selecting a High-School Curriculum

In some American high schools, the freshman student still has little to choose from in terms of curricula. In such schools, there is really only one curriculum; this curriculum is usually

---

[3] *Ibid.,* pp. 274-276.

made up of the courses that fulfill the entrance requirements of most liberal arts colleges. These courses usually include English composition and literature, history, civics, biology, chemistry, physics, algebra, geometry, and certain foreign languages. Valuable as these courses may be to the student who expects to enter a liberal arts college, some of them are relatively worthless to the boy or girl who is interested in preparing for a commercial position after graduation, for example.

In many high schools, however, the entering freshmen can select a curriculum from the variety that is available. In a four-year high school, he may choose any one of the following curricula: college preparatory, business, secretarial, scientific, home economics, technical, vocational or trade, and general. In a large city, some of these curricula may be offered only in certain high schools. One high school may have curricula that prepare its students for jobs in the manual trades; another, curricula that prepare its students for advanced training in professional fields such as engineering.

If a high school offers a wide range of choice among curricula, some students may decide quickly and easily which curricula they want to take. Such boys and girls know, or at least think they know, what curricula are best for them. Other students, however, may have difficulty in making appropriate selections. All these youth need help in choosing the high-school curricula that meet their needs and abilities.

To assist any youth in his choice of a high-school curriculum, the counselor should first inform himself about this counselee; to get this information, the counselor can employ the techniques already discussed in Chapters 6 and 7. These techniques yield many significant informational items that both the counselor and his counselee should consider. Among these items are the counselee's basic mental abilities, his strongest interests, his special aptitudes, his level of motivation, his ambitions, his family's background and its financial resources, and his personal qualities.

On the basis of the foregoing information and of the information related to the available curricula, the counselee with the counselor's assistance may decide upon the curriculum that appears to be best for him. Even so, this counselee may still have other decisions to make, usually at a later date. For example, after considering the facts, a boy may choose the science curriculum. After starting work in the courses in this curriculum, he may be faced with such a question as this: "Should I direct my training toward preparing for advanced study in the more theoretical or the more practical phases of science?" The former, the counselee learns, may lead to a career in teaching or research in a university; the latter, to a career in engineering in some industry.

However, even if the counselee delays his decision as to his eventual career, he will find that the courses in the science curriculum are valuable to him. Such courses usually include algebra, plane geometry, advanced algebra, solid geometry, trigonometry, chemistry, and physics. By taking these courses and by making good marks in them, this youth can probably gain admission to a school of engineering or to a college offering a major in science.

As a general rule, the high-school boy or girl who is promising "college material" but who is still uncertain about his college plans should probably take the college preparatory curriculum. This curriculum includes courses in subjects that cover the main fields of knowledge. Through his experiences in these courses and in the light of his personal circumstances, such a youth develops a sound basis for deciding what he should do after high-school graduation. In his senior year, he may decide to enter a four-year liberal arts college. Or, he may decide to attend a junior college, a business school, or a technical institute. Or, he may decide to terminate his formal schooling and to obtain a position as a learner or apprentice in a trade.

Selecting a College

Assume that a high-school senior and his family have decided that he will go to college. Then, such questions as these arise: What is this student's specific educational and vocational goal? Should he attend a neighboring junior college for two years and then transfer to a four-year college? Or, should he enter a four-year institution that may not be near his home?

Organizing Information about Colleges and Other Schools

In advising a high-school senior as to which college to attend, the counselor should have at hand a wide variety of source materials. For instance, he should have a widely representative collection of catalogs and other publications issued by colleges, universities, and other post-high-school educational institutions.

These materials may be on file in the guidance office or in the high-school library. Wherever available, these materials should be arranged alphabetically by name of institution or geographically by location. To promote their use, the counselor or librarian should time and again call these materials to the attention of students, particularly juniors and seniors.

Both the counselor and the librarian should keep in mind that students may have difficulty in reading and comprehending the typical college catalog. Therefore, they should guide students, in groups or individually, in the reading of college catalogs and in the understanding of the technical terms therein.

To aid counselors and students in making effective use of the file of college catalogs, the counselor should prepare an accompanying card file and folder file. Each of these files should have such subject headings as these: liberal arts colleges (men's, women's, and coeducational); professional schools (medicine, dentistry, nursing, engineering, and law, for example); junior colleges (men's, women's, and coeducational); business schools; and trade schools.

The counselor should keep the card file and the folder file that are related to colleges and their catalogs up-to-date. He should make notations on the cards and add cards as needed. He should also enter pertinent information in the folder file. These entries, of course, represent the information that the counselor personally gathers over a period of time.

The counselor should constantly look for information other than that appearing in college catalogs. As he obtains this information, he should enter it in his card file or folder file, for later reference in his counseling work. Such information may come from a variety of sources. The counselor, for example, can interview or correspond with young men and women (particularly those from the local high school) who are attending a given college or who are graduates of it. Thereby he can obtain their reactions to the college as a whole, or to its educational offerings, housing accommodations, or social life. Moreover, the counselor can determine the attitudes of employers and others toward the college. Through personal visits, the counselor can get first-hand information about the college. By reading professional publications, he can get further knowledge of the institution.

Working alone, the counselor in a typical high school will find it difficult to collect the catalogs wanted or the other information needed. However, if his high school has a librarian, this staff member can help assemble and file catalogs and other published materials. Moreover, if his school has a staff member who performs the functions of a registrar, this "registrar" can provide considerable information about particular colleges, universities, and other post-high-school institutions.

In addition to the sources previously mentioned, the counselor should have at least some of the publications that appear in the list at the end of this chapter. These publications help the counselor to complete the store of information that he should have at hand. Without these publications, both the counselor and counselee are definitely handicapped.

FACTORS IN CONSIDERING AN EDUCATIONAL INSTITUTION

Assume that a high school has assembled a body of information about post-high-school educational offerings. Drawing upon this information, a student works to solve his problem of deciding which institution to attend after graduation. Suppose that this student has determined, at least tentatively, what his educational goal is. Then he must consider or reconsider such significant factors as these: his educational needs and wants; his personal characteristics; the requirements for admission to an institution; the expenses of attending that school; the opportunities for partial self-support; the availability of scholarships and loan funds; the location of the institution; the living accommodations there; the job placement services for

graduates and former students; the student extracurricular organizations; and the accreditation status of the school.

Matching Abilities and Requirements

In considering a post-high-school institution, the counselor and counselee usually give their principal attention to
its educational offerings; they slight or ignore other important
factors. These other factors may be crucial in some situations.
To illustrate, a college's requirements for admission and its
scholastic standards may be very high—in fact, so high that the
counselee probably cannot meet them. In other words, the
counselee's general and specific abilities, his previous scholastic achievement, and his promise of future attainment do not
measure up to that college's present requirements. If the counselee, by chance, were admitted to the college, he would probably encounter disappointment, frustration, and failure. For
this reason, the counselor should always help the counselee to
examine and to relate two main factors in choosing a college—
the counselee's scholastic abilities, and the college's academic
requirements.

Personal Preferences and Needs

Also, in considering a future educational institution, the
counselee should take into account his personal inclinations.
One counselee may prefer a woman's college; another, a man's
college; still another, a coeducational college. Also, one counselee may favor a church-related college; another, a secular
college.

The counselee's need for social development may be a significant factor in choosing a college. One counselee may be a
reserved, shy person who lacks aggressiveness. He needs to attend a college that will stimulate him to participate in social
and extracurricular activities, activities that contribute to his
all-round development. Another counselee may be a person to
whom social life comes very easily. As a result, he tends to
spend too much time in activities outside the classroom. Such
a counselee needs a college that emphasizes academic work.

The foregoing statements are, of course, general ones.
Conclusions concerning any one individual need to be con-

sidered in the light of the individual's total personality and his life goals.

Financial Costs

Every youth who is selecting a post-high-school institution obviously should consider the financial costs. A student can usually obtain definite figures or estimates of such costs as tuition fees, room, and board from the catalogs of most schools.

To these costs, the student must add the cost of transportation between his home and the school, keeping in mind the number of round trips he will probably make during the academic year. This total anticipated transportation cost may be an important factor in selecting a school. If the student cannot finance all of his expected school costs, he should obtain from the school information about the availability of scholarships and part-time employment.

Placement Services

All too frequently, the high-school counselor and his counselee neglect to find out about the job-placement services of an educational institution; these services, of course, are designed to help graduating students and graduates to obtain full-time positions.

The extent to which a school renders effective job-placement services to a graduate or former student is an important factor in evaluating that institution whether that evaluation is made by a prospective student or by someone else in the outside world. Other things being equal, the high-school student should favor an institution that has numerous contacts with prospective employers and a good record of job placements. Although an institution's job-placement services are usually more important to a young person immediately after graduation than later, these services deserve careful attention and evaluation on the part of a prospective student.

Accreditation

In advising a high-school senior, the counselor should have reliable information about the general educational standing of the institution under consideration. More specifically, he should know whether that institution is accredited. In the United States, there are various national, regional, and state accrediting agencies. Among these agencies are associations of secondary-schools and colleges. Each association has set up certain educational criteria. If an institution meets these criteria, the association accredits or approves it.

During the past 25 years, the accrediting associations have constantly improved their methods and raised their standards of accreditation. For some time and at present, these standards have been in terms of such important criteria as these: purposes of the institution; competence of faculty and other staff personnel in terms of training and experience; quality of administration; financial stability; library and laboratory facilities; character of the general plant with reference to the aims of the institution; and extent and quality of student personnel services.

In the earlier years of rating educational institutions, the typical accrediting association tended to place too much emphasis on the extent to which an institution met exact quantitative standards, such as the number of volumes in the library, the average number of students per class, and the amount of productive endowment per student. For the past 15 years, however, the typical accrediting organization has increasingly stressed the degree to which the institution through its available procedures and facilities is fulfilling its stated objectives.

In evaluating a particular school, an accrediting association makes wide use of rating scales that cover various important aspects of that school. The association then compares that school's ratings with the average ratings of like schools. Although that school may be somewhat deficient according to ratings in certain aspects, its over-all rating may compare favorably with those of other schools. If so, the school is classified as accredited. One leader in this newer approach to accreditation has been the North Central Association of Colleges and Secondary Schools.

For some types of institutions such as private schools for diesel engineers or television servicemen, there are as yet no recognized agencies of accreditation. Even so, a counselor should not question the reputation of a particular school solely because it is not accredited. Rather, he should try to obtain reliable and complete information about that institution. This information may include acceptance of the school's graduates by employers, by other schools, and by others; quality of the instructors' training and experience; available facilities for instruction; financial policies with reference to students; and general stability of the institution. On the basis of this information, the counselor is able to give sound advice to interested high-school students and their parents.

APPLYING FOR ADMISSION

Most high-school seniors and their parents need and welcome suggestions from counselors concerning the procedure of applying for admission to another school. Many seniors do not know what a high-school transcript is; many do not know that they themselves must ask the high school to send their transcripts to the admissions office of the institution where they are applying for admission.

In some instances, high-school seniors need help in filling out application forms for admission to other institutions. In providing this help, the counselor should make sure that a student who is filling out such a form provides accurate and complete information on all the items therein.

If the application form calls for the names of references, the counselor should advise the student as to the types of persons to be listed. For example, the student should give as references the names of persons who are well-acquainted with him; only if this is the case can that person write in specific not general terms about the applicant. Before listing a person as a reference, the student should obtain that person's permission.

If the application form calls for an autobiography, the student should make sure that his autobiography is clearly outlined and thought-through in advance; he should then write the autobiography carefully, making certain that it is easy to read and is free from errors in grammar or spelling. If the application form specifies the content and length of the autobiography, the student should observe these specifications. In this aspect as well as in all others of the application for admission, the student will be wise to follow specifically all instructions with reference to the application form.

CHOOSING COURSES OF STUDY

After a student has been admitted to a school, he has the problem of selecting an appropriate curriculum—this, of course, is a problem that often requires educational guidance. If the institution is a professional or technical school, the curriculum is usually prescribed; therefore, the student does not confront the problem of deciding which curriculum to follow. However, if the institution offers a variety of curricula, the student may decide which curriculum is best for him. Although this curriculum specifies many required courses, it also may offer some elective courses.

In the latter situation, the counselor again has a real opportunity to help the counselee to make wise decisions. In deciding which elective courses to sign up for, the counselee should be encouraged to consider these factors: the courses he should take to obtain a general, all-round education; the courses he needs to explore different subject-matter fields, fields that may be new to him and that may help him to develop broader interests; and the courses he should study to supplement or complement his major interests and abilities.

Both in a junior college and in a four-year college, the student is faced with the need to choose his major field of specialization. When the student enters as a freshman, he usually makes a tentative choice. Later, he may find it necessary or desirable to re-examine that choice; through this review, he may confirm his earlier choice or replace it with another choice.

Whatever a student's chosen field of specialization in college, that student knows that he must be self-supporting upon graduation. With this in mind, he should consider carefully the educational program that will best prepare him for a field of employment. In thinking through this program, the student should realize that he has limited time, finances, and other resources to devote to it. In the light of the foregoing, the counselor should from time to time help the student to review all the information considered during any earlier appraisal. This

information, of course, includes data about his abilities, potentialities, and interests. On the basis of this review, the counselor may arrange for the student to take additional tests, to
seek further occupational information, and to relate the findings from these two sources.

HANDLING EDUCATIONAL WEAKNESSES

Counselors in high schools and post-high-school institutions often realize that the educational problems brought to
them by students require diagnosis in terms of the strengths
and weaknesses in the student's educational preparation.

Consider, for example, the high-school sophomore who is
having a very difficult time in meeting the teacher's requirements in a course in literature. Although the student is interested in the subject, is well-motivated, and works diligently,
he is in danger of failing the course. As a result, both the student and the teacher feel frustrated if not at a complete loss.

As the *first* step in improving the situation, the counselor
diagnoses this student's educational problem. His analysis shows
that the student has the following weaknesses: a very slow rate
of silent reading, much below that of the average high-school
sophomore; an inadequate vocabulary; and lack of effective
techniques for outlining and taking notes on assigned reading.
The counselor's analysis also reveals that the student is strong
in the ability to express critical evaluations of literature. But
this strength is more than outweighed by the aforesaid weaknesses.

As the *second* step, the counselor and the English teacher
plan and carry out a remedial program designed to help the
student to overcome his weaknesses. They give the student
exercises to increase his rate of effective reading; special training to expand his vocabulary; and instruction to improve his
methods of studying. If the school has a remedial teacher, this
teacher, of course, takes an active part in this step.

In both the diagnostic and remedial steps, it should be
pointed out, the counselor takes into account the student's
earlier educational preparation as it bears on the latter's current problem. This type of problem, that has its roots in the

past, is commonly confronted by counselors at all levels of education.[4, 5]

The educational problems of college students are often due to their previous school experiences. In the elementary school, they as pupils may not have made normal progress because they did not master fundamental skills in reading, writing, and arithmetic. Even so, they may have been promoted regularly from grade to grade. When these pupils entered high school, they may still have been below-standard in the three basic skills just mentioned. And the same may have been true when they graduated from high school. Because these students never developed the necessary skills in the "three R's," they entered college with handicaps that jeopardized their chances for academic success.

Uncorrected educational deficiencies are more serious at the college level than at the high school level. This is because the requirements for succeeding in college subjects are usually exacting. The college student, for instance, must cover relatively difficult material. If he has educational weaknesses in basic skills or subjects, he is unable to do assignments or to pass examinations.

To reduce if not to eliminate the incidence of academic failures, the counselor should give a battery of tests to new students just before or soon after they enter his institution. The results of these tests indicate the strengths and weaknesses in the academic abilities of these students. For these students, the counselor should also obtain information about their study skills and habits and about their abilities in such fields of communication as speech, reading, and writing. By using the aforesaid information, the counselor can identify the students who are in need of remedial instruction in fundamental skills and of special assistance in subject-matter areas. Also by employing this information, the counselor can locate the students who are better-than-average in the skills, habits, and knowledge required for academic success.

---

[4] Shirley A. Hamrin and Blanche B. Paulson, *Counseling Adolescents* (Chicago: Science Research Associates, 1950), pp. 203-205.

[5] C. Gilbert Wrenn, *Student Personnel Work in College* (New York: The Ronald Press Company, 1951), chapters 5 and 6.

OVERCOMING LACK OF MOTIVATION

A student's educational problem may be due to the level of his motivation.[6] The student who has little or no academic motivation, for example, attends school not because he wants to go but because his parents make him do so. Or, he hates school because it is not the one he wanted to attend. Or, he dislikes the subjects he is taking because he has little interest or success in them. Or, he fails to take his studies seriously because he has no clear-cut educational goal. A student's low motivation in school may also be due to his strong preference for nonschool activities.

However low the student's educational motivation and whatever its causes, the counselor has the responsibility, *first,* to search for the roots of the student's problem and, *second,* to attempt to secure the student's cooperation in working out a solution. In an extreme case, the low-motivated student may refuse to cooperate even after numerous opportunities to do so. Then the counselor may have to recommend that the student be transferred to another school. If such a student is at or below the maximum age for compulsory school attendance, he *must* be kept in school—his present school or another school. If the student is above that compulsory attendance age, he may leave school voluntarily. If not, he may be asked to withdraw.

Whether the low-motivated uncooperative student is to stay in his present school or not, the counselor should try to help him to develop an educational plan. This plan, to illustrate, may include arrangements to transfer to a school that better fits the youth's abilities, interests, and resources.

The wise counselor recognizes that the administrative actions just suggested are negative and therefore should be used as the last resort. He holds the attitude that most cases of lack of motivation can be cured or improved by positive means. He makes every effort to determine the underlying cause of a student's lack of motivation. He then employs every available technique to assist that student toward making a satisfactory educational adjustment, an adjustment that at least keeps the youth in school.

---

[6] By permission from *Counseling Adolescents,* by E. G. Williamson. Copyright, 1950. McGraw-Hill Book Company, Inc., pp. 268-271.

In the light of the foregoing, the counselor may arrange to have the student transferred at the end of the semester to a different curriculum or to different elective courses. Or, he may help the student to obtain a more satisfying social situation. For example, the youth may join a new club, run for a class office, or, if a college student, find new rooming or boarding accommodations. Through suggesting or providing such new situations, the counselor may assist the student to revise his goals or to modify his attitudes. These changes, in turn, may help to motivate the student and to enlist his cooperation.

The importance of the student's degree of motivation for academic study cannot be overemphasized. This motivation definitely involves the student's emotions. If the student feels that a certain course of study is valuable to him and that active and serious participation therein is desirable, he is likely to gain much more from that course. In the course, the student may be taught better methods of study; he may be given individual assistance by the teacher. But the student will not cooperate to the fullest extent possible unless he is motivated by drives within himself to do his part in the learning process.

OVERCOMING LACK OF INTEREST

Closely related to motivation is interest. If a student has a strong internal drive to reach a goal, his interest in the activities required to achieve it are usually high. But if this student has little motivation toward that goal, his interest in the necessary activities usually is low if not absent. For this reason, a student's expression of lack of interest should be taken seriously by the teacher and counselor. Neither should brush aside the expression with a comment that the student is "lazy," "dull," or "foolish." Rather, both should look for the cause of the student's lack of interest and should then take steps to improve the situation.

Building Interest through Teaching Changes

Consider the case of Howard, who was taking a civics course. Howard felt himself getting bogged down by the detailed descriptions of the machinery of government. At the start, he was enthusiastic about the course. As the course proceeded, however, he began to lose interest. As a result, Howard applied himself less and less to the course; he soon fell behind in his work. This situation worried him so much that he discussed the problem with his teacher.

After talking with Howard, his teacher immediately took stock of her methods of handling the subject, her classroom activities, and her assignments of homework. On the basis of this stock-taking, she decided that part of the blame for Howard's lack of interest and success in the course rested on her. For instance, she began to realize that her approach to teaching the machinery of government was dry-as-dust and not close enough to real life.

Soon thereafter, Howard's teacher dropped her formal presentation of the branches of the federal government; instead, without the use of a textbook, she started her students on the search for facts about the government of their local community. Their first project was a visit to the city hall. Almost at once, Howard's interest in the civics course went up. And so did the interest of other students in the class.

While the students were gathering local information and were discussing it in class, they were reading books, magazine articles, and newspaper stories on local government. The students' interest reached its peak when the class wrote up as a group project an extensive description of the government at work in their own community.

After the students had developed this background of information and insight into local government, their teacher had little difficulty in holding the attention of the class. She readily led Howard and his classmates to study their state government and the national government.

In this situation, Howard was fortunate in having as a teacher one who met his problem by analyzing her own teaching methods and by modifying them. All too often, subject-matter teachers do not take similar steps to arouse the interest of their students.

Building Interest through Counseling

As another example, consider the case of Barbara, who was enrolled in another civics class. She flatly said that she saw no reason for a girl to be concerned about the organization and operation of government. Barbara's teacher referred her to the counselor. During the interview, Barbara stated that her sole aim in going to school was to prepare herself to be an efficient secretary. Nothing else interested her.

During interviews with Barbara, the counselor discussed the ways in which government influences the daily life of every citizen. He also pointed out the opportunities and the responsibilities of citizenship. Near the end of the third interview, Barbara haltingly but voluntarily acknowledged that there were good reasons for a girl who is a prospective secretary to have a basic understanding of the workings of the local, state, and federal governments. As an outcome of counseling, Barbara's attitude toward the civics class improved markedly and she completed the course satisfactorily.

Building Interest in Required Courses

It is a common observation that the more *attention* a person gives to an activity, the more likely he is to become *interested* in it. In Howard's case, the teacher modified her approach to civics. As an outcome, the boy's attention was attracted to the subject under study and his interest in the course was increased. In Barbara's case, the counselor helped her to focus her attention on the practical reasons for studying civics. As a result, her interest in the subject was aroused.

There are situations, however, when a student who lacks interest in a subject must discipline himself to do the assigned work therein. Even if this student's reading and other work is distasteful to him and appears to be somewhat superficial to his teacher, such work may result in his accumulation of valuable bits of information. As the student gradually builds up his knowledge of the subject, he may develop greater interest in it.

At some time or other, nearly every student has had to study a subject or to acquire a skill that originally was of little or no interest to him. Because of this lack of interest, he had to discipline himself to pay attention to the subject under study or to the skill to be mastered. With regard to a subject, such attention is likely to yield some information; this information, in turn, tends to stimulate interest; and increased interest begets more attention. Thus, through attention, the student gains interest and acquires knowledge or skill. And the learning process itself becomes both voluntary and satisfying.

In high school or college, students most commonly lack interest in the prescribed subjects of study. This is probably due to the fact that all students, without exception, must take these subjects. Lack of interest in a required subject bothers the counselor quite as much as it troubles the counselee. As Williamson has written: [7] "To the counselor the prevalent notion that all students must take the same required courses of study is a contradiction. Even the most casual diagnosis of a pupil reveals peculiarities and idiosyncrasies which preclude satisfying and satisfactory adjustment in a standard curriculum whether it is in the kindergarten or in the graduate school."

Until an educational institution changes its regulations so that a student can choose alternative required courses, that student will have to make the best of the situation as it is. To adapt himself to this situation, the student may pursue one of the following lines of thinking or action: He will accept the required courses as necessary parts of his education. Or, he will attempt to discover how the required courses can contribute to his particular field of interest, either directly or indirectly. Or, he will force himself by sheer self-discipline to give serious attention to the unwanted, uninteresting courses. Any of the foregoing lines may help the student to develop a genuine and growing interest in such courses.

DEVELOPING STUDY SKILLS AND HABITS

Among high-school and college students, a common educational problem is lack of good study techniques. To do good schoolwork, a student must be proficient in certain study skills and habits. These are not acquired by chance; they are the result of training as are those needed to operate a typewriter competently or to play golf expertly. If a student is to develop the efficiency that is essential to his academic success, he must have opportunities to learn and to practice good study skills and habits.

[7] *Ibid.*, p. 266.

All too many students do not have the "know-how" of effective study; they lack the skills needed to prepare their school assignments quickly, accurately, and completely. All too many also do not have the persistent drive to study efficiently; they lack the habits required to perform their schoolwork systematically and conscientiously.

The Need for a How-to-Study Course

Because so many students have inadequate study skills and habits, a school or college should make definite provisions for training all its students in study techniques. This training should preferably be offered early in the freshman year. It may be given as a unit in a freshman course in English or as a short noncredit course. In this unit or short course, students may use to advantage such publications as *Study Your Way Through School* [8] or *Studying Effectively.* [9]

At the college level, freshmen often are briefed in how-to-study techniques during Freshman Week. They then are trained in these techniques in an orientation course or in a special unit in an English course. In either type of course, the students may read and discuss a how-to-study book, for example, *A Guide to College Study.* [10] Whether students use such a book or not, they should learn better study methods by actually practicing them.

Students can be helped to improve their study methods through group instruction. A few of these students, namely those who are having special difficulties in studying, may need individual counseling assistance. Nearly all students, however, can gain much of value toward improving their study techniques by taking a short course in how-to-study, particularly if the classes therein are relatively small.

In a how-to-study course, the teacher should provide a variety of activities that include a series of practical lessons, discussions, demonstrations, and tests. Most of these activities

[8] C. D'A. Gerken, *Study Your Way Through School* (Chicago: Science Research Associates, 1953).

[9] C. Gilbert Wrenn and Robert P. Larsen, *Studying Effectively* (Stanford, California: Stanford University Press, 1949).

[10] Robert W. Frederick, Paul C. Kitchen, Agnes R. McElwee, *A Guide to College Study* (New York: D. Appleton-Century Company, 1947).

should deal directly with the study problems that students are facing in their regular subjects of study. For example, the teacher should give students actual practice in good study methods of reading a chapter in a social studies textbook for the next day's assignment, of outlining a novel for an oral report in English, and of conducting a review for a written examination in science.

At the start of a how-to-study course, the teacher may give all students the "Study Habits Inventory" that appears in *Studying Effectively,* by Wrenn and Larsen. In their book, this inventory is printed twice, at the beginning and at the end. By checking the inventory early in the course, a student gets information as to his study strengths and weaknesses; this information includes clues that are helpful to him in his efforts to improve his study skills and habits. By checking the inventory again near the end of the course, the student obtains information with reference to his total gain in study power and his further study needs.

As just implied, the Wrenn-Larsen inventory is arranged in such manner that the student can obtain an indication of the points in which he is strong or weak. For each of its items the inventory gives the page or pages in the book that a student should read to get more information on that item.

In instructing a how-to-study group or in counseling an individual student on study methods, the teacher or other staff member typically gives attention to such important matters as these:

1. Budgeting the student's time
2. Conditions for effective study (internal and external)
3. Problems of concentration
4. Efficient reading techniques
5. Learning difficulties
6. Problems of remembering
7. Note-taking methods
8. Maintenance of a notebook
9. Use of the library
10. Review and other preparation for examinations

With further reference to the foregoing discussion, the following point should be emphasized again: *Many high-school students and college students need help in developing more effective study skills and habits.* If these students take a how-to-study course early in their freshman year, they will acquire study abilities that not only benefit them immediately in their present courses but also have carry-over values into succeeding school or college years.

In assessing the need of students for how-to-study training, the experienced teacher or counselor can cite many examples of students whose educational problems were basically due to their lack of adequate study skills and habits.

In some instances, the student does not use his time wisely. To illustrate, consider the case of Joe, a high-school student. To complete his homework in all subjects, Joe needed to become a better manager of his time. Because he had a great interest and ability in English, he always studied that subject first. In fact, Joe liked English so much that he slighted his other subjects, such as algebra and Latin. To improve this situation, Joe prepared a systematic time schedule. This schedule specified certain hours day by day for studying his various subjects and for carrying on his other school-related activities. By following this schedule, Joe was able to keep up-to-date in all his subjects.

In other instances, the student does not realize that the environment in which he is attempting to study interferes with his achievement. This student may be doing his homework in the dining room where others of the family are distracting influences. He may be dividing his attention between studying and listening to the radio or watching television. He may be trying to study in a bedroom that is too cold or too hot for comfort. In still other instances, the student is disturbed by internal factors. While studying, he may be worrying about another problem. These are some of the many external and internal conditions that prevent effective study.

Occasionally a student does not study efficiently because he does not abide by the recognized laws of learning. He, for example, fails to concentrate on what he is studying. He studies passively—not actively; he "reads" a textbook chapter but cannot recall what he has read. Or, he neglects to review material carefully just before he is to take a test on it. If the teacher or counselor knows the laws of learning, he can help such a student to replace poor study skills, habits, and conditions with good ones.

HANDLING THE PROBLEM OF ACADEMIC FAILURE

The failure of students to meet the required standards of scholarship is a problem that is common to all educational institutions. Such failure is indicated in a variety of forms, as follows:

1. The student receives failing marks at the end of a marking period—at mid-term, for example.

2. The student receives failing marks at the end of a term.

3. The student unexpectedly fails his courses after one or more terms of satisfactory marks.

4. The student fails to achieve up to his capacity.

In handling such a student, the administration of a school or a college must answer questions such as the following: Recognizing that the student's failing marks in and of themselves constitute a kind of punishment, should the administration levy any other penalty against this failing student? Should such a penalty be imposed without counseling the student? If a penalty is imposed, should it be determined *after* the student has been counseled? Should the penalty be based upon the findings and recommendations of the counselor? [11]

A college's policies toward failing students depend upon a number of different factors, including these: the points of view of the teaching and administrative staff; the purposes of the school; the established traditions and the academic reputation of the college; the minimum-ability level that applicants had to equal or exceed to be admitted to the college; the necessity of maintaining a high level of enrollment; and the possible overcrowded condition of the college. Some but not all of these same factors influence a high-school's policies toward failing pupils.

Based on such factors as the foregoing, the typical college sets its standards of scholastic achievement. If a student fails to meet these standards, the college may ask him to withdraw. Or,

---

[11] Williamson, *op. cit.*, pp. 86-100.

the college may give him a second chance; it may place him on scholastic probation, say, for a term. If the student's work continues to be of unsatisfactory quality, the college may ask him to leave. After a lapse of time, the college may or may not readmit this student.

The Role of the Counselor

In dealing with failing students, the counselor is, of course, expected to work within the framework of the policies adopted by his high school or college. In the cases of certain students, the counselor may believe that the academic regulations of his institution are too inflexible, too strict, or too high. In such cases, the counselor may be able to gather and present data that may persuade the policy-makers to revise their policies.

Whether the counselor feels that his institution's academic standards are too high or that its academic policies are too rigid with reference to a failing student, he must seek answers to such questions as these: What can I do to help this failing student? If this student is fundamentally able to meet standards but has failed temporarily to do so, what can I do particularly for him? If this student is not working up to his capacity, how can I help him to improve his work? If this student has failed time after time, what should I recommend to him and to the administration? If this student does not have the ability to meet minimum standards, what positive suggestions should I make to him? If this student asks permission to withdraw from school, what actions should I take?

In a high school, the student who fails repeatedly but who according to law must stay in school cannot be dropped. However, if this failing student is above the age of compulsory school attendance, the school can drop him or he can withdraw voluntarily. But whether a failing student can or cannot leave school, the counselor should do all possible to aid him. Through studying the student's cumulative record, through conferring with his teachers, and through interviewing the student, the counselor should make every effort to assist that student in raising his marks from unsatisfactory to satisfactory levels. The counselor should also do all in his power to encourage the student to stay in school until he has graduated.

No student likes to fail at school or elsewhere. When a student receives failing marks, his pride in himself is hurt; his confidence in himself is undermined. He fears that the label of "failure" may be permanent. As a defense mechanism, some failing students appear to be quite undisturbed by low marks; a few even boast about these marks. Such students, however, are the exception, not the rule.

In working with failing students, the counselor often finds that the mores of a particular group or gang of students are important. According to the gang's mores, members may try to pass courses with as little effort as possible; they also may accept failure with a kind of braggadocio. In the case of many such boys and girls, their actions and attitudes are actually superficial. Inside, they are disappointed in themselves. They really want help, but they are not likely to seek it.

Techniques of Counseling the Failing Student

In order to assist a high-school or college youth who is failing for whatever reason, the counselor should take such steps as these:

1. Review the available information about the student's academic past and present; much of this information is on file.

2. Supplement this information by consulting teachers and others.

3. Collect information about the student's activities outside his regular program of study.

4. Analyze all the foregoing information to discover the probable reasons for the student's failure.

5. Interview the student. Through counseling, give him the opportunity to understand himself and his situation and to assume responsibility for his future course of action.

In reviewing a student's record, the counselor, of course, should devote special attention to that student's successes and failures. If the student has failing marks on his record, the counselor will seek answers to questions such as these: In which subject or subjects did the student receive failing marks? Did he get low or failing marks in the same subject over a period of years? In general, did this subject require the same or similar mental abilities for satisfactory work at successive steps of the school ladder? Are the student's low marks in a subject due, at least in part, to poor communicational abilities (reading, listening, speaking, and writing) or to inadequate study skills and habits? Answers to these questions aid the counselor in giving practical assistance to the failing student.

The counselor should also examine carefully the failing student's total school program, both curricular and extracurricular activities. With reference to these activities, he should ask: Is the student carrying a heavy, average, or light program of courses? What subjects is he taking? Are these subjects hard or easy for him? Does he have a part-time job? If so, what are his hours of work each day? Does this work leave him sufficient time for study? To what extent is he participating in extracurricular activities? How do these activities affect his academic work?

After answering the foregoing questions, the counselor should pursue more detailed lines of investigation. These lines are indicated by the following questions:

1. What specific items in the course being failed appear to cause the student particular difficulty?

2. Is the student handicapped by lack of preparation in fundamental skills or by poor work in the courses that are prerequisites for the one in which he is having trouble?

3. Has the student been absent excessively? Has he tried to make up the work thus missed?

4. Does the student have ready access to textbooks and other necessary learning aids?

5. Does the student have a budget for his time and is he observing the budget?

6. How many hours per week does the student study? Should he spend more hours in study?

7. Under what conditions does the student do his studying? Are these conditions favorable?

8. Does the student use the library to best advantage?

9. Has the student developed adequate skills in note-taking?

10. How well-motivated is the student? What are his attitudes toward the course he is failing?

11. Does the student have a physical disability? If so, can he make better adjustments to that disability?

12. Is the student under unusual mental and emotional strain? What are the reasons for this strain?

As the counselor works with a failing student, the counselee will probably help answer the aforesaid questions. He also will reveal his own point of view regarding his problem and the reasons for it. In his own mind, the counselor can then match the counselee's statements with the conclusions he has reached. If there is lack of concurrence, the counselor and the student should re-examine the evidence to discover where each has drawn incorrect inferences. This counseling should lead to a clear analysis of the fundamental reasons for the counselee's academic failure, to a definite plan for improving his situation, and to a diligent execution of that plan.

After two or three weeks, the counselor may ask the counselee's teachers for reports as to this student's most recent educational status. On the basis of these reports, the counselor may hold another interview with the counselee. If the teachers' reports show progress, the counselee will be encouraged. He may not need further counseling with reference to his academic work. But if the teachers' reports are unfavorable, he will need further assistance toward solving his problem. During a follow-up interview, the counselor may find that the counselee has not been pursuing the plan of action agreed upon; or, that the counselee has encountered new hindrances to his academic improvement. Whatever the cause of the counselee's failure to improve, he and his counselor may need to review the entire situation and to work out a more promising plan of action.

DEALING WITH INAPPROPRIATE EDUCATIONAL GOALS

Counselors in high schools and colleges often confer with young persons who are directing their energies toward inappropriate educational goals. The counselor, for example, finds that a counselee's record of earlier academic achievement and his standings on tests and inventories all indicate clearly that this student's educational goal is not fitted to his scholastic abilities and occupational interests. Such a counselee may have made his educational decisions because of his parents' insistence, because of his admiration for someone else, or because of his ambition to enter a given profession.

In working with this counselee, the counselor faces a delicate problem. He must tactfully present all of the pertinent evidence to the counselee; he must lead the counselee to recognize that his present educational goal is inappropriate for him. Then he must encourage the counselee, of his own accord and through his own insight, to develop a more fitting goal and plan.

From the point of view of the counselee who has an inappropriate educational goal, the sooner he realizes this fact the better for him. Otherwise, he may continue to pursue that goal, experiencing failure after failure as he goes along. This wastes his school time and may cause serious maladjustment in his personal life.

Sometimes the counselee who is experiencing this type of difficulty goes immediately to his counselor for assistance. If he does not do so, the counselor should soon call him in for an interview. If the counselor is quite sure that the student has made an error in his educational decision, he should discuss that error and what to do about it with the counselee. If the counselee is sensitive about his problem and if that problem requires the determination of new facts, the counselor may delay raising the question of inappropriateness of goal until a later interview.

During the first two or three years of high school, depending on the situation, the counselor may permit the counselee to develop his own educational plan and to pursue it. But if that plan does not work out, the counselor may rightly discuss with the counselee the question as to whether the latter's educational goal is suitable. In raising and discussing this matter, the counselor should be tactful and foresighted. He should give as much positive assistance as the counselee will accept.

ANSWERING QUESTIONS ABOUT THE VALUE OF A COURSE

At times, the typical student questions whether a particular course or curriculum has genuine value in helping him to train for a career and to succeed in it. The more mature the

student is, the more likely he is to raise such a query. Whatever the maturity of the student, he wants to know exactly
how his course of study bears directly or indirectly on his
general educational and vocational goal.

When a counselee questions a course, his counselor should
not give stock answers of the type, "The course is good for
you." Such an answer is obviously insufficient and inconclusive.

Every counselee is entitled to complete and logical answers—the best that the counselor can provide. During an interview, suppose that the two are discussing a prescribed
course in the high school's curriculum. At that time, the counselor should have full and accurate information as to the basic
reasons for the required course. He can then present this information to the counselee.

Again, suppose that the counselor and the counselee are
considering the reasons for an elective course. The counselor
can then point out the potential values of this course to the
counselee's future activities. He, for instance, can cite the
relationship between what the elective course offers and what
the counselee needs or wants. On the basis of such relationships, the counselee can decide whether or not he should take
that course. In reaching this decision, the counselee may
rightly consider the extent to which the elective course fits
into his total program of courses, past, present, and future.

A counselee often questions a course in which he is making low marks. Because of these marks, he may begin to doubt
whether he has the personal qualifications required to pass
the course. If standardized tests and other data indicate that
the counselee lacks the requisite qualifications, he may rightly
conclude that he can get little if any value by continuing the
course. But if the counselee appears to have the needed qualifications, he may wisely look for ways to use them to better
effect—through improved study habits, for example. All too
frequently, such a student possesses the abilities necessary to
succeed in a course, but does not have the other characteristics
required. The latter include knowledge of the real values of
the course, and internal drives to do well in it.

In adult life as well as in school life, a combination of
many different personal characteristics is necessary for success.

For example, if a man is to be eminently successful in business administration, he must have an unusual combination of personal characteristics such as these: a reasonably high level of aggressiveness; ability to get along well with people outside his organization, particularly to secure their cooperation; ability to work harmoniously with persons under his supervision, at his same level of responsibility, and above him in the organization; a good measure of self-assurance; ability to pursue his course of action in the face of criticism, deserved or undeserved; and ability to persuade others to his point of view, by the spoken and written word.

The student who is training for a specific career within the field of business administration may stand high in many but not all of the aforementioned characteristics. Perhaps the missing characteristics are very important to success in that particular career. Perhaps also they are difficult for this student to develop. If so, the student may wisely choose another career either in the field of business administration or in another field. In either case, he should select a field in which his low standing in certain characteristics will not interfere with his training or reduce his chances for success. In working with such a student, the counselor is dealing with a situation that involves not only the counselee's educational problem but also his personal and vocational quandaries.

HELPING THE SUPERIOR STUDENT

The student who has achieved an academic record that is much better than average is sometimes overlooked by the counselor. The typical counselor has to devote most of his attention to the pressing demands of helping students who are having academic difficulties; these are the students who are getting low marks, including failures, in their courses. As a result, the counselor has relatively little time to give to the superior student. In all too many schools such a student may not be interviewed even once during an entire academic year.

The Need for a Long-Term Goal

Superior students often need counseling services, for they, too, have educational problems. To illustrate one type of such problems, consider the case of Janet, a better-than-average student. In all her eleventh-grade courses, Janet was always well-prepared for classroom discussions and for tests. She always handed in written assignments on time. She was never tardy or absent. To the teacher, Janet presented no problems. The girl appeared to be satisfied with her courses and with her achievement in them. Therefore, she was given no counseling attention.

Janet, however, was troubled by an educational problem. She felt somewhat uncertain of and upset by the fact that she lacked a definite, long-range educational goal and plan. In short, she felt that she was "just going along" in the curriculum without any particular aim. Because Janet was fundamentally a reserved, shy girl and because she was not yet sufficiently impelled by her educational uncertainty, she did not, on her own initiative, go to a counselor.

In a casual conversation one day, the teacher caught a hint of the perplexity in Janet's mind. Then, tactfully questioning Janet, the teacher led the girl to talk about her subsurface problem. She then found it easy to persuade Janet to ask one of the counselors for assistance. That counselor soon helped Janet to develop her own long-term educational goal and program.

The Need for Early Counseling

To illustrate a second type of problem confronted by a superior student, consider the case of Dick, a first-semester college sophomore. Dick knew that he would have to choose his major field of study before the end of his sophomore year. Because Dick had done so well in all his courses, he knew that he could probably succeed in any one of a variety of possible fields. This knowledge made it difficult for Dick to choose a major field of specialization.

In working on his problem, Dick showed foresight. Early in his sophomore year, he went for help to the office of guidance services. Had he postponed this visit until later, he would have felt more and more disturbed about his problem. Through the assistance rendered by the guidance staff, Dick chose his field of specialization. In making this choice, he systematically studied the matter and methodically developed a plan.

Unlike Dick, other superior college sophomores do not seek help from a counselor early enough. Such a student may wait until the end of the college year before going to the guidance services office. At that time, he must choose a field of specialization, in a hurry and without preparation. As a result, this student is likely to make a quick choice, a choice that is based on insufficient consideration of the pertinent information. If he by chance makes a wise choice, he is fortunate indeed. Whether this student makes a good choice or a poor choice, he has certainly lost valuable time. During that time, moreover, he may have experienced emotional uncertainties that an earlier counseling interview might have helped prevent. For this student's unhappy situation, the guidance services staff must assume a sizable share of the responsibility.

The Need for Extracurricular Participation

The third type of problem that a superior student often faces is related to participation in extracurricular activities. If such a student devotes nearly all his time and energy to studying, he thereby loses the opportunity to develop a well-rounded personality. In many instances, the superior student, who does nothing but study, desperately needs the benefits that can be gained only through participation in activities outside the classroom. Without such participation, the student remains a "narrow" personality—a personality who is ill-prepared for achieving the level of all-round success in adult life that he might attain.

The counselor should be aware of the fact that a superior student, in all probability, will achieve much on his own, but will attain much more if he is given counseling assistance. Therefore, the counselor should give such a student as much help as, if not more than, he gives to the failing or probationary student. From the standpoint of both the individual and society, the development of the superior youth is highly important. Toward his development, a school or college should allocate sufficient personnel and time. If this institution does so, its guidance staff will stimulate the growth of an individual who can gain much from his schooling and who can contribute much after graduation.

Furthermore, if the institution's guidance services are devoted in major part to the students who are having educational difficulties, other students get the impression that such services are designed solely for students who are in trouble. As a result, the students who are succeeding in their schoolwork and elsewhere never voluntarily seek the assistance of the guidance staff. That is the reason the guidance department, by word and by deed, should make it clear that its services are available to all students, scholars as well as nonscholars.

SUMMARY

Helping students solve their educational problems is one of the most frequent yet most important services that the guidance department of a school or college is called upon to render. To answer this call, the department should offer its services to all students, including those who are failing and those who are superior academically.

Educational problems usually appear within a complex of other problems—vocational and personal, for example. These problems are often interrelated. For this reason, counselors must be able to handle students' educational problems competently not only in terms of the problems themselves but also in terms of their impact on other types of problems.

The counselor can employ a student's educational problem to open up that student's other problems. For example, a student brings his educational problem to the counselor; usually he is willing to discuss this problem freely and frankly. The student may also have a personal problem, a problem that he is reticent to discuss with the counselor. If the counselor is understanding and skilled, he can lead the student's discussion of an educational problem into a discussion of the latter's personal problem. Likewise, during an interview, the counselor can guide the student's discussion from an educational problem to a vocational problem, the subject of the succeeding chapter.

SOURCES OF GENERAL INFORMATION ABOUT HIGH SCHOOLS AND HIGHER INSTITUTIONS

Secondary

Sargent, Porter. *Handbook of Private Schools.* Boston, Mass.: Porter Sargent, 11 Beacon St.

U.S. Office of Education (Mabel C. Rice, compiler). *Directory of Secondary Day Schools, Showing Accredited Status, Enrollment, Staff, and Other Data, 1951–52.* Washington, D.C.: U.S. Government Printing Office, 1952.

List of high schools accredited or recognized, in one's own state, issued by the State University or State Department of Education.

List of high schools accredited by the association of one's own region—for example, the lists issued by the North Central Association of Colleges and Secondary Schools. (There are four other similar regional associations.)

Catalogs and pamphlets of private secondary schools, day and evening, in one's own community or near-by large cities.

Higher Institutions

A Handbook for High School Counselors. Valparaiso, Indiana: Association of College Admissions Counselors, Valparaiso University, 1952. (A 1953 supplement is available.)

Bogue, Jessie P. (ed.). *American Junior Colleges.* Washington, D.C.: American Council on Education, 1952.

College Blue Book. Deland, Florida: College Blue Book. (Descriptions of catalogs of American colleges, universities, and professional schools; entries organized according to kinds of institutions and geographical location.)

Irwin, Mary (ed.). *American Universities and Colleges.* Washington, D.C.: American Council on Education, 1952.

Karl, S. Donald, and Diehl, Barbara L. (eds.). *The College Handbook.* New York: College Entrance Examination Board, 1953.

Lovejoy, Clarence E. *Lovejoy's College Guide.* New York: Simon and Schuster, 1952.

Lovejoy's College Digest—Monthly Supplement to Lovejoy's College Guide. New York: Times Tower Building, Times Square.

Wilkins, Theresa B. *Accredited Higher Institutions, 1952.* U.S. Office of Education, Bulletin 1952, No. 3. Washington, D.C.: U.S. Government Printing Office, 1952.

Special Schools

Catalogs, pamphlets, lists, and other descriptive materials covering such educational opportunities as these in one's own or neighboring communities: trade and commercial; courses of study offered by business and industrial organizations; schools for the handicapped (blind, hard-of-hearing, orthogenic); classes for foreigners.

Directory of Business Schools in the United States—A Handbook for Vocational Advisors and Guidance Officers. Washington, D.C.: National Association and Council of Business Schools, 1950.

Publications of General Value to Counselors

College and University, the Journal of the American Association of Collegiate Registrars and Admissions Officers. Editorial office is Office of Registrar, Miami University, Oxford, Ohio.

Directories and lists of educational opportunities issued by local agencies for adult education. Some communities have an organization known as the Adult Education Council.

Educational Record. Washington, D.C.: American Council on Education.

The journal, or proceedings, issued by the school-accrediting association for the region in which the counselor lives. (For example, the *North Central Association Quarterly* is published by the North Central Association of Colleges and Secondary Schools, Ann Arbor, Michigan.)

School Life and *Higher Education.* Washington, D.C.: United States Office of Education. (Order these periodicals through the Superintendent of Documents.)

SUGGESTED READINGS

Anderson, Ruth E. "An Annotated Bibliography on School and College Information," *The Bulletin,* XXXVI, No. 188. (October, 1952), 170-208. Washington, D.C.: National Association of Secondary-School Principals.

Baber, Ray E. *Marriage and the Family.* New York: McGraw-Hill Book Company, Inc., 1953.

Barnard, Mildred B., and Blair, Waddington. *You, Your College and Your Career.* San Francisco: Lithotype Process Company, 1950. Pp. 17-93.

Bennett, Margaret E. *College and Life: Problems of Self-Discovery and Self-Direction.* New York: McGraw-Hill Book Company, Inc., 4th ed., 1952.

Dunsmoor, Clarence D., and Davis, Oliver C. *How to Choose That College*. Boston: Bellman Publishing Company, 1951.

Frederick, R. W., Kitchen, P. S., and McElwee, Agnes R. *A Guide to College Study*. New York: Appleton-Century, 1946.

Froehlich, Clifford P. *Guidance Services in Smaller Schools*. New York: McGraw-Hill Book Company, Inc., 1950. Pp. 81-103.

Greenleaf, Walter J. *What School or College?* Washington, D.C.: Federal Security Agency, Office of Education, Misc. 3276, 1948.

Hamrin, Shirley A., and Paulson, Blanche B. *Counseling Adolescents*. Chicago: Science Research Associates, 1950. Chapter 7.

Strecker, Edward A. *Basic Psychiatry*. New York: Random House, 1952.

Traxler, Arthur E., and Townsend, Agatha (eds.). *Improving Transition from School to College*. New York: Harper and Brothers, 1953.

Turngren, Annette. *Choosing the Right College*. New York: Harper and Brothers, 1952.

Williamson, E. G. *Counseling Adolescents*. New York: McGraw-Hill Book Company, Inc., 1950. Pp. 78-100.

Williamson, E. G. (ed.). *Trends in Student Personnel Work*. Minneapolis: University of Minnesota Press, 1949. Pp. 80-104.

Wrenn, C. Gilbert. *Student Personnel Work in College*. New York: The Ronald Press Company, 1951. Pp. 274-292.

CHAPTER TWELVE

Helping Students Make Wise Vocational Choices

ACCORDING TO a statement made in 1937 by a committee of the National Vocational Guidance Association, *the process of vocational guidance entails assisting the individual in his efforts to choose his occupation, to prepare himself for entrance into it, to enter it, and to make progress in it.*[1]

At first glance, this statement indicates that the process of helping the individual to solve his vocational problems is relatively simple. But in reality, that process is often extremely complex.

To note the complexities of the process, consider the statement's emphasis on *assisting* the individual. In an earlier statement, issued in 1924, the National Vocational Guidance Association defined the process as *giving* the individual "information, experience, and advice in regard to choosing an occupation."[2] The contrast between the 1937 statement and the 1924 statement is sharp and revealing—for example, *assisting* the individual versus *giving* him information, experience, and advice. This contrast reflects a fundamental change in point of view or emphasis in the field of counseling. In earlier years, the counselor usually had the attitude that he should *tell* the counselee what to believe, think, or do. More recently,

---

[1] Report of the Committee of the National Vocational Guidance Association, "The Principles and Practices of Educational and Vocational Guidance," *Occupations*, XV (May, 1937), 772-778.

[2] George E. Myers, "A Quarter Century of Vocational Guidance," *Occupations*, XII (May, 1934), 35.

the counselor has taken the position that he should *assist* the individual to gather and interpret information and to choose his vocation, all largely through the counselee's own efforts.

WHY VOCATIONAL GUIDANCE IS COMPLEX

With the foregoing emphasis in mind, consider next the reasons why the process of helping people to solve their vocational problems is complex.

First, the process of vocational guidance is complex because of the element of time. In the guidance field, the word "process" often connotes a continuous and progressive series of activities that occur over a period of time. In vocational guidance, the process of assisting an individual to choose an appropriate occupation usually cannot be consummated quickly. Rather, this process requires time; it extends from the individual's initial approach to the problem of occupational choice into his taking a position in some gainful occupation. And even after the individual is working in that position, he may need time to adapt himself to the tasks required.

Second, the process is complex because it involves an individual whose personality is complex. No matter who he is, his personality has many facets. These include his abilities, interests, and other personal characteristics. Because these characteristics are unique whether considered singly or in combination, this individual has his own ideas about his vocational aptitudes and interests, his own attitudes toward particular jobs and occupational fields, and his own insights into ways to prepare for and to enter the career of his choice. Because the individual often changes his ideas, attitudes, and insights as he matures, he tends to become a more complex person. Therefore, the process of guiding him vocationally also becomes increasingly complex.

Third, the process is complex because it deals with a highly complex and fast-changing world of work. This world is made up of thousands of different occupations that vary more or less in their requirements for entrance and for success. In general, there is a wealth of information about a number of specific occupations, particularly those that attract many young people. Although this information is ready at hand, information about many other occupations is relatively hard to obtain. Assuming that the counselor has the occupational information needed, he must tailor that information to the needs of the counselee; together they may relate job facts to the characteristics of the counselee—to help the youth prepare for entrance into a selected occupation and to progress in it thereafter.

Fourth, the process is complex because it usually entails not only a vocational problem but also educational and personal problems. More specifically, the individual who is choosing a career must consider the educational program required to prepare for that career. He must also have in mind certain personal considerations that bear upon his career choice. These considerations include the financial resources of his family, the attitudes of his parents toward particular occupations, and the adjustments called for in social relationships.

ESSENTIAL STEPS IN CHOOSING AN OCCUPATION

The steps that are essential to the wise choice of an occupation can be summarized, simply and briefly, as follows:

The first step. Secure as complete information as possible about the counselee, including facts about his occupational interests and aptitudes.

The second step. Obtain detailed, authentic information about the occupations that appear to be most promising for the counselee.

The third step. Relate the types of information that were gathered in the first and second steps.

If properly executed, the third step may lead the counselee to select one of the vocations he has studied, or to investigate other possible occupations. In reaching a final decision, the counselee should carefully analyze and revaluate all the available information; he should then thoughtfully apply that information to his own situation.

The reader should not infer that the steps listed must be pursued routinely in the order given. In some situations, the counselor may take the second step first—he may help the counselee gather information about occupations. The counselor may then proceed to collect facts about the counselee. In some circumstances, moreover, the counselor may take both these steps at about the same time.

Ideally, the counselee should continuously relate what he is learning about himself and what he is learning about vocations. The former type of learning definitely stimulates the latter, and *vice versa*. Together they broaden and deepen the counselee's search for and application of information that is pertinent to his vocational choice. For these reasons, neither type of learning deserves priority over the other in terms of precedence or importance. Additional background on this matter appears in a thought-provoking book by Ginsberg.[3]

The sections that follow immediately will present the items that are essential to the understanding of any occupation and to the vocational guidance of any counselee. These sections will also discuss the sources of occupational information and the uses of such information.

ESSENTIAL ITEMS IN THE STUDY OF OCCUPATIONS [4]

Counselors are fairly well agreed that the principal items for consideration in the analysis of an occupation are covered by the following questions:

1. What is the nature of the work in the occupation? Specifically, what are the activities, duties, and responsibilities of those engaged in it?

2. What special mental abilities are required in the occupation?

3. What are the special educational prerequisites for entering the occupation? Does the occupation require grade-school, high-school, technical-school, or college training? How many years are involved in this special training? How much will this training cost? Are there any special qualifications for securing this training?

---

[3] Eli Ginsberg, *Occupational Choice: An Approach to a General Theory* (New York: Columbia University Press, 1951).

[4] For a detailed presentation of this important subject, see Max F. Baer and Edward C. Roeber, *Occupational Information: Its Nature and Use* (Chicago: Science Research Associates, 1951).

4. How can this occupation be entered? Is there an examination? Who conducts it? Are there any special clearing houses or agencies to handle placement? How much do they charge for this service?

5. Are there any restrictions as to those who can enter the occupation? What are these restrictions? Are they based on race, religion, nationality, background, or personal appearance?

6. What are the conditions of work? What are the regular hours of work? Is there much overtime? Are there any particularly busy seasons? Are there physical hazards or mental strains? In what form is the compensation—piece rate, hourly wage, salary, or commission? Does one work alone? Is the work routine?

7. What has been the general trend of employment in the occupation? Is the occupation growing or shrinking in importance? Does the demand for employees vary seasonally? Is there a large turnover in employment? In what areas of the country is the demand for workers heaviest? What is the demand in the local community and near-by areas?

8. What is the average income, and what is the income range in the occupation? What is the typical starting wage or salary? What are the chances for promotion in this occupation? How much job security does the occupation offer? Is there a pension or retirement plan? How are promotions obtained? Does a job in this occupation lead to better positions in related occupations?

9. In general, how may this occupation be rated as a life career? How does this occupation contribute to social progress and well-being? What effect does the occupation have on the worker's personal life?

All the items of information that answer the foregoing questions are important in the study of any occupation. The kind and amount of information that are available vary considerably from occupation to occupation. The counselor and the counselee may experience difficulty in gathering data that answer certain questions about a given occupation. Nevertheless, if the data are keys to the solution of the counselee's problem, the counselor should make every effort to obtain such data.

ESSENTIAL ITEMS IN STUDYING AN INDIVIDUAL

A high-school boy or girl, or even a college youth, often expresses opinions about another person's fitness for a given occupation. For example, he may say: "Joe's a good talker; what a lawyer he'd make." Or, "Betty is such a striking girl; can't you just see her working as a model?" These statements are usually based upon observation of relatively superficial characteristics—general appearance, dress, manner of speaking, and the like.

The counselor recognizes the fallacies involved in the foregoing statements of judgment. He realizes that an individual's personality is more than his outward appearance and overt behavior; that personality, in fact, is made up of all his characteristics. The counselor also knows that studies have shown that an adult must have certain characteristics to succeed in a given occupation; some of these characteristics are not among those which people commonly associate with success in that occupation.

In helping a student to make a wise vocational choice, the counselor should emphasize the importance of a detailed study of that counselee's personality. Specifically the counselor should assist the counselee to find out all that he can about his own personality, including such characteristics as these:

1. Physical characteristics
   a. Personal appearance (dress, grooming, bearing, posture, etc.)
   b. Voice and manner of speaking
   c. State of general health and level of energy
   d. Physical handicaps (if any) and their implications
   e. Age, height, and weight, and their relationships to specific requirements for jobs
2. Personal qualities
   a. Motives and goals
   b. Level of emotional stability and maturity
   c. Level of social development; degree of ability to get along with people; social poise; tendency to-

ward dominance or submission in relationships with others

3. Pattern of mental abilities (general and special)
   a. General ability to learn
   b. Verbal comprehension (ability to understand ideas expressed in words)
   c. Word fluency (ability to write and talk easily)
   d. Numerical facility (ability to think in quantitative terms and to work proficiently with figures)
   e. Visualizing or space thinking (ability to manipulate mentally objects in two or three dimensions)
   f. Facility in inductive reasoning (ability to work out rules or principles)
   g. Ability to memorize [5]

4. Pattern of occupational interests
   a. Outdoor
   b. Mechanical
   c. Computational
   d. Scientific
   e. Persuasive
   f. Artistic
   g. Literary
   h. Musical
   i. Social Service
   j. Clerical [6]

5. Aptitudes
   a. Manipulative
   b. Mechanical
   c. Clerical
   d. Artistic
   e. Musical
   f. Other

---

[5] This classification is based on Thurstone's work. L. L. Thurstone, *Primary Mental Abilities* (Chicago: University of Chicago Press, 1938). L. L. Thurstone and Thelma G. Thurstone, *Factorial Studies of Intelligence* (Chicago: University of Chicago Press, 1941).

[6] This classification of interests is suggested by Kuder. G. Frederick Kuder, *Kuder Preference Record—Vocational* (Chicago: Science Research Associates). Interests in specific occupations and occupational groups as suggested by Strong should also be taken into consideration.

6. School and nonschool achievements
   a. General level of scholarship; marks in specific school subjects
   b. Participation in extracurricular activities (school clubs, student government, athletics, etc.)
   c. Nature of and success in part-time or full-time jobs
   d. Relationships with other members of the family
   e. Participation in nonschool social groups (youth, religious, and other organizations)
   f. Pursuit of hobbies or other special interests

SOURCES OF OCCUPATIONAL INFORMATION

In the area of occupational information, there is a large body of materials—books, pamphlets, magazine articles, and other forms of publications. These materials come from varied private, public, and professional sources. Although the task is somewhat difficult and time-consuming, the counselor should be generally familiar with all the basic informational materials, particularly with those dealing with major occupations and occupational trends. In addition, the counselor should be well-acquainted with the best sources of information so that he can obtain reliable data as efficiently as possible. If the counselor has adequate knowledge of informational sources, he is able to facilitate the counselee's search for and interpretation of occupational information.

The foregoing was clearly emphasized by Baer and Roeber in the following statement.[7] The counselor "must have a general understanding of the world of work. In addition, he must know where to get detailed occupational information and how to use it whenever he is called upon to help specific individuals. Thus, the test of a good counselor in the area of occupational information is not necessarily the number of occupations about which he knows something. It is rather the extent to which he has a realistic understanding of occupational life in relation to individuals who come to him for help."

---

[7] Max F. Baer and Edward C. Roeber, *Occupational Information: Its Nature and Use* (Chicago: Science Research Associates, 1951), p. 3.

The World of Work

As the initial approach to securing this broad outlook on occupations, the counselor should orient himself in the total range of occupations. At first, he may feel bewildered by the immensity of this range—some 40,000 job titles and even more thousands of work activities. But as the counselor realizes that these occupations have been classified according to sensible and manageable categories, he is able to get an over-all understanding of the world of work. If the counselor has such an understanding, he can effectively orient the counselee. If the counselee is generally familiar with a wide range of occupations, he is in a good position to use intelligently the information that relates to the occupation or the occupational field that is of greatest interest to him.

In seeking an overview of the vocational world in the United States, the counselor may well think first in terms of the occupational structure and the industrial structure. The former refers to the various kinds of work activities. The latter alludes to the classification of the industries in which the occupations occur.

The Occupational Structure

A standardized classification of occupations according to the kinds of work involved has been set up by the United States Employment Service.[8] According to its classification, the seven major occupational groups and the code numbers thereof are as follows:

0—Professional and managerial occupations
1—Clerical and sales occupations
2—Service occupations
3—Agricultural, fishery, forestry, and kindred occupations
4 and 5—Skilled occupations
6 and 7—Semiskilled occupations
8 and 9—Unskilled occupations

---

[8] U.S. Department of Labor, Bureau of Employment Security, *Dictionary of Occupational Titles,* Second Edition, Vols. I and II (Washington: Government Printing Office, 1949).

The Industrial Structure

A standardized classification of occupations according to the industries in which these occupations occur has been developed by a technical committee made up of representatives of business and government.[9] This classification is particularly helpful to many counselees because typically they often choose an industry rather than an occupation. For example, a counselee first decides that he wants to work in the local steel mill (a manufacturing industry). Later, he decides on an occupation, or a group of related occupations, within that steel mill.

The Standard Industrial Classification was prepared by a committee composed of representatives of trade associations, agencies of federal and state governments, and private research agencies. According to this classification, industrial activities are grouped into nine major divisions, as follows:

Division A—Agriculture, forestry, and fisheries
Division B—Mining
Division C—Construction
Division D—Manufacturing
Division E—Wholesale and retail trade
Division F—Finance, insurance, and real estate
Division G—Transportation, communication, and other
           public utilities
Division H—Services
Division I—Government

The *Standard Industrial Classification Manual* assigns code numbers to the nine major divisions, and to the 91 main groups therein. Within these groups there are code numbers for 519 subgroups of closely-related industries and for 1,530 industries.

The United States Census of Occupations

Basic data concerning the distribution of workers in all occupations appear in the reports of the Bureau of the Census,

---

[9] The Technical Committee on Industrial Classification, Division of Statistical Standards, Executive Office of the President, Bureau of the Budget, *Standard Industrial Classification Manual*, Volume I, *Manufacturing Industries;* Volume II, *Nonmanufacturing Industries* (Washington, D.C.: Government Printing Office, 1942).

a part of the U.S. Department of Commerce. As provided in the Constitution, the United States Government takes a Census of population once every ten years. The Census of 1950 was the seventeenth in the nation's history. In the 1950 Census, interviewers asked a number of questions that dealt with an individual's employment.

After each census, the Bureau of the Census issues publications that summarize the information gathered. These publications give statistics on such characteristics of employment as the following: number of workers in each major occupational group, in certain subdivisions of each group, and for men and women separately; classifications of occupations by industries and the numbers of workers employed therein; distribution of employees by age; distribution of employees by income; distribution of workers by race (white and nonwhite, for example). These publications also present separate statistics for the several states.

Major occupational groups in the Census. The 1950 Census provides employment and related information for eleven major occupational groups, as follows: [10]

1. Professional, technical, and kindred workers
2. Farmers and farm managers
3. Managers, officials, and proprietors, except farm
4. Clerical and kindred workers
5. Sales workers
6. Craftsmen, foremen, and kindred workers
7. Operatives and kindred workers
8. Private household workers
9. Service workers, except private household
10. Farm laborers and foremen
11. Laborers, except farm and mine

These eleven groups include 446 titles of specific occupations. The professional group has the occupations of actor, dentist, dietitian, lawyer, nurse, teacher, physician, and engineer, to mention a few.

---

[10] U.S. Bureau of the Census, *U.S. Census of Population:* Vol. II, Characteristics of the Population; Part I, United States Summary (Washington 25, D.C.: U.S. Government Printing Office, 1953).

Industrial Classifications in the Census

The 1950 Census also includes an enumeration of employees according to industries. It gives 12 major industrial divisions, and 148 subsidiary categories. The major divisions are as follows: [11]

1. Agriculture, forestry, fishery
2. Mining
3. Construction
4. Manufacturing
5. Transport, communication, and other public utilities
6. Wholesale and retail trade
7. Finance, insurance, and real estate
8. Business and repair services
9. Personal services
10. Entertainment and recreation services
11. Professional and related services
12. Public administration
13. Industry not reported

Statistical Abstract of the United States

For basic employment and related data that supplement information appearing in census reports, the *Statistical Abstract of the United States* merits more extensive use by counselors. This publication, which is compiled and edited by the Bureau of the Census, appears annually. Each volume presents important summary statistics on the industrial, social, political, and economic organization of the United States. It includes a representative selection of important data from statistical publications, both governmental and nongovernmental. The *Statistical Abstract* is made up mostly of national data; it does, however, present some state data in summary form. The section of the abstract entitled "Labor Force, Employment, Earnings" [12] is of special interest and value to the counselor who is working in the field of vocational guidance.

---

[11] *Ibid.*

[12] *Statistical Abstract of the United States* (Washington 25, D.C.: Superintendent of Documents, U.S. Government Printing Office). See the most recent edition.

Dictionary of Occupational Titles

Among the many purposes served by the *Dictionary of Occupational Titles,* two in particular merit emphasis at this point. *First,* through its various classifications of occupations, the *Dictionary* provides an overview of the range of existing jobs in the United States. Thus it offers the counselor and the counselee the orientation to the field that they need and want. *Second,* the *Dictionary* presents job definitions of thousands of occupational titles. Because these definitions are authentic descriptions of specific jobs, they have practical value to the counselor and to the counselee in the study of occupations.

The content of the Dictionary. Based upon careful research sponsored by the United States Employment Service, the volumes making up the *Dictionary* were published as a series, beginning in 1940. The latest edition of Volumes I and II appeared in 1949. In Volume I, the foreword states that the book "contains 22,028 defined jobs, which are known by an additional 17,995 titles, making a total of 40,023 defined titles." Volume II of the *Dictionary* presents the titles of occupations arranged according to major groups, divisions, and subdivisions. Each group, division, and subdivision has an assigned code number.

In Volume I of the *Dictionary,* a job definition typically is composed of four parts: (1) the job title; (2) the industrial designation determined by the product made or process employed or by the type of activity carried on; (3) the coded definition (by numbers) or the uncoded definition (by a list of similar jobs); and (4) a brief description of the job. This description includes a statement of the duties, responsibilities, skills, requirements, and other significant aspects of the job. Some descriptions give information about working conditions.

As an illustration of the job definitions appearing in Volume I, here is the definition of *educational psychologist:* [13]

> Psychologist, Educational (professional and kindred) 0-36.23. Investigates processes of mental growth and development for the purpose of guiding individuals in selection of academic

---

[13] *Dictionary of Occupational Titles, op. cit.,* vol. I., p. 1039.

or vocational courses leading to a suitable career. Conducts personal interviews to determine educational programs for individuals. Administers and scores questionnaires and psychological tests which reveal intelligence, achievement, aptitudes, and interests of students. Evaluates personal qualifications, taking into consideration past records, test results, and pertinent facts derived from interviews. Suggests specific courses and activities. Analyzes causes of maladjustment of individuals in educational institutions and recommends corrective action. Develops and applies methods of instruction and training handicapped persons. May teach, conduct research, or perform administrative services.

Coding of Occupational Names

As noted in an earlier section of this chapter, the occupations appearing in the *Dictionary* are classified into seven major groups. Each major group is designated by the first code number—for example, "0" designates the "Professional and managerial occupations" group. Each of the first four major groups is broken down into two or four divisions. Each division is indicated by the second code number—"0-1" designates "Professional occupation." Each subdivision is shown by the third code number—"0-16" designates "Civil Engineer." Each smaller group within the subdivision is indicated by the fourth and fifth code numbers—"0-16.01" designates "highway engineers."

In addition to five-digit code numbers, such as the one just given, there are six-digit numbers. For example, the occupation of "Subassembly Installer (aircraft, manufacturing)" is indicated by the number "5-03.562." Here is what each of these code numbers means:

5-   Skilled occupations (a major occupational group)
5-03   Occupations in building aircraft (an occupational division)
5-03.5   Occupations in assembling aircraft (an occupational subdivision)
5-03.562   Subassembly installer (a smaller group within the subdivision)
           Engine control installer (a specific job within the smaller group)

Although space is inadequate to present all the details of the classification system employed in the *Dictionary*, two general statements about this system will be helpful to the counselor and the counselee. *First,* the more digits that different codes have in common (when reading from left to right) the closer is the relationship between the given occupations. For example, there are close relationships among 5-75.220 (Drifter I, construction), 5-75.270 (Cable Driller, petroleum production), and 5-75.280 (Tool Dresser, petroleum production). Note that for all these jobs the first four digits are identical.

Second, in the codes for skilled, semiskilled, and unskilled jobs, the digits for the major occupational groups indicate the *degree* of skill required. For example, the code 5-75.220 (Drifter I, construction) represents an occupation at the *skilled* level. In comparison 7-75.220 (Well-Driller-Operator Helper, construction) signifies an occupation at the semiskilled level. The other digits (75.220) indicate that the two jobs call for the same or a similar *kind* of skill.

Classification of Inexperienced Workers

Part IV of the *Dictionary* [14] presents a classification that is particularly helpful to young, inexperienced persons. This classification is based on *fields of work.*

Inexperienced or untrained persons cannot be classified in terms of specific occupations given in the job definitions appearing in Volumes I and II of the *Dictionary.* Therefore, the local offices of the United States Employment Service realized the need for another system of classifying occupations. To meet this need, a classification according to *fields of work* was developed and published as Part IV of the *Dictionary.* This part is organized so that an inexperienced or untrained person can be classified according to his potentialities—that is, on the basis of his personal characteristics and of his potential ability to learn a particular job.

The latest available edition of Part IV, published in 1944, includes approximately 6,000 entry occupations. These occu-

[14] U.S. Department of Labor, U.S. Employment Service, *Dictionary of Occupational Titles, Entry Occupational Classifications,* Part IV (Washington: Government Printing Office, 1944).

pations are classified according to the following occupational groups: [15]

0-X PROFESSIONAL, TECHNICAL, AND MANAGERIAL WORK

0-XI Artistic Work

0-X2 Musical Work

0-X3 Literary Work

0-X4 Entertainment Work

0-X6 Public Service Work

0-X7 Technical Work

0-X8 Managerial Work

1-X CLERICAL AND SALES WORK

1-X1 Computing Work

1-X2 Recording Work

1-X4 General Clerical Work

1-X5 Public Contact Work

2-X SERVICE WORK

2-X1 Cooking

2-X2 Child Care

2-X5 Personal Service Work

3-X AGRICULTURAL, MARINE, AND FORESTRY WORK

3-X1 Farming

3-X8 Marine Work

3-X9 Forestry Work

4-X MECHANICAL WORK

4-X2 Machine Trades

4-X6 Crafts

6-X MANUAL WORK

6-X2 Observational Work

6-X4 Manipulative Work

6-X6 Elemental Work

For each of the six foregoing groups, Part IV of the *Dictionary* lists the worker characteristics that are occupationally significant. These characteristics involve personal traits; leisure-time activities; casual work experience; and civilian and military training. For example, computing work (in the clerical group) calls for the following personal traits: speed and accuracy in making mathematical calculations; memory for detail; ability to concentrate; ability to grasp quantitative concepts.[16]

---

[15] *Ibid.*, pp. vi-xiv, 2.

[16] *Ibid.*, p. 161.

For a given youth, such personal traits are indicated by his leisure-time activities, his casual work experience, and his civilian and military training. By comparing his traits and experiences with those specified for a field of work as given in Part IV of the *Dictionary*, the youth is able to work out more intelligent and realistic plans for his career than otherwise.

Job Analysis

In order to name, define, and classify jobs systematically for the *Dictionary of Occupational Titles*, those who developed this important publication found it necessary to get basic facts about jobs. Toward this goal, they made comprehensive and exhaustive studies of jobs at the places where workers were engaged in these jobs. The data from these direct on-the-spot studies were supplemented by data gathered by labor unions, industrial organizations, professional associations, and other groups. These investigations, begun in 1934 by the U.S. Employment Service, yielded the exact and detailed information required for preparation of the *Dictionary*.

In studying jobs, considerable use was made of the technique known as *job analysis*. As defined by the War Manpower Commission, job analysis is "the process of determining, by observation and study, and reporting pertinent information relating to the nature of a specific job. It is the determination of the tasks which comprise the job and of the skills, knowledges, abilities, and responsibilities required of the worker for successful performance and which differentiate the job from all others." [17]

According to Shartle, job analysis includes the following major items: [18]

1. Identification data: name of job and specific location
2. Work performed: description of the tasks involved
3. Performance requirements: the demands which the job places

---

[17] U.S. War Manpower Commission, Bureau of Manpower Utilization, Division of Occupational Analysis and Manning Tables, *Training and Reference Manual for Job Analysis* (Washington: Government Printing Office, June, 1944), p. 1.

[18] Carroll L. Shartle, *et al.*, "Ten Years of Occupational Research," *Occupations,* XXII (April, 1944), 392.

on the worker for successful performance (responsibilities, job knowledge, mental application, dexterity, and accuracy)

4. Sources of workers, including essential training and experience
5. Comments: technical and general background of the job
6. Physical demands: working conditions and physical factors
7. Worker characteristics: estimate of the inherent characteristics of the worker which are called forth by the job

Job analysis, in various forms, has been employed by a number of industrial and commercial establishments. They have found that such analyses contribute, for example, to the setting of standards for selection of employees, to the planning of the content and methods of employee training programs, and to the determination of wage scales.

As just suggested, the items to be included in a job analysis depend upon the purposes of a given study. The range and depth of that study depend upon the given circumstances. A detailed listing of items that have been used in job analyses appears in a book by Shartle.[19]

Job Families

If the counselor is to help students to make wise vocational choices, he should be generally familiar with information about what are known as *job families*. According to Baer and Roeber, "a job family is a constellation of occupations. The occupations in the constellation are grouped together on the basis of one or more job or worker characteristics which they have in common." [20] Said another way, the members of a job family have many common elements that are manifested in such areas as these: the kinds of tasks required; the kinds of personal qualifications required; the kinds of work experience required; the kinds of special training required; and the kinds of special skills or knowledge required.

In helping a student to solve his vocational problems, the counselor finds that information about job families serves the following important purposes:

First, the counselee who has had no work experience gains

---

[19] Carroll L. Shartle, *Occupational Information: Its Development and Application* (New York: Prentice-Hall, 1952), pp. 34-38.

[20] Baer and Roeber, *op cit.*, p. 86.

a clearer idea not only of a given job but also of a group of related jobs. He learns that certain occupations have common elements. Therefore, through proper training he prepares to enter not a single job, but a number of related jobs within the world of work. For example, suppose that a youth decides to take the training necessary to become an accountant. After completing that training, he is prepared to become a junior worker in a public accountant firm, in the accounting department of a manufacturing concern, or in the trust or foreign trade department of a large bank. Or, he is prepared to become a specialized agent in the Federal Bureau of Investigation.

Second, the counselee who is physically handicapped is encouraged by the knowledge of job families. Although his handicap may bar him from one occupation within that family, it may not be an obstacle to obtaining another occupation within that same job family.

Third, the counselee is aware of the fact that he can obtain a position in any one of a number of the jobs belonging to the same family. If the counselee wishes to do so, he may transfer from one job to another where both jobs require the same kinds of ability and training.

Because of the value of *job family* information in counseling, the authors hope that the great interest and activity previously exhibited in this field will be revived. There is genuine need for determining a larger number and variety of job families, particularly in the fields of professional occupations, semiprofessional occupations, and clerical and sales occupations.

Other Sources of Occupational Information

The basic sources already mentioned give an overview of occupations in the United States. In addition to these sources, there is a voluminous body of occupational information materials. Because the existing titles are so numerous, the following paragraphs will merely cite the kinds of these materials that are available to the counselor.

Among such informational materials are the reports of special occupational surveys. These surveys, which contribute to the background knowledge of the counselor, cover the following types of subjects: nature and extent of unemployment; labor supply and demand; wages and hours; occupational outlook; local, state, and regional employment and training opportunities; follow-up of graduates of schools; employment problems of minority racial groups in the population; employment problems of older workers; employment problems of the physically handicapped; and legislation affecting labor.

The counselor who is helping his counselee to solve his vocational problem can draw on many sources of information that the counselee himself can study to advantage. These sources include the following:

1. Books describing a variety of occupations; occupational monographs; "occupational briefs," presenting information about separate jobs

2. Articles about specific jobs or fields of work activity appearing in popular magazines, journals of professional societies, and trade journals

3. Biographies and fiction dealing with persons engaged in certain occupations

4. Brochures and other materials on occupations published by businesses and trade associations

5. Catalogs and other materials published by training schools

6. Interviews with and talks by people who have had experience and success in their respective occupations or occupational fields

7. Correspondence with officers of trade, commercial, or professional organizations

8. Interviews with local employment agency personnel

9. Motion picture films and charts presenting occupational information

10. Radio and television programs devoted to vocational problems

11. Personal visits to offices, stores, and factories to observe people at work in different occupations

12. Try-out experiences in jobs, either part-time or full-time

13. Norms on various tests that indicate the levels of pro-

ficiency and the patterns of interest needed in different occupations

EVALUATION OF OCCUPATIONAL LITERATURE

Because of the variety, volume, and uneven quality of available literature about occupations, the counselor confronts the difficult problem of evaluating informational materials. He has the definite obligation to direct the attention of counselees to materials that present authentic and realistic information.

In selecting publications in this field, the counselor can make effective use of a monograph by the Publishers' Committee of the Occupational Research Section of the National Vocational Guidance Association (now a division of the American Personnel and Guidance Association). This monograph, entitled "Distinguishing Marks of a Good Occupational Monograph," [21] presents a list of criteria including the following:

1. Sponsorship: professional standing of the organization, group, or person who published the material

2. Time: exact information as to when the material was collected

3. Methods used: extent of library work; scope and nature of the search for data at the original sources

4. Complete coverage of the treated occupation or occupational field (The essential items for such a presentation have been published by the Occupational Research Section.)[22]

5. Scientific character: exhibited in method of collecting the data; unbiased, accurate, specific presentation of the material

6. Presentation of the occupation in its social and economic setting

7. Clear, concise, interesting style

8. Attractive format

In seeking occupational information, both the counselor and the counselee face the problem of finding materials that present up-to-date facts. If the counselee bases his occupational

---

[21] "Distinguishing Marks of a Good Occupational Monograph," *Occupations*, XVIII (November, 1939), 129-130.

[22] Occupational Research Section, National Vocational Guidance Association, *Occupations*, XIX (October, 1940), 20-23.

choice on outmoded information, his career decision may be
ill-advised and even harmful. To avoid this possibility, the
counselor should be continuously on the lookout for recently
collected data in published form; he should continually replace
out-of-date information with current data. If the counselor systematically reviews the informational materials on hand, say,
at least once every three months, he will be able to weed out
the materials that are no longer of value.

MAKING OCCUPATIONAL INFORMATION ACCESSIBLE

Although the counselor may have a wealth of occupational
information materials on hand, those materials should be readily available to students who are working on their vocational
problems. This means that the materials must be filed logically
so that any student can quickly find the exact publications that
he wants. In organizing the files of such materials, the counselor should seek the assistance of the librarian; together they
can work out the best plan—a plan designed to serve all students in the institution.

Occupational materials are varied in character; they are
used in a variety of ways. These two factors should be kept in
mind by the counselor and the librarian while they are planning the storage, display, and distribution of such materials.
For optimum handling of these materials, their plan may well
call for the allocation of a special section of the library or of
a special room.

Before materials are shelved, filed, or displayed, they
should be cataloged. The librarian can, of course, catalog occupational information books according to the library's regular
system. The librarian and the counselor, however, will have to
work out a plan for cataloging and filing booklets, pamphlets,
college and university catalogs, mimeographed documents,
magazine articles, and the like. These unbound materials may
be filed in heavy manila folders (letter or legal size). Such
folders may be stored in a regular filing case; or they may be
kept in cardboard file boxes that are stored on bookshelves.
For example, college catalogs and other booklets may be filed
in inexpensive pasteboard boxes of uniform size. The "back-

bones" of these boxes may be lettered by hand or may have typewritten labels to indicate the contents.

Special Card Files

As just mentioned, occupational materials may be kept on the shelves or in files in a separate section of the library or in a special room. Wherever these materials are placed, the counselor and his counselees need a special card file to locate quickly and exactly the publications desired. This card file should be primarily a subject-matter catalog—that is, it should list all the occupations on which the library has materials. This catalog should have a card for each book, pamphlet, or other publication; that card should have a code letter or number that indicates where the publication is located on the shelves or in the files. In some instances, the card file should have author cards in addition to subject cards. These author cards together with the cards listing books of general value in the study of occupations can be placed in a general section at the front of the card file.

Plans for Cataloging Unbound Materials

Whatever classification plan is employed for filing unbound soft-cover materials, the scheme should meet the four criteria suggested by Baer and Roeber.[23] *First,* the plan needs to be simple enough so an inexperienced person can find what is wanted primarily by his own effort. *Second,* the plan needs to be expandable. New materials and shifts in old ones can thereby be handled without impairing the established filing system. *Third,* the physical appearance of the shelves of books and catalogs and the file drawers of unbound items need to be attractive, neat, and orderly. *Fourth,* the plan needs to be psychologically appropriate. In other words, the filing plan should be based on the interests and abilities of the students who will use it.

The last criterion suggested by Baer and Roeber is all too often ignored. Materials are usually classified and cataloged solely on the basis of a relatively limited number of occupations

[23] Baer and Roeber, *op. cit.,* pp. 369, 370.

or of occupational areas. In such a card catalog, for instance, the student may find cards with headings like "Chemist," "Engineer," "Botanist." But he may not find the cards that deal with the occupations in which he is most interested and for which he has special aptitudes.

In developing the best possible filing plan, the counselor may use or get ideas from commercially-published plans. Such plans include the *Science Research Associates Occupational Filing Plan;* the *Michigan Plan for Filing and Indexing Occupational Information;* and the *New York Department of Education Plan.* For detailed information about these plans, the counselor should refer to the book by Baer and Roeber on *Occupational Information.*[24]

PRESENTING OCCUPATIONAL INFORMATION THROUGH INDIVIDUAL AND GROUP METHODS

Essentially, there are two principal means of presenting occupational information to students. The *first* is through individual contacts such as interviews. The *second* is through group contacts including classroom sessions.

With reference to the first means, the counselor deals with counselees individually when he feels that he can thus help them best to solve their several problems. For example, consider the counselee who is interested in the study of a specific occupation or a field of work that is of little interest to other students. In this case, the counselor will work individually with this counselee in interviews. Or, if this counselee has a very personal problem related to an occupation, the counselor will discuss that problem with him during an interview. This discussion obviously will be kept confidential.

From the viewpoints of conserving the counselor's time and energy, of serving the maximum number of students, and of holding institutional costs for the program at a reasonable figure, much of the important work of disseminating occupational information can be conducted through group activities. To illustrate, young people who are confronted by vocational problems need orientation in occupational information; spe-

---

[24] Baer and Roeber, *op. cit.,* p. 371 ff.

cifically, they need to be introduced to ideas in this field and to the sources of materials therein. Toward this goal, the institution can make effective use of group techniques—for instance, class discussions, assembly programs, and field trips.

Imparting Information through Interviews

Baer and Roeber have suggested four principal questions that the counselor should consider in using occupational information in counseling interviews.[25] These questions, together with the present authors' comments thereon, follow.

1. *What are the conditions under which occupational information is used in the counseling interview?* To make such conditions specific, consider the high-school junior who has shown keen interest in preparing himself to be a civil engineer. Should the counselor direct this student immediately to sources of information related to his occupational interest? Or, should the counselor delay until this student has learned more about his basic abilities or potentialities? Perhaps this counselee's problem lies in the area of personality; if so, his vocational quandary may be secondary, at least for the time being. On the basis of interviews with this student, the counselor may decide to follow two courses of action simultaneously. The counselor leads the student to explore particular sources of information in order to keep alive his indicated vocational interest. And the counselor helps the student to develop a keener insight into his situation and a more realistic appraisal of it. Thereby this counselee is more likely to become genuinely ready to deal with his vocational problem.

2. *How much assistance does the counselor give the counselee in his use of occupational information?* As Baer and Roeber point out, some counselees can proceed quite well on their own after being given access to printed materials. Other counselees, however, cannot do so. In working with the latter counselees, the counselor needs to direct their occupational reading and to discuss it with them. As such a counselee learns to be self-directive, the counselor decreases the amount of his assistance. Stated another way, the counselor adjusts the de-

[25] *Ibid.*, pp. 418-424.

gree of his assistance to the counselee's readiness to proceed on his own in the study of occupational materials.

3. *How does the counselor determine which occupational information materials are appropriate for the counselee?* To answer this question, the counselor needs to know the counselee's level of reading ability, his background of experience, his drive to read the available information, and his attitude toward his own vocational choice. In addition to the foregoing, the counselor needs to know the occupational information that is most appropriate for that counselee.

4. *How does the counselor evaluate the use of occupational information in counseling interviews?* In imparting information to the counselee through interviews, the counselor should be concerned with the degree of his effectiveness. In estimating this degree, the counselor should ask himself such questions as these: Does the counseling increase the accuracy, adequacy, and usefulness of the knowledge gained by the counselee? Does the counseling keep the counselee's interest at the pitch needed to bring the counselee back for additional interviews? Does the counseling terminate the contact with the counselee before or after he has achieved sufficiently high levels of self-knowledge and knowledge of occupations? Do follow-up studies of former counselees indicate that they made unwise vocational choices because they did not receive appropriate or sufficient occupational information during interviews? If so, what changes should be made in the kinds and amounts of occupational information being offered to present counselees?

Imparting Information to Groups

As suggested earlier in this chapter and in Chapter 8, information about occupations can be effectively and economically imparted through group techniques. These commonly-used techniques include class discussions and small group conferences.

To assist students in choosing vocations, the guidance worker can employ group methods in dealing with such important topics as these:

1. Orientation to occupations—the over-all view of adult work activities

2. General introduction to the basic sources of occupational materials that are appropriate for young people

3. Presentation of the three essential steps toward choosing an occupation: (a) securing information about occupations; (b) obtaining data about the counselee's characteristics; and (c) matching the foregoing types of information in the selection of a career

4. Discussion of occupational trends in the nation and in the local community

5. Development of the concept of occupational families

6. Consideration of the bearing of the individual's characteristics of personality on his success in a job

7. Presentation of information about the fields of work or specific occupations that are particularly significant to the students in the school

The role of courses. Ideally, the high school should make available to every sophomore or junior a regularly-scheduled and accredited course that covers the field of careers or occupational information. Through such a course, even the youth who believes that he has made a wise and final decision as to his life work can be stimulated to think the matter through again. By restudying his choice, he will broaden his occupational horizons. In the light of this fresh outlook, he may confirm his previous vocational decision—or he may make a new and better decision.

Some high schools offer an elective credit-granting course in vocational information or career choice. Because all students do not take such a course, this arrangement falls short of the ideal. Nevertheless, such an elective course on career choice can have real values; it is certainly far better than no such course at all. Suppose that this elective course is taught by a teacher who is interested, informed, and stimulating. Suppose also that it is placed in a desirable position in the general class schedule. Then the course in careers will tend to attract and to serve more and more students in the school.

Whether the course in careers is required or elective or whether it is offered at all, the school can include topics related to careers in different subjects of study. More specifically, an

English course or a civics course may include one or more units in the field of careers.

Desirable as such units are, they alone are insufficient. In the typical English or civics class, the teacher must cover the essential subject matter of the course. This means that he has relatively little course time to give to the study of careers. Moreover, if the teacher himself has little or no interest or background in the career training of youth, he is likely to treat the subject superficially in his class.

The homeroom program and extracurricular activities. In addition to or instead of the group methods just suggested, the school may attempt to offer career education through its homeroom program. For example, the teacher may conduct career discussions during the homeroom period. Seldom, however, can such a teacher carry on adequate activities in this field. The typical homeroom period is so short and so filled with other necessary activities that a thorough study of occupations is usually impossible.

High schools and colleges commonly offer occupational information in extracurricular activities. Whether such activities are as effective as class activities has not been conclusively proved. But these extracurricular activities undoubtedly can play an important part in the institution's program of vocational guidance.

The career conference. One of the most worth-while extracurricular projects in this field is that of the career conference. This is a favorite group vehicle for imparting occupational information in high schools and colleges. In an educational institution where the student body is large and varied, the career conference is likely to be elaborate. The conference program continues during all or most of two or three school days. In a school where the student body is small and homogeneous, such a conference is likely to be simple; the program is completed within not more than one school day. In one school, these career-related activities may be concentrated within a day or two; in another school these activities may extend over a longer period of time—a semester or an entire year.

Whether the career-conference type of program covers a short or long time span, its activities usually include the following feature: Men and women who are experienced and well-recognized in their vocations talk to students or preferably answer the questions that students raise in small group sessions. These adults may also arrange personal interviews with interested students.

If a good career conference is to be as effective as possible, it must be carefully planned by the staff and the student body of the institution. Well in advance, the institution sets up a committee that is responsible for developing the program, inviting speakers, handling publicity, and performing the many other necessary tasks.

To make sure that the conference deals with the problems of greatest interest to youth, the committee may give a questionnaire to all students. On this questionnaire, students not only indicate the fields of work in which they are interested; they also offer other suggestions as to the content and conduct of the conference. On the basis of questionnaire returns, the committee (in advance of the conference) "briefs" the speakers; it informs them, at least in a general way, as to what experiences and ideas the students would like to hear discussed.

The "College Day." Many high schools not only have career conferences but also have what is called a "College Day." In preparation for such a group event, the high school invites the representatives of colleges and universities that are of interest to the student body to be at the high school on a given day. On that day, each college representative meets with a group of high-school students. Together they discuss the college's educational programs, its extracurricular activities, its placement services, and the tuition and other costs involved. The representative then meets individually with students who are interested in attending his institution.

By cooperative, advance planning, the staff members who are responsible for a high school's "College Day" program can help many a student to select the college that is best for him. With the assistance of a college's representative, the student can explore that college's curricular and other offerings as these relate specifically to his vocational plan.

Other group methods. In orienting groups of students to

occupational information, high schools and colleges have employed additional means, such as the following:

1. *Display posters in prominent places—in the school's corridors, library, and classrooms, for example.* Students should help in constructing or choosing posters or other materials for display. Each display should have a definite theme; it also should be attractive. Thereby the display will catch the attention of the student body and will get its message across.

2. *On prominent bulletin boards, post such items as charts, other graphic materials, and announcements of publications and of special lectures.* The bulletin boards should give students information about where publications can be obtained—in the school or in the public library. The bulletin boards should also give the names, office hours, and room numbers of faculty counselors.

3. *Show motion picture films that present authentic occupational information.* Also, have an adult or a student tell a realistic story about a certain kind of work.

4. *Take field trips.* If possible, the group should visit a number of industries or commercial establishments. In conducting a field trip, the teacher should prepare in advance for it. He should brief his students and the hosts at the plant or office to be visited. For instance, students should know what questions to ask and what answers to look for.

5. *Use the subject-matter approach.* Each teacher of a subject of study should present the occupational information that relates to his field of specialization. He should point out exactly why and how his subject helps students to prepare for certain kinds of jobs.

6. *Organize student clubs.* Such clubs should be built upon students' interests in subject fields or in occupational fields. The program of each such club should be planned by the student members, with assistance from the faculty sponsor; he should, of course, be readily available if, as, and when needed.

Whether occupational information is imparted through individual interviews or through group methods, both techniques are helpful. Because each approach serves its own purpose and circumstance, neither can supplant the other. Therefore, neither should be used exclusively; rather, each should supplement the other.

Which approach should be employed in a given situation depends upon the resources of time, personnel, and money available in a school. In some situations, the individual approach is more practicable. In other situations, the group approach is more useful. In a school where the major work must be through group techniques, faculty members are called upon to exercise ingenuity to find the best possible ways to reach students.

INFORMATION ABOUT OCCUPATIONAL TRENDS

To the counselee who is engaged in choosing his career, occupational trends have considerable significance. With the counselor's assistance, this counselee should not only evaluate present opportunities within a given occupation or family of occupations. He should also forecast what those opportunities are likely to be when he is ready to enter that occupation. Therefore, the counselee should ask such questions as these: What is the trend in the employment opportunities in the occupation? Over a period of years, have these opportunities stayed about the same? Have they decreased? Have they increased? In the future, are these opportunities likely to increase or decrease? Will the product or service be in greater demand than formerly? Or will the demand probably fall off?

Questions that deal with the outlook for an occupation are often difficult to answer. Nevertheless, for a popular occupation, the counselor should strive to keep his information as up-to-date and as complete as possible. To do so, he should obtain the most recent reports of governmental and other agencies with reference to employment conditions within the occupation—for the nation, the state, and the local area. These reports including those issued by the Bureau of the Census yield key information on long-term occupational trends. With reference to such information, the counselor will find that he can usually obtain more authentic data about an occupational trend within the nation as a whole than within a state or a community.

The counselor should not expect to keep at his tongue's tip the detailed information about the occupational outlook for a large number of specific occupations. Instead, he should try to learn and remember the general trends within the larger fields of occupations. Toward this goal, he should gather both objective and subjective information related to the business world. His questions might include: Is business optimistic or pessimistic about the future? Is the steel industry expanding, stable, or contracting? Are large retail stores and mail-order houses experiencing good times or not? Is the oil industry expanding its personnel in a number of departments? The counselor should endeavor to answer these questions in terms of the national outlook, the state outlook, and the local outlook. He should then use the answers (the information obtained) to assist a counselee to solve his particular occupational problem.

The counselor and the counselee should carefully evaluate all data and all statements that purport to predict occupational trends. They should realize that such predictions are guesses as to what will occur. These guesses may be forecasts by governmental agencies. Because these agencies usually have extensive resources for collecting and analyzing information, their forecasts are among the best guesses as to the future. Even so, no matter what the occupational forecast is and no matter who makes it, that forecast usually involves some factors that are difficult to predict. Among such factors are those related to national defense requirements during a period of international tensions.

In interpreting forecasts of occupational trends, the counselor should also keep the following considerations in mind: [26]

1. Is the prediction short-term or long-term?

2. Does the forecast take due account of past employment trends in the occupation? Are the data for earlier years genuinely comparable?

3. Does the forecast adequately consider the factor of replacement of workers—due to retirement, death, or large movements to more promising fields?

4. Does the forecast recognize the general state of the nation's economy? (When economic activity is rising, there is an increasing demand for workers in almost all occupations.

[26] *Ibid.*, pp. 165-193.

However, the demand does not increase uniformly for workers in all lines of work.)

5. Does the forecast take into account the trends related to the size and the character of the population? (Such trends affect the demand for goods and services, as well as the supply of labor.)

6. What technological changes, if any, have occurred which may influence the forecast? (The creation of new industries, or the decline of old ones, significantly affects the demand for workers.)

7. What are the possible influences of legislation on the occupational forecast? (This legislation may regulate foreign trade—tariff laws; domestic manufacturing—the Prohibition Amendment; and the labor supply—immigration laws and child labor laws.)

8. What changes in the public's habits and style preferences are likely to affect the demand for labor in the production of certain goods and services?

9. For a new industry, are there workers available from related existing industries? Can these workers be trained quickly to perform the tasks required in the new industry?

10. To what extent do labor unions and professional societies regulate the opportunities for training and thereby the supply of potential workers?

11. Do higher levels of earnings and better working conditions draw labor to certain occupations?

Whatever the general outlook for a given occupation, the counselor and the counselee should consider that occupation in relation to the personal characteristics of the counselee (for example, his age, sex, race, and physical handicaps, if any) and to the locality where the counselee wishes to work. Such personal characteristics and desires often have an important bearing on the availability of a job to a particular counselee.

THE STUDENT'S CAREER NOTEBOOK

Over a period of several years, a student may gather considerable information about himself and about the occupations in which he is most interested. Yet he is likely to forget or ignore much of this information unless he has a systematic plan for organizing and applying it. As part of this plan, the student may well consider the use of a *career notebook*.

For his career notebook, the student should employ a standard ring binder notebook. Such a notebook, of course, has hard covers and holds punched 8½ x 11-inch sheets. These sheets can be moved from place to place within the notebook. The notebook should also have divider sheets with index tabs. These sheets divide the notebook's contents into sections; the tabs help the user quickly to locate a given section.

There is no one best plan for organizing a career notebook. In fact, each student should be encouraged to work out his own plan. Even so, students may well consider the inclusion of three main parts entitled as follows: "Information about Jobs," "Information about Myself," "Matching Jobs and Myself."

The first part headed "Information about Jobs" may have the sections: "General Occupational Information," "Information about Occupations of Special Interest to Me," and "Problems for Which I Need More Occupational Information."

The second part entitled "Information about Myself" may have these sections: "My Academic Record" (the marks made in various courses), "My Performance on Standardized Aptitude and Achievement Tests," "My Preferences for Occupations or Occupational Areas," "My Hoped-For Career," and "My Educational Plans."

The third part on "Matching Jobs and Myself" offers the student a special opportunity to use his ingenuity. In this part, for example, he can devote a section to graphic presentations in which he matches his characteristics and his occupational possibilities. In this and other ways, the student considers his abilities and other traits in their relationship to the requirements of one or more occupations.

The counselor should encourage the student to record the sources of the information reported in his career notebook. If the item of information is from a book, the student should record the title of the book, the name of the author, the publication date, and the page number or numbers on which the informational item appeared. If the item of information is from an interview, the student should record the date of the interview, the name and position of the interviewer, and the name of the company or other organization. By thus recording each source of information, the student can readily consult that source again if he needs to do so.

A student can enliven his career notebook by pasting in appropriate clippings (stories and pictures, for instance) from magazines and newspapers. Or, as suggested before, he can include colored charts or other illustrations that he himself has prepared.

COMMON MISTAKES IN CHOOSING A CAREER

Before citing the mistakes that students commonly make in choosing their careers, a constructive observation is appropriate. To make a wise occupational choice, a student should accept the idea that he must be as objective and as impersonal as possible in his analysis of his own qualifications in relationship to occupations. If the student does not accept this idea, he is likely to make an unrealistic vocational decision. Sooner or later this decision may lead to failure to get or to hold a job, and to accompanying feelings of disappointment, frustration, and inferiority. Because of this danger, the student should never gloss over serious limitations or minimize important difficulties.

Even so, the student should not quickly or lightly give up in the face of certain obstacles to his goal. Some of these obstacles may be more apparent than real; others, with effort, may be overcome. If the obstacle cannot be surmounted or by-passed, however, it is wiser for the student to recognize the situation, to accept it, and to change his goal.

With the foregoing in mind, consider next the commonly observed mistakes that youth make in choosing their careers. Some of these mistakes, the reasons for them, and their effects are described in the paragraphs that follow.

1. *Choosing an occupation that requires mental ability above that of the student or that has limited entry possibilities.* According to a number of studies of the careers chosen by high-school youth, an undue proportion of these youth select occupations that are "over their heads" or that are restricted in terms of employment potentials.

With further reference to the latter, all too many youth choose careers that are out of line with the numbers of adults who are actually engaged in the occupations chosen. For example, one study showed that 16 percent of a group of boys in the senior year of high school aspired to enter professions. Other studies have revealed even higher percentages. Compare the 16 percent of boys choosing professions as a career with the 7 percent of all men in the labor force (U.S. Census of 1950) who were professional and semiprofessional workers.[27]

Although some youth aspire to occupations above their mental abilities, others look toward occupations that demand levels of mental abilities below what these youth possess. If a youth enters and continues in such an occupation, he tends to develop increasing dissatisfaction with his work. By the time he decides to change occupations, he may find that he is too old to prepare for and to enter a new occupation, one that is more nearly in line with his mental abilities.

2. *Choosing an occupation for which the required levels of skill cannot be attained by the student.* Certain students who are superior in music in high school or college, for example, may think that they should become professional musicians—soloists, orchestra performers, or conductors. Other students who are superior in the field of art believe that they should become professional artists. Unless these students have outstanding skills in their chosen professions, they should think twice before pursuing these professions as careers. Even though these youth have additional training, they may be unable to build the skills necessary for professional success.

3. *Choosing an occupation for which the student does not possess essential skills in tool subjects.* A boy who is weak in mathematics may choose engineering as a career. A girl who makes many mistakes in spelling, punctuation, and grammar may want to become a secretary. Although a few such students may overcome these weaknesses, many students will find it difficult if not impossible to do so. Such students should consider changing their occupational choices to fields in which they are much more likely to succeed.

---

[27] Walter J. Greenleaf, "More About Occupations," *School Life,* 34 (October, 1951), 5.

4. *Choosing an occupation for which the student does not have the appropriate characteristics of personality.* If a boy is reserved or shy, he will probably not become a successful salesman. If a girl has little understanding of or sympathy for people in trouble, she is not likely to become an effective social service worker.

5. *Choosing an occupation for which the student lacks the required physical strength and endurance.* If a girl gets tired quickly, she should not choose a career in advertising or in department store buying. Either career requires considerable physical stamina and drive. If a boy is not physically fit, he should not seek to become a traveling salesman.

6. *Choosing an occupation because of its glamor.* Boys and girls often give first consideration to the surface features of certain occupations. They see these jobs through rose-colored glasses, ignoring completely the routine and less pleasant aspects of the work. A boy, for example, selects dentistry as a career; he believes that he will like the work and that he will earn a good income in it. But this boy has little or no idea of the training, skills, and patience required in this profession. A girl wants to become a movie or television actress. But she little realizes the training necessary to prepare for this profession or the abilities required to succeed in it.

7. *Choosing an occupation without considering financial limitations.* A youth may rightly select a career because he has outstanding aptitudes in that occupational field. He may, however, not give sufficient thought to the time and money required to train for such a career. Because the youth's family cannot finance his college education, he may, after high-school graduation, have to give up that career. This disappointment might have been avoided if the high school had previously helped the student to see his financial situation realistically.

8. *Choosing an occupation in which there are many more qualified candidates than there are openings.* In certain occupations, the relationship between the supply of and the demand for qualified personnel shifts. To illustrate, schools and colleges have been training a growing number of accountants. During the postwar manpower shortage, the demand for young men trained in the accounting field has been much greater than

the supply. Suppose, however, that the market becomes comparatively glutted with qualified candidates for accounting positions. If this happens a young man should think carefully before deciding to train in the field of accounting.[28] He should consider his abilities and interests in relationship to those of successful accountants. He should weigh the odds for and against his chances of obtaining an accounting job and of getting ahead in this field. After careful consideration, he may stand by his original decision. If he does so, however, he perseveres with his eyes open, recognizing that he may meet keen competition. This youth may become such an able prospective accountant that he secures a beginning position and later qualifies for advancement.

9. *Choosing an occupation on the basis of the wishes and ambitions of parents or friends.* For several generations, the head of a family may have been engaged in the same or in a similar occupation. Because of this, for example, a farmer wants his oldest son to become a farmer. That son may not have the interests and abilities required to become a successful farmer. If that is true and if the father forces his son to choose farming as a career, the son may before long become discontented with his vocation—a factor that may cause failure. For such a reason as the foregoing, parents, teachers, and other adults should not transfer their own ambitions to youth. Neither should they coerce youth to enter occupations in which these youth lack either interest or ability.

DESIRABLE ATTITUDES TOWARD VOCATIONAL PROBLEMS

To cite the implications for counseling of the foregoing discussion, here is a list of some of the desirable attitudes that the counselor should have in working with a counselee:

1. The counselor should have the sincere conviction that each counselee has abilities that will be useful and worth-while in the world of occupations.

2. The counselor should see that the counselee increas-

---

[28] He may, for example, find it advisable to take the tests made available through the accounting testing program of the American Institute of Accountants, 21 Audubon Avenue, New York 32, N.Y.

ingly takes the responsibility of gathering and applying information about occupations and about himself.

3. The counselor should help the counselee to develop his own insights concerning himself with reference to occupations.

4. The counselor should assist the counselee to develop the attitudes, skills, and other abilities needed for self-guidance.

5. All in all, the counselor should refrain from directing and dominating the counselee while the latter is making his decisions.

SUMMARY

The process of making wise vocational choices is complex. Toward making this process effective, the counselor and counselee should have knowledge of the essential steps in choosing an occupation: knowledge of the basic facts about occupations; and knowledge of the fundamental characteristics of the counselee. In addition, the counselor should know exactly where occupational information is available and how it can best be imparted to the counselee. This information should include up-to-date trends in various occupations. Furthermore, both the counselor and the counselee should know the mistakes that are commonly made in choosing careers in order to guard against such mistakes. After the counselor has helped the counselee to make a wise vocational choice, he should aid the latter to find a job. This is the subject of the next chapter.

SUGGESTED READINGS

Baer, Max F., and Roeber, Edward C. *Occupational Information: Its Nature and Use.* Chicago: Science Research Associates, 1951.

Barnard, Mildred B., and Blair, Waddington. *You, Your College and Your Career.* San Francisco: Lithotype Process Company, 1950. Pp. 129-169.

Bedford, J. H. *Your Future Job.* Glendale, California: The Society for Occupational Research, Ltd., 1950.

Bennett, Wilma. *Occupations Filing Plan and Bibliography.* La Porte, Indiana: Sterling Powers Publishing Company, 1951.

Carter, Harold D. *Vocational Interests and Job Orientation.* Stanford, California: Stanford University Press, 1944.

Cromwell, R. Floyd, and Parmenter, Morgan D. *Suggestions to the Teacher of Occupations.* Buffalo, N.Y.: Guidance Publications, Box 89, Niagara Square Station, 1949.

Forrester, Gertrude. *Methods of Vocational Guidance.* Boston: D. C. Heath and Company, 1951.

Forrester, Gertrude. *Occupational Pamphlets: An Annotated Bibliography.* New York: H. W. Wilson Company, 1948.

Greenleaf, Walter J. *Occupations: A Basic Course for Counselors.* Washington, D.C.: Government Printing Office, Superintendent of Documents, 1951.

Humphreys, J. Anthony. *Choosing Your Career.* Chicago: Science Research Associates, 1949.

Humphreys, J. Anthony. *Helping Youth Choose Careers.* Chicago: Science Research Associates, 1950.

Job Charts for College Women. Washington, D.C.: B'nai B'rith, 1952.

Kaplan, David L. "Occupational Information from the 1950 Census," *The Personnel and Guidance Journal,* XXXI (March, 1953), 368-370.

Michigan Plan for Filing and Indexing Occupational Information. Sturgis, Michigan: Library Division, The Sturgis Printing Company, 1948.

Occupational Filing Plan. Chicago: Science Research Associates, 1946.

Shartle, Carroll L. *Occupational Information: Its Development and Application.* New York: Prentice-Hall, Inc., 1952.

Smith, Glenn E. *Principles and Practices of the Guidance Program.* New York: Macmillan Company, 1951. Pp. 184-206, 230-251.

Stead, William H., Shartle, Carroll L., *et al. Occupational Counseling and Techniques.* New York: American Book Company, 1940.

Strong, Edward K., Jr. *Vocational Interests of Men and Women.* Stanford, California: Stanford University Press, 1944.

Super, Donald E. *Appraising Vocational Fitness.* New York: Harper and Brothers, 1949.

Thurstone, L. L., and Thurstone, Thelma G. *Factorial Studies of Intelligence.* Chicago: University of Chicago Press, 1941.

U.S. Department of Labor, U.S. Employment Service. *Dictionary of Occupational Titles,* Vols. I and II. Washington, D.C.: Government Printing Office, Superintendent of Documents, 1949.

U.S. Department of Labor. *Occupational Outlook Handbook.* U.S. Bureau of Labor Statistics, Bulletin No. 998, 1951. Washington, D.C.: Government Printing Office.

U.S. Department of Labor, Bureau of Labor Statistics. "Occupational Outlook Summary." (Series of leaflets published regularly.) Washington, D.C.: U.S. Department of Labor.

Webb, Maryann K. "The Ranking of Occupations on the Basis of Social Status," *Occupations*, XXVII (January, 1949), 237-241.

Wolfbein, Seymour L., and Goldstein, Harold. *Our World of Work.* Chicago: Science Research Associates, 1951.

CHAPTER THIRTEEN

Helping Students Find Jobs

THIS CHAPTER has three main purposes: (1) to discuss the ways in which young people can be aided in finding job openings and in applying for these positions; (2) to consider the various kinds of job placement agencies that are available; and (3) to point out the principal tasks that a school's placement services can and should perform.

One of the counselor's primary objectives in helping a student to solve his vocational problems is to assist that student to enter the occupation that is best for him. Such assistance is commonly referred to as placement, or more specifically, as *job placement.*

Job placement has become a technical undertaking that requires the services of thousands of trained and experienced men and women. The early assumption was that any college-trained or experienced person could function successfully as an advisor in job placement. This assumption has gradually been replaced by the sound idea that a person trained for placement services can best do this type of work.

Technically trained and otherwise competent personnel have replaced catch-as-catch-can placement with placement that is based on scientific research and systematic administration. Such personnel not only use the techniques already at hand but also develop new and better techniques.

Whatever techniques a counselor may employ, he has fulfilled his responsibility to his counselee only when he has helped this counselee (1) to select an occupation or a family of related occupations, and (2) to obtain a job that is in line with the counselee's interests and abilities.

JOB PLACEMENT AS AN OBLIGATION OF SCHOOLS

High-school and college administrators have different opinions about the degree of responsibility of their institutions for the job placement of graduates and of other former students. On the one hand, some administrative officers hold that their institutions have little responsibility, either directly or indirectly. Such officers may not be cognizant of the potential meaning and importance of guidance services to their students.

On the other hand, other administrators are convinced that their institutions do have the responsibility to provide placement services for both their present students and their former students. Such an institution may have a staff member who has the ability, the time, and the facilities to work actively on the task of discovering job openings for which students can be recommended. If not, that institution can at least give students information on the best methods of finding and applying for available positions.

Whether a school administrator recognizes it or not, job placement is one of the last practical steps in the formal educative process—a step that helps to make the student's education effective socially. For this reason, it would seem, every high school or college would accept if not welcome job placement as a genuine and high-priority obligation.

A high school or college may well consider placement services in terms of their many and varied benefits both to the student body and to the institution itself. The morale of students and graduates, for example, is enhanced by the knowledge that their school has sufficient confidence in them and in its educational activities to establish and maintain an active and effective placement office. If this office has directly assisted graduating students or former students to find vacancies and to secure jobs, these students have a special reason to feel loyal to their institution. Thus, the institution builds good will among many of its students and alumni—an asset that is desirable in and of itself and that may bring material benefits. Whatever these benefits, a school or college that offers placement services should endeavor to develop and draw upon all the resources possible to assist its students in finding jobs.

WAYS OF HELPING YOUTH TO FIND JOBS

As suggested earlier, whether an educational institution has its own placement office as such, it does have the educational responsibility to inform its students concerning the essentials involved in the process of securing positions. These essentials, for example, bear upon the "right" ways and the "wrong" ways of locating jobs and of attempting to obtain them.

Uncovering Job Vacancies

Quite logically the educational institution should see to it that its students are instructed as to the best means of uncovering actual or potential job vacancies. Prior to the student's search for a vacancy, the institution's counseling services should have aided him in determining rather exactly the kind of job or jobs that he desires. Such a determination is important for at least two reasons. *First*, this determination provides the focus for all job-seeking activities. And, *second*, it gives the job applicant more self-confidence, thus leading him to make better impressions in interviews with prospective employers or with placement agency personnel.

As pointed out earlier, the institution can assist its students in the processes and with the problems of job-getting by group methods such as class instruction and by individual methods such as counseling interviews. The latter, of course, enable the individual student to raise and to discuss his own personal needs and problems.

Whether a school employs group methods, individual methods, or both, it should initiate its placement assistance not later than the beginning of the latter half of the senior year. In some situations, a high school or college may start offering this assistance even earlier. In either case, the school should allot adequate time for this significant educational program.

In orienting students with reference to job-finding techniques, the guidance worker should familiarize them with readily available sources of information, such as the following:

1. The school's own job placement services
2. Public employment services (local and/or state)
3. Private placement agencies
4. Local placement bureaus maintained by semipublic agencies including youth and youth-service organizations
5. Placement service committees of local civic organizations (Chamber of Commerce, Kiwanis, Lions, Rotary, trade or labor unions and councils)
6. Relatives, friends, and acquaintances
7. Announcements of civil service examinations for positions in local, state, or federal governmental agencies
8. "Help Wanted" advertisements in local or near-by city newspapers
9. "Situation Wanted" advertisements in local or near-by city newspapers
10. "Help Wanted" or "Situation Wanted" advertisements in trade or professional journals
11. News items in newspapers and trade journals (Items that deal with such matters as new plants, expansion of old plants, and changes in personnel often reveal job openings to ingenious job-seekers.)
12. Classified telephone and commercial directories (These directories give the names of firms that specialize in certain kinds of activities or that render specialized services.)

Applying for a Position

With information in hand regarding an actual or potential job vacancy, the counselee is interested next in making effective application. Toward doing so, he can obtain realistic assistance from a counselor. The counselor may present and discuss the four principal means of applying for a job. These means are as follows:

1. By personal interview
2. By letter of application
3. By filling out an application blank
4. By carrying on a direct-by-mail campaign

In using any of these means, there are desirable and undesirable approaches. For this reason, some counselor in the school should take the responsibility for explaining each of the means, for pointing out its advantages and disadvantages, and for citing the precautions to be observed in employing it. As implied, each one of the means just listed has its unique characteristics. For information about these characteristics, the student can refer to several books.[1]

Because so much depends on impressions made by the job-seeker in his interviews and letters of application, the guidance worker may well arrange for groups of students to learn job-finding techniques. Such a student group can stage simulated interviews between an employer and an applicant for employment; after each interview, members of the group can offer comments and suggestions on the applicant's appearance and behavior. The student group can also read aloud and discuss letters of application that were written by its members or by others who were successful job applicants. The latter type of letters may be borrowed from local businessmen. In considering such letters, students should keep in mind that the letter itself is seldom a decisive factor in job-getting. Rather, it is an instrument that helps clear the way for an interview.

Preparing for and Participating in the Interview

In the group's discussion of the interview, students should consider such "pointers" as the following:

1. Prepare for the interview.
   a. Make a definite appointment for the interview well in advance.
   b. Organize information about yourself—your schooling and other training; your work experience; your occupational interests; your special aptitudes; your list of references. Type this information, in outline form, on a single sheet of paper.
   c. Get ready for the questions that will probably be

---

[1] Paul W. Boynton, *Six Ways to Get a Job* (New York: Harper and Brothers, 1940).

Mitchell Dreese, *How to Get the Job* (Chicago: Science Research Associates, 1948).

J. Anthony Humphreys, *Choosing Your Career* (Chicago: Science Research Associates, 1949).

James C. Worthy, *What Employers Want* (Chicago: Science Research Associates, 1950).

asked. For example, list the points that relate to such a request as: "Tell me about yourself." Also, list the important questions that you want to ask during the interview.

d. Just before the interview, check carefully upon your personal appearance—grooming, dress, cleanliness, and posture.

e. Get as much information as possible about the job for which you are applying and about the business organization in which you are seeking employment.

2. Appear for the interview shortly *before* it is scheduled to begin, but *not* too early.

3. Be thoughtful and considerate during the interview.

a. Be courteous. Good manners also help land the job.

b. Allow the interviewer to steer the conversation. Don't try to do this yourself.

c. Give short, clear, direct, and complete answers to the interviewer's questions.

d. Don't argue with the interviewer; and don't try to flatter him.

e. Be tactful. Behave with self-assurance, but not with cockiness.

f. Sense when the interviewer wishes to terminate the interview. Don't waste his time.

g. Check with the interviewer as to next steps. These may include the filling out and submittal of a job application form, if this has not been done previously; the arrangements for interviews with department heads; and the taking of a health examination.

Writing an Effective Letter of Application

In helping students learn to write a good letter of application for a job, the guidance worker should stress such points as the following:

1. Adhere to the accepted form of a business letter. Include the date, your home address, and perhaps your telephone number.

2. Make the letter neat in appearance and legible.

3. Be sure that the letter is free from mistakes in grammar, capitalization, punctuation, and spelling.

4. Check carefully on the content of the letter. Make certain that sentences and paragraphs are well-constructed, that colloquialisms are avoided, and that ideas are expressed with clarity, conciseness, and definiteness.

5. Make the letter as brief as possible, but cover all the main points that should be presented.

6. Make positive statements about yourself—avoid negative statements.

7. Give complete information about yourself; highlight information that you believe will be of interest to the employer.

8. Be specific about the position you are seeking and for which you think you are qualified. Discuss how you believe you can fill the job with competence.

9. Present full, but concise, information about yourself—your training; your experience; and vital statistics about yourself such as birth date, place of birth, height, weight, and health. (This information in outline form may be typed on a single, separate sheet that is attached to your letter of application to a prospective employer.)

10. Give a list of references. Include their full names, titles, and business addresses. (Before listing a person as a reference, obtain his permission to use his name.)

11. List your achievements that you believe are unusual.

12. Enclose a small, recent photograph of yourself. On the back of the photograph write your name and address.

13. Offer to provide any additional information about yourself, as requested.

14. Tactfully suggest a personal interview, if you have not had one previously.

15. Make your official signature as legible as possible. If you are a married woman, indicate that fact.

Filling Out the Application Form

The guidance worker should impress students with the importance of treating the application form as seriously and conscientiously as possible. Every job-seeker should appreciate the opportunity to fill out an application form; and he should fill out that form to the best of his ability. The potential employer, for good reasons of his own, may give little attention to the filled-out form; he may place it in his file for possible reference at a later date. Even so, the applicant should assume that the prospective employer desires the filled-out form and will use it within the near future. There is always the chance that the employer who does not consult the filled-out form immediately will consult that form later—and will then get in touch with the applicant.

To the employer, the application form is an essential tool. He or his employment officer has presumably constructed the application form on the basis of a careful study of the kinds of information about an applicant that are needed to select the best person for a job opening. For this reason, the applicant should take the attitude that every item in the application form is important to the potential employer. In the light of this attitude, the job-seeker should carefully answer every item in the form.

In orienting a student or other job-seeker relative to the application form, the counselor should offer such suggestions as these:

1. Before beginning to fill out the form, read the entire form quickly but carefully. This reading will give you a general idea of all the information requested.

2. Ask the employer for two copies of the form. Fill out the first copy in pencil and correct it. Then, from this copy, fill out the second copy in ink or on a typewriter. Submit this copy to the employer.

3. Write or print legibly. Write neatly. Make the filled-out form as attractive and as easy to read as possible.

4. Give the information requested in all the items of the form. If an item does not apply to you, draw a dash line to show that you have noted that item. But if that item calls for a "Yes" or "No" answer, enter that response rather than a dash line.

5. Make your responses to each item as complete, concise, and clear as possible.

6. List your references carefully. Choose references who

know you and your abilities or other traits reasonably well and who can give the employer the information he probably wants. List the exact number of references requested—no more and no less. If the form requests specific kinds of references (for example, former employer, professional person, banker, and minister), give such references.

7. If there is a section labeled "remarks" or "other information," provide significant data not already given. These data may include (a) your financial situation, such as insurance carried, savings plan, home ownership, and the like; (b) participation in church or other community activities; and (c) formal or informal specialized study that relates to the job sought.

8. Follow all directions carefully. For example, if the form requests a list of all your previous positions, enter first your present (or last) position, then your next to last position, and so forth in reverse chronological order.

Conducting a Direct-by-Mail Job Campaign

Under some circumstances, a person may conduct a direct-by-mail campaign to obtain a position. Although this job-seeker may have no information of actual vacancies, he can employ this device to make himself known to business or other organizations that may have job openings.

In using this approach, the job-seeker should try to determine in advance whether the organization probably employs persons with his qualifications or whether it has the kinds of positions of interest to him.

The direct-by-mail job-seeking letter should have essentials that are similar to those already mentioned for a letter of application. The letter, for example, should be legible, neat, attractive, and free from errors in spelling.

Although the direct-by-mail letter cannot refer to a particular vacancy, it can and should emphasize the possibility that the prospective employer may be interested in the applicant either now or later. If this employer has ready at hand information about the applicant and his qualifications, he may consider that applicant for a replacement position or for a newly-created position.

The direct-by-mail job-seeker should address and send his letter to the appropriate officer in the organization. This officer may be the director of the employment office, the personnel director, or the head of a department within the organization. In any case, the applicant will find it desirable to address his letter to a particular person within the organization rather than to the organization in general.

TYPES OF JOB PLACEMENT OR SERVICE AGENCIES

Counselees need to know that the two general types of job placement agencies are (1) those financed by the public from taxes and operated by nonprofit public agencies, and (2) those financed privately and operated by nonprofit or profit-making organizations. Both types of agencies aim to provide services to both employees and employers.

In the United States, the job placement services that are publicly supported and administered are provided by the United States Employment Service and by the state employment services in the several states. These public placement services will be discussed next; private placement services will be described later in this chapter.

Public Placement Services

Under varying arrangements and in varying degrees since 1918, the federal government and the states have cooperated in the provision of free, public placement services. At present, each state carries the primary responsibility for public job placement activities within its borders. Its state employment service, usually in the state department of labor, maintains, directs, and supervises branch offices in key localities. This service also cooperates closely with local private (both nonprofit and profit-making) placement agencies.

The United States Employment Service, a part of the U.S. Department of Labor, serves as a coordinating center of public job placement agencies for the entire country, as a research center for the development of improved placement techniques, and as a clearing house of state and national information.

Over the years, some job-seekers and some employers have

had an unfavorable attitude toward public employment services—local, state, and federal. Certain individuals and groups have criticized these public agencies, charging that they were a waste of taxpayers' money and that they were providing inferior services. One reason for this hostile attitude was probably the fact that public agencies did not charge a service fee either to job-seekers or to employers. To some people, a service is not regarded favorably if it has not been paid for directly.

Even so, the state employment services that have had the necessary financial support and that have maintained high standards in terms of personnel and operating techniques have functioned and still function satisfactorily. In the light of this fact, counselors should get well-acquainted with their nearest state employment service office. There they can find out what that office offers in the way of services. They can then pass this information along to their counselees.

State Help to the Handicapped

Nearly all states now have rehabilitation service offices that are charged with the responsibility of helping the physically handicapped (the blind, the deaf, and the crippled, for example) to secure the kinds of training and placement services they need to become self-supporting. To help support these services, the federal government makes grants-in-aid to the states. Using this federal grant and state-granted funds, the rehabilitation service office of each state allocates money to handicapped individuals to cover all or part of the expense of their rehabilitation programs. When, as, and if the handicapped person appears to be employable, the state rehabilitation service refers that person to the state employment service; the latter then tries to place him in a job that is suited to his abilities.

The effectiveness of programs for the rehabilitation and placement of handicapped persons varies from state to state. There can be no doubt, however, that in recent years many states have steadily improved their services to handicapped residents. These improvements have been due mainly to war and postwar experiences through which the states developed new techniques for working with the handicapped. These techniques have resulted in better specialized training and more selective placement of handicapped persons. Many states, furthermore, have rendered service to increasing numbers of the handicapped.

Civil Service Commissions

Civil service commissions, whether federal, state, or local, are not employment offices as such. Nevertheless, they are mentioned here because they indirectly render placement services to job-seekers. The main responsibility of these commissions is to recruit and certify candidates for other public agencies. For state governmental units, for example, the state civil service commission performs services that are similar to those provided by a personnel department for its business organization.

The federal government and each state or local government that uses the merit system for appointment of needed personnel has a civil service commission. The functions of such a commission are as follows:

1. To classify and to define positions according to a logical system

2. To set up the specifications of the work involved in particular positions

3. To determine the qualifications of the candidates required to fill these positions

4. To develop the necessary application forms and examinations for positions

5. To administer the necessary application forms and examinations to candidates for positions

6. To evaluate filled-out application forms, to grade examination papers, and, in some instances, to interview candidates

7. To rate candidates on the basis of the combined data— for example, test scores, training, experience, and other relevant information as given in filled-out application forms

In terms of the foregoing types of functions, a civil service commission is the mechanism whereby a government administration that operates according to the merit system tries to select the best possible candidates for open positions. Toward this goal, such a commission is charged with the responsibility not only of rating candidates but also of setting standards and procedures for the promotion or the transfer of employees. The commission, furthermore, usually has the task of administering whatever retirement plan has been established by the governmental body.

The United States Civil Service Commission (in existence since 1883) and many of the state civil service commissions have excellent records of public service. Through their work, these commissions have contributed significantly to the development of better personnel services in many private business organizations.

Private Placement Agencies

Privately financed and operated agencies may be divided into two main groups—profit and nonprofit. The agencies organized for profit charge fees for their services; they are ordinarily referred to as commercial placement agencies. Nearly all of the nonprofit agencies make no charge for their services; a few of them, however, charge fees that are usually nominal.

For the right to operate, commercial placement agencies must secure licenses from their states; thereafter, these agencies are subject to state regulation. Thereby, each state endeavors to protect the public against possible abuses, such as exorbitant placement fees and other unfair practices.

In nearly every large city, there are many commercial placement agencies. Because these agencies have operated honestly, competently, and efficiently, they have earned for themselves a respected and permanent place in the community. Such agencies render necessary and valuable services to both job-seekers and employers.

Although the community may have a public employment office that functions in a highly satisfactory fashion, it still needs the services of reliable commercial placement agencies. For some kinds of placement, for example, the private agency is fitted to render certain specialized services that the public employment office does not or cannot offer.

Nonprofit placement offices other than those of public employment services are maintained by a wide variety of organizations in the United States. Some of the larger public high schools have such offices, usually attached to the administration; these offices assist high-school students to get part-time or summer work before graduation or full-time work after graduation.

If the community does not have a local public employment office or commercial employment agency, the high school does have an obligation to operate a systematically organized placement service. Such a service is usually welcomed by local employers because through the high school they can obtain the name of a job-seeker and specific, authentic information about him. This information, of course, appears in the school's personnel files.

The larger colleges and universities operate placement services primarily for the benefit of their graduates. And so do private schools that offer specialized training in general business subjects, secretarial work, beauty culture, radio, television, diesel engines, and the like. Many of these colleges and business and trade schools have developed close contacts with potential employers. Some schools have been relatively selective in their recommendations of qualified candidates to employers. For such reasons, these educational institutions have built up a fine reputation for their placement services. As a result, employers actively seek the graduates of these schools. Moreover, the public increasingly recognizes that these institutions are rendering important services to society.

A large number of colleges and universities that should be offering effective placement services to their own students and to prospective employers are not doing so. Many of these higher institutions, for example, are not sufficiently aggressive in their placement efforts; many are not as efficient in their placement work as they should be. These colleges usually have a great deal of highly valuable and readily available information about the young men and women whom they have trained. Therefore, these educational institutions are in a particularly good position to carry on programs of selective placement.

Some associations of professionally-trained persons maintain placement services for their members. These services are usually made available through the information appearing in the columns of the associations' journals or through the associations' offices. The latter may have on file the records of candidates; they send these records to employers on request.

Placement services are rendered on a nonprofit basis not only by the institutions and groups already mentioned but also by such organizations as the following: trade associations, merchants' associations, chambers of commerce, and labor unions. Certain labor unions, for instance, have been especially effective in placing their members.

Specialization in Placement

Theoretically, state employment service offices do not limit their services to certain types of personnel. In actual practice, however, these public offices in some states have been most active in placing office workers, sales people, supervisors, foremen, skilled and unskilled workers, and domestic help. These offices have given little or no attention to placement in the professional and highly technical occupations.

Rather generally, the offices of private employment agencies specialize in the placement of certain kinds of personnel— for example, school teachers, supervisors, and administrators; general business workers and office workers; business executives; professional engineers; nurses and laboratory technicians; skilled workers; unskilled laborers; and domestic workers. In a large city, the names, addresses, and phone numbers of these specialized placement agencies usually appear under the heading "Employment Agencies" in the classified telephone directory (the yellow pages).

Reliability of Placement Agencies

Before referring students and former students to a private employment agency, the counselor should learn certain essential facts about the agency. These facts may well include the following: the name of the agency's owner or of its sponsoring organization; the reputation of the person or persons who head the agency; the standing of the agency according to the employers and the employees who have used its services; the financial integrity of the agency; and the provisions of the contract that its registrants (job-seekers) must sign.

Before signing such a contract, the registrant should read carefully and understand thoroughly all the detailed provisions of that contract. Thereby, for instance, the registrant can find out exactly what he must pay the agency for its services. These payments usually include the registration fee and the service fee or commission. The latter is customarily in the form of a certain percentage of the registrant's income from the new job during a given period of time—the first several weeks or months, or the first year. Most agencies permit the registrant who is placed to pay the fee or commission due on an installment plan.

By careful reading of the contract, the registrant can also determine whether he must pay the fee or commission in full, even though unforeseen circumstances prevent him from taking the position after he has accepted it. Moreover, the registrant can learn the maximum length of time that he can wait after receipt of notice of a vacancy before he must notify the agency whether he wants to be recommended for a position. The contract may have a clause stating that failure to reply to a vacancy notice before a given deadline obligates the registrant to pay the full commission whether or not he applies for the announced position.

Familiarity with Legal Regulations

For the benefit of his counselees and for his own protection, a placement officer or counselor should know the provisions of federal, state, and local labor laws and of the regulations thereunder—for example, laws governing the establishment, licensing, and operation of placement or employment agencies; laws pertaining to fair labor practices; laws controlling the working conditions of women; child labor laws; compulsory school attendance laws; social security laws; unemployment compensation laws; and workmen's compensation laws. If the placement officer does not know the legal regulations that bear upon placement activities and employment conditions, he may give his counselee incorrect information, information that may hamper if not harm the job-seeker. However, if this officer is familiar with such regulations, he is more likely to give the job-seeker sound advice.

SUGGESTIONS FOR A SCHOOL'S PLACEMENT SERVICES

Assuming that a high school or college has financed and staffed its placement office, that office may well conduct such service-related activities as the following:

1. Determine the kinds of positions and the kinds of registrants that the office will handle.

2. Publicize the office's services among present and former students and among prospective employers.

3. Set up a filing system that classifies available jobs and that has cross references to these jobs.

4. Establish cooperative relationships with prospective employers. To do this, a placement officer can write brief to-the-point letters to employers. Or, even better, he can telephone them. Or, best of all, he can visit and talk with them. By knowing employers personally, the placement officer is best able to develop cooperative working relationships.

5. From employers, obtain notices of their job vacancies and their specifications for these jobs. For each notice, make out a card and place it in the employers' card file.

6. Interview and register job-seekers. Secure as complete information as possible concerning the qualifications of each registrant. This information should include vital data (birth date, place of birth, sex, etc.); school record (major and minor fields and academic marks); offices held in school or community organizations; hobbies and other interests; and work experiences. The registrant should supply most of these facts when he fills out his biographical form.

7. Organize an efficient filing system of registrants' data. This system should include a registration or applicant's card and a file folder for each registrant. This folder should hold copies of the registrant's biographical form.

8. Secure definitive statements from the references listed by each registrant.

9. Check up on the accuracy of the information given by each registrant on his registration card and on his biographical form.

10. For a vacant position announced by an employer, select the registrants to be recommended by the placement

office. To do this, a placement officer should carefully screen all registrants; he should then recommend as candidates only those registrants who appear to meet the qualifications specified by the employer. If the placement officer recommends an unqualified person, this action may bring disappointment to the candidate and may alienate the employer.

11. Notify registrants of job vacancies and secure their approval before recommending them for these jobs.

12. Send to the prospective employer a copy of each recommended candidate's biographical form. Include a covering letter. In some cases, this letter may present the highlights of a candidate's qualifications.

13. Later, check with the prospective employer to find out (a) whether he offered the job to the recommended candidate and, if he did so, (b) whether the candidate accepted that job.

14. Record the results of a job application in the employers' card file and in the candidates' card file. In the active sections of these files, respectively, put the cards of unfilled vacancies and of unplaced candidates.

15. At the end of each academic year, prepare a summary report of the work of the placement office. In this report, include the number of registrants placed according to types of positions, the number of notices of job vacancies received, and the like. Give copies of this report to the school's administrative head and other staff members, to present and former students, to the parents of students, and to the press.

16. From time to time, conduct follow-up studies to evaluate and to improve the services of the placement office. These studies may include two types of questionnaires—one to be filled out by former students; the other, by their employers.

In handling the placement of students in part-time jobs or in summer jobs, the placement office does *not* have to carry on all of the foregoing activities. It does *not* need to collect detailed information about registrants or to supply such detailed information to prospective employers. For part-time and summer jobs, the office should have appropriate card files for candidates and for employers; these cards, however, need to contain only the most essential information.

NECESSARY CHARACTERISTICS OF THE PLACEMENT COUNSELOR

Whether the placement counselor is a staff member of a public or private agency, he should have characteristics and should carry on activities such as these:

1. He should be professional-minded. That is, he should be activated by professional motives and guided by professional standards of conduct.

2. He should give highest priority to the welfare of each job-seeker.

3. He should take whatever time is necessary to secure all the pertinent facts, to consider these facts, and to act on the basis of these facts.

4. He should employ the most reliable and valid devices to appraise the job-seeker's qualifications.

5. He should investigate thoroughly the reputations and the practices of the employers who wish to use his services.

6. He should recommend the job-seeker for a position that seems best in terms of the latter's qualifications and of the latter's situation.

7. He should cooperate in every way possible with each job-seeker and with each employer.

8. He should be objective-minded, honest, and fair in all his relationships with the job-seeker and with the employer.

SUMMARY

Placement service is among the most important of all guidance services. Its major purpose is to assist counselees to obtain positions that meet their interests, needs, and capabilities. The extent to which the placement service fulfills this purpose is a measure of the effectiveness of its work.

Placement service, of course, is one part of the total program of guidance services. Another part is the service rendered to students in the field of their personal problems, the subject of the next chapter.

SUGGESTED READINGS

Boynton, Paul W. *Six Ways to Get a Job*. New York: Harper and Brothers, 1951.

Froehlich, Clifford P. *Guidance Services in Smaller Schools.* New York: McGraw-Hill Book Company, Inc., 1950. Pp. 226-256.

Kirkpatrick, Forrest H., *et al. Helping Students Find Employment.* American Council on Education Studies, Series 6, Student Personnel Work, No. 12. Washington, D.C.: American Council on Education, 1949.

Reed, Anna Y. *Occupational Placement, Its History, Procedures and Educational Implications.* Ithaca, N.Y.: Cornell University Press, 1946.

Smith, Glenn E. *Principles and Practices of the Guidance Program.* New York: Macmillan Company, 1951. Pp. 288-335.

Tanneyhill, Ann. *From School to Job: Guidance for Minority Youth.* New York: Public Affairs Committee, 1953.

Wrenn, C. Gilbert. *Student Personnel Work in College.* New York: The Ronald Press Company, 1951. Pp. 349-411.

CHAPTER FOURTEEN

Helping Students Solve Personal Problems

HIGH-SCHOOL and college students confront many problems other than those related to educational and vocational matters. Such problems may be conveniently referred to as *personal problems.*

Many young people face certain problems that are so highly personal in nature that they bear their difficulties alone and in silence. These youth hesitate to discuss such problems with older persons or even with their closest companions. Youth also have certain other personal problems that they willingly talk about with others, with adults and with their peers. Yet, no matter what personal problems young persons face, the guidance worker should be alert to these problems and should be ready to assist in their solution.

PERSONAL PROBLEMS RELATED TO PROBLEMS IN OTHER AREAS

In the life of a young person, the area of personal problems is not isolated from other areas, such as those of educational problems and vocational problems. Rather, these areas sometimes overlap and are often interrelated. Nevertheless, for the purpose of study and discussion, each area has been treated in a separate chapter of this book. The present chapter, as its title indicates, focuses upon the personal problems of youth.

To illustrate the interrelatedness of problem areas, a high-school boy is making low marks in many of his subjects of study. This educational problem creates a vocational problem. The boy cannot gain admission to a college that will train him for the occupation of his choice. The boy's failure in school-work and his disappointment about his career cause personal problems. He has feelings of frustration and defeat because of his own apparent shortcomings. And he has feelings of unhappiness and hostility because of his parents' criticisms.

As already suggested, no hard-and-fast lines can or should be drawn between problem areas or between a problem in one area and that in another area. Even so, in dealing with the personal problems of youth, guidance workers have found that the classification of these problems by areas is extremely useful in counseling activities.

COMMONLY-OBSERVED PERSONAL PROBLEMS

A number of research workers have made studies of the problems of young people. On the basis of these studies, they have prepared lists of problems according to the frequency of occurrence. They have also classified the problems listed according to areas—personal, educational, and vocational, for example. These researchers have then prepared check lists in which students indicate the problems that are troubling them. Among such check lists are those developed by Mooney and by Remmers.[1]

Drawing upon the findings of Mooney, Remmers, and other investigators, the authors of this book suggest the following seven-fold classification of personal problems:

1. Problems related to *physical health* and *constitutional development*

2. Problems related to *social relationships* (nature and extent of participation in social, civic, and recreational activities; likes and dislikes for other people; degree of harmony in social relationships; personal satisfaction obtained)

3. Problems related to *emotional behavior* (general emotional tones and actions in various situations; freedom from

[1] Ross L. Mooney and Leonard V. Gordon, *The Mooney Problem Check Lists Manual* (New York: Psychological Corporation, 1950).

H. H. Remmers, A. J. Drucker, and Benjamin Shimberg, *SRA Youth Inventory Manual* (Chicago: Science Research Associates, 1949). Also, H. H. Remmers and Robert H. Baurenfeind, *SRA Junior Inventory Manual* (Chicago: Science Research Associates, 1951).

mental fears; mental and emotional self-sufficiency; feelings of self-confidence and self-reliance)

4. Problems related to *home and family relationships* (attitudes toward parents, brothers, sisters, or other relatives living in the home)
5. Problems related to *sex, dating, courtship, and marriage*
6. Problems related to *finances*
7. Problems related to *ideals, morals, religion*

CONCEPTS BASIC TO THE SOLUTION
OF PERSONAL PROBLEMS

As a counselor works to help a young person to solve his personal problems, he should have certain basic concepts in mind. The counselor should understand these concepts so thoroughly that he habitually applies them at every stage of his efforts to assist a youth to deal effectively with his personal situations. Each of these concepts and a discussion of it are presented next.

The first concept: Personality is both whole and complex.

As pointed out in Chapter 3, when a person reacts to a situation, his whole being tends to be involved in that response. This is because personality is a manifestation of a physical organism in action—an organism that responds both in a specialized or partial way and in a generalized or total way, at the same time.

Personality has a physical basis and that physical basis involves the structure and the functioning of the organism. Said another way, one's personality is affected by the condition of his body and by the state of his mind. Because body and mind are closely interrelated, a bodily disturbance such as a migraine headache or an upset stomach, for example, can render the mind less able to act up to its capacity. Or, a mental disturbance as displayed by a pessimistic, timid, or fearful attitude can produce a bodily ailment. The general mental or emotional tone of a person, moreover, can cause not only immediate physical discomfort but also prolonged physical malfunctioning.

The interdependence of body and mind, as it bears on

personality, is shown in the following cases. A person develops a chronic sinus condition; this may alter certain expressions of his personality. Such a person may become easily irritated by others; he may even become a hypochondriac. Another person is so anxious or worried that he develops such bodily ills as severe headaches or serious stomach ulcers.

The foregoing discussion implies not only the wholeness of personality but also its complexity. Both in structure and in function, the human body and the human mind are characterized most aptly by the word "complex." This fact is revealed by anatomical and physiological studies of the body including the brain and other parts of the nervous system. The fact is also evident in studies of human behavior ranging from uncontrolled observations to scientific mental measurements. Personality indeed is a highly complex phenomenon.

The second concept: A person's problems are often interrelated.

As suggested earlier, a personal problem seldom if ever occurs in isolation. Rather, it usually is in a setting that is composed of a cluster of problems—problems that interact one on another.

An example is the case of a physically handicapped high-school boy who faces the educational problem of staying in school until he graduates. He is under pressure from his family to earn money. This pressure, say, is due to the fact that the family is having trouble in making both ends meet financially. The youth's physical condition, however, makes it difficult for him to find a gainful job. This boy faces an educational problem that is interrelated with other problems—his own physical problem, his family's financial problem, his vocational problem, and his problem of getting along harmoniously with his parents.

As another instance of the interaction and interrelatedness of problems, consider next the case of the young woman who is a spastic. Despite her handicap, she has graduated from college. Her main problem then is vocational—to get a job that meets her interests and abilities. Due to lack of physical coordination, this woman writes with great difficulty; her speech and hearing are also impaired. She tried out as a library assistant, a job in which she worked alone. Although this young woman did her best, she was unable to meet the demands of her position; as a result, she lost the job. This young person faced not only a physical problem and a vocational problem but also a family problem. Her mother refused to try to secure work for herself; instead, she insisted that her daughter support her. As the family had no other source of financial support, the daughter was caught in a difficult and uncomfortable situation—a situation made up of a complex of interrelated problems.

The two cases just cited point out that, in helping a counselee to solve his personal problem, the counselor should recognize that such a problem often relates to and interacts with other problems.

The third concept: Personal problems have causes.

The counselor should have in the forefront of his thinking the fact that a personal problem always has a cause or causes. If he does so, he is more likely to focus his attention on causes than on symptoms. If he observes only symptoms, his counseling will probably be superficial.

Some causes of a problem may be fairly obvious; they can be determined from casual observations. Other causes may be relatively well hidden; they can be ascertained only by careful studies that go to the roots of the problem.

In searching for the causes of a student's personal problem, the counselor should recognize that there may be a number of causes, that these causes may occur serially over a period of time, and that, at any given instant, these causes have varying degrees of influence on the problem situation. No matter what the causes or their comparative bearing on the problem, the counselor should help the counselee to understand these causes and to weigh their relative importance.

To make the foregoing point concrete, some of the findings from an actual study of the case of Don are presented next. In working with Don, the counselor read reports and made observations that revealed the following symptoms of the youth's personal problem:

1. A tendency to expend effort only if driven by outside pressure

2. Ability to achieve a fair measure of success in a field in which he was actively interested (drama and related fields)

3. Lack of good work habits

4. A tendency not to keep his promises

5. A tendency to minimize or gloss over his failure to achieve even in a minimum degree

6. A tendency to dramatize himself, to push himself to the center of the stage, and to use other ways to bring himself to the attention of other people

7. Undue interest in his poor physical condition

After observing and analyzing the symptoms of Don's case, the counselor concluded that the basic or primary cause of the youth's personal problem was his physical weakness—a weakness due to poor general health over many years. Because of this weakness, Don lacked the physical energy required to adapt himself to new situations. Consequently, his personal growth was retarded and his social development was inadequate and incomplete. Although Don was a youth of college age, he showed many signs of early adolescence and, at times, of childishness.

In studying Don's case further, the counselor discovered that the contributory causes of the youth's personal problem were as follows:

1. Because of Don's poor physical condition, his mother had an overly protective attitude toward him; also, she often overindulged him. Don's home did not stimulate him to exert effort or to develop physically.

2. Don's older sister was mentally and physically quicker than he. She put forth greater efforts to succeed in school and elsewhere. Because of this, the parents continually cited their daughter as the model that Don should emulate.

As mentioned earlier, the counselor observed that Don's personal problem involved poor achievement in school subjects accompanied by immature emotional reactions. The counselor might have attributed this problem solely to the youth's lack of good work habits. But instead, the counselor traced Don's problem further until he believed that he had identified its root causes. Thereby, the counselor was able to help Don think back through his experiences and to discover for himself that his prolonged physical weakness was the primary cause of his personal problem.

The fourth concept: Personal problems always have emotional aspects.

Because the emotional aspects of personality are so important, the counselor should give them careful consideration in dealing with personal problems.

In an interview, the skilled counselor is alert to the emotional tones, the feeling states, and the attitudes of the counselee. The counselor looks and listens for answers to questions such as these:

1. What is the counselee's general attitude toward himself?

2. What is the counselee's typical attitude toward other people?

3. What does the counselee think the attitudes of people are toward him? What are their actual attitudes toward him?

4. Does the counselee's behavior indicate that he is living in a world of reality or in a world of fantasy? Does the counselee live solely within himself, with little or no attempt to participate in the outside world, a world of "give-and-take"?

5. In the counselee's day-to-day behavior, do his emotions ordinarily control his thoughts and actions? Or, do his rational processes serve as a governor of his emotional reactions?

As the counselor obtains answers to the foregoing types of questions, he gains increasing insight into the counselee's personal problem and into promising possibilities for its solution.

The fifth concept: The individual's self-concept is often the key to his personal problems.

As was pointed out in Chapter 3, each individual has a concept of self made up of his thoughts and feelings about himself. He tends to behave or wants to behave in a manner that is consistent with this concept.

While the counselor is working with a counselee in interviews, he should attempt to obtain a picture of the counselee's self-concept. He should also compare this self-concept with other information about the counselee—objective test data, interest inventory findings, school marks, anecdotal records, reports of extracurricular participation, accounts of interviews with parents, and the like. Through such data, the counselor is able to obtain as clear and complete a picture as possible of the counselee's self-concept—a picture that is of great value in counseling.

The role of the counselee's self-concept has been aptly described by Spache,[2] as follows:

> Each of us has a concept of self, an ego-ideal of what we are. This idea about ourselves and, consequently, our behavior undergoes gradual crystallization as we mature. It continues to be modified as we age and are forced to adjust ourselves to the realities of our physical status and our environment. Thus throughout our lives, our ideas of self, our habits and behavior, are constantly being modified by new experiences and by an attempt to assimilate and adjust these experiences to our concept of self.

As just implied by Spache, the individual's behavior is modified and his personality is altered by the influence of his environment, in which people are obviously an important part. In the process of solving personal problems, the individual engages in a continuous struggle between his self-concepts and the impact of his environment.

In normal behavior, the individual constantly attempts to resolve the differences between his internal standards, desires, and demands and those of his environment, particularly those of the persons and the groups with whom he is most closely associated. If the individual finds it difficult to resolve these differences through changing himself or his environment, he is likely to face personal problems that are new or that are more serious than before.

---

[2] George Spache, "The Learner's Concept of Self," *Education for the Preservation of Democracy,* pp. 97-99. A Report of the Thirteenth Educational Conference (New York City, October 28-29, 1948), under the auspices of the Educational Records Bureau and the American Council on Education (Washington, D.C.: American Council on Education, April, 1949).

In helping the individual to solve his personal problem, as the foregoing suggests, one of the counselor's main tasks is to lead that counselee to determine the nature and extent of the existing differences between his self-concept and the pressure of his environment. As the counselee makes this determination, he increasingly understands why he is what he is, why he has his particular problem. The answers involve two factors— the counselee himself, that is, his personal characteristics and experiences; and the counselee's environment, that is, the outside forces that are pressing upon him.

With such understanding, the counselee may find it necessary to adapt his behavior in order to gain the satisfactions that he wants out of life, both as an individual and as a member of society. Or, to obtain these satisfactions, the counselee may have to modify his environment—to make new friends, for example.

The sixth concept: The individual should develop his own insights into his personal problems.

According to this concept, discussed in Chapter 7, the counselor should counsel in such a way that the counselee gains in his understanding both of himself and of his problems. This means that the counselor does *not* tell the counselee immediately and directly what he thinks the counselee's problems are or what he believes the solution to any one of these problems is. Rather, it means that the counselor assumes a nondirective or permissive attitude—an attitude that encourages the counselee to develop his own insights and to make his own decisions.

AIMS OF COUNSELING AS A MEANS OF SOLVING PERSONAL PROBLEMS

In handling a counselee's personal problem, the immediate goal of the counselor and counselee is to arrive at the most satisfying solution as quickly as possible. Beyond such a goal, the counselor has other objectives in view. These objectives involve both the near future and the more distant future as these relate to the counselee's well-being.

The counselor, of course, works to help the counselee

reach an early adjustment to his personal problem. This adjustment may relieve the counselee's current difficulty through a solution of the problem; or, it may help him to live with his problem, at least for a while. At the same time, the counselor strives to assist the counselee in working out a long-term program for solving his personal problems—a program that develops both maturity and self-sufficiency.

In aiding an individual to solve his personal problems, the counselor should apply such principles as these:

1. Assist the counselee in recognizing what is generally considered normal behavior in a problem situation.

2. Assist the counselee in making acceptable adaptations to his current problem situation.

3. Assist the counselee in laying the foundations on which he can build acceptable adaptations during an extended period of time.

4. Assist the counselee in accepting responsibility for making his own decisions.

5. Assist the counselee in working out for himself a reliable pattern whereby he can analyze his personal problem situations and devise ways to meet them. Such a pattern should encourage and enable the counselee to solve his problems largely by his own abilities and efforts.

In line with these principles, the over-all aim of the counselor is to assist the counselee in achieving reasonably good solutions to his problems—solutions that contribute to personal happiness and welfare. If these solutions are in keeping with the counselee's self-concept and if they are acceptable to the key persons within his environment, they are more likely to bring him the greatest possible satisfactions. If not, these "solutions" may cause the counselee to experience internal frustrations and external conflicts.

At this point, the reader may well raise the question: How far should the individual go in adjusting his inner drives, ambitions, and attitudes toward himself to the demands and requirements of the environment? Assume that the individual's present environment is highly restricted and inflexible. He may be able to obtain an environment that is freer and more flexible in two ways. First, without changing his residence, the individual may find a more favorable environment. For example, he may join new groups of people who have ideas like his and who are accepted by the community. Or, the individual may seek out a new environment in a new locale. This environment may be more in harmony with his self-concept and more in line with his desired pattern of behavior.

The individual's specific self-concept and his general behavioral pattern are, of course, molded by his previous environment. The degree to which he can become independent of the influence of that environment depends on such factors as his chronological age, mental ability, and emotional maturity.

METHODS OF COUNSELING YOUTH ABOUT PERSONAL PROBLEMS

As pointed out before, personal problems are usually complex and interrelated. These problems differ from individual to individual. No two individuals have exactly the same cluster of problems. Although these individuals appear to have the same problem, say, undue timidity, each faces this problem as a unique personality in a unique situation. For the foregoing reasons, the counselor should not try to use identical procedures in working with his counselees. Instead, he should adapt these procedures to the personal problems and needs of each counselee.

Whatever procedures the counselor uses and however he adapts them, he should have in view certain guideposts. These guideposts, described later in this chapter, are not predetermined steps that the counselor should take. Rather, these guideposts are road signs that the counselor may well observe in aiding a counselee with his personal problems. The counselor, of course, will employ the suggestions accompanying these stated guideposts only when, as, and if these suggestions are appropriate to the counselee and his problem situation.

At this point, it should be emphasized, the processes of counseling with an individual about his personal problems are not exact sciences—and probably will never be. That is why the counselor should employ the principles, methods, and content not only of science but also of such fields as philosophy, art, psychology, history, and sociology. Using the various methods developed in all these fields, the counselor obtains both objective and subjective information about the counselee and his situation. Drawing upon his own background of knowledge and experience, the counselor develops the insights, intuitions, and hunches whereby he aids the counselee in solving his personal problems.

In its complete form, counseling in the field of personal problems consists of these aspects:

1. *Gathering facts:* Collection of information (a) about the counselee's problem and (b) about the counselee

2. *Diagnosis:* Careful analysis of the available facts about the counselee

3. *Prognosis:* Forecast of the outcome of the counselee's course of action

4. *Therapy:* Assistance to the counselee in working out a solution to his problem

5. *Follow-up:* Later check upon the counselee's success or failure in solving his problem

Searching for Information about the Counselee's Problem

Because the counselee comes to the counselor for help in a problem situation, the counselor's natural first step is to find out as clearly as possible just what that situation is. During the interview, the counselor should attempt to get at the roots of the counselee's situation. He should first attempt to establish rapport with the counselee; such rapport is essential to understand the counselee and to work with him. The counselor should then encourage the counselee to express himself freely and frankly about himself and his problem.

As the counselee talks, the counselor should be on the alert to sense whether the counselee is revealing all that he might and should. If the counselor does not obtain sufficient rapport with or information from the counselee, he should arrange for further interviews.

In the search for information about the counselee's problem, the counselor should look for such items as these:

1. The setting in which the counselee's problem exists

2. The involvement of other persons in the counselee's situation

3. The characteristics of these persons that have significance in the situation

4. The relationships of the particular problem to the counselee's other problems—that is, to other aspects of the counselee's life

5. The length of time that the problem has troubled the counselee

6. The nature and effectiveness of earlier attempts by the counselee to resolve his problem

On the basis of information such as that just outlined, the counselor can reach at least a tentative conclusion as to the general nature of the counselee's problem. In drawing such a conclusion, the counselor will find that many of the personal problems of high-school and college students are not deep-seated and do not involve serious emotional disturbances. For this reason, the crux of these problems can be rather easily identified.

At times, however, the counselor is confronted by a counselee whose personal problem is relatively complex. For example, a counselee appears to have a clear-cut financial problem. However, during an interview he reveals that this problem is complicated by other problems, such as emotional maladjustments due to strained relationships with his family. In such a case, the counselor should not make a quick, superficial determination of the counselee's difficulty. Rather, he should make a thorough analysis of the counselee's situation before deciding what the latter's basic problem is.

Searching for Information about the Counselee

The counselor should study not only the counselee's problem situation but also the counselee himself. In the process of securing facts about the counselee's problem, the counselor also obtains much additional information about the counselee. During an interview, the counselee often brings out new facts and opinions about himself and his problem. These data are highly useful to the alert, experienced counselor. Such a counselor, for example, makes mental notes of the counselee's expressions of attitudes toward himself and toward others. These expressions indicate the counselee's feelings of self-confidence or lack of it, of his hopes or fears; they also indicate his successes or failures, his acceptance or rejection by others. The alert counselor also observes the emotional tone of the counselee as disclosed during his statements about himself and his problem situation. Through the foregoing, the counselor obtains understandings and insights that are highly valuable to him in helping the counselee to solve his personal problem.

The counselor must decide how much information and what kinds of information he needs to aid the counselee. If the latter's problem is serious and complex, the counselor requires more data than usual. But if the counselee's problem is relatively simple and easy to solve, he needs only a few items of information.

Whether or not the counselor makes a complete case study of a counselee, he will find useful the following outline of the types of information that may be sought.

1. Physical history
   a. Age
   b. Sex
   c. Physical and mental health
      (1) General health
      (2) Special disabilities or weaknesses, if any
2. Family history
   a. Ancestry
   b. Parents
   c. Siblings
   d. Economic status (financial resources)
   e. Cultural status
   f. Relationships within the family (attitudes of family members toward counselee and of counselee toward them)
3. History of social development
   a. In school
   b. Outside school
4. School history
   a. Elementary school
   b. High school
   c. College
      (At each of the foregoing levels, investigate such

matters as successes and failures, strengths and weaknesses, and efforts toward remediation of the latter.)

5. Mental qualities
   a. Level of general mental ability
   b. Special mental abilities
   c. Aptitudes
6. Other personality traits
   a. Interests
   b. Emotional characteristics
   c. Motivations (ambitions, goals, and the like)
   d. Pattern of values (moral ideas and ideals, standards
      of personal conduct)
   e. Religious ideas and practices

Collecting Information during the Interview

During the interview, the counselor must decide whether
to make notes of what the counselee is saying. If he believes
that such note-taking will interfere with the development or
maintenance of rapport, he obviously should not make such a
record in the presence of the counselee. This note-taking, moreover, tends to prevent or to stop the counselee from talking
about matters that are highly personal and emotionally-
charged. The counselee may fear that his revelations as recorded by the counselor will be used later to his disadvantage,
say, to punish or to humiliate him.

When the counselee is discussing matters that are unemo-
tional or nonconfidential, the counselor may take notes during
the interview. To maintain rapport, the counselor may introduce his note-taking by a remark such as this: "You won't
object, will you, if I write down the important facts or ideas
you are giving me? Otherwise, we may forget or overlook these
important points." Usually the counselee will readily agree to
this arrangement. Then note-taking tends to strengthen rather
than to weaken rapport.

During any interview, however, the counselor should probably keep his note-taking to a minimum. If he needs a record of
routine but key information about the counselee, he should
have the latter provide this information by filling in a ques-

tionnaire in advance of the interview. Then, during the interview, he can encourage the counselee to talk freely; he also can give his full attention to what is being said.

Making the Diagnosis

Although no hard-and-fast line can be drawn between diagnosis and therapy, the counselor will often find it valuable to identify these two aspects of the counseling process. According to Wrenn, "the counselor seeks (1) to understand the student, and (2) to provide assistance to the student in the form of interpretation, direct psychotherapy, or opportunity for self-clarification. Sometimes Step (1) is thought of as 'diagnosis' and Step (2) as 'therapy.'" [3]

Through diagnosis, the counselor gains a deeper and broader understanding of the counselee's personal problem. In making the diagnosis, the counselor draws upon the various types of information about the counselee and about his problem situation. The counselor not only assembles this information; he also evaluates, interprets, and applies it. For example, from the mass of available data, he selects the items that are relevant or pertinent. He carefully analyzes these items. He then compares, relates, and combines these items, thus obtaining a synthesis—an over-all understanding of the *modus vivendi* of the counselee.

In conducting this analysis, the counselor and the counselee should try to distinguish between a symptom and a cause, never mistaking the one for the other. They also should attempt to determine the basic cause or causes of the counselee's difficulty. This process of diagnosis has been described by Williamson in the following paragraph: [4]

After collecting analytical data, the counselor and the student search for a pattern of consistency in them. Such a pattern may describe and explain the student's characteristics and indicate the possible and desirable treatment, therapy, or counseling which should be carried out by the student and the counselor.

---

[3] C. Gilbert Wrenn, *Student Personnel Work in College* (New York: The Ronald Press Company, 1951), pp. 78, 79.

[4] By permission from *Counseling Adolescents*, by E. G. Williamson. Copyright, 1950. McGraw-Hill Book Company, Inc., p. 178.

Such a diagnosis-pattern may also be defined as a terse summary of problems, their causes, and other significant and relevant characteristics of the student, together with the implications for potential adjustments and maladjustments. The process of searching for such a pattern is called *diagnosing*.

Closely related to the foregoing is Wrenn's point of view concerning diagnosis, as expressed in the statement that follows: [5]

Diagnosis in counseling becomes the process of arriving at a specific and penetrating understanding of a student's characteristics within the context of his life pattern. This includes the identification of his present state of adjustment in a specific enough manner to suggest causal factors. Unless the basic psychological condition (meaning either fundamental personality characteristics or causes of present poor adjustment) is uncovered, one cannot say there has been a diagnosis.

Summing up, the counselor takes these steps in diagnosing a counselee's problems. *First,* he collects the facts. *Second,* he analyzes, interprets, and synthesizes the facts. *Third,* he discovers basic causes. And *fourth,* he develops a "penetrating understanding" of the counselee's problem situation—an understanding that leads to prognosis.

Working Out the Prognosis

In prognosis, the counselor predicts what the counselee may do or what may happen to the counselee with reference to his particular problem. More specifically, the counselor forecasts the extent to which the counselee may or may not make a desirable or satisfying adaptation to his situation.

In working out a prognosis, the counselor is looking ahead— to the counselee's future. On the basis of all available information, the counselor estimates the probable outcome of a course of action that the counselee may take in attempting to solve his problem situation.

Because the relationship between a given course of action and its outcome is sometimes obscure, Williamson suggests the possibility of telescoping diagnosis and prognosis: [6]

---

[5] Wrenn, *op. cit.,* p. 83.
[6] Williamson, *op. cit.,* p. 189.

Actually, diagnosis and prognosis are quite separate steps in clinical work. This separation is especially true where research and experience have not yet indicated the probable outcome or future adjustment likely to grow out of certain situations. In other types of problems, knowledge is adequate for the telescoping of the two steps. For example, research and clinical experiences have revealed that the overwhelming proportion of low-aptitude students fail to succeed in difficult school work. When the clinician sees a low-aptitude score in the case history of a student, he will not state the diagnosis as "low-intelligence." Rather, he will say, "too low ability for difficult school work," or "almost certain failure will result if this student tries to become a doctor as he now desires to do."

The counselor should recognize that a sound prognosis does not emerge suddenly and automatically from the mass of facts, symptoms, causes, and interpretations that are at hand. Rather, he realizes that such prognosis is the outcome of logical thinking, examination of relevant literature (perhaps a study of similar cases), and consultation with other counselors or faculty members. All this implies that, in some cases, the counselor can make a reliable prognosis only by carefully reconsidering his original prognosis in terms of all the facts available, both then and since.

Each counselee brings a unique problem situation to the counselor. Therefore, the counselor's prognosis of one counselee's problem situation should be different from that of another counselee's problem situation. Although the counselor may look for and learn from the common elements in different problem situations, he should avoid any tendency to generalize in his prognoses, for example, from the case of a previous counselee to that of a present counselee.

Conducting Therapy

Therapy, the development of a satisfactory solution to a personal problem, is the goal toward which the counselor and counselee have worked from the moment of their first contact. This goal has given purpose and direction to all the steps taken previously. Through these earlier steps, the counselee and the counselor have gained new insights that they can now sharpen and apply toward helping the counselee to make needed adaptations.

The process of therapy may be easy or difficult, depending on the nature of the counselee and of his problem situation. In one situation, the counselee and the counselor may quickly see the way to a promising solution even during the first interview. In another situation, however, the counselee and the counselor may require a series of interviews to arrive at a reasonably satisfactory solution.

Ideally, in therapy, the counselee should accept the major responsibility for determining the course of action to be taken in solving his problem. If the counselee himself makes this determination, he is more likely to follow that course of action.

For a given problem situation, it is often wise to develop alternate courses of action, each leading to a satisfactory solution. Such alternatives are particularly desirable if the counselee's problem is marked by complexities that are difficult to understand or by circumstances that are difficult to control. Then the counselee can pursue the first alternative. If he succeeds, well and good. But if he foresees failure during the early stages, he can abandon the first alternative and pursue the second.

As already suggested, the counselor should not attempt to apply a single form of therapy to all personal problems. The counselees involved, the attending circumstances, and the possible solutions—all differ from case to case. In the light of the foregoing, the counselor should adjust his therapy to the personality and the needs of each counselee as an individual. To help one individual, the counselor may wisely assume a directive attitude. To help another, he may rightly employ the nondirective approach.

With reference to therapy, Wrenn points out that "the kind of assistance to be given must be adapted to each individual. Diagnosis, or even a faltering attempt to understand the individual, has little practical value unless it leads to some development in the individual. For this reason the assistance provided is always a function of any diagnosis that is made." [7]

---

[7] Wrenn, *op. cit.*, pp. 80, 81.

Carrying on the Follow-Up

The counselor should follow up a counselee to determine the outcome of the latter's attempt to solve his personal problem because of at least two basic reasons—the welfare of the counselee, and the improvement of the counselor's professional effectiveness.

The counselor who has a real and continuing interest in a counselee actively seeks answers to such questions as these: Did the counselee's course of action prove to be both practical and satisfying? Did the counselee achieve relief from his problem situation? Did he achieve the goal he had set for himself?

The counselor who wishes to learn professionally from experience tries to follow up the case of each of his counselees. Thus, the counselor acquires knowledge that enables him to evaluate his work—the steps taken and the techniques used. If the counselor finds that a counselee has subsequently failed or succeeded, in whole or in part, he can and should review every aspect of his handling of the counselee's case. From this review, the counselor will discover the probable reasons for failure or for success. By studying these reasons, the counselor may be able to develop many improvements in his services.

In the field of helping individuals solve their personal problems, counselors up to now have lacked a sufficient body of complete and detailed case records—records that include follow-up information. As a result, counselors have had too little specific information as to the eventual outcomes of their counseling. They have not improved their counseling techniques and procedures as much as they should have. It is only the rare counselor who has adequate summaries of his cases and thorough evaluations of his devices.

As counselors give increasing attention to the follow-up of their former counselees, they will render greater assistance to their present counselees. They will also raise the levels of their professional competence.

No matter how competent the counselor, he should recognize that therapy is not the function of the counselor exclusively. He may collect the facts and make the preliminary diagnosis of a counselee's personal problem. In one school, for example, the psychologist who also served as the guidance chairman provided assistance to a student with a personal problem of ordinary difficulty. But in the case of a student with an involved problem, the psychologist and the school psychiatrist worked together. After making a tentative diagnosis, the psychologist turned over his report to the psychiatrist; the two discussed the report in a conference on the case. Thereafter, the psychiatrist handled the therapy for and the follow-up of the case.

SUMMARY

Helping students to solve their personal problems is one of the counselor's most difficult, most complex, and most challenging tasks. To perform this task well, the counselor should be skilled in various counseling techniques. He should know the mechanisms of personality. He should be able to think clearly and logically, and to make sound and discriminating judgments. The counselor, moreover, should have a strong belief in the worth of the individual. He should accept the counselee as he is and should strive to understand the latter's outlook.

In a given counselee's situation, the counselor should apply the available techniques that appear to be most appropriate. In this application, the counselor should use an individualized approach. He should not have one or even several preconceived patterns for dealing with all counselees' personal problems. Rather, the counselor should treat each counselee's problem as unique. If he does so, he will adapt his techniques both to the counselee and to the latter's problem situation.

In working with each case, the counselor should endeavor to collect and to relate all the facts, ideas, attitudes, and conditions that are relevant to the counselee's problem. He should sift and interpret all the evidence, although this is sometimes a difficult and laborious process.

During the course of counseling, the counselor should look for additional facts and new relationships; both help to illuminate the case. The counselor should be ever willing to review his interpretations and diagnoses. If the counselor has made incorrect interpretations or unsound diagnoses, he should be ready to make corrections—all designed to help the counselee to achieve a desirable and satisfying solution to his personal problem.

In working with a counselee whose personal problem is complicated by emotional involvements, the counselor should keep in mind such points as the following. *First,* the counselor should have a thorough understanding of the role of the emotions in personality. He should know the accepted facts and theories concerning the basic emotions—for example, how emotions develop and how they influence human behavior. *Second,* if the counselor has had some training in the psychology of emotions, he should be able to distinguish between so-called *normal* and *abnormal* reactions. "Borderline" reactions, of course, can be so classified only by the highly trained psychologist or psychiatrist. *Third,* unless the counselor has had exceptional training and experience, he should not attempt to diagnose or to treat the case of a counselee who is seriously disturbed emotionally. In such a case, the counselor should refer the counselee to a professional person who is thoroughly qualified to make the necessary diagnosis and to conduct the proper therapy.

From the foregoing, the counselor should not conclude that he has little or no responsibility for handling the cases of counselees whose personal problems have emotional complications. Neither should the counselor assume that he can make no contribution to the solution of these problems. The counselor, as just stated, works with seriously disturbed cases; he soon refers these cases to a psychologist or psychiatrist. The counselor also works with cases who have emotionally-charged problems, problems that he himself is able to handle. The latter group of cases is more typical—that is, most counselees are relatively normal in terms of their personal problems.

SUGGESTED READINGS

Barnard, Mildred B., and Blair, Waddington. *You, Your College and Your Career.* San Francisco: Lithotype Process Company, 1950. Pp. 95-128.

Carroll, Herbert A. *Mental Hygiene—The Dynamics of Adjustment.* New York: Prentice-Hall, Inc., 1951.

Cattell, Raymond B. *Personality.* New York: McGraw-Hill Book Company, Inc., 1950.

Kraines, S. H., and Thetford, E. S. *Live and Help Live.* New York: Macmillan Company, 1951.

Malm, Marguerite, and Jamison, Olis G. *Adolescence.* New York: McGraw-Hill Book Company, Inc., 1952.

Sadler, William S. *Mental Mischief and Emotional Conflicts.* St. Louis: C. V. Mosby Company, 1947.

Symonds, Percival M. *The Dynamics of Human Adjustment.* New York: D. Appleton-Century-Crofts Company, 1946.

Thorpe, Louis P., and Katz, Barney. *The Psychology of Abnormal Behavior.* New York: The Ronald Press Company, 1948.

Thorpe, Louis P. *The Psychology of Mental Health.* New York: The Ronald Press Company, 1950.

Williamson, E. G. (ed.). *Trends in Student Personnel Work.* Minneapolis: University of Minnesota Press, 1949. Pp. 136-158, 221-232.

Wittenberg, Rudolph M. *So You Want to Help People.* New York: Association Press, 1947.

PART IV

Administration of the Guidance Program

CHAPTER FIFTEEN

Organization of Guidance Services

AS BACKGROUND for discussing the organization of guidance services, consider some of the cardinal points of previous chapters, as presented next.

First, in a school or college, student personnel services are the systematically organized and operated program for rendering assistance to the individual. The main objectives of this program are to help the individual (a) to make the best possible adjustments to his problems and situations, and (b) to realize the highest possible achievements within his aptitudes. Toward these objectives, the program serves the individual in all the important phases of his personal development.

Second, guidance services, the major part of the program of student personnel services, are the activities that assist the individual to grow in self-understanding, to make wise decisions, and to plan his life.

Third, guidance services both supplement and complement classroom instruction in fostering the all-round development of the individual and his personality.

Fourth, student personnel services (including guidance services) are one of the three main functions of an educational institution. The other two are instruction and administration. All three functions should have equally important places in the total educational program.

GUIDING PRINCIPLES OF ORGANIZATION

In the light of the foregoing points, the principles that should be observed in organizing a guidance services program are as follows. Each principle is expressed in the form of a suggested course of action:

1. Prepare a clear-cut statement of the objectives of the guidance services program. These objectives should take into account the characteristics and needs of the student body. They should be in line with or consistent with the objectives of the educational institution as a whole.

2. Determine precisely the functions of the guidance services program—that is, what the program shall do for students.

3. Assign specific duties to the personnel who are to participate in the guidance services program. Allocate tasks to individual staff members on the basis of their individual qualifications for the work. Give them definite responsibilities for performing these tasks.

4. Give each staff member assigned to a task in guidance services the authority commensurate with his responsibility.

5. Define clearly the working relationships (a) among the staff members who are responsible for guidance services and (b) between these staff members and others in the institution. Recognize that some staff members will work directly and full-time in the field of guidance services; others will work directly and part-time in the same field; and still others will work indirectly and during a small share of their total work time.

6. Set up a form of organization that is best adapted to the institution's purposes, characteristics, personnel, size, and financial resources.

7. Keep the plan of organization and its operations as simple as possible.[1]

As the principles just presented indicate, the guidance services program should be oriented primarily toward students. At the same time this program should contribute to the welfare of the educational institution itself. As was pointed out in Chapter 4, if guidance services personnel cooperate closely with the administrative and instructional staffs, the guidance

---

[1] See also Robert Hendry Mathewson, *Guidance Policy and Practice* (New York: Harper and Brothers, 1949), pp. 140-141; and C. Gilbert Wrenn, *Student Personnel Work in College* (New York: The Ronald Press Company, 1951), pp. 36-52.

program aids in building a stronger institution. In short, the better the guidance services, the more they enhance the over-all quality of the institution.

If the functions of guidance services are to be stated precisely, those responsible for these functions must think through the guidance program in terms of its purposes and methods. If guidance functions are stated clearly and definitely, they can be carried out more efficiently; they also can be evaluated in terms of their effectiveness in the total guidance program.

The institution that has good organization and administration of guidance services assigns specific guidance tasks to staff members on the basis of their abilities to perform these tasks. Thus, each staff member knows exactly what his responsibility is. At the same time, the institution gives each staff member the authority he needs to meet his assigned responsibility. Otherwise, he is not in a position to carry out that responsibility.

If an institution's guidance services program is to operate smoothly and efficiently, it must have well-defined working relationships among the personnel of the department mainly responsible for these services and between this department and every other department. The guidance staff can provide many, but not all, of the services that students need and want. For this reason, guidance staff members must have the active assistance and cooperation of other staff members—the administrative head, deans of men and women, department heads, classroom instructors, and librarians, to mention some.

In the guidance organization and program, coordination and integration do not occur spontaneously or automatically. These essential features are an outcome of many factors, particularly of the willingness of all responsible personnel to cooperate.

Toward developing cooperation between the guidance staff and other staff members, the institution should have a clear, specific, and detailed plan of organization of its program of guidance services. A chart of this plan should give the responsibilities of each department and of the key staff members therein; the chart should also show the relationships among the staff members and departments. This plan and its accompanying chart help the institution to specify, coordinate, and integrate its various guidance services.

In developing a plan of organization, an institution should not copy the set-up used in some other institution. Rather, that institution should work out its own plan, based on its purposes, characteristics, size, existing personnel, and financial resources. Thus, the school has an organizational plan that best suits its particular situation.

If an institution is initiating a guidance services program, it must adapt its plan to the departments and offices that are in existence at the time. In a high school, for example, the plan may rightly take into account the fact that the school has a dean of boys and a dean of girls; also that each dean, who is charged with certain duties, is highly competent.

If the school has just employed a guidance director, he should organize an over-all program in his field of responsibility. Toward this goal, the director should carefully outline the purposes, functions, and responsibilities of the new office of guidance services. He should seek the active cooperation of the school's deans and of other staff members in preparing an organized guidance plan. Furthermore, the guidance director should make every effort to fit the new function (guidance services) into the existing situation.

To initiate an effective guidance program, the director may sometimes find that he must work to introduce changes in the current situation. According to such changes, an established office or department may give up certain functions or take on new ones. Regarding these changes, the chief administrative officer, of course, has the responsibility of rendering the final decisions.

An institution may develop a complex organizational plan for guidance services. This plan may look good on paper; it may favorably impress some people. But such a plan is undesirable from a practical point of view. It usually provides for too much machinery, too many committees, too many checks and balances on the activities of personnel. Moreover, such a plan is likely to hamper rather than to facilitate guidance services for students. For these reasons, an institution should have a simple plan of organization, a plan that best serves the purposes and advances the functions of its guidance program.

THEORIES OF ORGANIZATION

In setting up and in conducting its guidance services program, an institution may employ one of three main types of organization: line, staff, and a combination of line and staff.

The Line Organization

In the line organization, within a public school system, for example, the direction and control of guidance services flow from the chief administrative officer (the superintendent of schools) in a straight, vertical line down to his main assistants (the school principals). From these assistants the direction and control proceed in a straight line to their subordinates (the classroom teachers). By this means, the chief administrative officer maintains a high degree of centralization of authority; he assigns responsibilities and checks upon their fulfillment.

The Staff Organization

In the staff organization, the chief administrative officer allocates activities according to functions. He assigns each function or group of related functions to a department head; this head is directly responsible to the school's chief officer. One important advantage of this type of arrangement is that each department head is likely to develop a greater degree of specialization and efficiency in the performance of his function or functions.

In the staff as in the line organization, the ultimate control rests in the hands of the chief administrative officer. But in the staff set-up, this chief officer delegates definite responsibilities to department heads, staff specialists, and others, for the functions assigned to them. Each head is a specialist in his own field. Because this specialist serves as a staff officer to the chief administrative officer, he has an important role in the development of the general policies and procedures of the entire organization.

The Combined Line-and-Staff Organization

The combination of the two aforesaid plans is known as the line-and-staff organization. This type of organization combines the advantages of the line-type and of the staff-type organizations. Usually it is required in a large educational institution.

The staff of any institution, no matter what its size, will find helpful Gulick's observations regarding the two main types of organizations and their relationships. According to Gulick,[2] *staff* includes "all of those persons who devote their time exclusively to the knowing, thinking and planning of functions." *Line* includes "all of the remainder who are, thus, chiefly concerned with the doing functions. The overhead directing authority of the staff group, usually a board or committee, is the 'general staff.' Everything that the staff suggests is referred up, not down, and is carried out, if at all, on the responsibility and under the direction of a line officer."

Furthermore, Gulick observes that the "chief value of the line and staff classification is to point to the need (1) of developing an independent planning agency as an aid to the chief executive, and (2) of refusing to inject any element of administrative authority and control into such an agency."

SAMPLE CHARTS OF ORGANIZATION

A school or college will want to develop its own plan of organization for guidance services. Even so, this institution may get valuable leads from the organization charts that are presented next.

A Guidance Plan for a Small School

A simple line organization that a small school or a small school system can use in organizing its guidance program is illustrated in the chart appearing in Figure 9. The solid connecting lines show the flow of authority and responsibility from the superintendent of schools (the chief administrative officer)

---

[2] Luther Gulick (ed.), *Papers on the Science of Organization* (New York City: Columbia University, Institute of Public Administration, 1937), p. 31.

down through the principals, to the teachers, and eventually to the pupils. The broken lines show informal and cooperative relationships, not lines of authority. Neither the group of teachers nor the committee on guidance services (made up of some of the teachers) has authority over the other. To plan and

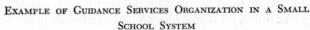

FIGURE 9

EXAMPLE OF GUIDANCE SERVICES ORGANIZATION IN A SMALL
SCHOOL SYSTEM

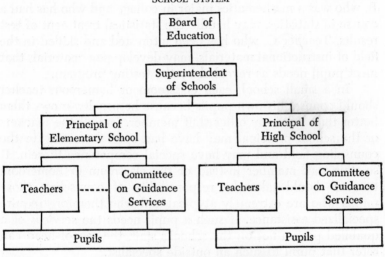

SOLID LINE: DIRECT LINE OF AUTHORITY
BROKEN LINE: COOPERATIVE RELATIONSHIP

carry out effective guidance work, the teacher group and the guidance committee must establish and maintain full and free cooperative relationships.

Because the school is small in terms of the number of pupils and staff members (teachers and administrative officers), it probably cannot afford a complete staff of specialized guidance workers. Even so, this school can develop an efficient guidance program if the following conditions exist: (1) The school has active interest in guidance. (2) The school heads are eager to take leadership in the guidance program; they also want other staff members to participate in planning and conducting the program. (3) The staff sets up a working committee to stimulate and coordinate guidance activities.

According to this organizational plan, all teachers render guidance services; they may do this as a part of, or as an emphasis in, their regular courses, or as special units of study or work. Because certain teachers have particular interests and abilities, they may well become "specialists" in different aspects of guidance. To illustrate, Teacher A, who has had experience and training in the field of psychological tests, may plan the testing schedule and direct the administration of tests. Teacher B, who was a mathematics major in college and who has had a course in statistics, may handle the statistical treatment of test results. Teacher C, who has been interested and skilled in the field of instructional materials, may develop new materials that meet pupil needs as revealed by the testing program.

In a small school, each classroom or homeroom teacher should counsel his own pupils because he usually knows them better than does any other staff member. One of the teachers or the school principal may have had special training in the counseling field and may have special competence therein. If so, this staff member instead of the classroom or homeroom teacher should take the responsibility of counseling those pupils who are extremely atypical and who therefore require specialized assistance. If such a pupil needs the services of a qualified person not on the school's staff, the school head can refer that pupil to such an outside specialist.

The organization of the guidance committee and its work in a small school merits further discussion. The school principal usually appoints as committee members those teachers who are actively interested in guidance services. The committee may select its chairman, or the principal may appoint him. This chairman may well be the teacher who is particularly enthusiastic about guidance—a teacher who is doing guidance work in his classroom and who has taken some college courses in this field. This teacher should be relieved of at least some of his teaching duties; thereby, he will have time to devote to the development of an effective guidance program. As part of his responsibility, this teacher should work to coordinate the efforts of all the teachers who are participating directly and indirectly in guidance activities.

One of the first functions of the committee, led by its

chairman, is obviously to devise the school's plan for a total guidance program. In making this plan, the committee should select the best qualified person to take responsibility for each of the various phases of the program. The principal, of course, should have the final responsibility of approving the plan and of conferring with the selected teachers to obtain their agreement to perform the duties suggested for them.

The guidance services committee may be thought of as carrying on a staff function within the school. That is, this committee acts as an advisory body to the principal; it also plans and operates specified guidance functions.

The simple organizational chart in Figure 9 does not show all of the important services that the school should make available to pupils. These services, for example, should include periodic physical examinations. Such examinations, given to all pupils at least once a year, often reveal defects or diseases that should be called to the attention of parents. They can arrange to have physicians, dentists, and oculists provide the necessary corrective or remedial treatment.

A Guidance Plan for a Large School

The simple type of guidance organization just presented is considerably different from the set-up required in a large school system, as shown in Figure 10. For the large school, a fairly elaborate organization of *staff* and *line* is essential.

In Figure 10, the five assistant superintendents are directly responsible to the superintendent; they serve as his advisory staff. As such a staff, the assistant superintendents (for administrative research, for pupil personnel and special services, for instruction, for school personnel, and for business) devote their attention primarily to the creative planning of the functions respectively under their direction. They make suggestions to the superintendent or refer the suggestions of others to him. He then decides what actions he wishes to take with reference to the suggestions submitted. The superintendent, on his own initiative and within his authority, may direct that certain new policies and procedures be adopted. Or, he may recommend to the Board of Education that it approve the new

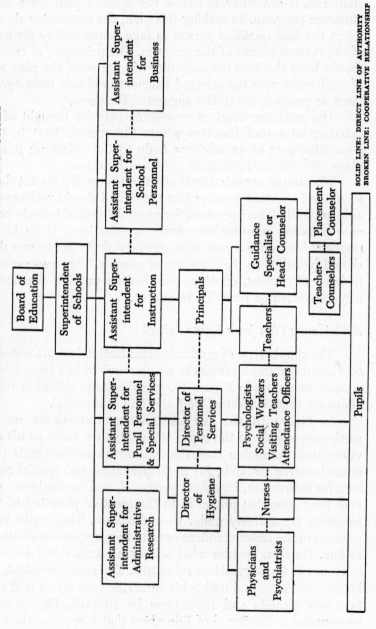

FIGURE 10

EXAMPLE OF GUIDANCE SERVICES ORGANIZATION IN A LARGE SCHOOL SYSTEM

SOLID LINE: DIRECT LINE OF AUTHORITY
BROKEN LINE: COOPERATIVE RELATIONSHIP

policies and procedures; if it does so, he directs his staff and line officers to carry out such policies and procedures.

As Figure 10 shows, the Director of Hygiene, the Director of Personnel Services, and the principals are line officers when they function in relationship to their immediate supervisors and to those whom they directly supervise. But they are staff officers when they operate in an advisory or cooperative relationship with other officers at their same level in the administrative set-up.

Because this book is concerned with guidance services (part of pupil personnel services), Figure 10 shows in detail only the organization of these particular services. In the chart, note that under the Assistant Superintendent for Pupil Personnel and Special Services are the Director of Personnel Services and the Director of Hygiene. These two heads may be regarded as staff officers who develop and direct their particular functions; they may also be considered as line officers who through their subordinates carry out the policies and procedures given them by their supervisors. In their roles as staff officers, moreover, the directors of personnel services and of hygiene have planning and advisory functions at their own level. In their roles as line officers, they pass their ideas and recommendations up to the Assistant Superintendent for Pupil Personnel and Special Services. They also supervise their own personnel in carrying on the detailed, daily operation of their offices.

The broken horizontal lines in Figure 10 indicate cooperative relationships, not direct responsibilities. For the effective conduct of guidance functions, there must be close cooperation between the director of personnel services and the principals of individual schools.

As pointed out earlier, each school system should develop its own organizational plan—a plan adapted to its needs and resources. In some systems, for example, the Director of Personnel Services supervises the Director of Hygiene.

A Guidance Plan for a College or University

Figure 11 illustrates the organization of student personnel services in a college or university. The plan shown is only one

FIGURE 11

EXAMPLE OF GUIDANCE SERVICES ORGANIZATION IN A COLLEGE OR UNIVERSITY

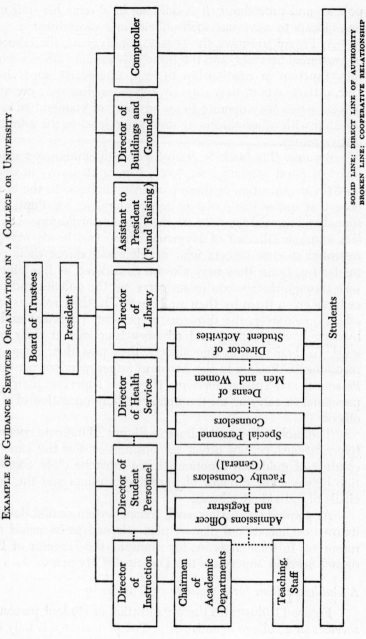

SOLID LINE: DIRECT LINE OF AUTHORITY
BROKEN LINE: COOPERATIVE RELATIONSHIP

among many—every institution should have its own plan, a plan that is unique in many respects. In many institutions, the deans of men and women are directly responsible to the president or to another administrative head. Therefore, they are co-ordinate with the director of student personnel services.

Note that the Director of Student Personnel Services is directly responsible to the President. Also, that this arrange-ment of officers according to functions provides (1) for cen-tralization of authority in the supervision of personnel services and (2) for some measure of decentralization of responsibility in the conduct of those services. Thus, the arrangement gives clear direction to those responsible for the personnel services program; it also stimulates wide staff participation in the pro-gram and helps coordinate staff efforts in this important field of education.

The broken lines in Figure 11 indicate cooperative rela-tionships among staff members. With reference to this matter, Wrenn states:

> Coordination . . . means not only the placing of student per-sonnel services under a personnel director (line relationship), but the development of appropriate staff relationships with other services and other departments of the institution. From another point of view, a coordinated personnel program is one in which all personnel services are integrated under the direction of one man or one agency, some having a line and some a staff relation-ship to the coordinating agency. This agency not only coordi-nates the existing services to prevent overlap and wasted effort, but it also assumes responsibility for recommending the pro-vision of new services as need for these becomes apparent. A coordinated program is a complete program, coordinating needs and services as well as coordinating the services themselves.[3]

Due to the relative newness of student personnel services and particularly of guidance services, some colleges have found it wise for the chief administrative officer to set up a student personnel council and a committee on student personnel work.

As Wrenn has pointed out,[4] a student personnel council is

---

[3] C. Gilbert Wrenn, *Student Personnel Work in Colleges* (New York: The Ronald Press Company, 1951), p. 40.

[4] *Ibid.*, pp. 48, 49.

made up of the heads of the various types of activities in the total student personnel program. As members, it also has other administrative officers who have or should have significant relationships with the program. This council constitutes a "cabinet" that advises the head administrator of personnel services. For example, it helps the administrator plan the organization to be set up and the procedures to be followed; it also assists him in carrying out the agreed-upon policies.

The committee on student personnel work is composed of the heads of the personnel services office and related offices plus the instructional department heads and the instructors who are keenly interested in the student personnel program. This committee determines the main features of the total program and sets the boundaries thereof. It states the policies under which the program is to be developed. And it defines the specific jobs to be done.

In a large city school system such a committee may include the director of guidance services as chairman and other important staff officers, representative principals, and interested teachers as members.

ORGANIZATION OF HIGH-SCHOOL GUIDANCE PROGRAMS

In an extensive national survey of secondary schools, Reavis [5] found four general types of organization of guidance programs. Although Reavis made his study in 1931 and changes have undoubtedly occurred since then, many of his findings help illuminate the present situation.

According to Reavis's survey, the four types of guidance service programs were as follows:

1. *A centralized bureau of guidance for secondary schools in large city systems is responsible directly to the superintendent of schools for pursuit of guidance service.* The director of this bureau or department has these tasks: (a) to formulate the policies of the guidance program for the city system, with the approval of his superior officer; (b) to organize the department as a clearing house for problems in personnel service and for re-

---

[5] W. C. Reavis, *Programs of Guidance*, Bulletin No. 17, National Survey of Secondary Education Monograph No. 14 (Washington, D.C.: U.S. Office of Education, 1932), pp. 135-144.

search; and (c) to provide in-service training of assistants who give expert guidance in schools that desire such assistance. The central department provides the specialized services and aids the principals of the high schools in organizing the schools' guidance programs and in integrating the various activities. The assistants in the central bureau visit schools when called, conduct group work, and hold interviews with individual pupils.

2. *A centralized organization for personnel service in a city system with the individual secondary school the unit places the responsiblity for the program on the chief administrative officer of the secondary school.* The central organization renders only consultant service to the principal and specialized help to the guidance functionaries in the local school. The officers of the local school have the task of administering the school, including the program of guidance. The principal approves the plans for personnel services formulated by the local director of guidance. The counselors, homeroom heads, and teachers carry out the program. The director of guidance carries on basic research, interprets the guidance program to the teachers and the community, and performs guidance activities which demand skills not possessed by other members of the staff. Under this plan, as contrasted with the central bureau type, it is more certain that a complete program of personnel service is developed in each school, not just in those schools which seek the service of the central bureau.

3. *A centralized guidance organization in individual schools has a staff set up as a structural part of the school's organization.* The director and his staff may carry on all of the guidance activities or he may pursue certain activities and allocate to the school's administrative officers other tasks, while he retains the supervisory oversight. This arrangement is similar to the type of central bureau of large city systems. However, it has the advantage of concentrating its activities in one school. In operation, this type resembles the organizations in city systems which emphasize the individual schools as units. It differs from them in that it has its own staff of personnel officers rather than utilizing the regular administrative officers and teachers.

4. *A central guidance organization in individual schools uses regular officers and teachers as functionaries.* There is no centralizing or coordinating agency in the main office of the school system. The principal or trained counselor acts as director of the program. Other administrative officers and teachers perform the activities required by the program of guidance. Par-

ticular care must be taken that the work of the functionaries is coordinated. This type of organization is especially well adapted to the smaller secondary school, where the full-time, or even part-time, service of a fully trained worker cannot be justified. The program of guidance can be developed by the principal, supervised by him, and carried on by the teachers. In-service training of the teachers who act as guidance functionaries is particularly important under this kind of organization.

STEPS IN INITIATING A PROGRAM
OF GUIDANCE SERVICES

Initiation of a program of personnel or guidance services in a high school or college requires careful preparation. This preparation includes a preliminary study that canvasses the entire situation—all of the present functions of the school, for instance. On the basis of this canvass, the school personnel responsible develop a step-by-step plan for the guidance services program.

The Two Main Steps in Starting a Guidance Program

To illustrate how such a program can be developed, here is a description of what an educational institution might do.

The first step. The administrative head of the school appoints a guidance services committee. The members of this committee represent all of the institution's functions that may conceivably be related to the new program. The committee pursues three preliminary lines of inquiry: (a) It surveys the guidance service activities that already exist in the institution. (b) It surveys students' needs to ascertain which of these needs shall be served. (c) It surveys individual staff members to determine the nature and extent of their interest in guidance work, their willingness to participate in this work, and their qualifications for performing such work.

The second step. The guidance services committee drafts a suggested program and organizational plan. It works out the proposed objectives of the program. These objectives are in line with the fundamental purposes of the school; they are based on surveys of the characteristics and needs of the students.

In the light of these objectives, the guidance services committee prepares a tentative master chart of the organization. This master chart shows the main departments and the chief officers therein for operation of the program. The chart also indicates the lines of authority and of cooperative relationships among the various offices or officers. The committee next drafts subsidary charts that portray the details of organizing and operating the program—for instance, the specific types of jobs to be performed by various school personnel.

Finally the guidance services committee submits its recommended program and organization to the entire staff at a faculty meeting. At this meeting, staff members ask questions about and make comments on the committee's proposals. Later the committee revises these proposals in terms of faculty suggestions.

The Need for Staff Cooperation and Participation

With reference to the two steps just mentioned, note that the head administrator makes certain that the guidance services committee includes representatives of all guidance and guidance-related activities within the school. These representatives are either directors of these activities or their designees. Note also that from the beginning the head administrator and the guidance services committee encourage staff participation. The administrator makes sure that the committee truly represents the whole staff. Because the committee is representative, it is able to plan guidance services in a broad and realistic frame of reference. Also for this reason, the committee is able to develop good will among staff members and to enlist their enthusiastic cooperation in the program.

It is impossible to overemphasize the point that if the guidance services program is to be successful, it must have the wholehearted support and active cooperation of the head administrator and of all key personnel. If even one key official is skeptical, he will tend to impede the development of an effective program. Likewise, if any other faculty member is doubtful, he may retard the growth of the program. For these reasons, the guidance services committee should make every effort to convince key officials, teachers, and other staff members of the necessity for a comprehensive guidance program.

In all its activities, the guidance services committee should take the position that all staff members have the right and the responsibility to participate in planning and conducting the guidance program. Thereby, the committee develops better plans and smoother operations than otherwise. Thereby, it gains greater acceptance of its plans.

From time to time in its deliberations, the guidance services committee should call in representatives from the student body. During such meetings, the committee should invite these student leaders to give their reactions to the guidance plan and their suggestions for the guidance program. In this way, the committee improves the guidance services offered; it also builds student confidence in and support of these services.

The Role of the Chairman

The success of the guidance services committee depends in no small part upon its chairman. The chairman should be a person who is wholeheartedly enthusiastic about guidance. He should be well-grounded in the basic principles and practices of different guidance services. Preferably, he should have had both training and experience in this educational field. Furthermore, the chairman should have the respect both of the committee and the rest of the school's staff. And last, but not least, he should display real leadership in all phases of the developing guidance program.

If the administrative head of the school has the foregoing qualifications and the time to serve in the capacity, he may be chairman of the guidance services committee. If not, the committee may choose as chairman any staff member who appears to have the desired characteristics. With reference to this chairmanship, there should be a clear distinction between the guidance functions and the disciplinary functions within the school. The principal or other staff member who is mainly responsible for disciplining students is many times not in the best position to guide students toward solving their personal and other problems.

If a school or college has a director of guidance services, he is the logical chairman of the guidance services committee. This director, of course, has been appointed to his position by the institution's head administrative officer. With administrative approval, moreover, the director has assumed a variety of guidance-related duties. Because this director is well-trained in the guidance field and because he has the responsibility of leading the development of the school's guidance program, he is usually the ideal person to chair the guidance services committee.

In advancing the guidance services program, the guidance director with the help of the committee should not only plan and conduct the institution's guidance program. He should also carry on a public information program. This program should inform students about the guidance services that are available to them and about the benefits that they can obtain therefrom. The program should also inform the general public —the parents of students and local employers, to mention two important groups.

A school or college that provides personnel or guidance services should continuously inform all persons who come into contact with these services either directly or indirectly. By informing its own student body and the public about its guidance services, the institution builds an understanding of its guidance program. It also develops the cooperative working relationships that are so essential to the success of this program.

A Job Analysis of Educational Personnel Workers

For an over-all approach to the organization and administration of guidance services, attention is directed to an important report by the Study Commission of the Council of Guidance and Personnel Associations.[3] (This Council was the forerunner of the present American Personnel and Guidance Association, Inc.)

The Study Commission's report contains analyses of a number of jobs in the field of personnel work. For each job, it gives: alternate titles; job summary; work performed; qualifications; training; and relationships. Whether a school already has a sys-

---

[3] An Interim Report by the Study Commission of the Council of Guidance and Personnel Associations. "Job Analyses of Educational Personnel Workers," *Occupations*, XXX (October, 1951), Part II—Special Report.

tematically organized program of guidance services or not, this report is valuable as a guide to future development. The report helps to orient a prospective personnel worker to the field. It also presents worth-while ideas with reference to staffing a program of guidance services.

COMMON MISTAKES TO BE AVOIDED

In planning the organization of guidance services, a school should look for and should avoid certain mistakes. If the school does not do so, its guidance program can be hampered or even jeopardized. According to the experiences of many educational institutions, here are some mistakes that commonly occur in the development of a guidance services program.

1. Lack of precise definitions of the program's functions or of the boundaries of its services

2. Division of the same responsibility among functionaries

3. Absence of clear-cut lines of responsibility and authority

4. Failure to specify the working relationships among the guidance services staff and between these staff members and the other functionaries of the institution

5. Failure to take sufficient account of the jealousies and rivalries among personnel with reference to the assignment of guidance functions

6. Failure to publicize the program, in the initial stages and continually thereafter, among those who have contact with that program

This chapter has presented suggestions with reference to the over-all organization of a school's guidance services program. The next chapter will consider the staff needed to conduct this program.

SUGGESTED READINGS

Brouwer, Paul J. *Student Personnel Services in General Education.* Washington, D.C.: American Council on Education, 1949. Pp. 155-170.

Crow, Lester D., and Crow, Alice. *Introduction to Guidance: Principles and Practices.* New York: American Book Company, 1951. Chapter 5.

Erickson, Clifford E., and Smith, Glenn E. *Organization and Administration of Guidance Services*. New York: McGraw-Hill Book Company, Inc., 1947.

Froehlich, Clifford P. *Guidance Services in Smaller Schools*. New York: McGraw-Hill Book Company, Inc., 1950. Pp. 10-80.

Hamrin, Shirley A. *Initiating and Administering Guidance Services*. Bloomington, Ill.: McKnight and McKnight Publishing Company, 1953.

Harden, Edgar L. *How to Organize Your Guidance Program*. Chicago: Science Research Associates, 1950.

Humphreys, J. Anthony. "Toward Improved Programs of Student Personnel Services," *Junior College Journal*, XXII (March, 1952), 382-392.

Kitch, Donald E., and McCreary, William H. "Improving Guidance Programs in Secondary Schools." *Bulletin of the California State Department of Education*, XIX, No. 8, 1950.

Romney, A. K. "Development of a University Counseling Service," *School and Society*, 70 (November 19, 1949), 330-331.

Rothney, John W. M., and Roens, Bert A. *Guidance of American Youth*. Cambridge: Harvard University Press, 1950. Pp. 151-201.

Smith, Glenn E. *Principles and Practices of the Guidance Program*. New York: Macmillan Company, 1951. Pp. 82-122.

Strozier, R. M. "The Office of the Dean of Students," *Proceedings of the Institute for Administrative Officers of Higher Institutions*. Chicago: University of Chicago Press, 1947.

Wrenn, C. Gilbert, and Dugan, Willis E. *Guidance Procedures in High School*. Minneapolis: University of Minnesota Press, 1950. Pp. 1-11.

Wrenn, C. Gilbert. *Student Personnel Work in College*. New York: The Ronald Press Company, 1951. Pp. 29-54.

CHAPTER SIXTEEN

Staffing the Guidance Services

AN INSTITUTION'S plan of organization of its guidance services, as discussed in the preceding chapter, determines in good part the staff required to provide these services. Such a staff is usually composed of two types of professional personnel—*generalists* and *specialists*. If a school has both types of personnel, if both are actively engaged in guidance work, and if both are cooperating closely with one another, the school is most likely to achieve the goals of its guidance program.

Because generalists and specialists are so important in the guidance field, the nature and role of each type are described next.

THE GENERALISTS

The generalists, as the name implies, include those persons who exercise general supervision of the institution's guidance services. In a school system, such generalists are the top administrators—the superintendent, the assistant superintendents, if any, and the principals. In a college or university, the generalists are the president, the vice-president, and the deans.

The degree to which the generalist participates in the administration of guidance functions varies from school to school. In an institution that has a competent guidance director on its staff, the school head usually gives this specialist full responsibility for the operation of guidance services. At times, however, this head may be so keenly interested in the guidance program that he becomes involved in the day-to-day conduct of the program.

For the sake of an efficient and smooth-running program,

the generalist should *not* exercise too close supervision of the detailed management of guidance services. If the generalist has appointed a person who is well-qualified by professional training and experience to head up these services, he should assume that such a person is fully able to direct and manage the guidance program.

With reference to a school's guidance program, the generalists also include teachers. These teachers have a special interest in their subjects of study and a general interest in the field of guidance.

Demands Made on the Generalist

For realization of the aims of the guidance services program, the generalists face three essential demands. *First,* the generalists must have the guidance approach in their relationships with other staff members and with students. That is, the generalists must have the point of view that recognizes the worth of the individual and that helps the individual to achieve the fullest possible development of his personality. *Second,* the generalists must have at least a basic knowledge of the principles and procedures of guidance services. Only with such knowledge can they make their maximum contributions to the guidance program. *Third,* the generalists must be willing if not eager to give wholehearted cooperation to the specialists who direct their guidance services program. Such cooperation is a *sine qua non* of effective guidance operations.

THE GUIDANCE SPECIALISTS

Within an educational institution, the guidance specialists are those persons who are technically trained and experienced in the field of guidance work or in some particular aspect of it. These specialists usually include the guidance director who heads up the guidance program; his assistant heads who are in charge of certain aspects of guidance services; and counselors who work directly with students.

Specialists in the guidance field have various titles. Among these, the titles most commonly used are as follows: director of guidance; director of personnel service; dean of students; dean of boys (or men); dean of girls (or women); faculty advisor;

counselor; teacher-counselor; vocational counselor; placement counselor; educational counselor; veterans' counselor; homeroom (or division) teacher; visiting teacher; psychologist; director of student activities; and director of student life.

As the titles imply, each of the aforenamed professional workers provides one or more specialized types of guidance services within an educational institution. In the typical school or college, full-time guidance specialists represent a small minority of the entire staff. If these specialists are to be effective, they must have the active assistance of the overwhelming majority of staff members, who, of course, are classroom teachers.

THE TEACHER IN THE GUIDANCE PROGRAM

Some educational administrators believe that all teachers should be relatively expert in the field of guidance. Ideally, these administrators express a defensible position—they look toward a goal that teachers should strive to reach. Practically, however, their position is somewhat unrealistic.

Regarding the role of the teacher in the guidance program, here is a description of the situation in a typical school and of the possibilities for improving it.

First. Some teachers are more interested in subject matter than in students. Such teachers want only those contacts with students that are definitely related to their regular courses. In general, these teachers consider that they have fulfilled their educational obligations when they have delivered lectures, conducted class discussions, made work assignments, administered subject-matter tests, graded these tests and other written work, and assigned academic marks. To such teachers, students are little more than names and grades in their class book. These teachers tend to change their attitudes toward students very slowly; this change, however, may be accelerated as a result of "exposure" to a dynamic guidance program.

Second. Many teachers have not had the opportunity to become informed and skilled in the field of guidance services. Some teachers may have had such an opportunity but did not take advantage of it. All these teachers may increase their competence in the guidance field if their school has an in-service training program.

Third. Many teachers may appear to lack the personal characteristics that are essential to successful guidance work with students. In actuality, however, most teachers have these characteristics or can develop them, either on their own or through a well-designed training program.

Fourth. Some teachers have such heavy teaching loads that they apparently cannot participate in guidance work. Without increasing their teaching burdens, however, most of these teachers can include guidance emphases in their regular course work.

Good teachers do much more guidance work in their classes than they commonly realize. This was pointed out by Hoppock in an address entitled "Guidance Aspects of Classroom Teaching." [1] He stated:

Any classroom teacher doing a thorough job of teaching his subject has already done a good deal of guidance work, whether anyone recognizes it or not.

He has contributed to the guidance services of his schools:

1. In helping to determine who would be admitted to his courses and after what prerequisites;
2. In orienting his students to the new subject they are about to study;
3. In planning his course work to take account of individual differences in ability and interest, in need for the subject, and in probable use of it;
4. In encouraging and helping students who show superior ability in the field;
5. In treating all students like human beings, helping them to get what they need and want from his subject, and not putting them through unnecessary busy work;
6. In showing students both the cultural and the vocational uses of the subject; and
7. In talking with students who have asked his advice on everything from how to pass the examination to whether or not to kiss the girl on his first date.

As Hoppock has suggested, teachers should have a real and continuing interest in students as individuals. This interest

---

[1] Robert Hoppock, "Guidance Aspects of Classroom Teaching." (An address before the Michigan Guidance Conference at Lansing, Michigan, October 4, 1947). Bulletin published by the Lansing Public Schools.

can be stimulated by the school's guidance specialists. But until teachers themselves see students as individuals to be educated or "guided," they will not have a genuine relationship to the guidance program or contribute to it what only they can.

Most teachers, as is to be expected, are interested mainly in the intellectual aspect of their students' personalities. Through this aspect, the teacher can perform a real service in the guidance program. For example, the teacher who knows the psychology of learning can apply this knowledge to the guidance of his students through a particular subject of study. This instructor asks and tries to answer such questions as these: (1) What are the best methods of conducting my course? (2) What typical learning difficulties do my students have? (3) What special learning difficulties do individual students have? (4) What can I do to aid students to overcome these difficulties?

While working out answers to these questions, the teacher is likely to gain in his understanding of the factors that influence or condition learning. These factors include the varied characteristics of a student's personality and the various aspects of his environment. Both factors affect the student's academic efficiency.

Up to the present time, too large a proportion of subject-matter teachers have had too little training in the psychology of the learning process. This is particularly true of college teachers; many of them have had little or no formal training in the psychology of learning as it applies to their fields of instruction.

At whatever academic level he works, the typical teacher tends to minimize, overlook, or neglect aspects of personality growth other than that of intellectual development. In contrast, the guidance-minded teacher takes the welfare of "the whole student" into account. Such a teacher tries to find the reasons for a student's academic failures. This student may be handicapped in his academic work by certain emotional factors. More specifically, he may have frequent and serious clashes with his parents over his homework and his school marks—clashes that hamper academic progress. Or, this student may have little or no spontaneous inner drive spurring him on to academic achievement; he may feel that school is a complete waste of time. Or, this student may be failing to progress academically because of an unhappy social life at school or a financial problem at home.

If the teacher is sensitive to nonintellectual factors, such as those just mentioned, he will almost surely have greater insight into the lives of his students. This teacher, moreover, will seriously consider these nonintellectual aspects of personality and environment as he adapts his teaching methods to the needs of his students. Such a teacher is interested in more than the routine of his work—recitations, discussions, laboratory exercises, examinations, and assignment of marks. He is concerned with the over-all guidance of his students.

The teacher who wants to help develop the student's total personality recognizes that he has varied functions to perform —not only as an instructor inside the classroom but also as an advisor or counselor both inside and outside the classroom. This teacher realizes that the student needs not only intellectual training but also training in other aspects of personality. Although the teacher may continue to emphasize the student's intellectual development, he takes a broader attitude toward that student. As a result, this teacher tends to narrow the gap that formerly existed between the instructional and the guidance features of his work. In fact, he may not just bridge this gap—he may actually close it.

THE ROLES OF THE TEACHER AND THE GUIDANCE SPECIALIST

No matter what guidance services a teacher may provide, he should understand the general relationships between the instructional staff and the guidance staff—the specialists who are mainly responsible for the guidance program. Both the guidance-minded teacher and the guidance specialist are working toward the common goal of assisting the individual student to develop himself as an individual person. Both are concerned with the student's entire personality—his intellectual life, his social relationships, his educational and vocational plans, and his personal problems. Both are attempting to make available to the student those experiences in school or college that will contribute most to his total personal growth. In short, the teacher and the specialist are partners in a joint project. They understand that, if this project is to be successful, classroom activities and extracurricular activities must be directed and coordinated toward the same goal—the guidance of each student as a personality.

The Guidance Tasks of Teachers

Although teachers and specialists have a common objective, each group has its own guidance aims and techniques. Consider, first, the role of the teaching staff in a school or college guidance program. This staff conducts such activities as the following:

1. Teachers construct, administer, correct, and grade tests in their regular academic courses. They employ the results of these tests in guiding their students.

2. Teachers administer and interpret standardized tests of reading abilities. They use the findings from these tests to ascertain the reading abilities of their students and to adapt their courses accordingly.

3. Teachers train their students in the study skills and habits that apply to their particular courses. Thereby, they help students to learn the best ways to study for class discussions and for periodic examinations.

4. Teachers instruct their students in the taking of notes, in the making of outlines, in the writing of term papers, and in the giving of short talks. All are essential communication skills.

5. Teachers guide students in the proper use of the school or college library—their best source of information.

6. Teachers inform students in group discussions or in individual conferences concerning educational and vocational opportunities. Each teacher, for example, points out how his field of specialization relates particularly to the careers that his students are interested in. Thereby, he assists his students in planning their educational programs.

7. Teachers report or refer students who are having special learning difficulties to the school's guidance department. Teachers then work with this department on programs designed to help these students solve their educational problems.

8. Teachers refer to the guidance department those students who apparently need the types of counseling service that teachers themselves cannot render. Teachers have so many first-hand contacts with students that they are in a strategic position to notice the students who have problems requiring special attention. Some of these students have sensory and motor difficulties—for instance, poor vision, faulty hearing, speech defects, and walking handicaps. Others of these students have serious mental and emotional disturbances. Only if teachers refer such students to the guidance department is that department able to assist these students to ease their difficulties and to achieve more satisfactory adjustments. When making such referrals, teachers should give as accurate and as complete information as possible about these students to the guidance department.

9. Teachers report to the guidance department the content of the significant interviews that they have had with individual students, unless this content was confidential in nature.

10. Teachers participate in the selection of certain standardized tests and in the evaluation of the results therefrom. On the basis of this evaluation, teachers may make adjustments in their courses of study and in their methods of instruction. They may recommend changes in the sectioning (if any) of students on the basis of tested abilities, in the courses and curricula offered, in the prerequisites for and sequences of courses, and in the guidance services provided by the instructional staff. By participating in the foregoing activities, teachers may make real contributions toward bringing nearer together the instructional and the guidance activities of the school.

11. Teachers assume responsibilities for the organization and the operation of extracurricular activities, particularly of those activities that are closely allied to their subject-matter fields or to their other interests. Many of these activities contribute to the guidance of students.

The Guidance Tasks of Specialists

As pointed out earlier, guidance specialists have definite responsibilities for a school or college guidance program. This program is often conducted by a department of the institution. This guidance department usually engages in the following types of activities:

1. The department sets up the organization for carrying on the guidance program. It operates this program in such a way as to achieve the maximum cooperation of the entire faculty. Throughout its work, the department seeks to coordinate and integrate the guidance and guidance-related activities of all staff members.

2. The department supplements the guidance activities being carried on by the teachers, wherever necessary or whenever possible.

3. The department facilitates the instructional and guidance activities of the teaching staff.

4. The department gathers from many sources the most significant information about each student. It records this information and makes it accessible to the faculty through the student's cumulative record.

5. The department plans and supervises the administration of all standardized tests and inventories. These include instruments that measure general scholastic ability, special aptitudes, personal adjustment, and vocational interests. Classroom teachers may assist in the administration of the tests that make up the school-wide testing program.

6. In secondary schools and colleges that have selective admissions policies, the department makes studies for and recommendations to the admissions officer.

7. The department organizes the program of orientation of new students. In planning and carrying out this program, it seeks the full cooperation and participation of the entire staff.

8. The department organizes and operates each of the following services: special diagnostic work related to educational and vocational problems; counseling of students; and placement assistance.

9. The department advises in the over-all organization

and general supervision of the extracurricular program of student activities. (In many schools, the direction of this program is the responsibility of the instructional staff rather than of the guidance department.)

10. The department plans and conducts research projects that bear upon guidance services. It makes the findings from these projects known to teachers, particularly to those who are especially interested in or in need of the data and conclusions.

11. The department serves as a referral agency for those students who are in need of specialized services not available in the school. If the school does not have a full-time or part-time psychiatrist on its staff, the guidance department may logically refer students in need of psychotherapy to outside experts and agencies who are qualified to render this type of service.

The Joint Tasks of Teachers and Guidance Specialists

The foregoing discussion leads naturally to the important question: What activities in the guidance program should be handled jointly by the instructional staff and by the specialists in guidance?

In the initiation and later pursuit of guidance activities by teachers and by guidance workers, both groups should display a spirit of mutual understanding and helpfulness. This spirit is particularly essential in working with students, either by the individual or the group approach. For example, if the counseling program is to be adequate, there must be close cooperation between teacher-counselors (usually part-time counselors) and other instructors and between these counselors and the full-time guidance staff.

Both the instructional staff and the guidance staff should be flexible in outlook and in temperament, because this flexibility is essential to a genuine sharing of responsibility. If teachers or guidance workers insist on exclusive and narrowly-defined rights of operation, neither can conduct effective guidance services for students. Whether in the guidance department or in the instructional departments of the school, all staff members must be ready and willing to make adjustments in terms of the needs of students and of the resources available for meeting them.

A SUMMARY OF THE ROLES OF THE GUIDANCE DIRECTOR, THE TEACHER, AND THE COUNSELOR

To sum up the foregoing discussion, here is a point-by-point statement of the respective guidance responsibilities of the administrator, teacher, and counselor, as presented by Erickson.[2]

The Role of the Administrator

1. The administrator helps the staff concentrate its attention on the problems, needs, and characteristics of the pupils.
2. The administrator has the responsibility for providing personal leadership in developing better guidance services.
3. The administrator helps the staff understand the "shared responsibility" of all for pupil growth. He helps them understand their mutual concern and the changing proportions of responsibility in different situations.
4. The administrator helps to define the administrative structure, clarify line and staff operations, and define job descriptions.
5. The administrator provides the time, scheduling, and facilities so staff members can work more effectively.
6. The administrator helps to interpret the program of guidance services to the school and to the community.
7. The administrator helps, by providing in-service training facilities, teachers and counselors to acquire greater skill and security.
8. The administrator helps the staff organize the guidance program to provide maximum improvement through the utilization of the guidance program.
9. The administrator selects competent counselors and places them in an educational setting so they can operate effectively.

The Role of the Teacher

1. Teachers, as teachers, are primarily concerned with the problems and needs of their pupils.
2. Teachers are the first line of detection of the emerging maladjustments of pupils.

[2] *The Role of the Staff in the Guidance Program,* Institute of Counseling, Testing, and Guidance (Clifford E. Erickson, Director), Michigan State College, East Lansing, 1951.

3. Teachers have an opportunity to provide most of the school situations for maximum pupil development.

4. Teachers have an opportunity to implement many of the decisions made as a result of the pupils' contacts with counselors.

5. Teachers have an opportunity to provide many group therapy activities.

6. Teachers have an opportunity to provide many instructional services closely related to the needs and problems of pupils.

7. Teachers have an opportunity to acquire much information and many insights about pupils and their experiences.

8. Teachers develop many effective contacts with parents and community agencies. These contacts have important possibilities in the complete guidance program.

9. Teachers have many personal contacts with pupils. These "rapport" relationships place them in an extremely strategic position to help children.

The Role of the Counselor

1. The counselor has a designated responsibility for counseling. Much of this counseling is supplemental to the work of the teachers in helping pupils with their problems and their plans.

2. The counselor accumulates and organizes basic data about pupils for staff use.

3. The counselor helps teachers with pupil problems which the teachers find difficult.

4. The counselor helps the staff organize their contacts with parents.

5. The counselor helps the staff to identify and utilize community referral resources.

6. The counselor helps teachers develop instructional activities more closely related to guidance needs of pupils.

7. The counselor helps the staff develop many of the important guidance services of the school: orientation activities, placement services, testing programs, pupil personnel records, follow-up services, etc.

8. The counselor helps the staff gather, organize, and use educational and occupational information needed by teachers.

9. The counselor helps the staff carry on research and evaluation studies.

QUALIFICATIONS OF GUIDANCE WORKERS

Because schools differ somewhat in the guidance services that they want and can afford, they also differ in the qualifications that they desire of the persons who carry on their guidance work. Nevertheless, experts agree in general upon the qualifications of guidance workers; these experts have stated these qualifications in terms of standards. According to the standards, some workers are highly qualified for their tasks. Others are fairly well-qualified. And still others are poorly equipped for guidance activities.

A school or college should establish its own standards for the selection of guidance workers; its standards, of course, include a list of the minimum qualifications that such staff members must have. Although the institution may not be able to obtain guidance workers who have all of the qualifications specified in its standards, it can have these standards in view and can work toward reaching them. Without such standards, the institution is handicapped. It has no definite yardstick for selecting its guidance personnel or for evaluating its present personnel.

During the past few years, professional associations and federal and state educational agencies have made careful studies of the qualifications of counselors—of the characteristics, the experience, and the training desired. The National Vocational Guidance Association, for example, conducted one of these studies and reported its findings in the manual entitled *Counselor Preparation*.[3] This manual presents the aims of counselor preparation, the areas of training therefor, and the courses to be organized therein.

Because the N.V.G.A. manual summarizes the cooperative thinking of leaders in a number of professional organizations, it is an excellent guide for the counselor, whether he has had little or much experience in this field; for instance, it directs him specifically toward the goal of preparing himself for increased competence. The manual is also valuable to any school head or to any classroom teacher who is interested in this field.

The N.V.G.A. manual proposes qualifications for guidance workers according to the levels of their respective responsibilities in the guidance field. To illustrate, part-time counselors (many of them teacher-counselors) need not have the range

---

[3] *Counselor Preparation* (Washington, D.C.: National Vocational Guidance Association, 1949).

and depth of qualifications that full-time guidance workers should have. But as the former acquire the qualifications set for the latter, they improve the guidance services that they are rendering in their schools.

The N.V.G.A. manual discusses the essential and the desirable qualifications of counselors in terms of four different categories as follows: background in general education; specialized education; previous work experiences; and personal characteristics. Each of these categories, as given in the manual, is presented next.[4]

General Education

The counselor should have had a broad, general education, representative of the principal areas of knowledge. In the biological sciences he should have some contact with zoology, as well as with human anatomy. The social sciences are particularly important: economics, sociology, political science, and history. Also the physical sciences—chemistry, physics, geology, and astronomy—make their own contribution to the education of the counselor. To complete the widening of his mental horizon, the humanities are necessary. Included in this field are literature, modern language, philosophy, appreciation of art and music.

It is particularly essential that the counselor view human knowledge in its relationships to the end that he may have a more complete understanding of people as individuals and as members of a group. Such an approach gives broader insights into the problems of individuals and possible solutions of their problems.

Moreover, the counselor who has studied the main fields of knowledge has gained a first-hand feeling for the kinds of mental effort required for thinking in these areas. He develops a keener appreciation of the mental characteristics necessary for successful work in different subjects and occupations. The counselor acquires also a broader vocabulary and enough knowledge—although superficial in some aspects—to talk intelligently with a variety of counselees. Rapport in a wide variety of situations is made more certain.

Specialized Education

The counselor's knowledge of *psychology*, both theoretical and applied, must be extensive and intensive because it is the

---

[4] *Ibid.*, pp. 6-7.

discipline which leads to basic understanding of human personality and behavior. It is particularly important that the counselor have command of the theory and applications of individual differences, and of the nature of the learning process and of motivation. Such knowledge is based on general psychology and educational psychology.

Quite obviously the more effective counselor is well-versed in *individual and group measurement* and appraisal of human abilities, aptitudes, interests, and personality traits. He knows not only what reliable objective measuring devices are available, but also how they are used and how the results may be appropriately interpreted. Hence the counselor should know the theory and applications of statistics for his kinds of problems.

Greater skill in the use of these tools of guidance and in interpretation of the results arising from use of these devices can be more fully achieved by extensive *experience in clinics* during the course of training. There is today increasing recognition that the traditional didactic method of classroom study and the approach through isolated laboratory experimentation do not give adequate training to the counselor. He ought to have experiences in a guidance clinic, beginning with observation of the professional activities of experts and progressing finally to the bearing of some responsibility himself for the handling of actual counseling situations. The clinical approach is needed for learning the techniques of counseling and interviewing.

Of significant value to the counselor is thorough grounding in the *psychology of personality*. First, there must be familiarity with the normal functioning of personality and the nature of the adjustment process. All aspects of human growth and maturation —physical and mental—should be understood by the counselor. This goal entails study of physiology and neurology, of the role of heredity and environment in the origin and development of human behavior.

In the field of specialized education, the counselor should also have some knowledge of abnormal human behavior. With this knowledge, the counselor should be able to recognize the symptoms indicating that a person has serious mental or emotional disturbances. When the counselor confers with such a person, he realizes that he does not have the training or the experience necessary to handle the case. Therefore, he refers the case to a psychiatrist for diagnosis and treatment.

In this connection and as an important part of his background, the counselor should have some first-hand observation of individuals who have serious personality disorders. He can arrange to observe such individuals in a mental clinic or in a mental hospital.

In his training, the counselor should study *social psychology*. Through this study, he learns about the behavior of individuals as members of groups—the interactions that go on among individuals within a group, and the problems that arise out of these interactions, for example. With knowledge of social psychology, the counselor can better understand the individual—his setting (his social and physical environment) and his nature (his characteristics and motives).

For effective work on the job, moreover, the school or college counselor should be familiar, at least in a general way, with the most common types of *business organization and administration*. He should be informed about the operation of representative commercial and industrial enterprises; he should know the important features of industrial personnel work and of industrial relations.

In the field of guidance services, the counselor-specialist and, so far as possible, the teacher-counselor should take a series of courses. These courses should cover the entire guidance field and should emphasize one or two specializations therein. They should treat specifically such important areas as these: the principles and practices of counseling, the nature and uses of occupational information, the methods of analyzing students, and the organization and administration of guidance services.[5]

Previous Work Experiences

A counselor who wishes to render maximum service in an educational institution should have a diversified background

[5] With further reference to these areas, the reader will find these books of practical value: Shirley A. Hamrin and Blanche B. Paulson, *Counseling Adolescents* (Chicago: Science Research Associates, 1950); Max F. Baer and Edward C. Roeber, *Occupational Information: Its Nature and Use* (Chicago: Science Research Associates, 1951); and Clifford P. Froehlich and John G. Darley, *Studying Students: Guidance Methods of Individual Analysis* (Chicago: Science Research Associates, 1952). Other valuable books are listed at the end of this chapter.

of work experiences. Within the key field of education, he should have had some classroom teaching and some experience in educational administration. Through teaching experience, the counselor gets first-hand contact with students and their problems, and with classroom methods, practices, and difficulties. Through administrative experience, even if in a minor capacity, the counselor obtains an understanding of administrative procedures and problems. Without such teaching and administrative experience, the counselor may offer suggestions or make recommendations that are impractical or unrealistic. He is certainly less well-prepared than he should be to deal with the problems of individual students.

In addition, the counselor should have some background, varied if possible, outside a school or college. For instance, he should have had experience working for business, industry, or government. Through this experience, the counselor learns directly about the problems of employers and of employees; in short, he "gets the feel" of jobs outside the school. As a result, he is able to render better guidance services to his students.

Essential Personal Characteristics

Because the counselor is a professional worker, he should be of *irreproachable moral character,* in all aspects of his personal living and in all his relationships with others. The counselor like a physician should abide by a code of ethics—a code that includes respect for the confidences of his counselees.

The counselor should have *better-than-average intelligence.* He should have a breadth and variety of intellectual interests. He should be mentally alert; he should have the ability to do abstract thinking. He should be capable of analyzing situations and of developing promising solutions to problems. He should have better-than-average skill in expressing ideas, both orally and in writing. If the counselor is reasonably gifted in all the foregoing attributes, he is more likely to succeed in his guidance work.

The counselor, moreover, should be genuinely *scientific in his point of view.* He should be objective in his attitudes and in his approach to problems. He should look for and depend upon authentic evidence. At times, the counselor may have to make recommendations and decisions on the basis of common sense, drawing upon years of varied personal experience and observation. Even then, however, he should attempt to be scientific in his selection and application of pertinent data.

As just implied, the counselor should be a person who has a high level of *common sense* and *good judgment*. He should be practical and realistic. All these traits contribute to his effectiveness as a counselor.

The counselor, furthermore, should have *broad rather than narrow interests*. Everything that exists is potential grist for his mill. This means, specifically, that the counselor should have contacts with a wide variety of people, situations, occupations, and areas of human knowledge, all in order to carry on his day-to-day work efficiently. The counselor should also view problems in their perspective; for example, he should see clearly the interrelationships among an individual's traits, social contacts, and past and present situations. If the counselor observes these interrelationships, he is more likely to make sound judgments in working with his counselees.

If the counselor is to provide the best possible guidance services, he should possess a wholehearted, genuine *interest in and liking for people*, particularly young people. He should have respect for the worth of the individual, no matter who that individual is. The counselor, in addition, should have a sympathetic understanding of people—a sensitivity to their thoughts and feelings, and to the situations they face. The counselor should be friendly and easily approachable; his personality should be warm and attractive.

At all times, the counselor should respect the confidences of his counselees; he should not reveal these confidences to others. The counselor should never go into the counselee's personal affairs unnecessarily, say, solely out of curiosity; moreover, he should not even give the impression that he is trying to do so. True, the counselor should become thoroughly informed about the counselee and his situation, but he should try to secure this information by means that are understood and accepted by the counselee.

Because of the kinds of demands made upon the counselor, he should have *good health,* both physically and mentally. He should have reserves of physical energy. He should also have emotional stability and mental maturity; in short, he should be well-adjusted in all aspects of his personal and social life. Only if the counselor has "a sound mind in a sound body" can he develop and maintain the guidance services that he should render to his counselees.

In addition to the qualities already mentioned, the counselor should be *sincere, open-minded, tolerant, and flexible.* More specifically, the counselor should be sincere in his attitudes and actions, in all his relationships with counselees and others. The counselor should treat all counselees fairly; he should keep his mind open to new ideas and methods; and he should be tolerant in all his contacts. His processes of thinking and acting should be flexible.

The counselor should have *cooperative attitudes* toward his fellow staff members. He should take the initiative in establishing friendly personal and working relations with his colleagues. If the counselor cooperates with them, they are more likely to exert their best efforts in the institution's guidance program.

The counselor may lack certain desirable personal characteristics or certain desired professional knowledge and skills. If so, he should not take a cocksure attitude to conceal his lacks, or a defeatist attitude with reference to them. Rather, the counselor should frankly recognize his own limitations. He is then better able to adjust to these limitations and to take steps to overcome them. Such a counselor sees his limitations as a caution against "going beyond his depth" in his counseling activities and as a challenge to improve his competence as a guidance worker.

In the typical school or college, the part-time counselor or teacher-counselor is usually less well-trained for and less able in guidance work than is the full-time specialist in this field. Just as rapidly as possible, however, the institution should endeavor to raise the competence of each of its part-time counselors. A school or college can do this in two ways. *First,* it can conduct a systematic in-service training program for these counselors. And *second,* it can select teachers who have already had some training and experience in counseling work.

SUMMARY

A school or college needs generalists in the field of guidance services. These include the head administrative personnel and the teaching staff, who conduct most of the institution's total educational program. If such personnel realize the importance of guidance services, and if they have had some training in this field, they are in the best possible position to advance the guidance program for the students in their institution.

An educational institution also needs specialists in the guidance field. If these specialists have had adequate training and experience, and if they have the appropriate personal characteristics, they are most likely to provide the optimum guidance services for all students.

A successful guidance program requires close and wholehearted cooperation between the generalists and the specialists within an institution. Only through such cooperation can these generalists and specialists agree upon the basic objectives of guidance services and carry out an effective guidance program.

In efforts to stimulate and facilitate full staff cooperation in a school's guidance program, the specialists should take the initiative; they should be willing to go more than half way in this matter. Without such cooperation, nonspecialists will tend to feel that guidance services are "fads and frills" of the institution's educational program. But if their cooperation is obtained, they will increasingly agree with the specialists that guidance can be and should be an essential and integral part of the total program of their educational institution. As a matter of fact, guidance is becoming a significant part of the total educational programs in an increasing number of schools and colleges, as the next chapter on future trends will indicate.

SUGGESTED READINGS

Berdie, Ralph R. *Concepts and Programs of Counseling.* Minneapolis: University of Minnesota Press, 1951. Pp. 27-55.
California State Department of Education. "The School Counselor:

His Work and Training," *Bulletin of the California State Department of Education*, XX, No. 7, 1951.

Council of Guidance and Personnel Associations, Study Commission of. "Job Analyses of Educational Personnel Workers," *Occupations*, Part II, Special Report XXX (October, 1951), 1-22.

Crow, Lester D., and Crow, Alice. *An Introduction to Guidance: Principles and Practices*. New York: American Book Company, 1951. Chapters 6, 7.

Federal Security Agency, Office of Education. *Counselor Competencies in Counseling Techniques*. Washington, D.C.: Office of Education, Misc. 3314-5, March, 1949.

Federal Security Agency, Office of Education. *Counselor Competencies in Occupational Information*. Washington, D.C.: Office of Education, Misc. 3314-3, March, 1949.

Federal Security Agency, Office of Education, Division of Vocational Education. *Duties, Standards, Qualifications for Counselors*. Washington, D.C.: Office of Education, Misc. 3314-1, February, 1949.

Froehlich, Clifford P. *Evaluating Guidance Procedures*. Washington, D.C.: Federal Security Agency, Office of Education, Misc. 3310, January, 1949.

Institute for Human Adjustment. *Training of Psychological Counselors*. Report of conferences held at Ann Arbor, July 27, 28, 1949, January 6, 7, 1950. Ann Arbor: University of Michigan Press.

Strang, Ruth. *The Role of the Teacher in Personnel Work*. New York: Bureau of Publications, Teachers College, Columbia University, 3rd ed., 1946.

Williamson, E. G. *Counseling Adolescents*. New York: McGraw-Hill Book Company, Inc., 1950. Pp. 241-281.

Wrenn, C. Gilbert. "The Selection and Education of Student Personnel Workers," *The Personnel and Guidance Journal*, XXXI (October, 1952), 9-14.

Zerfoss, Karl P. *Readings in Counseling*. New York: Association Press, 1952. Pp. 573-606.

PART V

The Future of Guidance Services

CHAPTER SEVENTEEN

Keynoting the Future

I N CHAPTER after chapter, this book has pointed out the principal developments in the field of guidance services. In this, the final chapter, the book will summarize these developments. It will also discuss such leading questions as these: In guidance, what will the emphases and tendencies probably be in the near future? In this field, what may guidance workers look forward to with reasonable assurance? The answers to these questions are indicated by the six main guidance trends that are presented in the following sections.

TREND NO. 1: GUIDANCE WILL BE AN EXPANDING FUNCTION OF EDUCATION.

At all levels of education, there is abundant evidence of expansion of the guidance function. In elementary schools, for example, principals, teachers, psychologists, and other staff members are working to provide more and better guidance services. Their objective is to improve the services rendered to the individual pupil; toward this objective, they are devoting greater attention to all aspects of the child's development. In high schools, staff members are increasingly cognizant of the need for more effective guidance programs and are working toward building such programs. So, too, the faculties of junior colleges, colleges, and universities are expanding and improving the guidance services offered to students within their institutions.

As the foregoing developments indicate, guidance services will assume an increasingly prominent position among all the educational functions provided by schools and colleges.

And this will be true at successive rungs of the academic ladder. As a result, an ever-growing number of children and youth will be guided better in a greater variety of ways.

Life Adjustment Education

A recent example of the expanding role of guidance in the schools is the so-called *life adjustment education movement.* For some years, leaders in the field of guidance services have emphasized the importance of developing educational programs that are specifically designed to meet the varied needs of young people. As an outcome of this emphasis, school personnel have worked to make significant adjustments in school curricula and in other school activities so that these better serve the needs of all youth. In comparatively recent times, guidance leaders have referred to such educational trends as the life adjustment education movement. This movement, of course, has important implications for guidance services. For instance, it calls for an expansion of these services; it places larger responsibilities on guidance workers.

Although life adjustment education was provided by a number of schools scattered throughout the country, there was a real need to stimulate this type of education among all schools and school systems. Therefore, in 1947 the United States Commissioner of Education appointed a National Commission on Life Adjustment Education, composed of one representative from each of nine educational associations.[1] At that time and since then, *School Life* and other publications of the Office of Education [2] have reported the development of local, state, and national programs of life adjustment education.

---

[1] These organizations were: American Association of School Administrators, American Association of Junior Colleges, American Vocational Association, National Association of High-School Supervisors and Directors of Secondary Education, National Association of Secondary-School Principals, National Association of State Directors of Vocational Education, National Catholic Welfare Conference, National Council of Chief State School Officers, and National Education Association.

[2] Federal Security Agency, Office of Education, *Life Adjustment Education for Every Youth,* Superintendent of Documents, U.S. Government Printing Office, Washington 25, D.C.

Guidance Offices in State Education Departments

An earlier example of the expansion of guidance was the movement in which federal, state, and local educational agencies cooperated to introduce and to improve guidance services.

Prior to 1947, state after state officially recognized the crucial role of guidance in the schools. Such a state set up a division of guidance services within the state department of education; to head that division, the state provided a state supervisor of guidance services. At present, the education departments of 44 states, of the District of Columbia, and of the territories of Hawaii, Puerto Rico, and the Virgin Islands each has an office of guidance supervisor.[3]

State guidance services offices were established and maintained as a direct result of state initiative and federal assistance. The latter was in two main forms: *First,* the federal government made grants-in-aid to the states for their offices of state guidance supervisor.[4] And *second,* the U.S. Office of Education, especially its Occupational Information and Guidance Service, provided considerable advice and other professional aid to the guidance services offices within state education departments. These state offices have worked closely and intensively in many different communities. Therein, the state guidance supervisors have helped local public elementary and secondary schools to organize, staff, and conduct increasingly effective guidance programs for their pupils.

Guidance Officers in Schools and Colleges

Still another example of the expanding nature of guidance services appears in Froehlich's survey of the number of public schools that had guidance officers.[5] Within the high schools reporting, the total number of counselors employed in 1945–46 was 8,299, nearly three times as many as in 1939–40. In this

[3] Glenn E. Smith, *Principles and Practices of the Guidance Program* (New York: Macmillan Company, 1951), p. 354.

[4] Harry A. Jager, "The George-Barden Act as an Influence in the Further Development of Guidance Work," *Occupations,* XXV (May, 1947), 483-489.

[5] Clifford P. Froehlich, "Counselors and Guidance Officers in Public Secondary Schools," *Occupations,* XXVI (May, 1948), 522-527.

period, the number of schools having counselors tripled. According to the U.S. Office of Education, 18,197 counselors were serving junior or senior high schools, or full school systems in 1952–53—double the high-school total in 1945–46.

As high schools, especially, have created guidance services positions, there has been an increasing demand for professionally trained persons to fill these positions. To train such personnel, many colleges and universities have expanded their offerings of courses that provide technical preparation in the guidance field.[6] The placement offices in these institutions have helped graduates to obtain guidance services positions. Such placement assistance is also rendered informally by the American Personnel and Guidance Association and the American College Personnel Association.

Colleges and universities, as well as high schools, have been devoting more and more attention to guidance services. This increasing attention is indicated by the following two facts: *First,* the American College Personnel Association has grown in total membership and in the diversity of its membership. *Second,* the American Association of Junior Colleges, whose membership includes both private and public colleges, has established a standing research committee on student personnel problems. Reports by this committee appear, from time to time, in the Association's *Junior College Journal.*[7]

Other evidence of the expansion of guidance in schools and colleges is the increased emphasis on the participation of all staff members in the guidance program.[8] According to this emphasis, every staff member within an institution must contribute to guidance if the entire student body is to receive the assistance needed.

---

[6] Clifford P. Froehlich and Helene E. Spivey, *Guidance Workers' Preparation* (Washington, D.C.: U.S. Office of Education, July, 1949).

[7] J. Anthony Humphreys, "Facts Concerning Student Personnel Programs," *Junior College Journal,* XIX (September, 1948), 8-13.

Charlotte D. Meinecke, "Placement and Follow-up in Junior Colleges," *Junior College Journal,* XIX (October, 1948), 58-67.

William A. Black, "Student Personnel Relationships of High School and Junior College," *Junior College Journal,* XIX (November, 1948), 145-150.

[8] Arthur E. Traxler, "Emerging Trends in Guidance," *School Review,* 58 (January, 1950), 14, 15.

TREND NO. 2: THERE WILL BE INCREASING COOPERATION AND COORDINATION IN THE PROVISION OF GUIDANCE SERVICES.

Whenever the experts assemble to discuss the organization and development of guidance services, they agree upon the necessity for both cooperation and coordination. And the same need is emphasized in nearly all the articles that appear in professional guidance journals. The consensus is clearly as follows: If guidance services are to become widespread and effective, there must be cooperation among staff members within a given institution, among different institutions, and among various associations concerned with personnel matters. There also must be coordination of the efforts and activities of all those engaged in guidance work.

Cooperation within an Institution

To be more specific, in an educational institution that has developed a highly successful program of guidance services, the guidance staff has obtained the cooperation of many if not all of the teachers and other staff members. The guidance office or department does not consider itself the exclusive guidance agency within the institution. For this reason, its specialists seek the active assistance of the *generalists*—the head administrators and the classroom teachers, for example. The *specialists* in the guidance office and other specialists on the school's staff work cooperatively—not in competition. On every possible occasion, they endeavor to coordinate their services to a student or to the student body. What such an educational institution does toward achieving cooperation and coordination helps to integrate its guidance services program.

Cooperation among Institutions and Organizations

An educational institution or its staff working alone cannot build the best possible guidance program. It can develop such a program only through cooperation with other institutions, usually institutions that belong to the same association of schools or of colleges. Its staff members can work toward better guidance services through cooperation with the staff members of other institutions, usually by means of professional associations.

Looking toward the improvement of cooperative relationships within the guidance field, a number of professional associations of guidance workers have set up committees to make special studies and to prepare specific recommendations. These committees have tried to reduce or to eliminate wastes due to duplication of services. They have warned against over-organization—the establishment of too many guidance committees or of highly complex guidance procedures, for instance. These committees, moreover, have emphasized the need for better integration of the guidance services offered at a given level and at successive levels of the educational ladder.

Toward more effective coordination and integration of the guidance services provided within a school, school system, or college, and between a lower school and the next higher school, the American Personnel and Guidance Association was organized. The A.P.G.A. has five principal constituents, including the National Vocational Guidance Association and the American College Personnel Association. The A.P.G.A.'s official magazine is entitled *The Personnel and Guidance Journal;* it is the successor to *Occupations* (The Vocational Guidance Journal).

In connection with the goal of developing better-integrated guidance programs, Super[9] made a preliminary analysis of the interests of educational institutions and professional organizations in various aspects of guidance services. His analysis serves as a map whereby the inexperienced guidance worker can orient himself as to the nature and magnitude of his tasks. It also serves as a chart whereby the experienced guidance worker can view his varied responsibilities as a whole and in detail. For either worker, this analysis can help bring about better coordination of guidance services.

Cooperation within the Community

Within many a community, groups of businessmen, educators, and social service workers, for example, have increas-

---

[9] Donald E. Super, "Charting Our Field," *Occupations,* XXVI (March, 1948), 346-348.

ingly recognized the need of out-of-school youth and adults for job placement and other guidance services. For years, many of these persons have not had an established place where they could obtain help in solving their occupational and personal problems.

On the whole, commercial and industrial employers have lacked the time, the facilities, and the other resources required to render adequate guidance services to prospective employees or to employees who are being dropped from payrolls.

Occasionally, school people as individuals have taken a personal interest in out-of-school youth; they have been able to assist a few of these youth, usually outside school hours. Generally, however, young people have had to fend for themselves; consequently, they tended to drift along and to make unnecessary mistakes.

During the depression of the early 1930's, scattered communities set up local councils that provided free guidance and placement services for out-of-school youth and adults. Made up of representatives of education, commerce, industry, and social welfare organizations, these councils aimed to help unemployed persons to find suitable jobs. Toward this goal, the councils conducted fairly effective programs; these programs included informational services, testing and counseling, and personal adjustment assistance. Those responsible for carrying on this work found that some of the problems of individuals arose not only from inability to obtain gainful employment but also from failure to attain personal maturity.

Among the most important supporters and contributors to the guidance services programs of community councils were such organizations as social welfare agencies, men's service clubs (Kiwanis, Lions, and Rotary, for example) and women's clubs. Others who rendered invaluable assistance in this work were interested individuals—leaders in business, in the professions, and in educational institutions.

In New York City, this type of work was carried on by the Adjustment Service, sponsored by the American Association for Adult Education. This free community counseling service for adults was a noteworthy example of cooperation among a number of local adult organizations. The service operated from February 1, 1933, to May 31, 1934. During that time, it helped over 12,000 men and women. Similar services were offered by councils of social agencies in Chicago and in Cincinnati.

Cooperative community projects designed to serve local youth were stimulated and assisted by the American Youth Commission. This commission was set up and sponsored by the American Council on Education, Washington, D.C.

The staff of experts of and advisors to the American Youth Commission made thorough local and regional surveys of the status of out-of-school youth. They also worked with local communities in the establishment of youth service councils. Descriptions of the work of the American Youth Commission and reports of its findings appeared in publications issued during the years 1937 to 1942. These publications suggest policies, procedures, and patterns that any community may well consider in developing an effective youth-serving program.

During World War II, American communities gained new experiences in cooperation that proved of real value in the post-war planning of community activities for helping returning veterans, displaced war workers, and out-of-school youth to achieve satisfactory adjustments. Long before the end of the war, educational and other leaders in some localities and staff members in some state offices of guidance services began working to establish agencies that provided community counseling services. An account of such community work and of the steps required to carry it on was prepared by the Out-of-School Guidance Committee of the National Vocational Guidance Association.[10]

Beginning in the latter part of 1943, a number of cities provided community counseling services for adults. The programs, methods of operation, and problems of these counseling services were described in an article by Jager and Zeran.[11] Such counseling services were initiated locally with the assist-

---

[10] Out-of-School Guidance Committee, National Vocational Guidance Association, "Organizing the Community for Vocational Guidance," *Occupations,* XXII (November, 1943), 102-108.

[11] Harry A. Jager and Franklin R. Zeran, "Community Adult Counseling Centers," *Occupations,* XXIII (February, 1945), 261-308.

ance of state education departments and of the Occupational Information and Guidance Service (Division of Vocational Education) of the U.S. Office of Education. This federal service provided much of the leadership in the nation-wide movement to aid adults through local counseling agencies.

A few years later, the adult organizations in some communities cooperated in the establishment of Veterans' Guidance Centers and local offices of the Rural Rehabilitation Agency. These centers and offices carried on significant counseling projects. The Veterans' Guidance Centers, set up in numerous communities, did outstanding work in aiding veterans to make postwar adjustments—to find satisfactory civilian jobs, for example.

TREND NO. 3: THE SCIENTIFIC APPROACH WILL BE INCREASINGLY EMPLOYED.

Within the field of guidance services, there is a growing emphasis on the scientific approach. This trend appears in the increased use of objective tests and inventories, in the improved methods of appraising individuals, in the application of statistical devices to predict success or failure, and in the development of better case study techniques.[12]

Although all guidance work cannot be conducted according to rigorous scientific procedures, more and more of this work can and probably will be scientifically approached. This will be due to the fact that, in recent years, guidance workers have increasingly acquired and applied scientific attitudes. These workers also have had better instruments for testing and otherwise appraising human behavior.

The pioneering in the development and use of scientific methods and devices that has been going on and that is continuing promises well for the future. As a result, guidance workers, year by year, will have at hand more reliable knowledge and better techniques. These will help such workers to improve and extend their services, including those related to different aspects of human behavior.

The scientific approach to guidance will be advanced by

---

[12] Arthur E. Traxler. "Emerging Trends in Guidance," *School Review,* 58 (January, 1950), 14-23.

the work of the specialized divisions that have been created within the American Psychological Association. Such divisions are entitled: counseling psychology; measurement and evaluation; school psychologists; and psychologists in public service. These divisions have as one of their primary goals the fostering of scientific development within their specialized areas. A similar goal is among the aims of some of the sections of the National Vocational Guidance Association.

Without too great a stretch of the imagination, we may envisage more systematic planning and pursuit of scientific research and evaluation in the field of guidance services. This will be an outcome of the cooperative efforts of individual investigators on the staffs of various institutions, agencies, and business concerns. It will also be a result of the committee work within different professional associations. Through scientific research, all these specialists and organizations, individually and cooperatively, will contribute to the improvement of guidance services—for children, youth, and adults.

TREND NO. 4: COUNSELING SERVICES WILL BECOME MORE EFFECTIVE.

During the past decade, guidance workers have continually endeavored to improve their counseling techniques. For many years, they have employed so-called *directive counseling*. In this type of counseling, the counselor mainly directs the content and course of the interview. In recent years, counselors have increasingly used nondirective counseling, an approach developed and advocated by Carl R. Rogers. In Rogers' method, the counselee directs the interview, the counselor taking a permissive attitude.

In the future, the majority of counselors will probably take a middle-of-the-road position between the foregoing two types of counseling. In short, they will be wise to employ what Hamrin and Paulson refer to as *eclectic counseling*—a type in which the counselor uses a directive technique or a nondirective technique depending upon which is more appropriate to the counselee and his current situation.

With further reference to the improvement of counseling

services, Traxler [13] indicates that the following tendencies are apparent:

1. Orderly accumulation and recording of a variety of information concerning each individual
2. Increased use of objective measures for appraisal of counselees
3. Recognition of relationship between remedial work and guidance
4. Use of improved case-study techniques
5. Use of better sources of occupational information
6. Use of follow-up studies

TREND NO. 5: THE DEMAND FOR PROFESSIONALLY-TRAINED GUIDANCE WORKERS WILL INCREASE.

The fifth trend is the rising demand from the field for guidance workers who possess both extensive and intensive professional training. The typical school or college will no longer be satisfied, say, with a full-time counselor whose main qualifications are reasonably good intelligence and enthusiasm for guidance. Rather, that institution will require that a counselor shall have had adequate training in the total area of guidance services.

According to Wrenn,[14] the professional training of a counselor will include the following:

1. The dynamics of individual personality
2. Appraisal of aptitudes and personality characteristics
3. Clinical skill in relating data and making diagnoses
4. Skill in therapy, using varied approaches
5. Statistical evaluation of personal and group data
6. Mental hygiene procedures
7. Diagnosis of educational and social maladjustments
8. Knowledge of predictive criteria and skill in prognosis

"These are unique to the professional personnel worker," states Wrenn, "when they are in combination with each other and with knowledge and skill in other areas."

---

[13] *Ibid.*, 14-23.
[14] C. Gilbert Wrenn (edited by E. G. Williamson), "Appraisal of Professional Status," *Trends in Student Personnel Work* (Minneapolis: University of Minnesota Press, 1949), 276.

TREND NO. 6: THERE WILL BE HIGHER PROFESSIONAL STANDARDS FOR GUIDANCE WORKERS.

The next clearly evident trend is the development of guidance functions as professional services. As in the profession of medicine, the profession of guidance will have rising standards for the certification of workers and an increasingly better code of ethical practices. Leaders in the professionalization of guidance and in the certification of guidance workers have been two national associations, the National Vocational Guidance Association and the American Psychological Association.

Certification

The National Vocational Guidance Association, in cooperation with other organizations, has set up standards for the preparation of counselors.[15] It has established two classes of membership—professional members and general members. State associations affiliated with the N.V.G.A. have worked for state certification laws or regulations. At present, 17 of the 48 states have certification requirements for qualified counselors.[16]

Similar steps have been taken by the American Psychological Association with reference to psychologists. Moreover, some state associations affiliated with the A.P.A. have been active in introducing bills in state legislatures to require certification of practicing psychologists.

While relatively few states have passed laws requiring the certification of counselors and psychologists, the movement toward this goal is gaining momentum. In the not too distant future, many if not all states will have such certification laws or regulations. This desired legislation will probably be a direct outcome of the continued efforts of professional associations.

Code of Ethics

One hallmark of an established profession is the existence of a code of ethical practices. In a given field, of course, such

---

[15] *Counselor Preparation* (Washington, D.C.: National Vocational Guidance Association, 1949).

[16] Glenn E. Smith, *op. cit.*, p. 360; and Benjamin G. Kremen, "Counselor Certification in the United States," *Occupations*, XXIX (May, 1951), 584-586.

a code is developed by the association of professional people who are working in that field.

The Committee on Professional Practices and its predecessor, the Ethical Practices Committee, of the National Vocational Guidance Association, for example, has set up standards for guidance or counseling agencies. This N.V.G.A. committee has examined some 200 agencies; it has found that a large proportion of these agencies met its standards. The names of these approved agencies are listed in the *1951 Directory of Vocational Counseling Agencies* [17] and in the *1953 Supplement* [18] to this directory.

By developing and applying criteria of quality and performance, the Committee on Professional Practices cites the counseling agencies that are providing services according to professional standards. This committee also helps all agencies to raise the competence and fairness of their services.

The code of ethics of a professional guidance association is beneficial in many ways. For instance, the ethical practices cited in such a code help guidance workers to develop professional attitudes toward their work and to conduct this work according to professional standards.

As guidance workers improve their code of ethics and practice that code in their daily relationships, they will increase their standing as a profession. Thereby, the guidance profession will take its place alongside well-established professions; and guidance workers will be respected as professionals by leading citizens of the community.

SUMMARY

Guidance workers have reason to look to the future with optimism. They provide services that meet genuine needs in educational institutions and elsewhere. Because of what these professional workers are doing, society is increasingly recognizing the value of their services.

To do their jobs well, however, guidance workers should

---

[17] "Ethical Practices Group Reports on Investigations," *Occupations,* XXIX (May, 1951), 645.

[18] "Ethical Practices Committee Gets New Name, Considers New Problems," *The Personnel and Guidance Journal,* XXXII (October, 1953), 106, 107.

think in terms of the optimum possibilities rather than in terms of the minimum essentials.[19] Toward this goal, they should seek to find and use all of the available resources that will aid them in helping people. They should try to employ the best tests, devices, and techniques. They should endeavor to locate or create the conditions that are most favorable to an individual's growth and maturity. And these workers should continually seek to improve themselves, particularly in their chosen technical fields.

Guidance staff members, working alone, cannot do the entire guidance job. That is why they should, at all times, try to cooperate with administrators, teachers, students, and parents, with other specialists inside and outside the school, and with all interested individuals and organizations in the community. Only if guidance workers seek and obtain the whole-hearted cooperation of the foregoing persons and groups will they be able to render the best possible services to their counselees.

To give over-all direction to their activities, guidance workers should have a point of view that recognizes the uniqueness and worth of the individual person. With this point of view, these workers can and will achieve the essential aims of guidance services.

[19] E. H. Hopkins, "The Essentials of a Student Personnel Program," *College and University*, 23 (July, 1948), 549-567.

Index

Index

Abilities and requirements, relationships between, 39-40

Abnormal persons, counseling of, 52-56; main dangers to avoid in, 54-55

Academic failure: counseling of, 261, 271-275; indication of, 271

Accreditation, 257-259

Achievement tests, 89, 131-132: sources of information on, 227

Adjustment, 9, 10, 50: counseling for better, 169-170; process of, 66-69; psychology of, 47-48

Administration of school, services rendered to, 68-69

Administrator in guidance program, role of, 402

Advising, not same as counseling, 164

Allen, Richard D., 197

American Association for Adult Education, 421-422

American Association of Collegiate Registrars and Admissions Officers, 97

American Association of Junior Colleges, 418

American College Personnel Association, 18, 86, 418

American Council on Education, 93, 96-97, 149, 422

American Institute of Accountants, 101

American Personnel and Guidance Association, 86, 418, 420

American Psychological Association, 18, 424, 426

American Youth Commission, 422

Anecdotal method, 139

Applying for a job, 329-335

Aptitude and interest, correlation between, 133-136

Aptitude tests, 137-138

Association of Collegiate Alumnae, 80, 81

Attitudinal orientation, 189, 190-191, 197

Australia, guidance movement in, 106-107

Autobiographies, 120

Baer, Max F., 32 fn., 215 fn., 288 fn., 292, 302, 309-310, 407 fn.

Behavior, explanation of, 56-57

Binet and Simon, 88

Bingham, Walter VanDyke, 45-46, 160

Black, William A., 418 fn.

Boston: "cradle of vocational guidance," 72; early guidance work in, 74-75, 85, 86

Boynton, Paul W., 330 fn.

Brouwer, Paul J., 5

Buros, Oscar K., 155

Canada, guidance movement in, 107-108

Careers. *See* Occupations

Carnegie Foundation for the Advancement of Teaching, 94, 98, 99, 101

Cathartic-supportive therapy, 192

Certification of counselors, 426

Character, measurement of, 141-142